MICHAEL W. ALLISON

FOREWORD BY ANTHONY TRUCKS

I0560237

BREAK THE BOTTLE

Shatter Limitations, Master Solutions Thinking, and Achieve Extraordinary Success

SHINE
PRESS
Tampa, Florida

S H I N E
—— P R E S S ——

Publisher: Shine Press
4522 W. Village Dr. #1294
Tampa, Florida 34624
Shine-Press.com | Jodi@Shine-Press.com
Shine Press is an imprint of Jodi K Costa, LLC.

For speaking engagements, event invitations, bulk orders, and other author requests, please contact the author: mallison@theadversityacademy.com

F I R S T   E D I T I O N

Paperback ISBN: 979-8-9993665-5-9
Hardcover ISBN: 979-8-9993665-6-6
Ebook also available.

CONTENTS

Dedication 7

Foreword 9

Introduction 13

PART 1: DECISION Shatter Limitations & Break The Pattern **22**

1: The Bottles We Carry 27

2: The Turning Point — Why You Must Decide 43

3: Owning Your Past Without Letting It Define You 63

4: Breaking the First Seal — Committing to Change 83

PART 2: DIRECTION Mastering Solutions Thinking & Choose The Path **96**

5: The Alpha Project — War-Torn Roads and the Map Forward 101

6: The Mindset Shift — From Problems to Solutions 125

7: The Enemies of Progress 153

8: Cultivating Resilience — The Ultimate Advantage 179

9: The Power of Perspective—Seeing Opportunities Where Others See Obstacles 225

10: Designing the Blueprint for Your Future 259

PART 3: DESTINATION Achieving Extraordinary Success & Own The Future
....**282**

11: Becoming Unstoppable..287

12: The Leadership Paradigm—Owning Your Role in Your Life and Business.......................313

13: The Confidence Code — Unleashing Your Boldest Self..345

14: Mastering Momentum — Sustaining Long-Term Success 373

15: The Final Break—Live Free - Lead Boldly - Your Time is Now.......................................419

Acknowledgments 449

References & Resources 455

About the Author...459

DEDICATION

To the silent fighters—the ones carrying invisible battles while wearing brave faces—this is your book. To those who have been told they're too broken to be brilliant, too far gone to come back, too scared to lead and has allowed limitations to hold them back—this book is for you.

To the 1 in 5 adults silently battling mental health challenges…
To the nearly 60% of people who feel disengaged in their work, unfulfilled by their potential…
To the survivors of trauma, the dreamers haunted by doubt, the leaders who show up for everyone but themselves…You are not alone.

This book is dedicated to the single mother pulling double shifts and still showing up for her kids. To the veteran navigating civilian life with unseen wounds and unspoken questions. To the entrepreneur who built something from nothing and still feels like an impostor behind the wheel.
To the young man in the back of the room who hasn't said a word, but is carrying the weight of the world inside. To the executive who looks successful on paper but feels like they're running on fumes.

You've survived things that would've broken others. You've carried pain that never had language. You've doubted yourself, sabotaged yourself, and questioned your worth—and yet, here you are. Still standing. Still breathing. Still becoming.

This book is not just about me breaking the bottle. It's about you smashing every lie, limitation, and label that has ever tried to define your future by your past.

Let this be your moment.
Not just of inspiration—but activation.
Let this be the season you choose *resilience over regret, identity over insecurity, clarity over chaos.*

To my brothers and sisters who've worn uniforms, titles, and masks…To those who've rebuilt after loss, found faith after failure, and dared to dream again after devastation…

You are why this book was written.

And finally, to every person who dares to believe they were made for more —

May these pages remind you:
You're not broken. You're becoming.

Now… BREAK THE BOTTLE.

— Michael W. Allison, MBA

USMC Purple Heart Veteran, International Keynote Speaker, Founder & CEO - The Adversity Academy and Break The Bottle™ Coach & Consultant

FOREWORD

When I first met Michael Allison, I knew immediately that he wasn't just another man with a story—he was a man with a mission. There was an intensity in his eyes, a conviction in his voice, and a weight in his words that told me this was someone who had been to the depths and decided not only to climb out, but to bring as many people with him as possible.

Michael didn't just want to **"motivate"** people. He wanted to help them **break free**—to shatter the patterns, beliefs, and cycles that were quietly destroying their lives, their dreams, and their sense of self. He had already fought his way through that battle himself. He knew the terrain. He knew the traps. And he knew the urgency.

What struck me most was how clear he was on his calling. Michael understood that he wasn't here by accident—that the pain he had endured and the darkness he had overcome had equipped him for a greater purpose. He didn't just "want" to help people break the bottles in their lives… he felt a deep **duty** to do it. And he wasn't waiting for the perfect time or the perfect circumstances. He was already in motion.

That's what I admire most about him. Michael has a **go-getter's mentality** that doesn't just talk about transformation—it **embodies** it. He lives in alignment with the message he shares. There's no gap between his words and his walk. Every story in this book, every lesson, every strategy—he's lived it. He's proven it in the hardest of environments. And he's applied it not just to himself, but to countless others whose lives are now better because of his influence.

From the Battlefield to the Stage

Michael's story is unlike anyone else's I've ever met. From his early years in Jamaica, through the chaos of childhood separation and survival, to serving as a U.S. Marine in one of the most dangerous combat zones in Iraq—his life has been shaped in fire. Those experiences left him with deep scars, some visible, most hidden. But where many would have allowed those wounds to define them, Michael made a different choice: he would **use them**.

He returned from war with more than medals—he carried the weight of unspoken trauma, identity loss, and emotional battles that raged long after the physical ones ended. He knows what it's like to feel "high-functioning" on the outside while silently unraveling on the inside. He's been through the nights when it feels like there's no way forward. And he knows the courage it takes to finally face what you've been avoiding.

That's what makes him so credible. He's not writing this book from a safe distance or an academic perspective—he's writing it from the trenches of real life, with the wisdom earned through lived experience. This isn't theory for him. It's survival.

The Bottles We All Carry

If you've never heard Michael talk about **"the bottle,"** you're in for a life-changing concept. The bottle represents all the pain, limiting beliefs, and emotional baggage we've sealed up over time. Sometimes we know what's inside it; sometimes we've buried it so deep we can't even see it clearly. But whether we acknowledge it or not, it shapes everything—our relationships, our confidence, our decisions, our future.

Michael doesn't just explain the bottle—he hands you the tools to break it. His **3D Framework™—Decision, Direction, Destination**—isn't a motivational soundbite. It's a blueprint for rewiring your identity, reclaiming your power, and rebuilding your life from the inside out.

And here's what I love: Michael doesn't try to sell you on an easy process. He's honest about the reality—that breaking the bottle requires courage, discomfort, and consistency. He calls you to face the truth without flinching, to make decisions with discipline instead of emotion, and to lead yourself before you try to lead anyone else.

Why This Book Matters

There's no shortage of self-help books on the market. You can find thousands of pages about mindset, success, and positive thinking. But this book? This book is different.

It's different because it's **born of real battle**—both the kind fought with weapons and the kind fought in the mind and heart. It's different because Michael has done the internal **"skunkwork"** he talks about. He's put in the behind-the-scenes labor of confronting his own pain, rewriting his belief system, and conditioning himself to thrive under pressure.

It's different because he's lived on both sides—he knows what it's like to be stuck, and he knows what it's like to be free. That's why the strategies in these pages work. They aren't built on hype—they're built on healing.

As someone who has worked with Michael and seen his heart up close, I can tell you this: he is the real deal. He doesn't just want you to feel better. He wants you to **be better**. He wants you to walk into the version of yourself that you know exists but may have felt out of reach for far too long.

A Personal Challenge to You

If you're holding this book right now, I believe it's because a part of you is ready. Maybe you're tired of wearing the mask. Maybe you're exhausted from pretending you're fine. Maybe you've accomplished some impressive things but still feel disconnected from who you really are. Or maybe you've been living in survival mode for so long that you can't remember what thriving feels like.

Whatever your reason, I want to challenge you the same way I know Michael would: don't just read this book—**work it**. Engage with it. Let it confront you. Let it stretch you. Let it disrupt the patterns that have kept you in place.

Because here's the truth—your life doesn't change because you read the right words. It changes when you decide to live them.

Michael Allison is a soldier in more ways than one. Yes, he's worn the uniform and served his country in combat. But today, he's still on the front lines—fighting for the hearts, minds, and futures of those who are ready to break free. He's taken the discipline, courage, and resilience forged in the military and now applies it to the greatest battle any of us will ever fight: the battle for our own identity and destiny.

You're about to step into a book that can change your life if you let it. Michael will hand you the tools, but you'll have to pick them up and use them. He'll point you toward the door, but you'll have to walk through it. And when you do—when you break the bottle—you'll discover that everything you've been searching for was never lost. It was just waiting for you to set it free.

So read with openness. Read with courage. And most importantly, read with the willingness to act.

Michael has walked this road ahead of you. Now it's your turn.

— Anthony Trucks
Former NFL Athlete, International Speaker, Founder of Dark Work, and Identity Shift Coach

INTRODUCTION

There comes a moment in life—quiet, devastating, and unforgettable—when the belief of the framework you've built your identity around suddenly collapses. It could be a choice. A loss. Rock-bottom. A moment of reckoning. One that shakes you to your core and leaves you staring at the wreckage of what once felt stable. One that makes the stories you used to tell yourself impossible to keep believing.

You live in this world, and you make choices.
Choices you try to justify under a belief system.
For yourself. For your family. For your legacy.
And for a while, it works. You manage. You endure. You survive.
Until one day—it doesn't.

Until you make a choice—or life hands you one—that shatters everything you thought you knew, leaving your old truths feeling hollow… like a beautiful lie you can no longer believe.

A decision you can't explain away.
A mistake you can't forgive.
A fracture you can't seem to heal.
And it takes everything.
Your family. Your friendships. Your sense of self.

And all you're left with is…
Nothing.

Nothing but a shadow. Ghosts of who you were. A phantom of who you could've been. An invisible unfulfilled future you were too hurt, too numb, too lost to reach for.

The Invisible Barriers Holding You Back

You smile for the camera.
But you can't meet your own gaze in the mirror.
You check the boxes, chase the milestones, manage the performance—
Yet deep down, something feels… off.
Something feels trapped.
Something feels like it's screaming to be acknowledged, but you don't know how to listen. It could be fear, doubt, anxiety, grief, guilt or some other limitation holding you back.

This book is for that *purpose*.

Adversity is not a detour—it's the path. No one gets through life unscathed. There is no success story untouched by suffering. No breakthrough that didn't come with breaking. The real question is not whether you'll face hardship—but what you'll *do* with it. Because the difference between those who rise and those who remain stuck… is what they choose to do when adversity knocks.

Some people become *defined* by their wounds.
Others become *refined* by them.

The Story You Keep Telling Yourself

Every night, millions of us go to bed selling ourselves stories soaked in fear, shame, and self-doubt—only to wake up the next morning as the first customer to buy them.
It's a vicious loop: inner narratives rooted in insecurity that shape how we see, speak, and show up in the world. And we don't even realize it's happening—because we've normalized it.

Science has a name for this: negativity bias—our brain's built-in tendency to give more weight to negative experiences than positive ones. Research shows that nearly 78% of our thoughts are negative, and the vast majority are repetitive. That means we're not just thinking harmful thoughts—we're rehearsing them like scripts.

And the cost is real.

More than 70% of adults report experiencing at least one major traumatic event in their lifetime. But trauma isn't the only wound we carry. Millions silently bottle up and battle with low self-worth, anxiety, depression, burnout, addiction, and identity confusion—not because they're weak, but because no one ever taught them how to fight back with emotional intelligence, clarity, self-awareness, and resilience.

We've been conditioned to master performance.
To produce.
To push through and perfected survival.
To silence pain.
To smile through dysfunction.
To bury what's breaking us because "there's no time to fall apart."

So let me ask you:

What if the real barriers in your life aren't external?
What if they're internal contracts—unseen, unspoken pacts you made with pain, comparison and performance?

What if the only thing standing between who you are and who you're meant to be… is a bottle?

But what if…

What if everything you've been chasing—your breakthrough, your peace, your purpose, your clarity, your confidence, your connection to your family and loved ones—wasn't lost?
What if it was just *trapped…in a bottle*?

Trapped behind old pain.
Behind your silence.
Behind the stories you've accepted as truth for too long.
Behind that bottle.

And what if, on the other side of breaking that bottle, lived the version of you you've always known existed—the one who leads with power, lives with purpose, and shows up fully in your life, relationships, business, and calling?

What would you be willing to do to meet that version of you?

What would you be willing to break... to finally break through?

As we journey through these pages, you're going to see me—the real authentic, vulnerable transparent me—laid bare in all my raw, unfiltered vulnerability. We'll travel back to my childhood in Jamaica and the gritty streets of Overtown, Little Haiti, Opa-Locka and Carol City in Miami, Florida. You'll walk beside me through my years in the military, the transition back to civilian life, and the lingering trauma of war. You'll hear about my run-ins with the law, the mental breakdowns that nearly broke me, and my climb through the ranks of corporate America. You'll see me as a single father, navigating marriage in a blended family, facing the heartbreak of divorce, and finding love again. You'll witness how my faith was challenged and how it re-anchored me, how I pursued the unpredictable path of entrepreneurship, the turns into medical research, and the return—the full circle—that has brought me right here. To you. To this book. To this very moment.

We've been taught to perform, to endure, to keep going—but never how to truly heal. And you can't heal what you refuse to face. You can't break free while pretending you're fine. The truth is, your potential is often trapped behind unspoken agreements with shame, perfectionism, fear, survival, and silence.

The turning point comes when you decide that your healing is worth the disruption—when you choose to stop running from the pain, the silence, and the truths you've avoided. That choice changes everything.

That's what this book is about—not just the breakdowns we hide, but the decisions we make in their wake. The moments we try to outrun. The emptiness we try to fill. The truths we try to bury. And most importantly, the healing we must choose for ourselves—because no one else can do it for us.

Whether it's trauma, regret, addiction, grief, moral injury, burnout, or the quiet ache of unrealized potential—we've all bottled something. And the longer we keep it sealed, the more it poisons our progress, our relationships, our identity, and our future.

This book was born out of necessity—not theory.
It's about breaking that bottle—metaphorically—to challenge your BS... your *Belief System*... and everything you've bottled up inside—boldly, bravely, and permanently.

It was created because too many of us are silently struggling—high-functioning in our pain, performing strength while privately unraveling. I know, because I lived it. I was the man who looked successful on the outside but was quietly imploding on the inside. I wore the uniforms, earned the accolades, built the résumé—but none of it could heal the fractured identity I carried underneath.

Break the Bottle was created as a response to the invisible battles people fight every day—shame, trauma, fear, self-doubt, burnout, addiction, and loss of identity. It's not just a book; it's a manual for inner transformation. It was created for those who have survived but never learned how to live. For the ones who have achieved but still feel unfulfilled. For the leaders who give everything to others but don't know how to show up for themselves.

I created this book because I needed it myself—a blueprint that merged science with soul, truth with tools, story with strategy. I needed more than motivation—I needed a method. And when I found my way back from the edge, I knew I couldn't keep what I'd learned to myself.

This book is the result of that journey—a fusion of lived experience, trauma-informed insight, mental health research, leadership coaching, and raw, unfiltered truth. It was created for those who are tired of wearing the mask. For those ready to make a decision, choose a direction, and own their destination.

Because the world doesn't just need more leaders. It needs more healed ones. It's about finding clarity in chaos. Identity in the ruins. Healing in the work.

You're not here by accident. You're here because you're ready to reclaim your power and **break your bottle**.

- Ready to make a **decision** and break the patterns.

- Ready to choose a **direction** and choose the path.

- Ready to discover your **destination** and own your future.

What It Means to Break the Bottle—and How It Can Transform Your Life

This book isn't here to entertain you with polished tales or give you a short-lived surge of motivation. It's here to equip you—with truth, with tools, and with a proven framework—so you can move from stuck to unstoppable. It's here to reflect what you've been too busy, too afraid, or too overwhelmed to face, and to give you the system to finally face it head-on.

Breaking the bottle isn't about smashing glass—it's about shattering the invisible container that's been holding you back. That bottle is built from the narratives you've inherited, the lies you've adopted, and the wounds you've never named. It's forged in childhood pain, hardened by trauma, and sealed shut by the performances you've perfected just to feel safe, accepted, or worthy. Inside it are every version of "I'm not enough," every internalized doubt, every quiet breakdown that never got language. It holds your protective masks, your coping mechanisms, and the unspoken apologies you make for existing too loudly or needing too much.

And while that bottle may look intact, it's quietly leaking—into your relationships, your leadership, your decisions, your identity. To break it is not an act of destruction, but a declaration. It's standing in your truth and saying, *I will no longer shrink to fit the life my pain designed for me.* It's leading from authenticity, not armor. Building from intention, not insecurity. Rising not in spite of your story, but because you finally owned it.

This isn't about one dramatic breakthrough—it's about reclaiming the blueprint of your life. It's about reconstructing your inner architecture so your future is no longer held hostage by your past. It's about choosing healing over hiding, ownership over avoidance, and transformation over performance. That's what the **3D Framework™—Decision, Direction, Destination**—is designed to do. It's a mirror, not to show you who you've been, but to reveal who you are becoming.

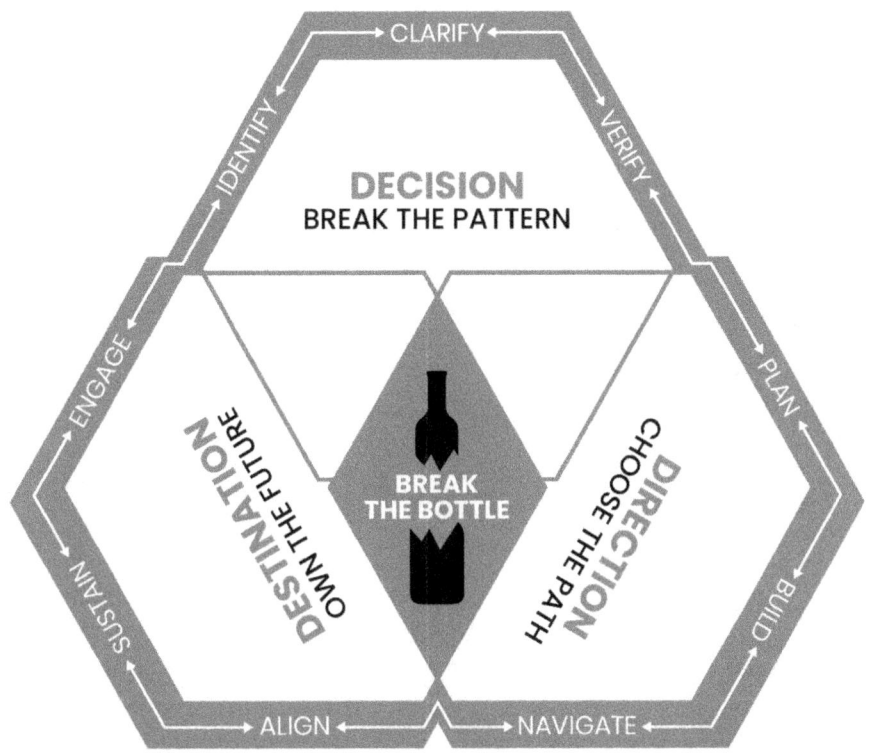

Through this framework, you'll recalibrate your mindset, reclaim your energy, and reestablish your identity around truth, not trauma. You'll stop negotiating with fear and start leading your life with purpose. You'll walk away not just inspired, but mentally and emotionally equipped to live free, lead boldly, and finally own the version of you the world's been waiting to meet.

I know this because it's the path I've walked—not in theory, but in survival. From the battlegrounds of Iraq to sleepless nights of self-doubt, from the weight of leadership to the breaking point of burnout, I've tested every principle I now teach. As a keynote speaker, leadership trainer, resilience coach, and business consultant, I've seen this framework transform lives in every arena—because it isn't abstract. It's grounded in lived experience, backed by neuroscience and psychology, and proven in real-world resilience.

Inside these pages, you'll find the language for your pain, the tools for your breakthrough, and the strategies to turn your healing into lasting momentum. You'll stop settling for surface wins and start building a life of deep alignment and legacy. You'll no longer react out of fear—you'll respond with clarity.

This journey will not be soft. But it will be worth it. If you're willing to confront what's been keeping you stuck, this book won't just change how you think—it will rewire how you lead, how you build, and how you live.

This isn't just a book.
It's your blueprint.
Welcome to the next level of you.
Let's begin.

DECISION

SHATTER LIMITATIONS & BREAK THE PATTERN

You have the power to choose. Imagine living your entire life bottled up—not just emotionally, but mentally. Bottled thoughts. Bottled potential. Bottled dreams. You carry the pressure you never talk about, the pain you hope will fade, the questions you never dare to ask. And maybe, like me, you've learned to function while fragmented. You've mastered the art of compartmentalizing and survival—but haven't yet discovered the rhythm of truly living.

For me, that survival looked like a string of decisions I thought would make me whole. Some were reckless—like chasing quick wins, staying in toxic environments, or trying to prove my worth through titles, relationships, or recognition. Others were simply reactive—made in moments of pain, fear, or pride. I thought I was moving forward, but I was really running in circles.

It wasn't until much later that I learned a hard truth: **your life is shaped less by what happens to you and more by the decisions you make in response to it.**

It has been an extraordinary journey, not just walking through my own process of breaking the bottle, but sitting front row to the courageous transformations of others. Over the past 40 plus years of my life, I've watched people from every walk of life rise from adversity—not because life got easier, but because they got intentional. I've seen healing happen in raw, unpolished moments. I've seen teenagers, parents, business leaders, and veterans stare down the parts of themselves they once feared. And every time someone broke through, I asked myself a deeper question—not just on their behalf, but on mine: *What separates those who rise from those who remain stuck?*

The answer that kept surfacing was simple, but life-changing: solutions thinking. The people who break through are not the ones who avoid failure or escape pain. They're the ones who make the decision to act with purpose and learn to ask better questions. They don't fixate on what's broken—they aim at what's possible. Instead of obsessing over what they don't want, they stop asking, *"Why me?"* and start asking, *"What now?"* they take ownership of what they *do* want. They name what they want with clarity instead of defining their lives by what they're trying to avoid.

It sounds obvious, but most people never ask that question. They become experts in complaint and avoidance, skilled in listing what's wrong—yet strangers to the clarity of what's right. Think about it: when you step into a taxi, the driver doesn't ask, *"Where do you not want to go?"* He asks, *"Where are you headed?"* Life works the same way. You can't move toward something you've never dared to name.

Breaking the bottle is about naming it—everything you've sealed inside: the fear you've silenced, the pain you've carried, the stories that no longer serve you. It's about doing the deep excavation to uncover the truth beneath the layers of conditioning, fear, and performance.

For me, that meant making new decisions that felt uncomfortable at first—setting boundaries I'd avoided for years, leaving environments that looked good on paper but were killing my spirit, confronting habits that kept me small, and letting go of relationships that didn't align with who I was becoming.

Making a decision is not a single moment of courage—it's a lifestyle of choosing courage over comfort again and again. It's not dramatic. It's not loud. It's not always public. It's transformative. And it begins with one bold question: *What do I really want to build with my life?*

That's emotional intelligence—not just feeling deeply, but directing those feelings with purpose. Asking questions that empower you, not limit you. I've stopped running from challenges because I've learned to see them as teachers. Every crack in the bottle reveals more of who I really am. Every obstacle is an invitation to rise, not recoil. With every setback, I've gained clarity, humility, and strength. Not because I deserved it—but because I chose it. I chose to own my transformation. To lean into the tension. To become responsible for the future I say I want.

This is the difference between emotional decisions and disciplined decisions. Emotional decisions feel good in the moment, but they rarely lead you anywhere lasting. They're reactive. They shift with the weather of your feelings. Disciplined decisions, though, are rooted in your vision. They prioritize long-term fulfillment over short-term comfort. They require saying "no" to distractions, "yes" to boundaries, and "not yet" to impulse. They're not made *for* you—they're made *by* you, guided by the person you're becoming, not the emotion you're feeling.

But this kind of transformation isn't accidental. It starts with intention. You must decide what kind of life you're building. What kind of legacy you want to leave. Who you want to help. How you want to wake up each day—with dread or with direction? That level of clarity doesn't come to the passive. It comes to the ones who are bold enough to ask, *"What do I really want my life to stand for?"*

To live fully is to struggle intentionally. It's to wrestle with pain, not to be consumed by it, but to be shaped through it. And every time life places you at a crossroads, you have a decision to make: will you retreat into reaction, or will you lead yourself with intention? When you ask, "What difference will this make?" It means making the boldest decision of all: to become who you were created to be—on purpose. In the face of challenge, you don't just gain clarity—you access the emotional fuel that powers purpose.

But here's what I've learned: **transformation is never accidental.** It starts with a decision—one you live, breathe, and anchor your life to. Decision is where you stop waiting for change and start creating it. It's where you reclaim your power, not from fear, but from truth.

The process begins with **Identify**—naming what's been holding you back. You can't change what you refuse to see. That means confronting the habits, fears, excuses, and limiting beliefs that have been silently scripting your life.

Next, you **Clarify**—digging deep to understand where these patterns began. Were they shaped by past experiences? Someone else's expectations? Moments of pain that left a scar? When you trace the roots, confusion turns into understanding, and understanding opens the door for change.

Finally, you **Verify**—separating truth from lies. Every limitation carries a message. Some hold truth, but many are distortions rooted in fear or old wounds. Verification is the moment you decide which narratives get to stay and which ones you're ready to shatter for good.

This is the power of Decision: breaking the pattern, disrupting old stories, and rewriting your future with clarity and conviction. It's not a single moment of courage—it's a lifestyle of choosing courage over comfort again and again. And once you decide, everything else begins to shift.

1

THE BOTTLES WE CARRY

"You don't just wake up trapped in a pattern—you inherit it, reinforce it, and carry it like a bottle no one told you could break."

— Break The Bottle

Identifying Your Personal Bottles

We don't trip over mountains; we trip over the pebbles in our shoes. Not because they're loud, but because they're constant. The real weight of life isn't in what's ahead of us—it's in what we carry silently inside: the shame we never processed, the beliefs we never challenged, the pain we buried so deep we forgot it was still shaping us.

I call these our "bottles."

Just like a tightly sealed container, these bottles hold emotional pressure: fear, anxiety, self-doubt, insecurity, past traumas, and false stories that have been told so many times we've mistaken them for truth. And here's the hard part: they don't just disappear over time. They explode—leaking into our relationships, sabotaging our success, eroding our confidence, and showing up in moments that matter most.

When I was eight years old, I remember watching my uncle, a tough, stoic man who had survived more than most, quietly break down one night at the kitchen table. He never talked about what haunted him, but you could feel it in the silence. That silence taught me something: not all pain screams. Some pain just sits with you, tight-lipped and heavy, and you carry it everywhere you go. That's a bottle.

If you're going to rise, you have to break the bottle.

We all carry bottles—some dark, some clear. The dark bottles are the ones we keep hidden—filled with pain, secrets, trauma, or shame we never dared to examine. The clear bottles aren't lighter because the past was easier—they're lighter because we've done the hard work. We faced what was inside, labeled it, healed from it, and decided what to carry forward.

But here's the truth: it's hard to see the label when you're inside of the jar. When you're submerged in your own story—your own patterns, pain, and perception—it becomes difficult to step back and name what's actually weighing you down. You become both the contents and the container. You're swirling in emotion, memory, fear—and until you rise above it, clarity remains elusive.

That's why the work of identifying your personal bottles takes courage. It's a process of stepping outside yourself—seeing your life from a higher shelf, with a fresh perspective. It's choosing to stop marinating in old mindsets and start examining what's been fermenting in the background for years. You can't clean what you won't confront. You can't label what you refuse to look at. But once you do—once you name it—you gain power over it.

So, I'll ask you:

What's in your bottle?

Is it fear? Scarcity? Resentment? Worry? Anxiety? Stress? Bitterness?

Don't just name it. Face it.

Breaking the Bottle You Pretend Isn't There

You can't break what you pretend doesn't exist. And you can't lead with purpose if you're leaking pressure. Bottled emotions don't disappear—they detonate. You may think you're managing it, but that pain is quietly shaping every decision you make, every risk you avoid, and every opportunity you sabotage.

Let's get one thing straight: **the bottle is not what happened to you.** The bottle is what you believed about yourself because of what happened.

Maybe you buried trauma beneath ambition. Maybe someone told you that you'd never make it, and even though you brushed it off, somewhere deep down… you believed them. So you overcompensate. You play small. You keep people at arm's length before they get too close. That's the bottle talking.

And here's the thing about change—it rarely whispers. Most of the time, it hits like a truck. It's not a tidy shift in circumstances—it's a full-body shock to your system. The first thing you feel isn't logic. It's not a strategy. It's raw, visceral, heavy emotion.

Change can flood you with sadness, anger, fear, confusion, or numbness—all at once. Suddenly, getting out of bed feels impossible. Making the call feels like lifting a thousand pounds. Stepping into that gym or walking away from the bottle or the barstool feels like climbing a mountain with no oxygen.

And it's not just in your head—your body feels it first. Your chest tightens. Your stomach drops. Your limbs feel heavy. Before your brain can even assess what's happening, your heart, gut, and nervous system have already sounded the alarm.

This is why change feels so overwhelming—especially the kind you didn't choose. It disrupts your known world. It shakes the routines, identities, and comfort zones that used to anchor you. Your nervous system treats that disruption as a threat, pulling you back toward the familiar—even when the familiar is destroying you.

So you stay on the couch even though you crave a breakthrough. You avoid the conversation even though the silence is suffocating. You go numb even though you're desperate to feel alive again.

And here's the most painful truth: what feels like protection is often prevention. It's not shielding you from pain—it's keeping you from healing, freedom, and forward movement.

So what do you do when the bottle finally breaks and the flood comes rushing in? You don't fight emotion with force. You move through it with awareness. And that movement begins with a decision:

- **Name It** – Emotions lose their grip when they're brought into the light. Say it out loud: *"I feel sad. I feel overwhelmed. I feel scared."* Naming isn't weakness—it's power.

- **Normalize It** – Emotional shock is normal. You're not broken—you're human.

- **Don't Wait to "Feel Better" to Start Moving** – Movement creates momentum. Brush your teeth. Walk outside. Call a friend. Remind your body: *"We're not stuck."*

- **Use the Emotion as Fuel** – Emotions are messengers. Anger can reveal a boundary crossed. Sadness can point to a loss you haven't grieved. Anxiety can show you where your future feels uncertain—which means there's something worth fighting for.

- **Create a Ritual for Momentum** – Small, consistent actions— making your bed, writing your truth, saying your affirmations— build the energy to tackle the big things.

The key to breaking the bottle isn't avoiding pain—it's confronting it with clarity. Because the moment you stop reacting and start deciding, you stop being a prisoner of your past and become the architect of your future.

The Three Bottles We All Carry

Every invisible weight you carry can usually be traced back to one of three bottles:

1. **Limiting Beliefs** – These are the quiet scripts that whisper, *"You can't."* They disguise themselves as logic—*"I'm not a leader."* *"Success is for people with connections."* *"If I fail, I'll be worse off."*—but they're really protective illusions that keep you "safe" by keeping you stuck.

2. **Fear-Based Conditioning** – This is where fear pretends to be caution. It convinces you to stay in the job that's draining you, delay writing the book burning in your chest, avoid the stage, or shrink your brilliance to keep others comfortable. Most people aren't paralyzed by the fear of failure—they're terrified of being fully seen.

3. **Emotional Baggage & Generational Programming** – Some bottles aren't even yours. They were passed down like unwanted heirlooms: unspoken shame, survival-based thinking, or perfectionism disguised as love.

My Story – Where It All Started

I was born in Jamaica—a land as breathtaking as it is bruised. My earliest memories are a mix of beauty and struggle: the sound of rain against a tin roof, the smell of freshly cut sugarcane, the laughter of cousins playing barefoot in the yard—and the ever-present shadow of hardship.

In 1988, Hurricane Gilbert tore through the island with a force I can still feel in my bones. It ripped apart homes, uprooted trees, and scattered lives in every direction. Our family lost more than a roof—we lost our sense of stability. We were displaced, split apart, and thrust into survival mode. At that age, I didn't have the language for it, but I understood the lesson: safety was temporary, and pain could arrive without warning.

Not long after, in the late '80s, my family began the long and complicated journey of immigration—first to New York City, then to Miami. When I was just seven, my parents left to work in New York, while my siblings and I were sent ahead to Miami. I still remember that day at the airport—my small hand wrapped around my grandmother's, my eyes scanning the chaos around me. Planes roared overhead, voices echoed over the intercom, and everything in my world felt like it was moving too fast.

We landed in Overtown Projects—a place with its own kind of storms. The streets were loud, the buildings worn, and opportunity felt like something you had to steal before it disappeared. I didn't sound like the other kids. My patois accent marked me as different. I didn't walk like them. I didn't carry the same rhythm. And in a world that punished difference, I quickly learned how it felt to be an outsider.

I was a shy, introverted kid who wanted to disappear into the background, but difference doesn't let you hide. I endured relentless bullying—mocked for my accent, my clothes, my face, my weight. Even the places that were supposed to give me safety—the Boy Scouts, art school, football—came with their own hardship and bruises. I experienced abuse in the Boy Scouts that no child should ever experience. I fought on playgrounds and sidewalks. I collected emotional scars before I had the maturity to understand them.

But I didn't process any of it. I learned to compartmentalize, to smile when I was supposed to, to "man up" before I was even a man. I became fluent in survival—functioning on the outside while feeling fractured on the inside.

Some of that came from my environment. Some of it came from what was passed down to me. My grandmother—a brilliant, fiercely independent woman—believed asking for help was a weakness. It was a belief she carried with pride, but it trickled down through the family like an unspoken rule: carry your load alone. I didn't realize how deeply I had internalized that until years later, when I found myself breaking quietly under the weight of trying to handle everything without ever reaching for a hand.

Looking back now, I see the bottles I inherited before I even knew I was carrying them:

- **The scarcity mindset**—born from generations who learned to survive with less.

- **The perfectionism**—handed down as a form of love, but rooted in fear of failure.

- **The silence**—taught by people who had never been taught how to speak their pain.

Whether inherited or absorbed, those patterns shaped me. And here's the truth: you can't lead, love, or live fully while carrying what was never meant for you.

The Skunkwork of the Soul

Skunkwork isn't glamorous. It's not public. It's not praised. It's the hidden mission—the messy, uncomfortable, behind-the-scenes labor of growth. It's the part of transformation that smells bad, feels raw, and happens when no one is clapping, no one is watching, and everything inside you wants to run.

I call it *skunkwork* because that's where the real transformation happens— just like the secretive, high-autonomy engineering projects it's named after. In engineering, skunkwork teams work away from the spotlight to innovate. In life, skunkwork is your private, relentless battle with your deepest fears and your most unfiltered truths. If you've ever been near a skunk, you know the smell isn't just bad—it's unforgettable. It lingers. It clings to you. You can try to mask it, but it's still there. It's not polished or pretty. It's not something you post online for applause. It's the kind of work that gets under your skin, forces you to face what you've been avoiding, and leaves you permanently changed. Skunkwork is doing the dirty work no one else sees.

- It's crying on the floor after another failed relationship.

- It's finally admitting your addiction.

- It's calling out your excuses.

- It's writing down the truth you've never dared to say out loud.

- It's late-night journaling when you'd rather scroll your phone.

- It's the hard conversations you've put off for years.

- It's the therapy session where you finally say the thing you swore you'd never speak out loud.

- It's confronting the parts of yourself that smell so bad you've been holding your nose for years just to survive.

And if skunkwork is the smell, peeling back the layers is the process. Think of it like peeling an onion: the deeper you go, the more your eyes water. Sometimes you cry because of the pain. Sometimes you cry because of the relief. But either way, every layer you remove gets you closer to the core—the root cause that's been running the show from behind the scenes.

That's the power and the pain of skunkwork. It demands honesty. It demands vulnerability. It demands transparency—not with the world at first, but with yourself. Because you can't heal what you won't admit, and you can't break free from a bottle you refuse to open.

If you're willing to endure the smell, the sting, and the mess, you'll find something worth far more than comfort: the truth. And once you have the truth, you can finally build a life that isn't just functional on the outside, but free on the inside.

The paradox? Most people want transformation, but resist skunkwork. Why? Because facing yourself—really facing yourself—is the hardest work you'll ever do. The parts of you you've avoided? That's where the healing hides.

You can't fix what you refuse to face. You can't find the leak when you're underwater. That's why perspective is a gift—it shows up only when you step outside the story. And most of us can't do that alone. We need a mirror, a moment, or a mentor to reflect back to us what we can't yet name.

Think of your life like a jar. Is it half empty or half full? That question isn't just about optimism—it's about ownership. You don't even know what's really in your jar until you've done the skunkwork to unpack it. And when you do, you might find the "genie in the bottle"—your untapped power, your potential, your clarity. But it doesn't come out through comfort—it comes through confrontation.

If you want the magic, you have to go through the mess.

A Navy SEAL once told me, "The hardest mission is the one you do in your head—with no weapon, no safety net, no backup, and no exit strategy." That stuck with me because soul-work isn't about one burst of bravery—it's about daily honesty. If you don't confront what's bottled up inside, those toxins will leak into every part of your life—your work, your relationships, your leadership, your peace.

That's when identity erosion begins. It's rarely one big shatter—it's a slow leak. Drip by drip. Decision by decision. Mask by mask. You trade your truth for approval. Your authenticity for applause. And one day you wake up as a version of yourself that looks successful to everyone—except you.

I've lived this. There was a time when I wore resilience like armor, even when it was crushing me. I performed strength while I was crumbling. I outgrew that version, but for years I tried to resuscitate it because it was familiar. The turning point came when I stopped asking the world for permission to change and gave myself permission to evolve. That's when peace came—not from perfection, but from alignment.

But identity is just one layer of skunkwork. The second is *focus*—because where you direct it determines how you experience life. Most people live in the loop of "not enough"—fixating on what they lack, who hurt them, and what went wrong. That's a recipe for frustration, bitterness, and despair. If you want to change your reality, change your focal point.

The third layer is *conditioning*. You don't just need motivation—you need a nervous system that knows how to hold steady under pressure. Elite performers don't get hyped under stress—they get centered. That's biochemistry, not inspiration. I feel it every time I step on stage: I'm not performing, I'm anchored in presence. That comes from training, from surrounding myself with elevated energy, and from creating new neural pathways through intentional action.

Skunkwork is repetition meeting revelation. It's the discipline of asking yourself daily:

- "Is this action aligned with the identity I say I want?"

- "Is this decision reinforcing who I'm becoming?"

- "Is this thought creating traction—or distraction?"

It's not glamorous, and it's not Instagrammable—but it's the difference between inspiration and transformation.

I learned this the hard way.

One night in Stockbridge, Georgia, my phone rang. As a Trainmaster, emergencies were part of the job—but this one was different. The dispatcher's voice was flat: a suicide on the tracks. I arrived in the rain to flashing lights, reporters, a coroner, and a silence that felt heavy enough to crush you. Then I saw it—the body bag. Still. Lifeless.

Hours later, I sat in a boardroom being praised for my composure. "You held it together." "You're solid." They saw strength. I felt empty. That night, standing in my bathroom with my jacket still soaked from the storm, I stared into the mirror and didn't recognize the man looking back. Not because he looked different—but because he looked hollow.

That moment cracked something open. It pulled up a decade of buried trauma—combat tours, explosions, putting my best friend in a body bag. For over ten years, I told myself I was fine. But standing over those tracks, I saw the bottle I had sealed shut, and I couldn't unsee it.

And here's what I learned: the quiet beauty in struggle only shows up when you face what most people run from. Growth arrives in the tension—in the mirror—when everything in you wants to quit, but something deeper whispers, "Not yet."

Most people wait for a sign. A breakdown. A perfect moment. The ones who change don't wait. They decide this moment, this breath, this heartbeat is enough.

So I'll ask you:

What seeds are you planting with your words, actions, and beliefs?
Are you reinforcing a story of fear and lack without realizing it?
Who are you becoming by default?
And most importantly—what are you avoiding that will control you if you don't face it?

Skunkwork isn't just about healing the past. It's about building a future—a new "I AM"

Belief + Responsibility + Willingness = I AM

Here's the truth: rejection isn't the end—it's redirection. Every "no" life hands you is a detour toward something more aligned, if you're willing to listen instead of shut down.

The foundation of every transformation comes down to this simple but profound formula:

Belief + Responsibility + Willingness = I AM

At first glance, it might look like a motivational catchphrase. It's not. It's the blueprint for identity transformation—the anatomy of a breakthrough.

Belief is the ignition. Not hype, but the deep knowing that something better is possible and accessible to you. That even though your past shaped your patterns, it doesn't get to decide your future. You can't build a vision you don't believe in.

Responsibility is the anchor. It's not about blame—it's about ownership. You stop waiting for someone else to save, fix, or validate you. You pick up the weight of your own evolution. You own your time, your energy, your habits. You stop outsourcing your peace to your past, your parents, or your pain. Your life becomes your job.

Willingness is the bridge. The part most people miss. You can believe and take ownership, but if you're not willing to be uncomfortable, to take the first step without a guarantee, change will stall. Willingness is motion. It's showing up even when fear is louder than faith.

When belief, responsibility, and willingness collide, something shifts inside you. The old story starts to loosen its grip. You stop saying, "One day I will," and start living as, "I already am." Not because you've mastered it, but because your identity has been recalibrated.

"I AM" isn't ego—it's embodiment. It's a present-tense declaration backed by action. You stop chasing a future version of yourself and start acting like them now. That's where true confidence comes from—not after the results, but before them, when your actions and values are finally in alignment.

And if you're wondering why you still feel stuck, here's the hard truth: **inspiration without disruption changes nothing.** Reading quotes, reposting reels, or applauding someone else's breakthrough is easy. Real change begins when your comfort zone stops being comfortable. When the excuses lose their power. When the distractions stop working. It begins when you stop being impressed by transformation and start demanding it from yourself.

Transformation doesn't happen by chance—it's engineered through intention. If your patterns are passive, your growth will stagnate. If your habits are fear-driven, your success—no matter how impressive—will feel fragile, always one setback away from crumbling. And if you keep choosing comfort over courage, you'll never develop the resilience to sustain real, lasting change.

True transformation demands discomfort. It requires leading yourself with clarity when the world around you feels chaotic. And discipline—the kind that shows up consistently when motivation disappears—isn't punishment. It's the highest form of self-respect. It says, *"I know who I'm becoming, and I'm acting like it—now."*

Here's why that matters: self-sabotage isn't a sign you're broken—it's a sign your brain is doing what it was programmed to do—protect you. Your brain isn't designed for success; it's designed for survival. So when you step into something new—launching a business, speaking up, setting boundaries—it scans for danger. If it senses anything that feels like a past wound, it sounds the alarm. You procrastinate. You isolate yourself. You overthink. You self-sabotage—not because you can't succeed, but because your brain thinks it's keeping you safe.

As Dr. Bruce Perry's research shows, emotional memory lasts far longer than rational thought. That's why a single raised voice can trigger a reaction rooted in an old wound you thought you'd buried. The brain reacts before you even have time to think. And as a 2021 study in the *Journal of Personality and Social Psychology* found, people with internalized negative self-beliefs often avoid chasing their goals—not out of laziness, but out of fear that success will expose them as "not enough."

So if you've been feeling stuck, delayed, or distracted, it's not because you're incapable—it's because your operating system is still running on survival mode. And survival isn't where you were meant to stay.

This is your moment to rewrite the code. To stop letting the past drive your decisions. To train your brain to support your expansion instead of resisting it.

And it begins now—not when you have more time, more money, or more proof.

Because here's the truth—no one is coming to save you. But the moment you believe, take responsibility, and remain willing, you'll realize something life-changing:

You were the rescue plan all along.

BREAK THE BOTTLE CHALLENGE — Chapter 1

You don't need to fix everything overnight. You don't need to rewrite your entire life in one dramatic leap. But you do need to begin. And you begin by breaking just one bottle.

Here's how:

- **Step 1: Identify and Name It**
  List three limiting beliefs or emotional patterns that are keeping you stuck. Don't sugarcoat them. Be brutally honest. If you can't name it, you can't break it.

- **Step 2: Clarify and Trace It**
  Ask yourself: Where did this belief come from? Who modeled it for you? What moment cemented it? Pain leaves a fingerprint—look for it.

- **Step 3: Verify and Question It**
  Challenge the belief. Is it true? Is it helpful? Does it align with the future version of you you're working to become—or is it just keeping you emotionally safe in a story that no longer serves you?

- **Step 4: Reframe It**
  Replace the label with a new lens. For example:

  - From: "I always mess things up."

  - To: "I'm a work in progress—and that progress is power."

This isn't just semantics. It's neurological reconditioning. You're rewiring your brain to believe something new by feeding it new evidence.

- **Step 5: Act Against It**
  Choose one bold action within the next 24 hours that goes directly against your old pattern—and affirms your new belief. It could be making a phone call, submitting the application, having the hard conversation, or even just saying "no" for the first time without apology. Small action, massive momentum.

This Is the Beginning

You don't need another motivational speech. What you need is a new narrative—one that mirrors who you're becoming, not who you've been. One that calls you forward instead of chaining you backward.

When I finally broke one of my deepest bottles—the belief that I was only valuable if I was strong—it didn't come in the middle of applause or some big breakthrough moment. It came quietly during the skunkwork. It came in silence. It came with a single tear in the dark and the sobering realization that I had spent years trying to earn something that was already mine: worthiness.

That moment didn't just shift my mindset. It recharted the direction of my entire life.

So, break the bottle. Let what's been trapped inside finally breathe. And let the real you—the one who is bold, brilliant, and unbottled—finally rise.

RESOURCES

Download the Tool: Bottleneck Audit Checklist
Take a deeper inventory of the limiting beliefs, emotional blocks, and mental chains you've been carrying. Use this checklist to identify, confront, and begin releasing the internal bottlenecks sabotaging your momentum.

Available at: btbprograms.com/free-resources

2

THE TURNING POINT—WHY YOU MUST DECIDE

"Your next level will not be found in comfort. It will be forged in the fire of your decisions."

— Break The Bottle

The Psychology of Decision-Making

Every breakthrough begins with a choice. But the choice itself is rarely simple—it's a mental negotiation between who you've been, who you are, and who you dare to become.

Most people imagine decision-making as a clean, logical process: gather facts, weigh options, choose the best path. But the reality is far messier. Every decision is a psychological dance between your past experiences, your emotional triggers, your fears, and your vision for the future. At its core, decision-making is about navigating uncertainty—and here's the catch: your brain wasn't designed for success. It was designed for survival.

When you stand at a crossroads, your mind doesn't act like a neutral supercomputer. It runs every possibility through filters built from memory, past pain, emotional bias, and deeply ingrained safety patterns. You might believe you're weighing facts, but often you're wrestling with feelings—and those feelings can be far more persuasive than the numbers in front of you.

This is where cognitive biases quietly steer the wheel. These mental shortcuts help you make quick judgments but often lead you astray. Confirmation bias makes you seek only the evidence that supports what you already believe. Loss aversion makes you fear losing something far more than you value gaining something new. These tendencies don't make you weak—they make you human. But they also explain why so many people stay in toxic relationships, dead-end jobs, or self-sabotaging routines long past their expiration date. The brain will almost always choose the familiarity of pain over the uncertainty of possibility—unless you train it to do otherwise. I remember a mission in Iraq where our convoy's route was suddenly blocked by debris. We had seconds to choose: wait for clearance or reroute through unfamiliar terrain. The "safe" choice was to wait. But every minute on that road was exposure. My training told me one thing, my instincts another. In the end, we rerouted—and learned later that an IED had been planted on the original road minutes after we stopped. That moment seared into me the truth that "familiar" is not always "safe," and hesitation can be more dangerous than the discomfort of the unknown.

And then there's emotion. Many people think logic and emotion live on opposite ends of a spectrum, but neuroscience shows they are partners, not rivals. Your emotions don't just color your decisions—they shape them entirely. I learned this firsthand during my training at Rush Medical University when one of our instructors designed a simulation specifically for working with combat veterans. The scenario began in a controlled, clinical environment—fluorescent lights steady, vital signs stable on the monitor, and a patient mannequin dressed in fatigues lying on the bed. We had the medical protocol down cold. But then the instructor dimmed the lights, piped in the sounds of distant gunfire, shouted simulated commands over a loudspeaker, and added the faint, metallic scent of artificial blood. The heart monitor began to spike, alarms blared, and a recording of a soldier's strained breathing filled the room.

In seconds, everything changed. My training was still in my head, but my body responded differently—adrenaline surged, my hands hesitated, my vision tunneled. I wasn't just treating a mannequin anymore; my mind was reacting as if I were in the field under fire. That day, I understood in a visceral way: emotion isn't a side effect in decision-making—it's the steering wheel. And if you don't train yourself to manage it, it will steer you somewhere you don't want to go. Anxiety shrinks opportunity. Fear masquerades as wisdom. A choice made in panic will almost always be a defensive one, not a visionary one.

But not all emotions are liabilities. Emotional clarity—the ability to name and understand what you're feeling—is a decision-making superpower. People who can distinguish between sadness, fear, guilt, or frustration make more aligned choices because they aren't reacting from confusion. They're responding from awareness.

Memory plays its role too. Your mind doesn't just evaluate the present—it consults a vault of past experiences. Sometimes that saves you from repeating mistakes. Other times, it traps you in loops. You remember how failure felt, so you pick the safer option—not because it's right, but because it's familiar.

Personality, upbringing, and culture layer in even more complexity. Some are wired for impulsivity, others for methodical analysis. Some lean on faith, others on facts. There is no single "right" decision-making style—but there is a right decision-making awareness. The more you understand your own wiring, the more intentional your choices become.

Interestingly, mental shortcuts—or *heuristics*—can sometimes work for you. They allow for quick action when time is short. Other times, you need the deliberate slow burn of analysis. Wisdom is knowing when to trust your gut and when to slow down.

One model that explains this balance is **Fuzzy Trace Theory**—the idea that we make decisions using two paths: the "verbatim" route (details and facts) and the "gist" route (overall meaning and intuitive sense). As we mature, we lean more on gist. This is why you sometimes just *know* what to do—even when it defies perfect logic.

External forces shape your decisions too—social pressure, expectations, fear of judgment. Many unknowingly outsource their choices to the comfort zones of others—parents, partners, peers—until they've given away authorship of their own life. One of my clients, a talented graphic designer, spent years letting her parents' opinions dictate her career moves. She'd get offers to work with top brands but would decline if they didn't fit her family's idea of stability. Eventually, she realized she wasn't living *her* life—she was living *their* safety plan. The moment she stopped outsourcing her decisions and took a contract in a completely different city, her career and confidence skyrocketed. The irony? Her parents are now her biggest supporters. Sometimes the people who resist your decisions most are the first to admire you once you make them.

And here's the silent killer: indecision. People fear making the wrong choice, but in truth, most damage isn't from a wrong decision—it's from making none at all. Indecision drains momentum, erodes self-trust, and lets life move on without you.

The best decision-makers aren't those who always choose "right." They are the ones who decide, learn, adjust, and keep moving. They don't ask, *"Is this perfect?"* They ask, *"Is this aligned with who I'm becoming?"*

You are not broken. You're simply in the middle of a mental negotiation. But when you understand your biases, your emotions, and your wiring—when you realize you're not just reacting to life but actively choosing it—you step into a new kind of power.

Rewire Your Brain—The Biology of Transformation

Most people live on autopilot. They wake up, repeat yesterday's patterns, and wonder why life feels the same year after year. They consume information—books, podcasts, seminars—but the breakthroughs never seem to stick. Why? Because **information doesn't create transformation.** Repetition does.

Every action you take, every reaction you have, every belief you hold is directed by the most sophisticated system ever created—your brain. And here's the good news: you are not stuck with the wiring you have today.

Your brain contains roughly **100 billion neurons**—each sending signals at speeds faster than a Formula 1 race car. These neurons communicate through **synapses**, tiny junctions that form the "roads" of your mind. Every time you think a thought, feel a feeling, or choose an action, you send "traffic" down one of those roads. The more often you travel that road, the smoother and faster it becomes. That's how habits form. That's how beliefs get cemented. That's why fear can become your default setting—or why peace can take its place.

But here's the breakthrough: your brain is **plastic**. Not in the toy sense, but in the **neuroplasticity** sense—it can reshape, rewire, and reorganize itself in response to new information, focus, and repeated action.

Think of it like this: your mental highways aren't permanent. With enough repetition, you can close the old roads and pave new ones.

Let me show you how this works in real life.

A mechanical engineer named Destin, from the YouTube channel *Smarter Every Day*, once took on a strange challenge: ride a bicycle where turning the handlebars left made the wheel turn right—and vice versa. He'd been riding bikes since childhood, so logically, he knew what to do. But when he climbed on, he couldn't make it five feet without tipping over. His brain was wired for the "normal" bike.

For eight months, Destin practiced five minutes a day. At first, nothing. But then, one day, his brain clicked into the new pattern. The backwards bike no longer felt impossible—it felt natural. But here's the twist: when he got back on a regular bike, he couldn't ride it. The new wiring had completely taken over.

That's neuroplasticity in action. What was once impossible had become instinct—and the old instinct had vanished.

The same thing happens with your beliefs, your habits, and your emotional responses. Whether it's anxiety that spikes every time an unexpected bill shows up, or the reflex to reach for comfort food when you're stressed—

these aren't random flaws. They're the result of repeated neural traffic on the same mental roads.

The brain learns by association. Maybe as a child, comfort came in the form of food when you were upset. Or maybe your early experiences taught you that uncertainty equals danger. Over years, your brain dug deep ruts for those patterns.

But here's the hope: **any pattern that was learned can be unlearned**.

The process starts with **awareness**—spotting the pattern. Then you identify the **trigger**—the thought, feeling, or event that precedes the behavior. Beneath every destructive pattern is a **belief**—usually a lie. It might sound like, "I can't handle this," or "This is just who I am."

Once you see it, you can replace it. You begin to speak truth instead of lies. You rehearse the new truth, not just once, but over and over until your brain recognizes it as the new default. This is how peace becomes more familiar than panic.

One of your brain's gatekeepers in this process is the **Reticular Activating System** (RAS). Think of your RAS as the bouncer at an exclusive club—it decides what information gets in and what gets ignored. It bases its decisions on what you consistently focus on.

If you believe life is hard, your RAS will highlight every problem in your path. But if you train your mind to look for opportunities, it will filter for those instead. This is why gratitude works—not as a fluffy feel-good exercise, but as a way to reprogram your brain's filter. What you seek, your RAS will help you find.

The same is true for affirmations. When you declare, "I am capable. I am calm. I am growing," you are not just speaking words—you're sending your brain a construction order for new mental roads.

This alignment between science and scripture is striking. The Bible says, *"Be transformed by the renewing of your mind"*—and neuroscience shows exactly how that happens. Studies by cognitive neuroscientists like Dr. Caroline Leaf confirm that intentional thinking changes brain structure, healing the damage caused by toxic thoughts and reinforcing healthy ones.

Transformation is not about faking positivity. It's about daily, disciplined rewiring. It's about catching a thought, questioning it, replacing it, and rehearsing the new one until it sticks.

One client of mine, a high-level executive, came to me on the verge of burnout. He had the money, the influence, the resume—but inside, he was crumbling. He was living in survival mode. We didn't just fix his calendar. We rewired his mind. He began practicing gratitude, breathing through triggers, and challenging the lies he'd believed for decades. Six months later, he wasn't just surviving. He was leading his life with peace, clarity, and conviction.

That's the biology of transformation. You are not the thoughts you think— you are the person who chooses which thoughts to keep. But that choice requires training, and that training requires repetition.

Because when it comes to rewiring your brain, you don't rise to the level of your intentions—you fall to the level of your identity. Change that identity, and everything else changes with it.

The Power of Focus: What You Feed Your Mind Shapes Your Life

Every single day, your mind is consuming. Sometimes you choose the menu. Most of the time, you don't. Thoughts, conversations, headlines, scrolling feeds, music lyrics, office gossip—it all seeps in. And whether you notice or not, it all begins shaping something much deeper than your mood. It shapes your beliefs. It shapes your habits. It shapes the quiet, unseen architecture of your life.

This is why two people can live in the same city, work in similar jobs, and face similar setbacks—yet one steadily grows stronger while the other sinks deeper into frustration. The difference isn't talent. It isn't luck. It's the focus.

What you dwell on becomes the climate of your inner world. If you feed your mind fear, anxiety becomes the natural language of your body. If you feed it comparison, insecurity will take root in your identity. But if you feed it gratitude, your perspective expands. If you train it toward discipline, your energy compounds. Focus isn't just about what holds your attention in a given moment—it's the daily shaping of your mental and emotional foundation. What you consistently observe, you eventually absorb.

And this isn't just a poetic metaphor. It's biology. The same neuroplasticity that allows your brain to rewire for new habits also means it will reinforce whatever you keep putting in front of it—good or bad. If you pour garbage into your mind, your neural patterns will eventually normalize that garbage as reality. If you pour in truth, hope, and courage, your mind will begin building a life that reflects those things.

The challenge is that we live in an age where the noise is relentless. Since 2009, when smartphones and social media became the default way to connect, emotional health across generations has been in freefall. Anxiety, depression, self-harm, and suicide have all climbed sharply. Why? Because our attention is constantly under siege. We were never built to compare our lives to a thousand strangers a day. We weren't designed to chase validation through likes and filters. And yet, millions wake up and feed on a steady diet of curated highlight reels, outrage headlines, and digital distraction—all before they've even had breakfast.

But here's the empowering truth: focus is a choice. You may not control everything that shows up in your world, but you absolutely control what gets to stay in your mind. This is your lever for transformation. You can swap the highlight reel for purpose. You can replace passive scrolling with intentional learning. You can turn down the volume on noise so you can finally hear the voice of your own convictions.

One of my clients, Marcus, learned this the hard way. He was a talented graphic designer with a growing client list, but he spent hours a day comparing his work to others online. Every scroll chipped away at his confidence. By the time he sat down to create, his energy was already spent battling invisible competition. We did something radical: for one month, he deleted all social media from his phone and replaced that time with reading and sketching for himself, not for approval. By week three, his creativity had doubled. By the end of the month, he had signed two new clients—not because his skills suddenly improved, but because his focus shifted from "proving himself" to "feeding himself."

Focus is fuel. What you focus on, you strengthen. What you feed, you grow. And in this sense, transformation isn't about one lightning-bolt moment—it's about the repeated choice to feed the right things.

Still, even with the right focus, your mind will sometimes drift back toward old loops—the thought spirals, the "what-ifs," the invisible arguments. This is where **pattern interruption** becomes a weapon.

When you're stuck in a mental loop, you can't always think your way out. You have to break the pattern physically, emotionally, and mentally at the same time. Imagine sitting in rush-hour traffic, replaying a tense conversation, feeling your chest tighten. That's your brain defaulting to survival mode. Here's what I tell my clients: say it out loud—"I'm spiraling right now." Give the feeling a name—"I'm afraid of losing control." Ground yourself—feet flat on the floor, inhale for four seconds, hold for four, exhale for six. Then ask the truth—"What's real right now?" Finally, speak the new belief—"I am safe. I am grounded. I am capable of clarity."

Do this consistently and you're not just calming down in the moment— you're rewiring your nervous system. You're proving to your brain that peace is possible even under pressure.

Of course, your brain will still try to pull you toward the negative. It's called the **negativity bias**, and it's been with you since birth. Back when survival meant scanning for predators, that bias kept your ancestors alive. Today, it just keeps you on high alert for slights, mistakes, and worst-case scenarios. It's why one criticism can outweigh a hundred compliments.

You can retrain this bias, but it takes deliberate effort. One of the simplest and most effective tools is gratitude—not the vague "be positive" advice that gets thrown around, but intentional recognition of specific wins. Noticing you answered an email you'd been putting off. Noticing you made your bed when you didn't feel like it. Noticing you reached for water instead of soda. Small wins shift your RAS—the brain's filter—to start scanning for what's right instead of only what's wrong.

And here's something most people forget: **you are not your thoughts**. You are the thinker of your thoughts. Your mind can reflect distorted realities the same way a carnival mirror stretches or squashes your reflection. If you don't challenge those distortions, you'll start believing they define you. But you're not your worst thought. You're not the loop you're stuck in. You're the one who decides what stays.

That decision—to focus on truth over lies, opportunity over fear—is not a one-time event. It's a daily discipline. Champions in any arena aren't defined by moments of inspiration; they're defined by what they practice when no one's watching. That's where mental victory is forged—in the unseen repetitions, the small moments where you choose focus over drift.

When you live this way, peace stops being an occasional visitor and starts being your home base. And from that place, you make better decisions, you take bigger risks, and you create a life that reflects your highest identity—not your lowest reflex.

The Moment Everything Changes

Every breakthrough has a spark—but it's not talent. It's not luck. It's not even opportunity. It's the moment you stop negotiating with the life you don't want and start claiming the one you do.

The people you admire for their resilience, the ones who rise again and again despite failure, heartbreak, or relentless pressure—they share one thing: at some point, they made a non-negotiable decision about who they were becoming. They didn't tiptoe into change. They jumped. Fully. Boldly. Without a safety net.

My friend Ray is living proof. On paper, there was nothing remarkable about him. He'd failed out of college twice, worked jobs that drained him, and fought anxiety so heavy it sometimes kept him housebound. But one sweltering afternoon, parked outside a rundown gym, he whispered three words that changed everything: *No more waiting.* He didn't have a master plan or a perfect roadmap. What he had was a moment of emotional clarity so sharp it cut through years of mental fog. That same day, he walked into the gym—not to lift weights, but to lift his self-worth. Today, Ray coaches athletes, mentors young men recovering from trauma, and credits it all to one decision made in the shadows.

That's the truth about transformation: it's rarely explosive at first. It's often quiet. Internal. But when it's made with deep clarity and no exit strategy, it changes everything.

And here's why most people miss that moment—we make around **35,000 decisions every single day**. Most are small and forgettable: what to eat, what to wear, whether to check that notification. But research shows **up to 95% of those choices happen subconsciously**, driven by mental programming you didn't choose. That means the vast majority of your life is shaped by old patterns running on autopilot.

Think of your mind like a high-powered engine. It's constantly filtering and reacting through the lens of past experiences, emotional triggers, ingrained beliefs, and habits that may no longer serve you. You think you're making choices in the present—but unless you interrupt those automatic patterns, your subconscious is still steering the wheel.

Psychologist Daniel Kahneman's model explains this through **two decision-making systems**.

- **System 1** is fast, emotional, instinctive—running on old wiring and gut reactions.

- **System 2** is slower, deliberate, analytical—the part that weighs, considers, and chooses consciously.

Here's the problem: System 1 is running the show most of the time. Unless you become aware of its influence, you'll keep replaying the same habits, making the same compromises, and wondering why your life feels stuck.

That's why inner work matters. Confronting limiting beliefs, healing emotional wounds, and dismantling identity blocks isn't "just" personal development—it's rewiring the very machinery that shapes your daily choices. The moment you become conscious of what was once unconscious, you take back the pen. You stop reacting to life and start authoring it.

And when you do, decisions create separation. They mark the invisible line between who you were and who you refuse to be any longer. But most people never cross that line. They dabble. They debate. They delay.

Champions don't. They prepare in the shadows. They build resilient decision-making muscles when no one is watching. They show up to the unseen grind, when the work is thankless and consistency feels like a weight.

Take Erin, a burned-out nurse practitioner on the verge of her second divorce, drowning in debt. She didn't "find" her purpose—she created it through ritualized preparation. She woke at 5 a.m. to write intentions. She ended each day by naming her fears and declaring her future anyway. Within 18 months, she launched a wellness startup that's now changing lives across three states.

Her secret wasn't luck. It was training herself to choose—especially when fear screamed *stay safe*. That's the muscle you need if you want to stop negotiating with old patterns.

One of the most powerful tools for building that muscle is what I call **The Decision Matrix**—a mental filter to help you cut through the noise and choose in alignment with your future, not your fear.

Instead of relying on scattered pros and cons lists, the Decision Matrix pushes you to ask:

- **Will this decision expand me or shrink me?** (Growth Potential)

- **Is fear driving me, or informing me?** (Fear Cost)

- **What story will this choice write into my legacy?** (Legacy Impact)

- **Does this align with my deepest values—or just my conditioning?** (Value Alignment)

THE DECISION MATRIX

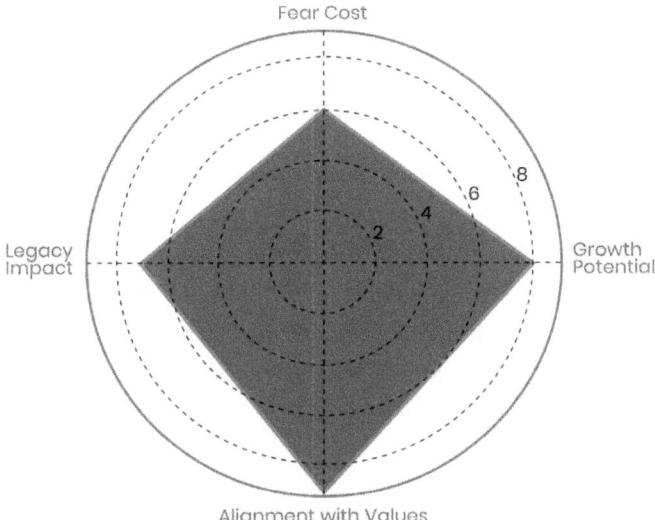

Use tools like: The Four Filters of The Decision Matrix

Decision Visualization: Mentally rehearse the moment of discomfort before it happens. Step into the tension. Prepare your response in advance.

When you're standing at a crossroads and unsure which path to take, clarity doesn't always come from thinking harder—it comes from thinking differently. The Decision Matrix is a powerful framework to assess any choice through four distinct lenses. Each filter brings a new layer of perspective, helping you cut through emotional noise and make decisions that align with your future, not your fear.

1. Growth Potential

Ask yourself: *"Will this decision expand me or shrink me?"*

This filter evaluates how much personal, professional, or spiritual growth a choice offers. It's about leaning into what stretches you—even if it scares you. Growth isn't always comfortable, but it's always clarifying. A decision with high growth potential may challenge your current identity, skills, or mindset—but that's exactly why it's worth considering. If a choice leaves you the same, it costs you more than you think.

2. Fear Cost

Ask yourself: *"Is fear driving this decision—or informing it?"*

Every meaningful decision triggers fear—but there's a difference between using fear as data and letting it become a dictator. This filter helps you assess the emotional tax of staying in comfort versus stepping into courage. If the only reason you're hesitating is because it's unfamiliar, uncomfortable, or uncertain, then fear may be costing you a breakthrough. Decisions driven by fear often create cycles of regret. Choose the path where fear feels like a sign of growth, not a stop sign.

3. Legacy Impact

Ask yourself: *"What story will this decision write into my legacy?"*

Legacy isn't about grand gestures. It's about the trail you leave in the lives you touch and the values you model. This filter asks you to zoom out and view your choice from a longer timeline. Will this decision make you proud ten years from now? Will it teach your children, your peers, or your community something worth remembering? Legacy-impact decisions shape character, integrity, and how you're remembered when you're not in the room.

4. Alignment with Values

Ask yourself: *"Does this choice reflect who I truly am—or just who I've been trained to be?"*

This is the anchor filter. When everything else feels muddy, alignment with values clears the fog. If your decision doesn't align with your core values— like freedom, faith, integrity, service, or creativity—it will eventually create friction. This filter helps ensure your decisions reflect your identity and principles, not just your obligations or external expectations.

When you run a decision through all four lenses, you're not just picking an outcome—you're deciding who you're becoming. And when the choice scores high on growth, aligns with your values, leaves a legacy you can be proud of, and only triggers fear because it stretches you—it's almost always the right move. Not the easy one, but the one that transforms you.

Preparation is what makes these moments count. While others wait for perfect timing, the prepared have already built clarity, rehearsed hard conversations, and anchored themselves in conviction. That way, when the moment arrives—and it always does—it won't politely ask if you're ready. It will simply expose whether you are.

How Indecision Breeds Mediocrity

Indecision is still a decision—it's the choice to stay exactly where you are. And it is the fastest, most reliable path to a life you never intended to live.

Your brain isn't designed to chase greatness; it's designed to seek safety. When you face the unknown, it triggers an ancient survival protocol. Cortisol floods your system. The amygdala—your brain's emotional alarm center—hijacks logic. Suddenly, you're not weighing options with clarity; you're negotiating with fear. And fear will always offer the same deal: stay here, stay small, stay safe.

I learned this the hard way in the desert of Iraq. My squad was ready—weapons checked, eyes sharp—when our orders changed mid-operation. In that split second, I assessed, recalculated, and moved. On the battlefield, you don't have the luxury of waiting for perfect clarity; hesitation is an opening the enemy will exploit. What struck me later, though, was how differently people approach decisions off the battlefield. In civilian life, that same urgency fades, and hesitation becomes acceptable—even normal. But while it may not cost lives, it quietly costs years.

That realization forced me to see a truth I'd been avoiding: waiting for perfect information isn't strategy. It's fear in camouflage. And I've seen that same disguised fear play out everywhere—in high-performing executives who could lead their industries but stall at the edge of innovation; in entrepreneurs sitting on game-changing ideas while they "get ready"; in soldiers who can execute a mission flawlessly but hesitate when it comes to shaping their own future. These people aren't short on talent or opportunity. They're trapped in negotiations with their own fear, clinging to familiar pain rather than risking unfamiliar purpose.

The cost? Regret.

More than **70% of people live with it**—not because they chose wrong, but because they never chose at all. It's the silent ache of the *What if?*, the one that follows you long after the window has closed. Comfort seduces you into believing you have more time. But comfort is a liar, and regret is the invoice it sends later.

Theodore Roosevelt captured it perfectly: "In any moment of decision, the best thing you can do is the right thing. The next best thing is the wrong thing. The worst thing is to do nothing."

Movement builds clarity. Action builds identity. Even a wrong step teaches you more than standing still ever will.

I think about Marcus, a young business owner I coached. He had a platform idea that could have reshaped his entire industry—solving a problem his competitors weren't even addressing. But Marcus wanted it "perfect" before launching. He kept tweaking, polishing, and running numbers until a year had passed. Then another company, bold enough to move without having every detail nailed down, launched first. They didn't just take the market; they took the momentum Marcus had been too cautious to claim.

The real loss wasn't the revenue. It was what happened inside Marcus. Every time you delay a decision you know you should make, you chip away at your self-trust. And when self-trust erodes, bold action becomes nearly impossible.

The antidote? Decide.

Even when it's messy. Even when the ending is unknown. Especially when fear whispers, *Wait*. Because clarity doesn't appear before you move. It comes because you moved.

You don't need the entire map. You need the courage to take the next step.

Turning points don't arrive with fireworks or fanfare. They pass silently, disguised as ordinary moments—and only in hindsight do you realize they were the ones that changed everything.

So the choice in front of you is not complicated: will you be the person who waits for certainty, or the one who creates it?

This chapter has shown you how your brain works, how focus forges your reality, how decisive moments define you, and how fear manipulates you into staying still. But knowledge without action is just another sophisticated form of hesitation.

This is your line in the sand. The moment to stop outsourcing your future to delay. The moment to stop circling the version of yourself you want to become and finally step into it.

Decisions crack the bottle. Indecision keeps it sealed.

Champion—transformation does not wait for permission. It waits for a decision. Make yours now.

BREAK THE BOTTLE CHALLENGE — Chapter 2

Let's make this real. No fluff. No waiting.

1. **Identify one decision you've been avoiding.**

   a. Not five. Just one. The one that keeps showing up. The one that stings a little. The one you rationalize away.

      i. **Be brutally honest:** What's the move you know it's time to make?

2. **Create your declaration.**

   a. Words create worlds. This is more than a sentence—it's a shift in identity.

      i. "I've delayed long enough. Today I decide to __, *because my future deserves it.*"

         1. Say it out loud. Write it down. Post it where you can see it. Make it real.

3. **Take one action within the next 24 hours.**
   Not next week. Not when the schedule clears. Now.
   That phone call.
   That boundary.
   That application.
   That conversation.
   That commitment to yourself.

It doesn't have to be massive. It just has to be movement. Because momentum isn't born from motivation—it's born from movement. Your future isn't waiting. It's watching.

Waiting to see if you'll finally break the bottle. Watching to see if this is just another chapter—or the moment you change your story. Let it begin here. Let it begin *with a bold decision*.

RESOURCES

 **Download the Tool: Daily Mindset Drills for High Performance**
Develop stronger internal focus, self-discipline, and direction with these practical daily mindset shifts designed to activate decisive action.

Available at: btbprograms.com/free-resources

3

OWNING YOUR PAST WITHOUT LETTING IT DEFINE YOU

"You can't change the past, but you can change the
meaning you give it—and that will change your future."

— *Break The Bottle*

Understanding the Root of Your Limitations

Every pattern has a starting point. Every fear has a birthplace. And every
bottle—those internal containers where shame, avoidance, and survival
instincts are kept—has a seal. Someone, somewhere, helped tighten it.
Maybe they didn't mean to. Maybe they did. But whether it came from
trauma or tradition, silence or shame, the bottle got sealed. And now, you're
holding it. But here's the truth that changes everything: you can't break what
you won't name.

Most of your core beliefs—the ones shaping your relationships, your self-
worth, your leadership style, your capacity to love and receive love—weren't
consciously chosen. They were inherited. Instilled. Embedded deep in the
nervous system long before you had the tools to question them. Before you
could ask, "Does this belief serve me?" you were already wearing it like skin.

These beliefs come from familiar places:

- Childhood experiences that taught you visibility wasn't safe.

- Cultural expectations that molded you before you could think for yourself.

- Schoolyard shame that made your voice feel like a weapon turned against you.

- The quietness of growing up in poverty where dreams felt like liabilities, not possibilities.

- Moments where you were overlooked, dismissed, or labeled too much—or never enough.

These things didn't just happen. They became code. Written into your nervous system. Wired into your perception of self and others. They didn't just bruise your feelings; they built a filter. A filter that decides whether or not you speak up in meetings. Whether or not you trust love. Whether or not you go after the thing you want—or talk yourself out of it before anyone else can.

I remember being eight years old, new to America, still learning the unspoken rules of how to blend in. My family had moved into a small apartment, and every day I stepped into a world that felt both exciting and overwhelming. My Jamaican accent was still thick, my clothes a little different, my lunchbox filled with food that didn't smell like anyone else's.

That morning, as I walked into class, my heart was already racing—not from fear, but from the silent pressure to fit in. I can still feel the way my hands clutched my pencil tighter than they needed to, the way my eyes scanned for the empty seat in the back. I wasn't thinking about academics; I was thinking about survival.

Halfway through the lesson, the teacher asked a question. I knew the answer—not just "I think I know" but that electric, confident certainty that made my hand shoot up before I could talk myself out of it. My chest filled with pride as she called on me. I opened my mouth, spoke my answer... and the room erupted in laughter.

They weren't laughing at my answer. They were laughing at how I said it. At the way my words carried the rhythm of a place they didn't know. In that split second, the pride in my chest collapsed into something hot and heavy. My ears burned. My heart pounded so loud it drowned out the teacher's voice. And without even realizing it, I made an unconscious agreement with myself: *Speaking up equals rejection. Being different equals being mocked.*

For the rest of that school year, my hand stayed down. It wasn't just a choice—it was wiring. What I didn't know at the time was that I had just experienced what psychologists call **schema formation**—the brain's fast-track process for deciding what's safe and what's not. In dangerous environments, these shortcuts can save your life. But in moments of potential, they can trap you in silence.

It would take me years to see how much that moment shaped me. How it followed me into boardrooms, into conversations, even onto stages. And I see this same pattern in my clients all the time.

Andrea, a high-performing executive, would have panic attacks every time she was promoted. Not because she lacked skill, but because she had internalized the belief that visibility was dangerous. Every time she stepped into the spotlight, her nervous system whispered, *This is unsafe.*

Elijah, a decorated Marine turned CEO, wasn't building his company from passion—he was building from pain. Deep down, he was still trying to prove wrong the father who once told him, *You'll never amount to anything unless you do it my way.* That script had followed him from the battlefield to the boardroom, driving his success but quietly eroding his joy.

Here's what I had to learn, and what I teach them: your blueprint may not be your fault, but breaking it is your responsibility. And here's the key— proving someone wrong is not the same as becoming who you were born to be. One is driven by survival. The other by vision. Until you understand the difference, you'll keep building a life around your wounds instead of your wisdom.

For years, I didn't even realize that moment in the classroom had left a mark. I thought I'd simply "grown out of it." But patterns have a way of hiding in plain sight. They show up in your hesitation before speaking, in the way you overthink emails, in the way you replay conversations long after they're over.

It wasn't until much later—after the Marines, after rebuilding my life more than once—that I began to see how much that early agreement was still running the show. And the first step wasn't to "get over it" or pretend it never happened. It was to get curious.

I started asking myself hard questions:
When did I first feel this way? Who taught me that being different was unsafe? What moments made me believe my voice was a liability instead of an asset?

At first, the answers came slowly. But I learned that clarity isn't a lightning strike—it's a series of steady flickers. Each time I traced a fear or hesitation back to its source, I could see the original wiring for what it was: a defense mechanism that had outlived its usefulness.

I remember one afternoon in particular during my transition from military life to civilian work. I was sitting in a leadership class at Rush Medical University, and the instructor asked each of us to introduce ourselves. As my turn approached, I felt the same tightening in my chest I had felt decades earlier in that third-grade classroom. But instead of retreating into autopilot, I noticed it. I named it. I told myself, *This isn't danger. This is just my nervous system remembering an old rule.*

That day, I didn't just speak—I owned my voice. And something shifted. The more I practiced this awareness, the clearer my internal map became. I could finally see which decisions were being made from vision, and which were still being made from survival.

This is why I tell my clients: clarity isn't just about knowing where you want to go. It's about understanding the invisible agreements you made years ago—and deciding whether they still deserve a seat at your table. Because once you can name the belief, you can challenge it. And once you challenge it, you can choose something different.

That's the work. Not erasing the past, but rewriting the meaning you've given it. Not silencing the old voice, but replacing it with one that serves your future. And every time you do that, you're not just making progress—you're reclaiming territory in your own mind.

Rewriting the Narrative of Failure and Fear

You can't build a new life with an old script. It doesn't matter how sharp your strategies are, how detailed your vision board looks, or how perfectly your goals are color-coded—if the story running underneath it all is still rooted in fear, it will sabotage you before you ever see the finish line.

Because it's never just *what happened to you*. It's the meaning you gave it. And that meaning quietly becomes your map.

Fear doesn't always shout. It narrates. Slowly. Relentlessly.
You failed once. You'll fail again.
This pain proves you're not meant for more.
Stay small. Stay safe.

That's the trap. Fear isn't content with delaying your decisions—it wants to rewrite your identity. And if you're not paying attention, you start to believe the hesitation is *who you are*.

I've coached high-level leaders, entrepreneurs, and veterans who look bulletproof on the outside—yet underneath, they're stuck in quiet panic: *If people saw the real me, they'd know I'm not enough.*

I know that feeling. After the DUI. After the divorce. After rebuilding my life for the second time. I remember walking into a high-level leadership summit to give a keynote. My suit was crisp, my notes memorized, my delivery flawless. The applause came, but afterward, a young man waited for the crowd to clear. He looked me in the eye and asked, "Do you really believe everything you just said?"

I froze. Not because I didn't know my material—but because deep down, I realized I was still leading through the lens of shame. My voice on stage was strong, but my inner narrator was still saying, *You've messed up too much to lead anyone.*

That's what fear does—it hides inside your history. It borrows the voices of coaches, parents, peers, or critics from your past and plays them on repeat until they feel like your own thoughts.

I've seen it in founders who build empires but can't rest without feeling like they're falling behind. In veterans who can command a battlefield but crumble when asked to share what they feel. In executives who keep the mask on so tightly that they can't remember what it's like to breathe without it.

And here's the truth: fear is clever. It dresses up as perfectionism, overachievement, people-pleasing, or control. Sometimes it even wears the mask of success so well that you forget it's fear underneath.

But there's a difference between rewriting your story and simply rewording it. Too many people try to "reframe" without re-emotioning. They slap a new label on the old bottle but never change what's inside. Real transformation happens when you don't just *say* you're enough—you train your body to feel it, so that peace no longer feels like a setup and success no longer triggers shame.

This is where clarity becomes non-negotiable. If you don't know the real story you've been telling yourself, you'll never know when fear is writing the next chapter for you. The work isn't to erase the pain. It's to strip fear of its authority to narrate your future.

The Power of Acceptance in Moving Forward

Understanding your past is not the same as healing from it. You can spend years tracing patterns in therapy, writing about them in journals, even teaching others how to break them—and still feel like you're carrying a hidden weight on your chest. That's because logic alone doesn't release pain. Insight without integration is just an elegant description of the cage you're still sitting in.

Healing doesn't begin when you name the wound. It begins when you accept it. Not to excuse it. Not to pretend it didn't hurt. But to finally loosen its grip on your identity.

I once worked with a former athlete turned corporate VP—sharp suit, sharper résumé—but there was a heaviness to him, like he was dragging a ghost into every meeting. During a leadership intensive, I asked, "What would it take for you to forgive yourself for the moment that broke you?" His eyes filled immediately. "I don't know how," he said.

That's when I realized: he didn't need another strategy. He needed surrender. He was still in a quiet tug-of-war with the past, trying to argue his way out of a moment that could only be released through acceptance.

Acceptance is not a soft landing—it's a turning point. It doesn't say, *What happened was okay.* It says, *What happened is no longer in charge of my future.*

The truth is, the more we resist what was, the more we re-anchor it in the present. We rehearse it in conversations, revisit it in our thoughts, reanalyze it late at night—and in doing so, we relive it over and over. Acceptance creates space. It introduces the pause between who you were and who you're now choosing to become.

But no one can force that moment on you. Readiness matters. I've coached people who knew exactly what was holding them back, but they weren't ready to let it go. Some still believed they needed to carry their pain—as proof of what they'd survived, as fuel for their grind, or as a shield against vulnerability. But transformation doesn't arrive while you're still negotiating with your trauma. It comes the moment you say, *I'm done carrying this.*

For me, that moment wasn't loud. It didn't happen under stage lights or during some cinematic life event. It came in the quiet stillness of a morning—the kind of morning where the world hasn't quite woken up yet, and the only sound is the low hum of the bathroom fan.

I'd stumbled out of bed after another restless night, moving on autopilot: toothbrush, water running, avoiding the mirror the way I'd done for years. I wasn't afraid of my reflection—not exactly. I just didn't want to deal with what was behind my own eyes. Looking at myself meant confronting the truth I'd gotten good at hiding: that I was still carrying every voice, every expectation, every impossible standard I'd ever been handed.

That morning, for reasons I still can't explain, I paused. I looked up. And there I was—not the version the world saw, not the speaker or the Marine or the guy who had it all together. Just me. Tired. Guarded. Still measuring my worth by performance.

It hit me like a slow wave: the inner critic staring back at me wasn't mine. It was stitched together from every teacher who told me to "tone it down," every system that made me earn my place twice over, every cultural script that said value comes from output, not from being.

I felt the instinct to look away—to go back to my morning routine and ignore the heat rising in my chest. But instead, I stayed. I did something simple, almost ridiculous: I asked myself, *Would I talk to someone I love this way?*

The answer was instant and obvious: no.

That was the start of a ritual. Every morning, I made myself meet my own gaze—not for two seconds, but long enough to get past the surface discomfort. The first few times were brutal. My jaw would tighten. My shoulders would creep up. My mind would look for the exit. But day after day, I stayed.

And something began to shift. The mirror stopped feeling like a courtroom where I was on trial for my failures. It became a meeting place between who I had been and who I was becoming—a space where I could acknowledge my flaws without making them my identity.

It didn't happen overnight, but slowly, that daily practice began to re-shape something in me. Each time I chose presence over avoidance, I wasn't just shifting my thoughts—I was changing the way I showed up for myself.

What started as an uncomfortable experiment became one of the most powerful tools in my healing. Because when you can look yourself in the eye—without judgment, without flinching—you stop outsourcing your worth to achievements, approval, or anyone else's opinion.

Over time, the mirror stopped being a reminder of where I'd fallen short. It became proof that I could meet myself exactly where I was and still be worthy of moving forward. That's when acceptance stops being a concept you talk about and becomes the ground you stand on.

That's what acceptance does. It doesn't erase your history. It changes your relationship to it. It allows you to walk into a room without dragging the past behind you. It lets you make decisions from clarity instead of reaction.

And here's the shift that matters most: when you stop fighting the past, you free up energy to build the future. Acceptance is the key that turns the lock. And once you turn it? Doors starts to open.

The Belief System Blueprint

Every one of us lives by a belief system. But here's the catch—it wasn't born with us. It was built. Piece by piece, silently, over time, shaped by experiences, influences, repetition, and exposure. Unless you've ever stopped to examine why you think what you think, chances are you're living by a mental blueprint someone else designed.

Think of it as your internal operating software—the quiet architect of your life. It governs your decisions, reactions, fears, and ambitions. It decides what you believe is possible, how much risk you'll take, and even what you think you deserve. It dictates whether you see challenges as threats or opportunities, whether you walk into a room like you belong or like you're trespassing. And most of the time, it's running in the background, invisible but in control.

Your parents' voices. Your teachers' warnings. The media you consumed. The sermons you sat through. The environment or the culture that raised you. Even the music that echoed in your headphones—all of these left fingerprints on your belief system, carving out the mental framework you now live by.

For me, one vivid example came during the Y2K panic. I was in high school, and it felt like the whole world had been put on a countdown clock. Every news broadcast had an ominous timer in the corner of the screen, ticking down to midnight on December 31, 1999. The anchors' voices carried that tense blend of authority and uncertainty, as if they were preparing us for impact but didn't quite know what form it would take.

At home, neighbors were stocking up on bottled water and canned food. I remember seeing one man wheel a brand-new generator into his garage like it was the most important purchase of his life. Families were discussing escape plans, and people spoke in hushed tones at grocery stores as if catastrophe might overhear. Even the church sermons shifted—preachers warning about the "end times," urging us to prepare our souls along with our pantries.

The disaster, of course, never came. Midnight arrived, the clocks rolled over to the year 2000, and the world kept spinning. But the urgency it planted in me didn't disappear when the fear did. It embedded itself deep in my wiring. Somewhere in my subconscious, a new rule had been written: time is short, disaster could strike at any moment, and the safest way to live is to stay in motion.

That belief fueled my ambition, but it also kept me in a constant state of tension—always bracing for the next hit, even when there was no hit coming. That's how belief systems work. They don't have to be logical to be powerful. They just have to be repeated enough times, in enough ways, until your body treats them like truth.

The danger is that they operate without your permission. If you believe you're not enough, you'll shrink from opportunity. If you believe life is a perpetual crisis, you'll live in a constant state of urgency. If you believe success is for "other people," you'll unconsciously disqualify yourself before you've even tried.

And here's the truth most people miss: no amount of behavior change will stick if it's built on an unchanged belief. You can hustle, grind, and discipline yourself into temporary wins, but if your core belief is rooted in limitation, you'll eventually circle back to the same wall. Long-term transformation doesn't begin with behavior modification—it begins with belief renovation.

One client, Rachel, came to me convinced she was "bad with money." Her parents had drilled into her that debt was dangerous, spending was irresponsible, and risk was reckless. While some of those lessons had value, they also planted deep fear. Rachel was financially stable but refused to invest in opportunities that could grow her business, because her belief system told her risk = loss. We didn't start with her bank account—we started with her beliefs. Once she replaced risk is dangerous with calculated risk is growth, she tripled her revenue in under a year.

In high-performance living, belief is a non-negotiable. You will never sustain what you don't believe you deserve. Doubt repels destiny.

If clarity gives you direction, belief gives you fuel. You can't sustain what you don't believe you deserve, and you won't reach what you aren't willing to reinforce again and again until it becomes your new normal. Belief is more than mindset—it's the software running your identity. And like any system, it must be upgraded if you want different results.

The truth is simple: your beliefs are either building you or breaking you. And not all beliefs are created equal. They fall into three distinct categories, each shaping the trajectory of your life in powerful ways:

1. **Limiting Beliefs—The Silent Saboteurs**
   These are the whispers that tell you what you *can't* do, usually dressed up as logic. Thoughts like: *I'm not smart enough. I don't have the right connections. I didn't come from the right background.* They sound rational, but in reality, they're fear wearing a mask. Left unchecked, they shrink your potential to the size of your doubts and convince you to settle for less than you were created for.

2. **Negative Beliefs—The Worldview That Holds You Back**
   These aren't just about you—they're about how you see others and the world. If you believe "rich people are greedy" or "success changes people for the worse," you'll unconsciously resist your own rise. Why? Because no one willingly becomes what they secretly resent. These beliefs don't just hold you back—they wire you to self-sabotage the very opportunities you pray for.

3. **Empowering Beliefs—The Catalyst for Momentum**
   These are the beliefs that shift everything. They're the declarations that prime your mind, body, and environment to align with your vision. Conor McGregor declared his private jet

long before he ever had one—not because he was delusional, but because belief always precedes reality. Empowering beliefs don't ignore obstacles—they anchor you to identity so deeply that obstacles lose their power to stop you.

The **Belief Blueprint** works because it transforms belief from a mental concept into a lived reality. It's not about saying affirmations once—it's about reinforcing the new story hundreds of times over. Whether it's 300 days of consistent practice, 300 intentional choices aligned with your vision, or 300 moments of catching yourself mid-doubt and rewriting the script, repetition cements identity.

You don't rise to the level of your goals—you fall to the level of your beliefs. And when you build the right blueprint, you don't just change what you think—you change who you become.

Everything ever built—from skyscrapers to movements—existed first as a belief in someone's mind. If you can believe it's possible for you, not just for "people like that," you've already started the process of making it real.

So let me ask you: What beliefs are running your life right now? Are they inherited or intentional? Are they expanding your future—or limiting it? Because belief isn't just the start of transformation—it's the foundation. And when you finally believe with certainty, not hesitation, that you were made for more, everything begins to shift.

The Cost of Holding Onto the Wrong Story

Every belief you hold writes part of your future. Whether it was whispered to you by a parent, carved into you through pain, or reinforced by the culture around you, these beliefs become the script you live by. But here's the real question: did you write the script, or did you inherit it?

The answer matters, because an inherited script often carries the weight of limitation disguised as wisdom. It sounds like:
"Good people don't ask for more."
"People like us don't get ahead."
"I'm not worthy of this opportunity."

These aren't just stray thoughts. They're subconscious contracts—quiet agreements you made long ago, often without realizing it. And the longer you keep them unchallenged, the more they dictate your choices, shrink your vision, and keep you circling the same walls.

To break the bottle, you have to break the contract. You have to decide that old versions of you don't get to make decisions for your current life. That means rejecting the instinct to disqualify yourself because of where you came from, what you've done, or what you've been told.

One of my clients, Donovan, carried an invisible story from his childhood in a low-income neighborhood. The message was simple: *People like us don't get ahead.* Even after earning a college degree and landing a high-paying job, he self-sabotaged every time a promotion opportunity came up. Not consciously—but through missed deadlines, "forgetting" to apply, or downplaying his achievements. The story was still in charge. It wasn't until we reframed his narrative from *I'm the kid who doesn't belong here* to *I'm the man who made it here for a reason* that his behavior shifted. Within six months, he not only accepted a promotion but began mentoring others who shared his background.

That's the power of rewriting—and the cost of refusing to.

The longer you hold onto the wrong story, the more it seeps into your identity. It doesn't just influence your actions—it changes your posture, your tone, your confidence. And here's the dangerous part: over time, you start mistaking the story for truth. You stop questioning it. You start defending it. And in doing so, you protect the very thing that's holding you back.

I remember visiting my grandfather several years ago in Jamaica. He lived in a modest home perched on a hill that overlooked the sea, the kind of view that could quiet even the loudest mind. We were sitting on his porch one humid afternoon, sipping ginger tea, when he told me a story about a neighbor who had tied his goat to the same short rope for years. The goat had plenty of space to roam, but over time, it stopped walking to the end of the rope. Even when the rope was untied and the animal was free to explore, it stayed in that same small circle—grazing on the same patch of grass, day after day.

"People do the same thing," my grandfather said, looking me dead in the eye. "They carry an old rope in their mind, and it keeps them in the same small circle even when the fence is gone."

It struck me then—how often we live inside limitations that no longer exist. How many of us are still measuring our reach by the length of an old rope, tied years ago by someone else's opinion, rejection, or fear. That's the danger of the wrong story: it doesn't just trap you in the past, it blinds you to the possibilities of the present.

Breaking that cycle requires disruption. Not gradual, not "when the timing is right." Immediate. Because every day you delay is another day you live someone else's narrative.

That disruption starts with clarity. If a belief or story doesn't serve the future you want, it's not neutral—it's costing you something. It might be costing you money. It might be costing you relationships. It might be costing you your peace. But it is always costing you time, and time is the one thing you never get back. Once you've identified the wrong story, the next step is to guard your clarity—because even a rewritten narrative can be derailed by subtle patterns that drain your focus.

The Three Clarity Killers

Clarity isn't usually stolen in one dramatic moment—it's drained in small, consistent leaks. Over time, certain patterns become so familiar you don't even notice they're sabotaging you. Three of the most common clarity killers I see in clients—and that I've wrestled with myself—are overcomplication, complaining, and anxiety. Each one might feel harmless in the moment, but together they can keep you trapped in the same cycle for years.

1. Overcomplication

For a long time, I equated complexity with intelligence. If an idea sounded impressive—packed with layers, jargon, and nuance—I assumed it was valuable. But here's what I learned the hard way: complexity doesn't create movement; it creates paralysis.

I remember designing a new training program early in my speaking career. I poured weeks into building elaborate frameworks, intricate slides, and "brilliant" multi-step processes. When I finally delivered it, the feedback was polite but clear: people didn't take action. It wasn't because the content wasn't good—it was because it wasn't clear. I'd given them a wall of information but no obvious next step.

The brain craves simplicity, especially when it's under stress. Most people can only hold onto a few actionable steps before overwhelm takes over. So if you want real change—in yourself or in those you lead—strip your beliefs, goals, and strategies down to their core essentials. Clarity beats clever every time.

2. Complaining

Complaining feels like release, but it's actually reinforcement. It's the verbal equivalent of hitting "repeat" on the same limiting story. And the more you complain, the more your brain wires itself to expect—and look for—what's wrong.

I saw this clearly in one of my mastermind groups. A highly talented entrepreneur came in every week with a new frustration: a slow client, a tech glitch, an unresponsive partner. Each story was valid, but she didn't realize she was rehearsing powerlessness. She wasn't venting to solve—she was venting to relive. And it kept her anchored to the very problems she wanted to escape.

The shift began when I asked her three questions:

- Is this complaint rooted in pain or pattern?

- Am I speaking to process or to reinforce?

- What's the opportunity in this moment?

Her energy changed. She started catching herself mid-sentence, reframing on the spot, and—most importantly—taking action. That's the key: complaining can't coexist with ownership. You can have one or the other, but not both.

3. Anxiety

Worry is one of the most convincing impostors of clarity. It feels like planning, like preparation, like being "realistic." But most worry is just rehearsing worst-case scenarios before they even happen.

I learned this lesson one afternoon in Iraq. It wasn't during combat—it was during downtime. I found myself spiraling over a hypothetical situation that hadn't happened. My heart rate was up, my shoulders were tight, and my focus was gone—all because my mind was scripting disaster in advance. That's when it hit me: my body didn't know the difference between a real threat and an imagined one. The stress response was identical.

The same is true in civilian life. One email. One vague text. One sideways comment, and suddenly you're on high alert for an outcome that may never come. The way out isn't pretending the fear doesn't exist—it's naming it, grounding yourself, and then acting anyway.

When worry walks in:

- Name it: *"I'm anxious right now. That's okay."*

- Locate the trigger: *"What just happened that pulled me into this?"*

- Interrupt it: breathe, move, go outside, take a shower, touch the ground, disrupt the loop.

Anxiety is not proof you're broken. It's a signal that your nervous system needs recalibration—and every time you respond with intention instead of panic, you're building that new baseline.

These three clarity killers all share one trait: they feed the wrong story. Overcomplication convinces you things are too hard to start. Complaining convinces you you're powerless to change them. Anxiety convinces you that danger is inevitable.

Break those patterns, and the old story loses its grip.

You Are the Rewrite

Every one of these patterns—overcomplication, complaining, anxiety—is just a symptom of the same root: a story you didn't write but have been living by. And here's the truth you need to feel in your bones: you don't have to keep it.

You weren't born with these beliefs. You weren't born second-guessing yourself. You weren't born bracing for rejection. You learned it. You absorbed it. And if it was learned, it can be unlearned. If it was absorbed, it can be released. If it was built by someone else's voice, it can be rebuilt by yours.

This is why I tell clients—and why I'm telling you now—the question isn't *"Can you change?"* The question is *"Will you stop protecting the old story long enough to write the new one?"*

That's the turning point. Not when you've got the perfect plan. Not when you've built up the courage for the whole journey. But right here—in this moment—when you decide to stop being the character someone else created and start being the author.

And let me tell you something I've learned after working with people in boardrooms, on battlefields, in therapy rooms, and across kitchen tables: the people who make that shift don't wait to "feel ready." They choose first, then they become ready through action. They understand that the gap between who they are and who they want to be is bridged not by hoping—but by deciding.

Your story isn't fixed. It's fluid. And you have the pen in your hand right now. That old belief—the one that says you're not enough, or too late, or too broken—it's just a paragraph. You can end it today. And the next line you write can change everything.

So here's the call: decide what your story says from this point forward. Decide it with the same conviction you'd have if your life depended on it—because in many ways, it does. Your peace depends on it. Your purpose depends on it. The life you've been circling but not committing to depends on it.

You are not a product of what happened to you. You are the architect of what's next. And when you choose to believe that fully—not just in your head, but in your nervous system, in your habits, in your posture—that's when the bottle starts to crack.

Not from rage. Not from luck. From truth. From ownership. From the refusal to live another day as anything less than the whole, capable, powerful human you were created to be.

You are the rewrite.
Now—write it.

BREAK THE BOTTLE CHALLENGE — Chapter 3

1. **Name It:** Identify one belief, mistake, or memory that still owns space in your mind.

2. **Reframe It:** Write a 1-paragraph reflection that gives it new meaning and power.

3. **Declare It:** Say this aloud:
   "That was a chapter. It's not the conclusion. And I own the pen from this point forward."

4. **Contradict It:** Take one bold action that breaks the pattern.

   - If your past made you feel voiceless—speak up today.

   - If it made you feel small—take up space.

   - If it made you feel broken—show up whole.

You are not who you were.
You are who you choose to become.
And that choice... starts now.

RESOURCES

Download the Tool: Identity Reset & Leadership Alignment Worksheet
Unpack your personal story, reset your core identity, and align with your purpose-driven leadership using this transformational 3-D Framework tool.

Available at: btbprograms.com/free-resources

BREAKING THE FIRST SEAL— COMMITTING TO CHANGE

"You don't break the bottle by hoping it shatters—you break it by throwing it with intention. Commitment isn't about trying harder; it's about eliminating the option to turn back."

— Break The Bottle

Why Half-Commitment Won't Work

There's a dangerous myth in personal development—the belief that making a decision is enough. That once you decide to change, the universe will start rearranging itself on your behalf. It won't. A decision is the spark, but commitment is the engine. And unless you fuel that engine with consistency, direction, and honesty, the spark burns out in silence. You don't need more intentions. You need more integrity—with yourself.

Half-commitment is a silent killer. It doesn't announce itself with alarms or warning lights. It seeps in quietly—in polite hesitation, in strategic delays, in well-phrased excuses dressed up as productivity. It's the gym membership you never use. The "yes" to growth that still negotiates with fear behind closed doors. It's calling yourself "in transition" while secretly building a nest in your comfort zone. From the outside, it looks responsible. It sounds ambitious. It checks boxes, attends webinars, fills journals—but nothing actually changes. Because you're not all in. You're not all out. You're stuck in the space between, where vision blurs and progress becomes optional.

That middle ground isn't neutral—it's corrosive. It wears down your resolve like water carving stone. The longer you live there, the harder it becomes to trust yourself. Not because you're a failure, but because every time you break your own word, even in small ways, your subconscious keeps the receipts: *You don't follow through.* One broken promise at a time, you start building an identity of "almost." Almost disciplined. Almost ready. Almost transformed. And when "almost" becomes your identity, "all in" starts to feel impossible.

I've lived that erosion more than once. After leaving the Marines, I told myself I was "all in" on entrepreneurship—but I kept a security gig on the side. Not for the money, but for the safety. Every time my business hit a rough patch, I would pour my energy into that job instead of solving the problems in front of me. On paper, I was moving forward. In reality, I was gripping the life I claimed to be leaving, too afraid to let go.

Years later, in Miami, I stood on the kind of stage I had dreamed about for years. The lights were hot, the applause was loud, and someone even said, "You just changed my life." But that night, in the quiet of my hotel room, I stared at the ceiling with a knot in my stomach I couldn't ignore. My health was slipping. My marriage was strained. My discipline had eroded. I had become an expert at *looking* aligned while quietly abandoning it in private.

That night wasn't a victory—it was a verdict. I grabbed my journal and wrote: *If you don't get honest, you're going to lose everything trying to look successful.* That was the moment I lit the match. I called my wife and told her the truth. I canceled three speaking gigs. I rebuilt my mornings from the ground up. I cut work that fed my ego but starved my soul.

In the Marines, we were trained to cut fallback communications on missions that required absolute focus. The signals from the rear would only confuse the operation up front. Verification works the same way: you can't keep listening to the voice that says, *You can always go back,* and expect to move forward.

Years later, I told my son this story after he came home from a football game feeling defeated. His eyes widened. "So you burned your bridge too, huh?" Yes, I told him. And I'd do it again—because burning the bridge wasn't about what I left behind. It was about reclaiming the authority to decide what came next.

The first two steps of Decision—Identify and Clarify—help you pull back the curtain on your patterns. You name the beliefs, habits, and fears that have been scripting your life, and you trace them to their source. But the final step is where most people stall. This is Verify—the point where you separate truth from lies, decide which narratives deserve to stay, and cut off any possibility of returning to the old story.

Verification isn't about proving you *can* change—it's about confirming, with absolute honesty, which parts of your history are worth carrying into your future and which must be shattered here and now. It's the moment you look your past in the eye and say: *Only the truth gets to come with me.*

Here's why it matters: a decision without verification is like signing a contract without reading the fine print. You might feel committed, but old agreements—the unspoken ones you made years ago—will still be running the show. If you don't tear up those contracts, they will quietly pull you back into the very cycles you swore you'd escape.

That's the danger of half-commitment—not just lost progress, but the slow erosion of your belief that you can keep your word. Until you burn the bridge to your old life completely, you'll always be tempted to cross back.

That's what verification gives you: the authority to stop asking your past for permission. The resolve to stop explaining your growth to people who preferred you stagnant. And the courage to live like the new version of you is non-negotiable.

If you're halfway in, you're already losing ground. The question isn't, *Are you ready to change?* The question is, *Are you done giving yourself an out?* Because if you are, then this is the moment you light the match. You're not waiting for the stars to align—you're becoming the force that moves them.

The Three Non-Negotiables of True Transformation

Every lasting transformation is built on three pillars. Remove one, and the entire structure wobbles until it collapses. These aren't motivational clichés—they are the skeletal frame of any real, sustainable change: **Identity Alignment**, **Environmental Integrity**, and **Consistent Execution**.

When these three are in place, you stop chasing transformation and start living it. Without them, you'll spend your life in cycles of high motivation and low follow-through.

1 – Identity Alignment

You can't live beyond the identity you believe is yours. Your behavior will always return to the person you think you are—even if your intentions are higher.

When I left the Marine Corps, I didn't expect the hardest part to be *identity whiplash*. I had spent years in a culture where your rank was on your chest, your role was clear, and your value was proven daily in the tightest of units. Then one day, I was standing in the parking lot outside the base, my gear in a duffel, realizing nobody out here cared that I had led Marines or navigated combat.

At first, I tried to replace the uniform with titles. Civilian job titles. Business cards. "Director of this." "Owner of that." But none of it stuck emotionally because inside, I still saw myself as "a Marine out of place"—not the leader I had become. That misalignment bled into my choices. I'd undercharge for work. I'd hesitate to speak up in rooms I was overqualified to lead.

The turning point came one afternoon when a mentor asked me, "If you met yourself today but knew nothing about your past, who would you say you are?" It stopped me cold. For the first time, I saw that I was defining myself by what I had *been*, not who I was *becoming*. That day, I wrote a new statement of identity—not a résumé, but a declaration: *I am a leader who builds people and systems that last.* Everything I've built since traces back to that realignment.

> **Your identity is the thermostat for your life—if it's set too low, you will unconsciously turn down your potential to match it.**

2 – Environmental Integrity

Discipline is easier when your environment supports it. If your surroundings—physical, relational, cultural—are wired for the old you, they will drag you back no matter how inspired you feel.

When I became Director for Military and Veterans Affairs at Florida Atlantic University, I inherited an office that looked more like a storage unit than a command center. Papers stacked. Furniture mismatched. Even the energy in the room felt like resignation. The staff was talented, but years of red tape and low expectations had worn them down.

If I had simply tried to "motivate" people in that space, it would have been like planting flowers in concrete. Instead, I started with the environment. We cleared every unnecessary item, reorganized the layout, painted the walls, and brought in visuals of mission, service, and pride. But it wasn't just the physical space—I shifted the relational space too. I invited student veterans to share their transition stories, created a culture of recognition, and made sure the office was a place people wanted to be.

Within months, the atmosphere changed. Morale went up. Attendance went up. People began taking initiative again. Why? Because environment shapes energy, and energy shapes execution.

> **If you want a new outcome, build an environment where the old outcome can't survive.**

3 – Consistent Execution

Momentum doesn't come from massive effort once in a while—it comes from small, non-negotiable actions stacked daily, even when no one's watching.

During one phase of my INC 5000 construction franchise, we hit a wall. Sales were flat, and the team was burning out. My first instinct was to hunt for a big, dramatic fix—a new marketing push, a flashy hire, something that would turn the ship overnight. But the truth was, the business didn't need a miracle. It needed a rhythm.

I sat down with my leadership team and committed to one non-negotiable: daily outreach. Every single person, from me to the newest hire, had to make a set number of meaningful contacts each day. No skipping. No "I'll make it up tomorrow." The number wasn't huge—but the consistency was absolute.

At first, it felt slow. Too slow. But within 90 days, the tide turned. We weren't chasing opportunities anymore—they were coming to us. Revenue climbed. Stress dropped. And the team learned something they carry to this day:

Consistency is the proof your future can trust you.

When **Identity Alignment**, **Environmental Integrity**, and **Consistent Execution** work together, you stop living on motivational spikes and start operating from structural stability. You're no longer relying on hype to keep you moving—your very life is set up to sustain the change you've decided on.

Your Decision Commitment Contract

The moment of Verify rarely announces itself. It doesn't arrive with fireworks or motivational music. It comes in ordinary moments when the noise stops, and you can finally hear the truth you've been avoiding.

One of mine came in the middle of a Thursday afternoon, sitting in my own office. I had just wrapped up a virtual meeting with a prospective client— the kind of deal that could have doubled our revenue for the quarter. I'd prepared for weeks, polished every detail of the pitch, and delivered it with the confidence they expected from me. The client smiled, said they'd "circle back," and the meeting ended on a high note.

As the screen went dark, I noticed my reflection in the monitor. The look in my eyes wasn't victory—it was hesitation. I knew I'd held back. I had avoided making a bold ask because I didn't want to risk losing the deal. I had kept the conversation in safe waters instead of steering it toward the transformation I knew we could deliver.

That was the same pattern I'd been running for months. Taking the meetings, delivering the work, hitting the numbers—but always leaving an escape route open. Enough effort to look committed, but not enough risk to make it irreversible. One foot in the vision, one foot in the fallback plan.

I swiveled my chair toward the window, watching cars crawl down the street. And it hit me: this wasn't about the client at all. It was about me still living with a "just in case" clause in my own future. Just in case this business failed. Just in case the bold move didn't land. Just in case someone told me I'd overreached. That kind of thinking doesn't build the future—it builds a waiting room.

So I opened my journal and wrote: *If you don't get honest, you're going to lose everything trying to look successful.*

And then I moved. I emailed the client back and made the ask I had been avoiding. I called a mentor and told him where I'd been playing small. I ended two contracts that were financially safe but strategically draining. I rearranged my entire calendar so my mornings were protected for high-impact work—no emails, no distractions, no fallback tasks.

Verification isn't glamorous. It's not a social media announcement. It's the quiet, irreversible step that makes retreat impossible. It's signing the lease before you've figured out how you'll make rent. It's committing to the launch date before the product is perfect. It's telling the person you've been avoiding, *"I'm in—and I'm not leaving room for an out."*

If you've ever said you were committed while secretly keeping a safety net, you've skipped this step. If you've made a bold declaration but left the old habit, relationship, or identity alive in the background, you've skipped this step. Skipping Verify is like buying a one-way ticket to your new life but also reserving a refundable return flight—you'll take it the moment things get uncomfortable.

The first two steps of Decision—Identify and Clarify—name the patterns and expose their roots. But Verify is where you strip those patterns of power. It's where you burn the bridge, close the account, hand over the keys, or take whatever action makes the old life impossible to return to.

That's what a Decision Commitment Contract really is—not a statement of intent, but a binding agreement with yourself. One that says: *Yes..yes..will not go back.*

Your 24-hour move? Do something today that takes away the option to retreat. Send the message. Cancel the subscription. Book the flight. Throw out the bottle. Make the call. Take one step that tells your nervous system, *"This time, we mean it."*

Because until you Verify, your "decision" is just an idea. Once you do, it becomes your reality.

The Break The Bottle Way

Transformation isn't born in a single lightning strike—it's built in the steady rhythm of days where your actions prove your intentions. The Break The Bottle Way isn't about hype or hollow declarations. It's about proof. It's about living so consistently in alignment that no one, not even your old self, can doubt your commitment. You don't just announce change—you *verify* it with every choice, every habit, every breath.

For me, this truth hit hard the year I came home from the military. I had the discipline, but not the direction. On paper, I was "fine." In reality, I was coasting—half in, half out. One Friday night, alone in an empty office, I caught my own reflection in a darkened window. The man looking back at me wasn't lazy—he was still negotiating with himself. That night, I made a choice: no more negotiation. I built a system that made coasting impossible—morning prospecting before anything else, Friday accountability check-ins, no excuses. That was the first moment I understood: the bottle doesn't break with talk. It breaks with proof.

Love, too, must be verified. Not with grand gestures, but with the unglamorous work of showing up. I learned this the day my son, crayons in hand, drew a picture of me—only calmer, softer, not mad. I realized then that being a father wasn't about shielding him from my flaws; it was about letting him see repair in action. Apologizing. Listening. Learning. Love isn't the absence of mistakes—it's the presence of presence.

Friendship works the same way. After leaving active duty, I drifted from one of my closest brothers-in-arms. Years passed before I heard he was struggling. I didn't text. I didn't "like" a post. I drove six hours, knocked on his door, and said, "I'm still here." That's what verification looks like—it's loyalty in the shadows, when no one's watching.

And work? Real work? It's not about proving you can grind—it's about proving you can align. My first business nearly burned me out because I was using hustle to verify my worth. But burnout will always tell the truth you've been avoiding. When I started filtering my decisions through one question— *Does this reflect my values, or just my ambition?*—my work stopped being a cage and became a craft.

Healing is verification in slow motion. I remember sitting in a VA counseling room, arms crossed, giving nothing. My therapist slid a paper toward me that read: *You can't verify your future if you keep protecting your past.* That was the first time I admitted I wasn't "fine." Healing didn't happen in a weekend—it happened every time I chose openness over avoidance, presence over performance.

The same principle applies to emotional mastery. Your life is shaped by the emotions you return to most. In deployment, I learned to set my state before the environment set it for me. Years later, in a tense business negotiation, I took 60 seconds in the hallway—breathing, grounding, choosing my posture.

That was verification in real time: proving I could lead my state instead of being led by it.

Verification also means rewriting the rules you live by. I once believed I'd feel successful when I earned six figures. The day I hit it, nothing changed inside. That's when I rewrote my rule: *I'll feel successful when I'm in alignment with my values.* That one shift turned my chase into purpose.

Patterns break the same way—through disruption. One of my clients couldn't finish her book because she was waiting for it to be perfect. I told her, "Stop verifying with perfect—verify with done." That week, she sent her half-polished draft to a publisher. That act didn't just change her behavior—it rewrote her identity.

Because that's the heart of The Break The Bottle Way: you stop keeping a spare key to your old life. You stop asking the past for permission. You live so that your choices *verify* your commitment—again and again.

And with each verified step, the energy shifts. You start moving faster, not because you're rushing, but because the weight is coming off. You're no longer dragging the dead body of your old identity. Every "yes" to your values is a "no" to the life that kept you small. And once that momentum catches, it's not a walk—it's a run. It's the sprint toward a life where your word and your walk are the same thing.

You don't need more time. You don't need more credentials. You don't need permission. You need alignment. You need to decide. You need to build. You need to begin—one breath, one boundary, one brave conversation at a time.

The bottle doesn't break by accident. It breaks when you throw it hard enough to hear the glass scream, when you watch the shards scatter in every direction, knowing there's no going back. That sound—that freedom—is the proof you've stopped negotiating with yourself. That's The Break The Bottle Way.

And your time isn't just now—your time starts the second you let it shatter.

BREAK THE BOTTLE CHALLENGE — Chapter 4

It's time to stop pretending you're in when you're really halfway out. This challenge isn't about declarations—it's about decisions. For the next seven days, choose one area of your life where you've been half-committed. You already know where it is. The project you keep postponing. The relationship you're still entertaining that's stealing your peace. The health decision you keep saying "next week" to.

Now do this:

1. **Name the Pattern** – Write it down. Be brutally honest. "I keep saying I'll ___ but I haven't." This is your moment of truth.

2. **Burn the Bridge** – Do one action that removes your option to go back. Cancel the subscription. Tell the person. Delete the file. Throw out the thing that keeps you stuck in the loop. Don't make it symbolic—make it structural.

3. **Establish a Daily Anchor** – Create a non-negotiable action tied to your commitment. Something simple but sacred. A 10-minute walk. A five-sentence journal check-in. One clean meal. One phone-free hour. Just one thing, daily, that becomes your proof.

4. **Share It** – Tell one person who believes in the future you're building. Don't just vent—declare. Let them hold you accountable.

5. **Sign the Contract** – Literally. Write this sentence: "I am committed to becoming the version of me who no longer gives partial effort to a whole calling." Sign and date it. Place it somewhere visible. This is your mirror check when excuses get loud.

This week, stop talking about breaking the bottle. Break it. Burn the fallback plan. Build from finality. And when you feel the tension rise, remember: that discomfort you feel? That's the sound of your old self losing power. Keep going.

RESOURCES

Download the Tool: Daily Affirmations & Declarations
Speak your truth into existence with affirmations designed to ground your commitment, build emotional strength, and disrupt old belief systems.

Available at: btbprograms.com/free-resources

PART 2

DIRECTION

MASTERING SOLUTIONS THINKING & CHOOSE THE PATH

I remember sitting in my car after everything had crumbled—marriage, money, mission. The engine was running, but I wasn't going anywhere. The GPS on my dashboard blinked, searching for a signal, as if mocking the reality of my life. I had no map. Not for where I was. Not for where I was going. And in that stillness, I realized: surviving was no longer enough. I needed direction. Not just movement—but meaningful movement. I didn't need motivation. I needed a method. A new way to think, lead, and live. That moment was the birth of what I now call *solutions thinking*—the ability to rise above reaction and lead yourself with clarity.

If you've ever taken a trip to somewhere unfamiliar, you know the irreplaceable value of a map. A map doesn't just point you forward—it orients you. It helps you navigate through what you've never seen, never experienced, and cannot predict. Life often feels like that—uncharted. We find ourselves in moments of transition, uncertainty, or even crisis, where what's behind us offers no guarantee of what's ahead. And when we're in that space, choosing a direction isn't just optional—it's vital. That's where solutions thinking begins. Not with perfect clarity, but with courageous intention. Choosing a direction means choosing to lead yourself instead of just reacting to life. It requires pausing long enough to ask: *What path aligns with who I want to become—not just what I want to avoid?*

Direction demands more than intellect. It calls for wisdom. And wisdom, I've learned, often begins with understanding the difference between belief and faith. While we often use those words interchangeably, they're not the same. Belief is intellectual—it's the mental assent to an idea we've accepted as true. Belief is grounded in logic, evidence, and adaptability. But faith—faith is deeper. Faith is trust. It's embodied. It moves even when the road is foggy. Belief might say, "I see the path." Faith says, "I'll walk it." Belief listens to reason. Faith listens to calling. Belief adjusts when facts change. Faith stays steady even when facts disappear. Belief thinks. Faith commits. To choose direction with solutions thinking, we need both: belief to understand the terrain and faith to move through it anyway.

But before we move forward, we must get clear. Most people don't fail because they didn't try hard enough—they fail because they lacked clarity. They ran fast, but in the wrong direction. They executed strategies for problems they hadn't properly defined. They chased answers to questions they never fully asked. In a culture obsessed with the right answers, we've forgotten the power of better questions. From childhood, we're trained to stop asking and start answering. Be right. Be quick. Be certain. But the people who lead, grow, and transform don't live in certainty—they live in curiosity. They ask, "Why?" "What if?" and "What truly matters here?" Solutions thinking begins not with declarations, but with inquiry.

When my son was small, he'd walk around pointing at everything asking, "What's that?" It wasn't just play—it was human programming at work. That kind of questioning builds connection, learning, and wisdom. But as we grow, society teaches us to abandon curiosity for correctness. Schools reward performance, not questions. Workplaces prioritize speed over understanding. Eventually, many adults stop asking altogether. But if you want to lead yourself through the storm—and to the next level of your life— you must return to that place. You must reclaim childlike curiosity. You must explore again. Listen deeply. Challenge assumptions. Sit in the tension of not knowing and still move forward with faith.

Solutions thinking is the discipline of asking. Great questions open doors. Poor ones shut them. Binary questions like "Is this good or bad?" or "Should I quit or stay?" flatten complex experiences into shallow choices. They trap us in either/or when life usually demands both/and. Real growth comes from expansive questions like, "What is this teaching me?" or "Where is the opportunity in this obstacle?" These are the questions that elevate our thinking and reframe our limitations as leverage points. The truth is, most of us don't need more advice—we need deeper reflection. Not more noise, but more stillness. We must stop assuming we understand—and start exploring what we've ignored.

My own life didn't change because I tried harder. It changed when I asked different questions. When I looked in the mirror and asked myself: *Am I chasing relief or seeking freedom? Am I avoiding pain—or building purpose?* These weren't easy questions. They didn't give me immediate comfort. But they cracked something open. They healed me. They made me face myself. That's where direction begins—with the truth we've been running from.

Solutions thinking doesn't ask you to fix everything. It asks you to align with what matters. It shifts your focus from chaos to clarity. From autopilot to awareness. From fear to trust. But here's the hard part: solutions thinking often asks you to pause. To breathe. To resist the urge to *just do something.* And in that pause, transformation begins. You stop being problem-focused and become purpose-driven. You stop reacting—and start choosing.

This is the essence of direction—and it unfolds in three movements: **Plan, Build, and Navigate**. Direction begins with **Plan**—defining exactly what needs to be done. This is where the fog begins to lift. Where vague dreams become concrete objectives. Where vision turns tangible and goals become priorities you can act on. The plan is not just about knowing what you want—it's about plotting the specific, strategic steps to get there. It's your blueprint.

Then you **Build**. This is where the plan moves from paper to practice. You begin gathering the tools, the people, the structure, and the internal systems you'll need to bring the vision to life. This part is less about dreaming and more about construction—crafting a framework strong enough to hold your transformation and flexible enough to grow with it. Dreamers imagine change. Builders execute it.

And finally, you **Navigate**. You start living the plan. You weave the vision into your daily habits, your relationships, your leadership. You stay alert, course-correct when needed, and hold your direction even when life throws curveballs. Navigation isn't just about knowing where to go—it's about adjusting with wisdom while staying aligned to where you've chosen to head.

Together, Plan, Build, and Navigate form the full spectrum of direction. Without all three, transformation lacks structure. But with all three, you gain not just movement—but meaningful momentum.

Every answer someone gives you is a sacred gift. When you ask, "What's that like for you?"—and mean it—you're not just having a conversation. You're creating connection. That's the soul of leadership. That's what changes culture. Listening with empathy. Sitting in the mess. Refusing to rush to conclusions. One great question asked with empathy will take you further than ten smart answers spoken without heart.

Choosing your direction is not a single decision. It's a way of life. It's the daily act of realignment. It's asking, "Does this choice honor my future—or just numb my present?" It's prioritizing peace over performance. Depth over distraction. Intention over inertia. And it's refusing to settle for a life that looks good but feels hollow. That's the heart of direction. The inner compass that calls you forward.

Here's the truth: when you hit rock bottom, what's next isn't about hustling harder. It's about moving smarter. With strategy. With solutions. With soul. Direction is more than momentum—it's a declaration. It's standing in your truth and saying: "I refuse to live on default settings. I will not carry recycled pain into a new season. I'm not going back to that bottle, that belief, that broken pattern." You don't need a hundred answers. You specifically need to know what you want. You need one powerful question. You need a map. You need your next right step.

This is how we choose the path forward. Not by waiting for guarantees, but by walking with intention. Not by needing certainty, but by reclaiming curiosity. Not by knowing everything, but by trusting what we *do* know— and acting on it. That's the power of solutions thinking. That's the heart of Direction.

5

THE ALPHA PROJECT—WAR-TORN ROADS AND THE MAP FORWARD

"They sent us where the maps blurred and the politics bled. But it wasn't about where we were ordered to go. It was about who we had to become to make it out—and what we brought back with us."

— Break The Bottle

The Recalibration of Direction

There comes a moment in every man's life when the soul undergoes a quiet but profound recalibration—a subtle shift that may go unnoticed by the world, yet rattles the foundation of everything within. For me, that moment didn't arrive in a therapist's chair or in the glow of quiet introspection. It came under the harsh sun of Fallujah, Iraq, when I was serving with 3rd AABN—3rd TRAX, ALPHA Company. It was September 13, 2004. The air reeked of diesel and death. The ground trembled beneath the mechanical thunder of our AAVs pushing through war-ravaged streets. The VBIED that detonated just seconds from where I stood, struck me with shrapnel, wasn't just an explosion—it was a crucible. It took lives I loved. It took parts of us we never got back. And yet, from that fire, something else emerged. Not just resolve. Not just rage. But awakening.

As a Marine, and as a Purple Heart recipient, I've carried those battlefield scars longer than most people have carried their careers. But the heaviest things I brought home weren't physical. They were questions. Questions that outlived the battles. Questions that still echo: What does it mean to lead? To kill? To follow? Where does courage end and trauma begin? And who do we become when the flags stop waving and the orders go quiet?

These questions didn't come from politics—they came from pain. And over the years, they led me to something most Marines don't talk about: consciousness. I began searching not for answers, but for frameworks—something to help me understand what I had seen, and what I had become. That search brought me to two models that reshaped my life: David R. Hawkins' *Map of Consciousness* from *Power vs. Force*, and the Graves Model—known to many as Spiral Dynamics. To some, these are theories. To me, they were survival maps. They revealed where I'd been in my soul—and where I needed to go to truly live again.

Power vs. Force opened my eyes to the hidden architecture of energy that runs beneath all human behavior. It revealed that most of humanity is stuck operating from low frequencies—survival, fear, shame, anger, ego. These are the forces that build armies, destroy marriages, start wars, and end lives. They get things done, but they burn everything in their path. They're the energies of conquest, not creation. In contrast, true power—real, transformative power—rises from higher levels of consciousness: love, courage, peace, reason. Power doesn't demand. It influences. It doesn't shout. It radiates. And in Fallujah, I witnessed both. I saw force unleashed on a city. And I saw power embodied in men who bore the burden of leadership with quiet gravity.

CLINICALLY PROVEN
"MAP OF CONSCIOUSNESS"

View on God	View on Life	Level Name	Level#	Emotions	Process
Self	Is	Enlightenment	700–1000	Ineffable	Pure Consciousness
All-Being	Perfect	Peace	600	Bliss	Illumination
		Spontaneous Healing			
One	Complete	Joy	540	Serenity	Transfiguration
Loving	Benign	Love	500	Reverence	Revelation
Wise	Meaningful	Reason	400	Understanding	Abstraction
Merciful	Harmonious	Acceptance	350	Forgiveness	Transcendence
Inspiring	Hopeful	Willingness	310	Optimism	Intention
Enabling	Satisfactory	Neutrality	250	Trust	Release
Permitting	Feasible	Courage	200	Affirmation	Empowerment

P O W E R ↑ (left)   **S T R O N G** ↑ (right)

Levels at or above 200 have Truth, Integrity, and support life.   CREATIVE

Levels below 200 are False, lack Integrity, and do not support life.   DESTRUCTIVE

View on God	View on Life	Level Name	Level#	Emotions	Process
Indifferent	Demanding	Pride	175	Scorn	Inflation
Vengeful	Antagonistic	Anger	150	Hate	Aggression
Denying	Disappointing	Desire	125	Craving	Enslavement
Punitive	Frightening	Fear	100	Anxiety	Withdrawal
Disdainful	Tragic	Grief	75	Regret	Despondence
Condemning	Hopeless	Apathy	50	Despair	Abdication
Vindictive	Evil	Guilt	30	Blame	Destruction
Despising	Miserable	Shame	20	Humiliation	Elimination

F O R C E ↓ (left)   **W E A K** ↓ (right)

POWER is self-sustaining, permanent, stationary, and invincible.
FORCE is temporary, consumes energy, and moves from location to location.

Logarithmic Energy Field Increases: **1** = 1; **2** = 10; **3** = 100; **4** = 1,000; **5** = 10,000; **6** = 100,000; ...etc.

All levels above 500 are "objective" and all levels from 500 to 1,000 are "subjective."

I still remember Capt. Venning, whose calm under pressure steadied our entire unit. I remember Lt. Colonel Renforth and Lt. Colonel Smith waiting for us after missions that almost destroyed us—not with applause, but with presence. Their eyes told us what words never could: You made it. And we will carry this weight together. And then there was General Mattis—a man who resisted operations he morally disagreed with, not through rebellion, but through disciplined clarity. These men taught me something I'll never forget: before we execute strategy, we must master presence. Before we rush to fix the world, we must first become anchored within ourselves. In war, they were more than commanders. They were stabilizers in the storm. And in a world addicted to urgency, they modeled what true leadership looks like: stillness in chaos, integrity under pressure.

But war didn't just break my body—it split open my psyche. And so, after the explosions stopped, my next battlefield became internal. That's where I encountered the Graves Model—a framework that helped me decode human development not just on the field, but in the soul. Spiral Dynamics taught me that humans evolve in layers, like tectonic plates of consciousness, each representing a worldview through which reality is filtered.

Level 1 is primal survival: "I need to live." You see this in those gripped by addiction, poverty, crisis. Level 2 is tribal: "We live through loyalty." It clings to rituals, myths, group identity. Level 3 is the warlord—the street hustler, the tyrant, the reactive self: "I take what I want." Then comes Level 4—order, religion, patriotism: "We must be responsible." It seeks structure, often rigid. Level 5 is the achiever: "I will win." It celebrates capitalism, personal growth, ambition. Level 6 is the empath: "We will rise together." Social justice, inclusion, shared humanity. Level 7 begins the leap—global systems thinking, innovation, cross-cultural wisdom. And Level 8? Harmony. Integration. Wholeness.

In Fallujah, I saw these levels clash in real-time. We weren't just fighting an enemy. We were navigating a battlefield of misaligned consciousness. Some insurgents were locked in Level 1 survival. Others fought from tribalism, legacy, shame. We moved as a Level 4 force—order, institution, structure. And when these worldviews collided, the result was not just war. It was confusion. Misunderstanding. Trauma that had nowhere to go.

GRAVES MODEL

LEVEL 08

Holisitc

Beginning: ? (macro), ? (micro). The Worldview is "our global."

LEVEL 07

Thought Leader

Beginning: ? (macro), ? (micro). The Worldview is "global." Focus: Galvanize around problem solving.

LEVEL 06

Ecology

Beginning ~20 years ago (macro), ? (micro). The Worldview is "our growth." Focus: Everyone has a voice. Civil rights.

LEVEL 05

Achievement

Beginning ~300 years ago (macro), ? (micro). The Worldview is "my growth." Focus: I'm going to get ahead. Capitalism.

LEVEL 04

Civilization

Beginning ~5,000 years ago (macro), 20's (micro). The Worldview is "institution." Focus: Let's be responsible. Most religions/patriotism.

LEVEL 03

Warlord

Beginning ~10,000 years ago (macro), teens (micro). The Worldview is "my needs." Focus: I want to be in charge. Seen in gang culture.

LEVEL 02

Tribal

Beginning ~50,000 years ago (macro), toddler (micro). The Worldview is "family." Focus: We want to live. Magic thinking turns formal.

LEVEL 01

Survival

Beginning ~150,000 years ago (macro), birth (micro). The worldview is "me." Focus: I want to live. (Uncommon in developed countries.)

And some will say, "That sounds like excuse-making." It's not. It's anatomy. The anatomy of belief. The anatomy of behavior. Understanding someone's worldview doesn't excuse their actions—but it does allow us to see the fuller truth. Without understanding, we don't change. We just repeat the same wars in different languages. The same domination, with different flags. And history shows us: when we fail to understand consciousness, we default to force.

After standing among the wreckage of 9/11, after surviving that VBIED blast, after years of suppressing grief under the banner of strength, I've come to believe this: the most dangerous war is not fought in streets—it's fought in the soul. It's the war between fear and love. Between dominance and presence. Between reacting and responding. If we do not shift how we think, how we feel, how we lead, we will carry conflict into every corner of our lives—even in peace.

And when I returned home, I saw it everywhere. In families. In churches. In schools. On social media. People at war with each other—not over facts, but over identity. Over unhealed pain. Over inherited shame. People reacting from Levels 2, 3, and 4—tribalism, ego, moral rigidity—unaware there's a better way to live, to lead, to relate. That's when I realized: Fallujah never left. We just changed the weapons.

The real mission now isn't out there—it's in here. It's in the willingness to climb. To evolve. To build from higher consciousness instead of reacting from broken instincts. It's in becoming a new kind of warrior—not one who fights for dominance, but one who constructs something better. A culture. A family. A self. Because pain will always knock. Chaos will always return. But when it does, who you are will determine what happens next.

The Weaponization of Presence

You don't need to be in a firefight to know what war feels like. You don't need sand in your boots or a rifle in your grip to feel ambushed by life. War, at its core, is simply chaos accelerated—and when that chaos erupts, whether in a combat zone, a conference room, or within the confines of your own home, there's only one force that brings gravity back into the room:

leadership. Not positional leadership. Not ranks. Not polished speeches or titles embossed on office doors. I'm talking about presence—raw, energetic, conscious presence. Leadership by vibration, by intention, by clarity that anchors others when the floor beneath them begins to shift.

It took years, and a brutal cost, for me to understand this. The deeper I studied David Hawkins' *Power vs. Force*, the more I saw leadership for what it truly is: a frequency, not a formula. Hawkins quantified it—fear vibrates at 100. Love? 500. Courage? 200. You cannot fake the energy you carry. And in the chaos of Iraq, that energy often meant the difference between disorder and unity, panic and precision. The moment you begin vibrating from the higher levels—love, courage, integrity—your very presence becomes a stabilizer. A weapon not of destruction, but of peace. Of clarity. Of forward motion. That's leadership. Not noise. Not bravado. Not control. But energetic stability rooted in truth.

I saw this embodied in Capt. Venning. It wasn't just what he commanded. It was how he existed in the middle of the storm. When the regional OPSO called and said no one else could take the ADOC mission—when it was clear we were not the perfect choice, but the only option left—his response was not panic. It was presence. Anchored. Unwavering. Intentional. That energy filtered through every one of us. In those moments, it wasn't firepower that carried us forward—it was alignment. His steadiness set the tone. His vibration became the command. And because of that, we didn't just endure the mission. We defined it. We set the bar. We shaped what followed. That's the power of presence. Not loud. Not flashy. But immovable.

We've been sold the lie that transformation happens in big moments. That change requires grand declarations or viral breakthroughs. But in reality, change happens in the invisible decisions—the pause before the reaction, the breath before the response, the quiet refusal to descend into fear. That's the new battlefield. That's where leadership lives now.

Years after I left Iraq, I found myself standing in a conference room, watching a team of high-performing executives verbally tear each other apart over a missed deadline. No bullets. No sirens. Just egos, blame, silence, and resignation. And yet—I felt it. The same heat in my chest. The same sense of fragmentation. That same chaotic energy I once felt in Fallujah, now wearing a suit and tie. That was the moment I realized: war doesn't end when the weapons are holstered. It morphs. It becomes emotional warfare, spiritual fatigue, culture collapse. And if we don't recognize it for what it is, we'll keep bleeding—just slower.

Most people never escape the chaos because they meet every problem with the same energy that created it. They respond to shame with more shame. To fear with more fear. They scream into the void hoping to find peace. But force never produces healing. Only power does. And power doesn't shout. It doesn't demand. It simply *is*. When you operate from power, your life reframes chaos. Your presence reorders energy. You don't need to control outcomes—because your vibration already anchors the environment.

This is why Spiral Dynamics—the Graves Model—became so pivotal to my understanding. It revealed that most of society isn't broken. It's just stuck. Caught cycling through outdated levels of consciousness—tribalism, warlord ego, rigid institutionalism. We think we're fighting ideologies. But we're actually fighting unresolved trauma. Consciousness that's never had a chance to evolve. Bin Laden wasn't just a terrorist—he was the manifestation of a Level 3/4 spiral: fear, shame, dominance, righteousness, tribal vengeance. His evil was real. His violence unjustifiable. But his actions didn't arise in a vacuum. They were the fruit of internal fragmentation, calcified into ideology. And understanding that doesn't justify—it clarifies. Because until we understand the consciousness behind the conflict, we will continue to fight symptoms while feeding the root.

That's the deeper war. And the new mission isn't about serving harder or protecting louder—it's about elevating. The mission now is consciousness. It's about training ourselves to operate from higher states. Asking better questions. Shifting the lens from control to curiosity. Instead of, "How do I stop this problem?" we must ask, "What energy birthed this problem?" Instead of, "How do I fix this person?" we ask, "What version of me do I need to become to no longer be triggered by them?" That's leadership. That's transformation. It's not reaction—it's creative consciousness.

In today's world, this kind of presence is not optional. It's required. In a society fractured by digital warfare, identity politics, and emotional disconnection, the ability to hold a regulated nervous system is now more powerful than any weapon. Veterans know this instinctively. We've been where structure failed. We've seen what happens when leadership disappears. We've lived through decisions where life hung in the balance. And those of us who've done the work to reintegrate, to process the trauma instead of passing it down, carry something sacred. Not just scars—but clarity. Not just memory—but insight. And that insight has value. It can't be outsourced. It must be embodied.

That's what the Alpha Project is. Not a campaign. Not a brand. But a new posture. A new ethos for what leadership and humanity can look like. It's the call to rise. To build. To no longer lead from force, but from aligned, embodied, empowered truth. To become the kind of person whose very existence shifts the atmosphere. Whose nervous system brings order to the room. Whose presence replaces panic with possibility.

There are no medals for this work. No accolades. No news segments. Just the deep, sacred mastery of a life lived with integrity. You won't be applauded for shifting your vibration. But the people around you will feel it. Your children will inherit it. Your teams will trust it. Your community will evolve because of it.

Because warriors don't just fight. They transform. And when the battle shifts from the field to the inner terrain, it's not your strength that wins—it's your stillness. That is presence, weaponized for peace.

The Misdirection—The Fog Behind the Fire

Leaving the Marine Corps was one of the hardest decisions I've ever made. Not because I was unsure about civilian life—but because I didn't know how to live it anymore. I walked away from the uniform with the weight of service on my chest and a silence in my soul. I lost my direction. I lost my identity. I lost my fire. But more than anything, I was haunted by a question I could never fully put down: Why were we sent to Iraq? Why Fallujah? Why not Afghanistan—the place where Osama bin Laden had been confirmed?

The very place where al-Qaeda orchestrated the attack that shattered American soil and our national psyche?

At the time, the answer was drowned in the noise of orders, urgency, and adrenaline. As Marines, we didn't ask why—we prepared, executed, and repeated. But with time, distance, and the sobering clarity of history, the fog began to lift. And what I saw on the other side of that fog wasn't easy to stomach. It wasn't clean, and it certainly wasn't comforting—but it was necessary. Because those of us who lived it deserve clarity, and so do the people who sent us.

In the raw aftermath of 9/11, the world stood still in a moment of shared grief and fury. Afghanistan was the natural target. It was the epicenter— the birthplace of the planning, training, and sheltering of the terrorists responsible. The Taliban gave sanctuary. Bin Laden found protection in its mountains. We struck first, yes. But we didn't stay focused. The narrative began to shift, subtly but surely, as if someone had turned the national spotlight onto another stage entirely.

Soon, the Bush administration began building a different case—one that pointed toward Iraq. They painted Saddam Hussein as a looming threat, claiming the existence of weapons of mass destruction, implying links to al-Qaeda, and suggesting—without outright saying—that he had a hand in 9/11. The American public, still bleeding emotionally, was primed to believe it. Fear, grief, and patriotism made fertile ground for redirection.

But I wasn't a policymaker—I was a warfighter. My world was made of dust, discipline, and duty. My days were filled with briefing rooms, leadership drills, and preparation for missions that could end in silence or glory. Even so, I remember the subtle shifts in atmosphere. The questions whispered behind closed doors. The sense that something didn't add up. Fallujah became our battleground—not because it was where justice led, but because politics did.

Eventually, the truth surfaced. There were no Weapons of Mass Destruction (WMD's). The intelligence was not only flawed—it was dangerously manipulated. The supposed links between Saddam and al-Qaeda were baseless, unproven, and in many cases, outright fabricated. The war had been sold under the guise of protection, but it was built on fear. Preemptive defense became the justification, but beneath it all was geopolitical ambition.

So why were we there? That's a question that still haunts the American conscience. On the ground, we didn't have the luxury of pondering it. We had orders, and we carried them out with honor, professionalism, and blood. But make no mistake—our battlefield was shaped not by justice but by strategy. Afghanistan was the crime scene. Iraq became the stage.

To understand that isn't to point fingers—it's to reclaim truth. It's to name the ghosts that still wake us up at night. It's to take ownership of a narrative that, for too long, ignored the voices of the men and women who lived it. Because we weren't chasing bin Laden through the mountains. We were navigating insurgent warfare through the dense and battered streets of Fallujah, fighting enemies that weren't connected to 9/11 but were born from decades of fractured history and foreign policy missteps.

Fallujah became more than a location—it became a symbol. A city stained with contradiction, courage, and confusion. And we fought not because we fully understood the mission—but because we understood each other. We didn't hold the line for politics. We held it for the men beside us. We fought for survival, for meaning, and for the kind of brotherhood that transcends explanation. Our stories weren't crafted in press conferences. They were carved into the dirt, the blood, and the silence between explosions.

I remember watching General James Mattis push back against the decision to commit the full Marine Division to Fallujah. He saw what many wouldn't: the lack of long-term strategy, the risk of politicized warfare, the danger of entering without a plan to stabilize. But ultimately, the decision didn't rest with him. It came from above—from the White House. President George W. Bush gave the order, and like always, boots hit the ground.

And we responded, because that's what warriors do. We stepped into fire, into ambushes, into missions that blurred the line between objective and survival. What followed was not clean or linear—it was brutal. It was costly. It was full of loss and resilience. Missions became memories we couldn't bury. And Fallujah, whether we chose it or not, became a chapter in our souls.

That's why direction matters. Because it isn't just a map—it's a soul contract. It's the decision point between purpose and pain, between wandering and legacy. And when direction is manipulated, miscommunicated, or politicized, the cost isn't only strategic. It's human.

As Marines, we never got to choose the battlefield—but we still deserved to understand why we were there. The world deserves to know what we carried. And more than that, we deserve to tell it ourselves.

History will debate the Iraq War for generations. But for us—for those who bled, broke, and survived on those streets—the truth is already written. Not in headlines. Not in reports. But in scars. In names. In the silence that follows a folded flag.

And so, this chapter remains not just a remembrance—but a reclaiming. Because war isn't only fought with rifles. It's shaped in boardrooms. It's launched with words. It's paid for by the people who had no vote in the matter—but every stake in its outcome. And long after the politicians retire, we carry what they started.

Let this be the anchor: Direction is forged through fire. And as we rise, rebuild, and repurpose that fire, our mission is no longer to simply survive it—but to ensure it never misleads another generation again.

My Break The Bottle Moment - From Combat to Community

After my darkest moment—my suicide attempt—I made a promise that changed everything: I would no longer live broken. I realized then that healing couldn't be only spiritual, motivational, or theoretical—it had to be practical. I had to participate in my own rescue. That conviction drove me into action.

I found myself immersed in training from some of the best at **Rush University Medical Center** in Chicago—on mental health treatment. For the first time, healing wasn't abstract—it was functional. I absorbed learning on PTSD, traumatic brain injury, cognitive therapy, neuro-linguistic programming, breathwork, art therapy, and more—everything structured around the real needs of warriors returning from battle, not textbook theory.

From Chicago, I went to the **Emory Healthcare Medical Center** in Atlanta—another hub of transformative care and part of the national **Warrior Care Network**, I studied prolonged exposure therapy, psychiatry, neurology, case management, wellness practices, and family support, all delivered through a blend of science and compassion, by a team that understood invisible wounds.

These weren't just educational experiences—they were lifelines. In those classrooms, clinics, and healing spaces, I discovered that courage without structure could crumble. I learned how to rebuild the brain without losing the soul. Therapeutic frameworks became safe maps back to myself. The clinical merged with the human. What I carried home from those programs wasn't just a deeper knowledge—it was a renewed capacity to heal others.

Because the worst wound isn't just what combat inflicts—it's what follows when you take off the uniform. I came home heavy. I returned without identity, wrapped in numbness, unraveling under the weight of invisible scars. I wasn't just unemployed or divorced—I was unmoored. My professional life looked seamless on the outside: I wore suits, led meetings, coached teams. But inside, everything was falling apart: I'd gained weight, I'd been arrested, I'd felt the seductive pull of despair more than once. The bottles I was carrying were invisible, but toxic: childhood wounds, guilt, loss, identity void, and unspoken expectation to be strong.

I lied to myself, to others, and to the mirror: "I can't afford vulnerability," "If I slow down, everything collapses," "I'm only as valuable as I'm useful." But over time, truth broke through. I started owning my story. I rebuilt, not with hustle, but with honesty. I rebuilt faith, family, business, identity—one careful choice at a time.

In my darkest moments, when therapy felt hollow and even leadership felt like weight, I returned to something primal—my faith. Not the polished sermons or the Sunday rituals, but the gritty, private kind of faith you whisper when no one's watching. I began praying not for outcomes, but for clarity. Not to be saved, but to be shown how to participate in my own salvation. That's when God became less of a distant commander and more of a divine strategist—helping me map not just where I'd been, but who I had the potential to become.

Here's what surfaced through my own journey—and what I offer to anyone who's ever felt fractured:

- **Authenticity**: You can't transform wearing a mask. Authenticity is the launching point.

- **Belief Systems**: Adversity isn't broken with force—but by dismantling the lies we've been conditioned to believe.

- **North Star Clarity**: When your mindset and mission align, momentum becomes inevitable.

Surviving war is one trial. Surviving what comes after—that's the harder fight. Reintegration isn't a return. It's a second battlefield, one made of silence, relational rupture, and emotional disconnection. Family, community—they may love you, but they cannot fully understand the wiring that now accompanies you. And that dissonance? It's not cultural. It's **consciousness-based warfare**.

It's here that I lean into the **Map of Consciousness**, which taught me that most people live in states like shame (20), fear (100), pride (175)—emotions that guarantee stagnation. But courage (200), neutrality, willingness, love, peace—those are operating systems. Real systems. Practical. Transformational. And the **Graves Model** taught me leadership isn't pushing someone to evolve. It's guiding them through levels: from tribal survival to civic responsibility to systemic empathy. You can't shortcut growth—but you can guide it.

That's become my purpose. Not conquest. Not status. Not applause. But quiet stewardship. Whether in homes, teams, communities, or organizations—I ask every room to shift its center of gravity: Is it operating from shame or from love? From force or from purpose?

Because systems replicate energy. Children raised in peace become emotionally literate adults. Companies built on empathy attract resilient teams. Communities rooted in authenticity cultivate trust.

This is the Alpha Project redefined. Not another campaign. Not another battle. But evolution: personal. Familial. Societal. You're not stuck. You're not invisible. You're the hinge in your lineage. You get to be the one who shifts the current.

Operationalizing Legacy—Frameworks for Personal and Community Mastery

Here's the truth few want to admit: without structure, transformation is temporary.

It doesn't matter how inspired you are after a retreat, how powerful a book you've read, or how deep a moment of clarity felt—if that insight doesn't become integrated into your daily operating system, it will dissolve under the pressure of survival. We fall back not because we're weak, but because gravity always pulls harder in the direction of what's familiar.

That's why healing—especially for veterans, leaders, and anyone trying to escape generational pain—requires more than motivation. It requires a **framework**. A structure strong enough to hold your growth, flexible enough to evolve with you, and simple enough to sustain when life hits hard.

Transformation isn't a weekend seminar. It's a mission. A daily recalibration with checkpoints, protocols, and accountability. Just like in the military—where every mission had clear objectives, sequencing, and strategy—so too must our healing. Because there's a world of difference between a motivational high and sustainable momentum. One fades with emotion. The other builds with intention.

That's why I built this model—because I needed something real. Something I could live by. Something I could teach. Something I could hand to a veteran, a father, a CEO, or a teenager and say, "Here. Start here."

"I'll never forget what one of my coaching clients told me after a session: 'You didn't just teach me how to lead my team—you taught me how to be present for my kids without trying to fix them.' That's when I knew the Alpha

Project wasn't theory. It was transformation in action. My son once told me, 'Daddy, you don't raise your voice anymore—you raise the room.' That's legacy. That's power."

I break it down into four essential layers: **Self, Relationships, Leadership, and Legacy**. These aren't steps—they're systems. And each one must be mastered to create a life that's not just successful, but significant.

1. Self—Recalibrating the Internal Operating System

It starts here, because everything starts here.

If you don't own your internal state, the world will own it for you. And let me be blunt—most of us were trained to survive, not to lead from within. Especially in the military, we were conditioned to compartmentalize, suppress, harden. That works in war. It destroys you in peace.

This is where **the Map of Consciousness** becomes more than theory—it becomes your compass. Every morning, I run a personal check-in: *Where am I today? Am I in shame? Fear? Anger?* Not to shame myself—but to steer. Because energy is measurable, and every state we live in becomes a strategy we repeat.

When I wake up low—grief, anxiety, resentment—I don't fake my way to joy. I name it. I sit with it. And then I choose—through breathwork, prayer, movement, journaling—to shift. Slowly. Intentionally.

This is where the **Tactical Consciousness Journal** comes in—a simple four-quadrant tool: Emotion, Trigger, Choice, Response. Every event becomes a data point. Not to obsess over feelings, but to **track transformation**. Because what isn't tracked can't be trained. This is my daily After Action Report—not on others, but on myself.

2. Relationships—Leading from Love, Not Codependency

This is where most people fail—not because they don't love, but because they haven't healed.

Unhealed leaders project. They control, manipulate, fix, or avoid—thinking they're helping. But what they're really doing is trying to resolve their past through their present partnerships.

Real power doesn't demand. It *regulates*.

This is why I train families like I trained fire teams. We hold **emotional state briefings** at home—not formal, but intentional. I sit with my wife and kids and ask: *Where are we emotionally? What's heavy? What's needed?* Because tactical readiness begins at home. And your family deserves a leader, not just a provider.

We don't use communication to confront—we use it to **co-regulate**. That means listening without defense. Speaking without blame. Leading not from fear, but from presence.

And here's what happens: when your house is in order, your mission expands. You speak clearer. You show up stronger. You lead with gravity, not noise. Healing at home scales into power at work.

TACTICAL CONSCIOUSNESS JOURNAL	
EMOTION	TRIGGER
CHOICE	RESPONSE

3. Leadership—Building Conscious Teams and Cultures

You don't need a title to be a leader. But if you have one, it comes with weight.

Whether you lead a company, a ministry, a school, or a squad—you are shaping **culture**. And culture isn't just about rules. It's about energy. Teams don't rise to their goals. They fall to their leader's level of self-awareness.

Traditional leadership is built on fear, metrics, and control. Conscious leadership is built on values, process, and emotional intelligence. It doesn't just ask *what are we doing?* It asks, *who are we becoming while we do it?*

This is where **Spiral Dynamics** becomes essential. If your team is operating from Level 3—ego, power, status—you'll see chaos, sabotage, and burnout. If they're stuck in Level 4—rigid systems—you'll see apathy, stagnation, and box-checking.

The goal is to help them evolve to Level 5 and 6—**personal mastery and collective empathy**.

That means:

- Hiring for alignment, not just experience

- Running meetings with energy check-ins

- Celebrating growth, not just performance

- Giving your team a language for their emotional states

We don't just need diversity in appearance—we need diversity in consciousness. And it's the leader's job to build the bridge.

4. Legacy—Engineering Impact Beyond the Individual
And this is where it all leads: **Legacy**.

Not the highlight reel. Not the resume. Not the followers or the bio. But the system you leave behind when you're no longer in the room.

Legacy isn't an accident. It's engineered.

I teach what I call the **Legacy Operating Framework (LOF)**—a three-part code to embed into your family, your business, your community:

- **Philosophy**—What you believe and stand for

- **Practice**—The rituals and habits that anchor those beliefs

- **Proof**—The evidence that it's working, in lives, not just numbers

Want to raise children who don't repeat your wounds? Create a family mission statement. Share your story. Write them letters they'll read after you're gone. Turn healing into heritage.

Want your business to outlive you? Systematize self-awareness. Create sacred feedback spaces. Make emotional intelligence as important as performance metrics.

Because here's the truth: people forget **acts**—but they replicate **systems**. If your system was built on survival, they'll survive. If it was built on power, they'll lead.

The Charge Forward—From Scars to Strategy

After two decades of carrying the weight of Fallujah—of mourning brothers lost, of reconciling the pain and purpose stitched into every scar—one undeniable truth has emerged: **scar tissue, when honored and understood, becomes strategy.**

The very moments that nearly took my life are no longer just painful memories. They've become planned blueprints. They've become fuel. The teachings of *Power vs. Force* and *Spiral Dynamics* didn't just expand my thinking—they **operationalized my purpose**. They transformed trauma into tactics, grief into growth, and survival into stewardship.

This is what I call **The Charge Forward**. It's not a sprint. It's not some hyped-up flash of motivation. It's a sustained, deliberate advance—anchored in clarity, moved by compassion, and led by courage.

I learned in the crucible of combat that **victory doesn't happen in the firefight**. Victory is **forged in preparation**—in the planned mental conditioning that precedes the chaos. When Alpha Company rolled into the ADOC under blistering sun and fire, it wasn't because we were the strongest unit. We were the **most prepared**. Captain Venning didn't wait for the pressure to rise before cultivating readiness—he embedded it in us through every patrol, every rehearsal, every breath we took before the battle came.

That kind of readiness—disciplined, grounded, strategic—is what true **operational power** looks like. It's not reactive. It's not impulsive. It is the **marriage of high structure and high consciousness**. And whether you're building a family, leading a team, or guiding a movement—this is the posture that wins the long game.

To **Charge Forward** is to say:
"I will feel the depth of my past, but I will not be defined by it."

You will carry your sorrow, your shame, your loyalty, your grief, your love. But you will also **build with it**. You will channel it into daily recalibration. Into courageous conversations. Into cultures that honor both the strength it took to survive and the vision required to grow.

Your first mission is this: **construct your Alpha Project Matrix**—a personal operating framework built on the four pillars we've just covered: **Self, Relationships, Leadership, and Legacy**. This isn't just theory—it's tactical living.

Set your **RECON protocols**:

- Daily: Check your emotional frequency. Journal your Tactical Consciousness.

- Weekly: Run your State Briefs with your family.

- Quarterly: Conduct Culture Checks with your team.

- Annually: Hold a Legacy Planning Session that defines who you are, what you stand for, and how you'll be remembered.

This isn't fluff. This is fieldwork. In military terms, it's **patrol, plug, and pivot**—surveying terrain, applying presence, and adapting with precision. If we had led with reaction in Fallujah, lives would've been lost. But because we led with structure, presence, and power—we prevailed.

And now, this is your battlefield.

Not with rifles—but with values. Not with firepower—but with frameworks. The boardroom. The neighborhood. The classroom. The church. These are the new frontlines—and they matter.

People are watching. People are listening. The way you carry your pain— whether healed or unhealed—will ripple across generations. The emotional state of your nervous system is contagious. When it's reactive, others retreat. But when it's trained—calibrated—**others follow**.

So here is my charge to you:
You don't have to be perfect.
You don't have to be pain-free.
But you must be **present**.
You must be **purposeful**.

Let the scars of your story remind you of your capacity to rise. Let the frameworks of consciousness give you something stronger than force: **the power to transform your world from the inside out**. Let your journey become a system others can trust, model, and inherit.

Because this isn't just the close of a chapter.
This is the beginning of your **inheritance**.
This is your mindful charge forward.

Let the mission begin.

BREAK THE BOTTLE CHALLENGE — Chapter 5

You've been through chaos. You've seen the fog, the fire, and the fractures—on battlefields, in boardrooms, or in your own heart. Now it's time to reclaim command. This isn't about reliving the trauma. It's about redeploying the wisdom. It's time to stop waiting for the external world to provide clarity—and start generating it from within.

Your mission over the next 14 days is to operationalize your power.

1. Create Your Alpha Matrix (Self – Relationships – Leadership – Legacy)
Map it out. Four boxes. One for each pillar. Write your current state of operation in each. Where are you reactive? Where are you powerful? Where are you still living from force? This is your battlefield recon. No fluff. Just facts.

2. Calibrate Daily with the Map of Consciousness
Each morning, identify your emotional state using David Hawkins' scale. Don't judge it—track it. Choose one method to elevate it: breathwork, prayer, journaling, movement, or stillness. This is your morning mission brief. It aligns your frequency before you lead anyone else.

3. Host One "State Brief" Conversation
Pick a relationship that matters—a spouse, child, team member, or mentor—and hold a deliberate, 15-minute check-in. Ask, "Where are we emotionally?" Not to fix them. To lead with presence. This is emotional reconnaissance.

4. Initiate Your Legacy Practice
Choose a ritual that will outlive you. A journal to your kids. A video message to your future self. A family

mission statement. Start it this week. Don't wait for significance—create it.

5. Adopt One Conscious Leadership Protocol in Your Organization
Introduce one new practice in your work environment that aligns with conscious leadership: emotional check-ins in meetings, values-based hiring, or celebrating growth over performance. Lead the shift.

You are no longer just the subject of transformation. You are now its architect.

This is not a challenge for the faint-hearted. It's for those ready to lead beyond wounds. To command not with fear, but with presence. To take scar tissue and turn it into sacred structure.

This is your Alpha Project in action.

Mission begins now.

RESOURCES

Download the Tool: Legacy Leadership Manifesto Template
Clarify the kind of leader you're becoming. Use this manifesto to define your values, mission, leadership code, and long-term impact.

Available at: btbprograms.com/free-resources

THE MINDSET SHIFT—FROM PROBLEMS TO SOLUTIONS

"You can't build a new future with an old mindset. Solutions aren't discovered—they're developed."

— Break The Bottle

The Mindset That Keeps You Moving

Now that you've broken the bottle, made your decision, and torched the bridge to who you used to be, you've stepped into something new— uncharted territory. You're not lost. You're just further than you've ever gone before. And this is where most people stall—not because they lack passion, but because they lack a plan. Decision is critical, yes. But a decision without direction? That's just emotional adrenaline. It feels good in the moment, but without structure, it fizzles into drift. I've seen it far too often: a moment of awakening, followed by weeks of circling the same cul-de-sac of frustration and shame.

They say all the right things—"I'm done playing small." "This is my moment." "Everything changes now." But then… life hits. The bank account dips below survival. The argument with the spouse turns cold. A dream gig falls through. And suddenly, that fire inside flickers under pressure. It's not because they're lazy or weak—it's because they changed their words, but not their wiring. They made a declaration, but never updated the operating system that runs beneath it.

This chapter isn't about hype. It's about architecture. Mental architecture. Because if the system that drives your thoughts hasn't been rebuilt, your decisions will always be short-term. And here's the truth most personal development books won't tell you: you can't build a new future with an old mindset. Motivation is a spark. Mindset is the structure that holds the flame.

Your mindset is the silent architect of your life. It's the hidden code behind your behaviors, your reactions, your self-talk, your relationships, even your income. It determines how you interpret hardship, how you show up under stress, and how you make decisions when clarity is nowhere in sight. If your foundational belief is "life happens to me," then every time pressure shows up, your nervous system will default to control, fear, and collapse. But if your belief is "I create, I respond, I lead," then your actions—over time—start to reflect that internal alignment. That's how your identity shifts. Not through talk, but through repetition.

And yet, most people approach mindset work like a side project—something they'll do when they're less busy, less overwhelmed, or finally feel "ready." They read the books. Listen to the podcasts. Repeat a few affirmations. But the truth is, they're trying to paint over broken drywall. Mindset work isn't surface work—it's foundation work. And that means digging up the old programming. The trauma, the shame, the beliefs passed down in silence. Because mindset is not about what you know. It's about what's running your show when life doesn't go as planned.

Let me make it plain.

When life sucker-punches you—when the contract falls through, when your name's not on the list, when your phone goes silent after you hit send—what's your first thought? Your knee-jerk reflex? Is it, "Why me?" or "Of course this always happens," or "I knew I wasn't enough"? Or do you pause, inhale, and say, "Okay. What's the next right step?" That moment tells the truth. Because that reflex isn't random—it's rehearsed.

And the good news? If it was rehearsed, it can be retrained.

I remember sitting in my car, gripping the steering wheel after a six-figure contract I'd been banking on collapsed in a single phone call. The silence in that car felt like betrayal. I could feel the pressure rising—financial stress, fear, shame, and that sickening voice saying, "You blew it again." Then from the backseat, my son's voice cut through: "Hey Dad, remember when you said it's not the fall, it's the bounce that matters?" I froze. Because right there, I realized something sobering—my reaction wasn't just mine anymore. My reflex was teaching him how to respond to loss.

That was the wake-up call.

In that moment, I had a choice. Reinforce the shame spiral. Or model the mindset I claimed to believe in.

That's what trained mindset does. It doesn't erase the fear—but it overrides the chaos. Not because the pain is easy, but because you've prepared for it. You've decided in advance how you'll show up when life doesn't follow the script.

Let's be clear: this isn't about being fake. It's about being formed. When you treat adversity as information—not condemnation—you reclaim your power. You stop spiraling and start strategizing.

That's the mindset that keeps you moving—not when it's easy, but when it matters most.

The Scarcity Trap: Shifting from Survival to Strategy

There's a silent thief at work in more lives than we care to admit. It doesn't break windows or empty wallets—but it hijacks futures. It's not always loud. In fact, it's most dangerous when it whispers. "There's not enough." "I'll never be enough." "This is my last shot." That thief is scarcity. And for years, it controlled me.

I remember one night vividly. I had just left my executive role, and my transition into entrepreneurship wasn't going as planned. I sat alone in the living room, lights off, blinds drawn. I was staring at a credit card statement, mentally calculating how much longer I could keep the lights on. My chest was tight. My thoughts were frantic. My entire nervous system felt hijacked by this gnawing sense of failure. It wasn't just financial—it was existential. I didn't just feel broke—I felt broken. I wasn't afraid of bankruptcy. I was afraid of becoming irrelevant, forgotten, useless.

In that moment, survival mode wasn't a metaphor—it was a prison.

Scarcity creates this illusion that everything is urgent and irreversible. It tricks your brain into thinking every setback is a dead end. It hijacks your identity and makes panic feel like productivity. But beneath it all is the lie that your worth is tied to your outcomes—and that any mistake could cost you everything.

That's the danger of a scarcity mindset. It fuels urgency but starves clarity. It tells you to *act now*, *react fast*, *push harder*, but never gives you a minute to breathe, reflect, or recalibrate. It's a loop. Hustle, crash, doubt. Repeat. You start patching your life with panic instead of building it with intention. You don't plan—you scramble.

But I want to tell you what I've learned standing in that space. The way out isn't hustle. The way out is **perspective**.

You see, scarcity thrives in chaos—but strategy is born in calm. And calm begins the moment you stop asking panic-driven questions and start asking powerful ones. Not "How do I fix this right now?" but "What's actually happening here? What's true? What's the pattern I'm repeating? And what is this pain trying to teach me?"

Because the truth is—most people live by default, not by design. They inherit beliefs they never challenge. They repeat behaviors they've never questioned. And they build lives that don't feel like theirs. Scarcity doesn't just limit your money—it limits your mind. It keeps you reactive instead of reflective. Surviving instead of strategizing.

Here's what I tell every client I coach—especially those who come to me feeling burnt out, anxious, or stuck: **"Slow down to speed up."** Scarcity wants you to spiral. Strategy wants you to simplify. And simplifying doesn't mean doing less—it means doing what matters **with clarity**.

The most grounded people I know don't make the fastest decisions—they make the clearest ones. They pause. They zoom out. They ask:

- What am I really responding to?

- Is this a real crisis or a learned panic response?

- What's mine to control?
  What needs to change—not out there, but in here?

These questions aren't philosophical—they're tactical. They break the spiral. They shift your nervous system from survival to creativity.

And that shift? It literally rewires your brain.

One tool that changed my life was silence. I don't mean just being quiet. I mean intentional, disruptive silence—the kind that separates you from the noise of the world and reconnects you to the truth inside. And I realized something in that silence: the root of scarcity wasn't just external. It was historical.

For me, scarcity was born in childhood. I was five years old when my family lost everything in a flood in Jamaica. A few years later, we faced a hurricane. Again—everything gone. Those early experiences taught me that safety was fragile. That peace was temporary. That loss could come without warning. That financial hardship can come like a thief in the night. So I started over-preparing. Over-achieving. Over-compensating. Not because I was ambitious—but because I was afraid.

I carried that wiring into my adult life. Into the military. Into the boardroom. Into marriage. Into fatherhood. It was always about *doing more* to protect myself from the feeling of being helpless again. That's the thing about trauma-based scarcity—it doesn't show up as fear. It shows up as overwork. As perfectionism. As trying to earn a sense of safety that never fully lands.

But healing began when I stopped trying to out-run the fear—and started listening to it. When I stopped asking, "What if I fail?" and started asking,

"What's possible now?"

That's the turning point. That's when you stop reacting to the world—and start creating your place in it.

Let me show you something I use with every client I coach—something I call **The Four Levels of Decision Consciousness**:

The Four Levels of Decision Consciousness

1. **REACTIVE**—"Why is this happening to me?"

    a. Focus: Blame. Victimhood. Emotion.

        i. (Scarcity lives here.)

2. **REFLECTIVE**—"What can I learn from this?"

    a. Focus: Growth. Perspective. Agency. Awareness. Insight. Personal Responsibility.

3. **REINVENTIVE**—"Who do I want to be because of this?"

    a. Focus: Identity transformation. Growth Mindset.

4. **RESOLUTE**—"What action must I now take aligned with who I'm becoming?"

    a. Focus: Momentum. Vision. Bold. Aligned Execution. Forward Momentum.

        i. (This is where Strategy lives.)

THE FOUR LEVELS OF DECISION CONSCIOUSNESS

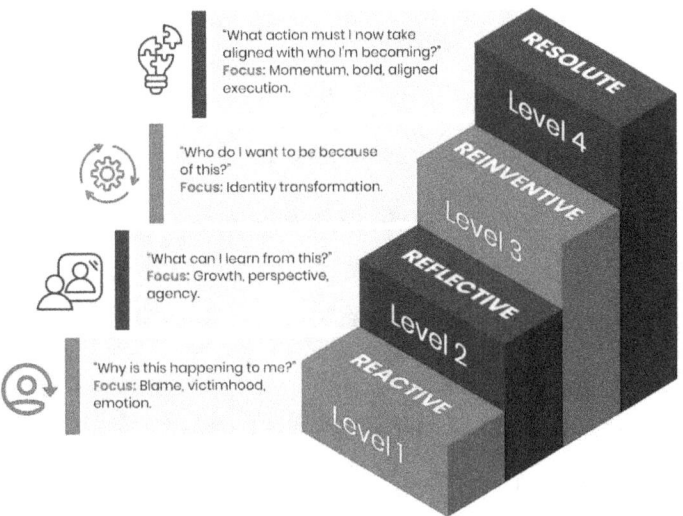

"What action must I now take aligned with who I'm becoming?"
Focus: Momentum, bold, aligned execution.

RESOLUTE — Level 4

"Who do I want to be because of this?"
Focus: Identity transformation.

REINVENTIVE — Level 3

"What can I learn from this?"
Focus: Growth, perspective, agency.

REFLECTIVE — Level 2

"Why is this happening to me?"
Focus: Blame, victimhood, emotion.

REACTIVE — Level 1

Your job is to climb these levels—until your questions reflect your future, not your fear.

I remember coaching a woman who had built a life around everyone else's needs. She was the backbone for her family, her company, her church. But behind the title and the smile, she was exhausted. Not just physically—spiritually. She had spent years helping others build their dreams while quietly disowning her own.

One day, she broke down in my office.

"I don't think I've ever made a decision just for me," she whispered.

So I asked her, "What would change if you did?"

She stared at me. Not blinking. Then her voice cracked:

"I might actually be free."

That moment wasn't emotional—it was sacred. Because what she realized wasn't just that she'd been surviving—it's that she was finally ready to **choose**. That's where the shift happens. Not in knowing the answers, but in learning to ask better questions. Ones rooted in identity, not fear.

Like:

- "What am I tolerating that's keeping me small?"

- "What boundary would protect my peace?"

- "What does success look like for me, not them?"
  "How do I build a life that feeds me—not just funds me?"

That's the work. That's the design.

And here's another powerful model to help you reinforce this mindset: **The Judger Path vs. The Learner Path**, developed by Dr. Marilee Adams.

The Mindset Shift: Judger Path vs. Learner Path

Judger Path:

- "What's wrong with me?"

- "Why can't I get this right?"

- "Whose fault is this?"

Learner Path:

- "What can I learn from this?"

- "What's the opportunity in this challenge?"

- "What new skill, boundary, or belief do I need?"

SHIFTING FROM THE JUDGER PATH TO THE LEARNER PATH

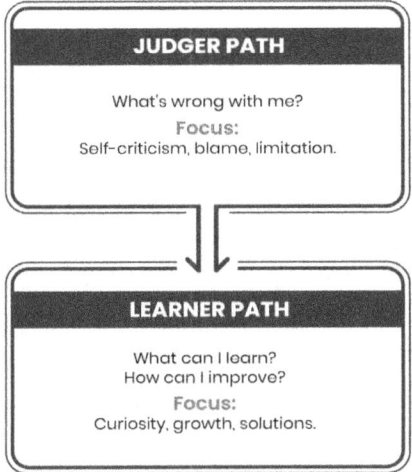

The difference between people who break through and those who break down? **Questions.**

And so I ask you right now:

What question are you living in?

Are you letting scarcity dictate your moves—or are you designing your life with strategy?

If you're reading this and haven't yet made a conscious decision to shift—make it now.

> "I am no longer driven by fear.
> I plan from vision.
> I build from peace.
> I respond with power."

Don't wait for certainty to give you permission. Strategy begins where survival ends. And survival ends when you stop patching your life and start building your path—brick by brick, belief by belief, decision by decision.

You were not born to react.
You were born to **architect your future.**

Now… what's your next question?

The Difference Between Fixed and Solutions Thinking

Fixed thinking is fear-based. It perceives challenges as proof of inadequacy. Fixed thinking is a mental cage dressed up as caution. It's fear dressed in logic. It waits for all the lights to turn green before making a move. It confuses delay with wisdom and silence with safety. It measures readiness by comfort. And most dangerously—it treats every challenge as evidence of personal failure. Fixed thinking doesn't always scream. Sometimes it sounds calm, calculated, even rational. But behind the scenes, it builds a life constrained by "what ifs," not what's possible. People living with fixed mindsets often don't even realize they're stuck—they've built an entire belief system around safety, control, and certainty. But control is not clarity. And safety, when idolized, becomes a self-imposed prison.

I remember sitting across from a military buddy at a retreat. No uniforms, no ranks—just two men trying to figure out what came after war. He leaned in, his jaw clenched like he was bracing for something. "Since I got out," he muttered, "it feels like I'm unraveling. Maybe I'm not built for this life." The pain in his voice wasn't just disappointment—it was identity crisis. He wasn't failing. He was simply trying to live a new life with the rulebook from his old one. And like many veterans, he had mistaken discomfort for dysfunction. That moment mirrored what I too had wrestled with.

After I transitioned out of the military, I believed my years of sacrifice had somehow earned me a smoother road. I'd paid my dues, fought my battles, and now—surely—I deserved a season of peace. Instead, what I got was a layered mess. PTSD that clung to quiet moments like shadows. A new marriage that felt unfamiliar and hard to navigate. A blended family dynamic that pulled me in ten emotional directions at once. Custody hearings that re-opened emotional wounds I hadn't prepared to face. I wasn't just battling external storms—I was confronting the parts of myself I'd buried beneath decades of discipline and duty.

And let me be honest—there were nights I didn't want to go home. Not because I didn't love my wife or kids, but because I felt like a failure in a story I was supposed to be leading. I'd sit in the car, engine off, wondering how I got here. A warfighter now fumbling through bedtime routines and visitation schedules. A decorated Marine, suddenly unsure how to communicate with a hurting stepson who didn't trust me yet. The guilt was heavy. The doubt, suffocating. And in that fog, I found myself asking the same disempowering question over and over: "Why can't I get this right?"

That's fixed thinking. It disguises itself as reflection but paralyzes action. It assumes that if you're struggling, you're sinking. That hard equals wrong. And that discomfort is a signal to stop, not stretch.

But there's another way to think. A better way. A **strategic way**.

It's called **Solutions Thinking**.

Solutions Thinking doesn't deny the presence of pain. It doesn't sugarcoat suffering or try to positive-think its way out of trauma. What it does is **zoom out**, identify patterns, ask better questions, and take ownership—not of the storm, but of the response.

My military buddy? The one who felt lost? He started journaling daily— not feelings, but frameworks. He'd break each challenge down: *What's the problem? What do I own? What are my options? What's one action I can take today?* Within six months, he launched a consulting business helping other veterans transition—*not* because he had all the answers, but because he stopped waiting for clarity and started building from chaos.

That's the shift.

Solutions thinkers aren't fueled by perfection. They're powered by progress. They make peace with uncertainty. They understand that momentum beats mastery. That clarity often comes after the action—not before it.

I applied the same mindset to my life. In the middle of our family chaos— new marriage, blended children, trauma still unpacking itself—I stopped asking, "How do I fix this?" and started asking, "What is this teaching me about love, leadership, and emotional safety?" I realized that my need to control everything was rooted in fear. Fear of being seen as weak. Fear of rejection. Fear of failing my family.

But when I surrendered that need to know everything, I discovered something radical: I didn't need a perfect plan. I just needed one courageous step at a time.

I had to become a student again—not of war, but of *emotional intelligence*. I studied myself like a mission. I learned when to lead and when to listen. When to speak, and when to apologize. When to step in with structure and when to lean in with softness. That season, more than any battle I'd fought overseas, rebuilt me from the inside out.

And it taught me this: **you don't need to change your identity—you need to change your lens**.

Solutions Thinking isn't optimism. It's **operational wisdom**. It's taking the mess and designing momentum. It's the refusal to let ambiguity become an excuse. It's the willingness to ask better questions, even when the answers don't come right away.

Questions like:

- "What's this tension trying to teach me?"

- "Who do I want to be when this season is over?"

- "What would courage look like today?"

- "What's the smallest step I can take in alignment with my highest self?"

And science backs this up.

Studies in post-traumatic growth reveal that individuals who engage in **positive reappraisal**—the ability to extract meaning from hardship—demonstrate significantly stronger emotional resilience and recovery. Why? Because when you tell a new story, your brain carves new neurological pathways. That's neuroplasticity in action. When you move from "Why me?" to "What now?", you literally start building a new mental highway—one that leads not just to healing, but to transformation.

Solutions thinkers don't wait for peace to act. They create peace through action.

And that doesn't just apply to trauma or major life events—it applies to parenting, marriage, business, and leadership. I saw it with my own son. He came home one day, crushed over a failed math test. "I'm just not good at this," he said, shoulders slumped, eyes dim. I saw myself in him—same voice, different script.

So I shifted the conversation.

"Let's talk about what you *don't understand yet*," I said.

That word—*yet*—changed everything. It turned a verdict into a variable. We sat down, unpacked the errors, and created a new plan. He didn't just pass the next test—he approached it like an architect. With questions. With curiosity. With confidence.

That's the essence of Solutions Thinking: it's not about having the answer—it's about knowing how to pursue it.

Dr. Carol Dweck's research proves this point. People with growth-focused, solutions-based mindsets are not only more resilient—they're more likely to thrive in the face of setbacks, because they've trained their brains to focus on *improvement*, not proof. They're not trying to validate their worth—they're building their capacity.

So let's make this plain:

- **Fixed thinking waits for perfect conditions.**
  Solutions thinking moves with what's available.

- **Fixed thinking asks, "What if I mess up?"**
  Solutions thinking asks, "What can I learn?"

- **Fixed thinking sees obstacles as evidence to stop.
  Solutions thinking uses obstacles as building materials.**

You don't need a ten-step master plan to begin. You just need to decide: *I'm done waiting. I'm ready to move.*

Progress isn't born from certainty—it's born from motion.
And the first step is yours.

The Art of Clear Thinking: Fast vs. Slow Strategy

If resilience is the foundation of high performance, then clarity is its compass. And clarity, contrary to popular belief, isn't just a feeling—it's a function. It's something you create intentionally, especially under pressure. High performers understand that the most dangerous moment isn't when the storm hits—it's when the mind gets foggy inside the storm. That's when people make reactive decisions, speak words they can't take back, or abandon strategies that were actually working. What separates elite thinkers from the rest is their ability to shift from reactive to reflective thinking in real time.

At the core of this mental discipline is a principle backed by cognitive science: the ability to toggle between fast thinking and slow thinking. Popularized by Nobel Prize-winning psychologist Daniel Kahneman in his groundbreaking book *Thinking, Fast and Slow*, this concept explains that the human brain operates on two systems.

- **System 1** is fast, instinctive, emotional. It's the autopilot. It jumps to conclusions, fills in the blanks, and reacts quickly— sometimes too quickly.

- **System 2** is slow, deliberate, analytical. It takes energy to engage, but it leads to clarity and precision.

Both systems are vital. But clarity requires that you know *when* to lean on each. The mistake most people make is relying on fast thinking in complex situations. They move with speed, but no strategy. And that's how good people make bad decisions.

The high performer doesn't eliminate fast thinking—they interrupt it. They know when to slow down, take a mental step back, and activate their higher reasoning. I witnessed this firsthand during a live military drill. A junior officer made a misstep that caused brief chaos in the field. Instead of yelling or escalating, the captain in charge took three deliberate steps backward. He physically distanced himself from the noise so he could mentally recalibrate. Then, in a calm voice, he issued clear, actionable commands that realigned the entire team.

Later, I asked him why he stepped back. His answer was simple but profound: *"Because leadership isn't about speed—it's about direction. And I don't make decisions unless my mind is clear."*

That's the art of clear thinking. The power to pause—not out of hesitation, but out of discipline. To resist the pressure to act from adrenaline and instead choose action from alignment.

In high-performance coaching, we refer to this as response flexibility—the ability to delay a reaction long enough to choose a better one. And it's not just a leadership tool. It's a life skill. In relationships, in business, in parenting—wherever emotions run high, clarity wins. Every. Single. Time.

But let me be clear—this isn't about overanalyzing or getting stuck in indecision. It's about intentional pacing. Because fast thinking, when unchecked, becomes impulsiveness. Slow thinking, when unpracticed, becomes procrastination. But when fused together, fast and slow thinking create strategic agility—the ability to move with speed and precision.

So how do you build this clarity muscle? You start by recognizing the triggers. The moments when you feel heat rise in your chest. When your vision narrows. When your thoughts start racing. That's your signal. That's when you must choose to shift gears. The goal is not to erase fast thinking—it's to reroute it through reflection.

And here's where the neuroscience gets exciting. MRI studies reveal that when people engage in reflective decision-making—activating the prefrontal cortex instead of the amygdala—they make decisions that are more aligned with their long-term goals, less influenced by fear, and more emotionally intelligent. Your brain literally lights up differently when you choose clarity over chaos.

That's why rituals matter. High performers create small, repeatable habits that create space between stimulus and response. Some use breathing techniques. Others use mantras or physical cues like stepping back or placing a hand on the heart. These aren't gimmicks—they're tools that re-anchor you in intention.

For me, before I make a big decision—whether in business or at home—I go through a quick mental check: "What do I know to be true right now? What emotions are coloring this? What would the clearest version of me do here?" That three-question pause has saved me thousands of dollars, preserved relationships, and redirected opportunities I would've otherwise missed.

The reason most people get stuck isn't lack of knowledge. It's cognitive overload. They're bombarded by input—social media, opinions, anxiety— and they lose the thread of what actually matters. Clear thinking is the act of cutting through that noise. It's surgical. It's precise. And it's learned.

So, when life gets loud, and the pressure is mounting, ask yourself: Am I reacting out of habit—or responding from clarity? That one question can buy you enough time to change your entire outcome.

Because ultimately, it's not your ability to think fast that makes you powerful. It's your ability to pause fast, *so you can think clearly.*

I've been thought that success loves speed, so let's get practical. Because theory alone doesn't transform you—training does. And when it comes to navigating high-pressure moments, most people don't need more time… they need more tools. Enter The Fast-Thinking Solution™, a tactical framework designed to help you disrupt spirals, regain mental footing, and make strategic moves even when emotions are running hot.

This method isn't about reacting faster—it's about regaining control faster. It gives you a repeatable path to clarity without overthinking. Because here's the trap most people fall into: they mistake fast thinking for good thinking. But fast thinking—when undirected—is just adrenaline chasing a storyline. It leads to catastrophizing, emotional misfires, and premature decisions. What The Fast-Thinking Solution™ does is rewire that instinct. It channels speed into structure. Emotion into alignment. Movement into meaning.

And it's not abstract. Each step is built around real-life patterns I've seen while coaching entrepreneurs, leaders, and high-stakes professionals—people who had everything to lose if they made the wrong call under pressure.

Step 1: Name the Real Problem—Fast

Your first move in a spiral is to strip away drama and drill down to truth. The brain loves complexity under stress—it makes things feel more important than they are. But clarity begins when you call the thing what it is. No fluff. No filters. No blame.

I once worked with a founder who said, "Everything's falling apart. My team isn't motivated. My revenue's slipping. I'm failing." But when we zoomed in, the issue wasn't the business—it was his fear of raising prices. That fear led him to overwork, undercharge, and eventually, burn out. When we named that fear—clean and clear—we finally had a problem we could solve. Remember: you can't shift what you haven't named.

Step 2: Feel It, Don't Fight It

Pause for thirty seconds. Let the emotion surface—without judgment. Anger. Shame. Frustration. Exhaustion. This isn't a weakness. This is intelligence. Because suppressed emotion doesn't disappear—it just leaks into your next decision.

A combat veteran once told me, "Sitting in emotion feels like losing." I told him: "Only if you think emotion is the enemy." In truth, presence is power. When you acknowledge what you feel, you remove its grip on your judgment. Neuroscience confirms this: labeling emotion activates the prefrontal cortex and lowers the intensity of the limbic system. You literally calm your brain by naming your pain.

Step 3: Delete the Noise

Before strategy, comes silence. Get quiet enough to hear your own voice—not your ex's, not your old coach's, not the algorithm's. The best leaders aren't the ones who think more—they're the ones who **think clearer.**

Use a four-minute mental reset:

1. **Mind sweep** – Dump every thought in your head onto paper or into a voice memo.

2. **Sort truth from noise** – Highlight what's real vs. what's imagined.

3. **Return to purpose** – Anchor to what actually matters.

4. **Create mental white space** – Silence gives strategy room to speak.

I use this weekly before every major keynote. If I don't, I'm not speaking—I'm reacting. Same goes for strategic decisions. You can't architect a vision from a cluttered mind.

Step 4: Ask a Better Question

Weak questions trap you in loops. Strong questions launch you forward. High performers don't just ask *if* something will work—they ask **how to move forward anyway.**

Instead of asking:

- "Why does this always happen?"

- "What if I fail again?"

- "Why can't I get this right?"

Shift to:

- "What's one thing I can control right now?"

- "What's this tension trying to show me?"

- "What would this look like if it were simple?"

One of my clients—post-divorce, financially unstable, and emotionally wrecked—pivoted her entire mindset with one question: *"What kind of woman do I want to become now that everything's changed?"* That question didn't just empower her. It redefined her.

Step 5: Anchor to Your Core

When the fog rolls in, your identity becomes your compass. Ask:

- **What do I believe about who I am—right now?**

- **What is my purpose at this moment?**

- **Who do I want to be on the other side of this?**

High performers don't make decisions from panic—they operate from principles. In the Marine Corps, I served as an AAV Section Leader, responsible for leading Amphibious Assault Vehicles—machines that demand precision, not just power. At the Assault Amphibious School in Camp Pendleton, there's an unspoken rule woven into every drill: Stabilize the vehicle before you strategize the mission. Whether you're cresting rough terrain or navigating open water, the first task is always control. Secure the platform. Anchor the machine. Only then do you assess, decide, and move forward.

That same mindset applies to life. Before you troubleshoot your circumstances, stabilize your state. Before you try to fix the chaos, ground yourself in clarity. Stability always comes before strategy. Because in high-stakes environments—whether it's combat or career—it's not the fastest thinker who wins. It's the calmest leader. The one who knows: panic doesn't drive progress. Presence does.

Step 6: Decide Without Debate

Set a two-minute mental timer. Make a call. Will you move or not? Don't wait for the perfect time or full certainty. Momentum is built through motion, not mastery.

Overthinking is just fear dressed up as wisdom. It wants you to believe that you're being smart—but really, it's just stalling growth. Decision is the knife that cuts through that paralysis. Make the call. Send the message. Commit to the next micro-step.

Step 7: Execute in Alignment

Now move. Not with doubt, not with drama—**with fire.** Call the client. Launch the idea. Walk into the room with power. Don't look back for applause. Move forward because it's who you've chosen to be.

One entrepreneur I worked with used this process to rebuild after a failed launch. He gave himself 30 minutes to redesign a product offer. Sent it to five former clients. One responded. That yes became momentum. That momentum-built confidence. That confidence sparked reinvention.

You don't need 100 green lights. You need **one clear next step**, taken in alignment with who you are and where you're going.

This is The Fast-Thinking Solution™. Use it when your emotions are loud, when your thoughts are racing, when the old reflex wants to scream or shut down. This process will bring you back—not to where you were, but to where you're meant to be.

It's not about control—it's about clarity.

And clarity is always your power position.

Once you've regained control using The Fast-Thinking Solution™, don't stop there. Emotional clarity without strategic action still leads to stalled growth. That's why we follow it up with The 7-Step Strategic Thinking Method—a framework that turns clarity into calculated, aligned movement. Think of it like this: Fast-Thinking brings you back from the storm. Strategic Thinking gives you the blueprint to build after it.

The 7-Step Strategic Thinking Method: Convert Clarity Into Movement

You've disrupted the emotional spiral. You've recentered yourself in clarity.

But clarity without a path leads to stall-out.

This is the point where most people stall—not because they lack intention, but because they lack strategy. They feel the breakthrough bubbling just beneath the surface, but they don't know how to channel that energy into movement. And here's where even high performers can fall short: they fail to transition from emotional clarity to operational precision.

That's what this method is for.

The 7-Step Strategic Thinking Method is designed to convert insight into alignment and alignment into action. It's not about whiteboarding your dreams. It's about building a tactical map to execute under pressure. Whether you're launching a business, leading a team, healing a relationship, or rebuilding after failure—this framework meets you where you are and moves you forward with structure.

1. Define the Problem – Without Distortion

Most people misdiagnose their issue. They conflate symptoms with source. They react to noise instead of identifying the signal. Strategic thinking demands ruthless clarity. You must strip your problem down to its core truth—not the drama, not the spin, but the exact pattern disrupting your momentum.

A client once told me, "My team is unmotivated." But with a few probing questions, the real issue emerged: his unclear expectations and lack of consistent feedback. Once we named that, the solution was simple. If you don't define the actual issue, you'll waste energy solving the wrong thing.

Precision begins with definition.

2. Split It Into Parts – Simplify the Complexity

Big problems often feel paralyzing because we see them as monolithic. But every big problem is just a collection of small ones wearing a trench coat. Strategic thinkers don't stare at the mountain—they segment it into actionable pieces.

Break the challenge into its components: Is it a people issue? A process problem? A resource constraint? Once you isolate the parts, overwhelm dissolves. Because what you can name, you can manage.

3. Analyze Each Part – Look for Pattern, Not Panic

Now that you have parts, analyze each one without judgment. Look at it like a surgeon—not a critic. Where is the system breaking down? Where's the friction? Where's the repetition?

Patterns always tell the truth.

Maybe every time you hit a growth phase, you self-sabotage. Maybe every time a project nears completion, you pivot to something new. The issue isn't momentum—it's your relationship to completion. When you start noticing your loops, you stop living in them.

4. Create Insight – Extract the Leverage Point

Insight is not knowledge. Insight is *applied awareness.* It's the "aha" that becomes a map. As you analyze the parts, you'll start to notice a leverage point—something small you can shift that creates maximum return.

Maybe it's a recurring delay in communication. Maybe it's an unclear KPI. Maybe it's the internal narrative you've believed about your capacity. This moment is about extracting that pressure point and asking: "If I shifted this one thing, what would ripple out?"

This is where strategy is born—not in massive overhaul, but in precise pivot.

5. Craft a Story – Connect Emotion to Execution

Humans move when meaning is present. And the fastest way to create meaning is through **narrative**. Strategic thinkers don't just solve—they reframe. They tell a new story that turns pain into purpose.

You're not "struggling to get your team aligned"—you're "designing a culture of ownership." You're not "fixing what's broken"—you're "rebuilding the foundation stronger." Craft the story your brain can believe and your spirit can own.

This step is critical because it engages the **limbic system**, which drives motivation and memory. If you want lasting transformation, the heart must be involved.

6. Make a Decision – Courage Over Comfort

Insight is worthless without decision. You've simplified. You've analyzed. Now comes the part most people avoid: *commitment*. Strategy dies in ambiguity. High performers know when to pull the trigger.

Ask yourself:

- What action aligns with this insight?

- What would boldness look like here?

- What am I afraid of—and is that fear based on truth or assumption?

Then decide. Not in a week. Not after more research. Now. Courage isn't the absence of fear—it's the refusal to be ruled by it.

7. Take Bold Action – Close the Loop

This is where the rubber meets the road. You take the insight, the story, the decision—and you execute. Not someday. Not "once the stars align." Now.

This doesn't mean a grand gesture. It means *one bold move* that aligns with your clarity. Send the proposal. Make the call. Outline the new SOP. Walk into the conversation you've been avoiding.

Momentum isn't mystical. It's mechanical. And action is always the lever.

Let me show you The Power of the Full Method and how this plays out in real life. I once worked with a client who was paralyzed after a partnership fallout. He couldn't trust himself, let alone new collaborators. Using this exact framework, we isolated the issue (he felt responsible for not setting boundaries early on). We split the problem (poor communication, lack of contracts, unclear expectations). We spotted the pattern (conflict avoidance). We created insight (his real fear was abandonment, not business failure). We crafted a new story ("I can lead with clarity and still be safe"). He made the decision to rebuild with clearer agreements. He took bold action by forming a new joint venture—with precise guardrails.

Six months later, he was thriving. Not because he avoided pain—but because he processed it strategically.

This method isn't just a mental exercise—it's a strategic protocol. It turns spirals into systems and emotion into execution. Use it when the stakes are high. Use it when clarity feels distant. Use it when you want to lead yourself through the storm instead of being dragged by it.

Because thinking well isn't enough.

You must think strategically.

And strategy, when paired with courage, always wins.

The Goal Isn't Slowness. It's Clarity. Let's make one thing clear: clarity is not slowness. It's not hesitation. It's not overthinking wrapped in good intentions. True clarity is the *precision of purpose.* It's the mental and emotional readiness to move—not in circles, not in reaction—but in a direction that aligns with your deepest identity and highest mission.

The world glorifies speed. Social media rewards hustle. Our culture celebrates fast results, instant responses, and 10X growth overnight. But high performers know a deeper truth: speed without strategy is erosion. Movement without meaning is noise. You don't win by going fast—you win by going *right.*

That's what clarity gives you.

It gives you the ability to separate the urgent from the important. To distinguish between noise and signal. To say no to what's shiny, and yes to what's strategic. And that kind of discernment doesn't just show up. It's cultivated. It's earned. It's trained through the practices we've outlined— slowing the spiral, structuring your thinking, aligning with identity, and executing in alignment.

And let's be honest—there will be moments when everything in you wants to rush the process. When fear tells you that speed will protect you. When doubt whispers that slow means stuck. But remember this: urgency is not clarity. Pressure is not alignment. Just because it's loud doesn't mean it's true.

Every true leader I've coached—CEOs, elite athletes, combat veterans, faith leaders, creatives—at some point had to master the art of slowing down long enough to hear the real question. The one buried beneath the panic. The one that breaks the cycle and unlocks the next move.

That question is always some version of:
"Am I moving from truth... or tension?"

Because here's what I've found: when your inner world is cluttered, your outer decisions will be too. And no title, tactic, or tool can compensate for internal chaos. You can read every book on performance. Attend every seminar on leadership. Hire the best strategist in the business. But if your inner voice is fogged by fear, you'll misinterpret the most critical data: your own instinct.

That's why we don't pursue slowness—we plan and pursue clarity.

Slowness for its own sake becomes paralysis. But clarity speeds you up *strategically*. It collapses time by removing distraction. It amplifies results by minimizing friction. When you're clear, your energy doesn't leak. Your message doesn't dilute. Your movements don't scatter. Everything tightens. Everything aligns.

I once worked with a nonprofit leader who was overwhelmed by decisions. Too many fires. Too many competing agendas. She said, "I just don't know what to focus on." Together, we took 20 minutes to strip the emotion, clarify her mission, and identify what truly mattered. By the end of the session, she had a 90-day action plan that restructured her entire team and revitalized her momentum. The key? She didn't get more productive. She got clearer.

And here's the irony: the moment she slowed down was the moment she accelerated everything.

That's the truth no one tells you: clarity is a force multiplier.

It magnifies your confidence. It streamlines your effort. It draws the right people to your vision. It builds a mental infrastructure that holds up under pressure. Clarity is not a soft skill—it's a leadership superpower.

So, when life gets loud…
When anxiety spikes…
When urgency feels like truth…

Pause. Breathe.
Ask yourself:
"Is this motion or mission?"
"Is this reaction or real direction?"

Because every leader—whether in business, in battle, in family, or in faith—will face a defining moment where they must choose between speed and strategy. And the ones who rise, the ones who build legacies that last, are the ones who train themselves to choose clarity over chaos.

You don't rise by thinking more.

You rise by thinking clearly—then moving boldly.

And that's what this whole chapter has prepared you for. Not just a better mindset. Not just more positive thoughts. But a new operating system—one that turns tension into traction, pain into performance, and setbacks into strategy.

The next time life presses you, don't just rise—**rise with precision**.

Rise with clarity.

Rise with a plan.

Because when you combine emotional command with strategic execution, you don't just bounce back—**you build forward**.

BREAK THE BOTTLE CHALLENGE — Chapter 6

If you're serious about stepping into the next level of your leadership, life, or healing—here's a challenge to ground it in practice:

Step 1: Identify the Loop

What's one recurring internal loop you keep revisiting? That same problem, thought, insecurity, or question that keeps circling back. Write it down—yes, physically. A client of mine wrote down, "I'm always falling behind," and she taped it to her wall—not to reinforce it, but to rewrite it daily.

Step 2: Reframe the Question

Take that old narrative and flip the question.
Instead of: "Why is this happening to me?"
Ask: "What strength is being built in me because of this?"
I coached a father going through divorce who once told me, "I feel like a failure to my kids." We worked to change that to: "What kind of consistent man do I want my kids to remember through this season?" That shift became the foundation of his recovery.

Step 3: Take One Aligned Action in the Next 24 Hours

Don't overthink. Don't over-plan. Take a step. Build the website. Send the message. Pick up the book. Call the coach. Go for the walk. One of my business clients created an entire product offer because I gave him five minutes to "act fast." One yes turned into momentum that changed his life.

Step 4: Anchor a Trigger Phrase

Choose a phrase that brings you back when your thoughts start spiraling.
It could be:

- "Pause. Pivot. Power."

- "We don't loop here."

- "Lead through, not around."

Say it out loud. Breathe it in. Move with it. You're Not Stuck—You're Just in Rehearsal

You're not broken. You're not too late. You've just been rehearsing the wrong story. But now you get to practice the right one. The one where you don't wait to feel better—you move in purpose. The one where you stop questioning your identity—and start building a life that reflects it. You've got what it takes. You're already in motion. The only thing missing is the decision to ask better questions and trust the power of your direction.

RESOURCES

 **Download the Tool: Confidence Habit Tracker**
Build habits that shape emotional resilience, discipline, and high-performance self-leadership.

Available at: btbprograms.com/free-resources

THE ENEMIES OF PROGRESS

"The cost of your next level is not just time or money—it's the courage to silence the enemies in your head."

— *Break The Bottle*

The Enemy Within: Where Fear Hides in Plain Sight

There comes a point when we have to quiet the noise—scroll fatigue, advice overload, and the endless hum of half-finished motivational slogans—and create space for something deeper. Not a scroll, not a swipe, not a hit of inspiration designed to evaporate in a minute. I'm talking about a pause. A space. A moment between you and me where the distractions fall away, and what's left is the truth you've been trying to outrun: you already know what needs to be done.

You don't need another productivity list. You don't need a flashy reel or another high-octane YouTube video telling you to hustle harder. You need alignment. You need clarity. And above all—you need to confront the invisible weight you've been carrying. Because despite all the affirmations you've whispered in the mirror, despite the journal pages filled with vision and strategy, despite the quiet commitments you've made in the dark—

something is still pulling you back. And it's not confusion. It's resistance.

It's the moment your hands freeze before clicking "publish." The quickening of your pulse when opportunity knocks—not because you're unprepared, but because some internal voice tells you you're still not enough. It's the loop you keep replaying, the hesitation dressed up as caution, the constant second-guessing that robs you of the peace you've earned.

This isn't just psychological fog. It's not just emotional static. It's a full-scale ambush—and it's happening inside your own mind. The battlefield isn't external anymore. It's internal. And the intruders don't wear masks. They wear your face. Your voice. Your memories. These internal saboteurs don't scream; they murmur. They don't break in; they're already seated at the table.

Their tactics are subtle, but deadly. They don't call you a failure. They just ask if you're "ready yet." They don't question your worth—they ask if you've really earned your place. They suggest waiting. They advise caution. They cloak fear in the language of wisdom and call hesitation a virtue. But it's not wisdom. It's sabotage in slow motion.

And here's the truth no one likes to admit: these voices are winning. Quietly. Consistently. They're stealing your momentum. Hijacking your courage. Polluting your vision. They feed off your doubts and multiply in silence. And if you've ever felt like the person holding you back is you, then you already know exactly what I'm talking about.

Let's stop pretending this is about needing more time. Or needing to learn "just one more thing" before you take the leap. This isn't a knowledge issue. This is an internal war. And it has names.

I remember sitting in the back corner of Mrs. Dawson's fourth-grade classroom, the one desk in the room that faced the wall. It wasn't assigned—it just felt safer there. I was the chubby kid with a stutter when I got nervous and hands that wouldn't stop sweating. My voice cracked when called on, even if I knew the answer. So I avoided eye contact, shrunk into my sweatshirt, and prayed no one would see me.

Recess was worse. While the other kids raced to the blacktop, I lingered by the fence pretending to tie my shoes. Again. Every day. I wasn't lazy—I was afraid. Afraid of the dodgeball that always seemed aimed at me. Afraid of the laughter when I ran too slow or missed the catch. I told myself I was just "observing" the game. But truthfully, I was negotiating with fear: "If I just stay quiet... if I don't mess up... maybe they won't notice me."

What I didn't realize back then was that this pattern—this quiet, nervous avoidance—was training my nervous system to equate visibility with danger. That every time I chose silence over speaking up, stillness over movement, hiding over risking—I was reinforcing a loop. A mental association that said: "Risk is unsafe. Being seen is unsafe. Don't step out, don't speak up, don't draw attention."

That loop didn't vanish with age. It just got more sophisticated. It started wearing a suit. It started calling itself "strategy." It told me not to pitch the idea until it was perfect. Not to speak unless I had the best insight. Not to take the opportunity unless I was certain I'd crush it. But it was the same scared kid behind the curtain, still tying his shoes at the edge of the game.

These are not abstract ideas. They're patterns with purpose—designed to keep you comfortable, and in doing so, keep you small. They are, by name and nature, the Three Enemies of Progress: Perfectionism, Procrastination, and Impostor Syndrome.

Perfectionism is the polished trap that tells you if it's not flawless, it's not worthy. Procrastination is the emotional con artist, whispering that delay is strategy. And Impostor Syndrome? That's the thief of identity—the voice inside that warns you not to be found out.

Each one of them is a master of manipulation. Each one plays a different angle, but with the same goal: to keep you in hesitation mode, waiting for some imaginary future where the conditions are finally right. But that future never comes. And while you wait, the clock keeps ticking, and your calling keeps fading into background noise.

This isn't a theory. This is data-backed. According to the American Psychological Association, more than 70% of people experience Impostor Syndrome at some point in their careers—including high-level leaders and executives. Research from the Journal of Behavioral Science highlights that nearly 20% of adults are chronic procrastinators, and many more suffer from situation-based avoidance that's tied to unresolved emotional stress. As for perfectionism, a 30-year meta-analysis shows it's increasing dramatically among younger generations, directly correlating with rising levels of burnout, anxiety, and depression.

This isn't just culture. This is a crisis. This is war at the level of identity—and it's happening in real time.

If you've ever felt paralyzed staring at a blank document, if you've ever postponed something deeply meaningful under the guise of "getting it right," if you've ever walked into a room and thought, "What if they find out I don't belong?"—then these enemies are already entrenched in your psyche.

And you're not alone.

Let me be clear: this is not a weakness. This is not a character flaw. You are not broken. You are not unmotivated. What you are—is under siege by internal forces that were trained into you: by outdated systems, unrealistic expectations, educational models that rewarded perfection over progress, and cultural programming that told you your worth was conditional.

But you're reading this right now, which means a different truth is already trying to surface.

The truth that you are not here to be perfect—you're here to be present. You're not here to delay—you're here to decide. You're not here to perform—you're here to build.

And to do that, you'll have to look these enemies in the eye—not to argue with them, but to unmask them. To expose their tactics. To reclaim the space they've been squatting rent-free inside your mind.

Because the only thing more dangerous than fear—is the kind of fear that hides behind logic.

It's time to end the negotiations. To stop mistaking self-protection for strategy. To silence the inner voice that's been masquerading as "wise" when it's really just scared.

You don't need more credentials. You don't need permission. What you need is truth. And truth only becomes power when it's activated.

So let's begin right here, right now—by naming the first enemy. Let's pull perfectionism out of its polished hiding place and put it under the light. Are you ready? Let's move.

ENEMY #1: Perfectionism—The Illusion of "Not Ready Yet"

Let's begin with the most deceptive enemy—the one that cloaks itself in the noble pursuit of excellence. Perfectionism doesn't show up as a brute. It doesn't kick down the door or announce itself with chaos. No, it wears the face of diligence. It whispers, "Let's just make it a little better." It offers the seductive lie that waiting is wisdom, and that excellence demands delay.

But perfectionism isn't really about standards. It's about safety. It's not driven by a hunger to serve, but by a fear of being seen—truly seen—before everything is polished. It masquerades as care, but it's really controlled. And beneath that control is the aching terror of rejection. What if they don't get it? What if they don't like it? What if it's not enough?

Perfectionism doesn't ask you to improve—it demands that you postpone. It trains you to tinker endlessly. To delay courage in the name of "preparation." You convince yourself you're being responsible, when in truth, you're hiding in plain sight. You're not refining the work—you're shielding your identity. And the longer you wait, the more your confidence corrodes in silence.

Because here's the real cost: momentum dies in perfection. Confidence fades in the quiet space between intent and execution. Identity itself starts to crack under the pressure of a standard that was never achievable to begin with. And when you finally do release something—if you ever do—it's not joy you feel. It's anxiety. Because you've trained yourself to believe that unless it's flawless, it's worthless.

I know this trap intimately. Early in my speaking career, I was given a small event—just 40 people in a community center. I prepped like a man possessed. I rehearsed every line, every transition. My slides were pristine. I had the stories, the cadence, the flow—all timed down to the second.

But five minutes in? My mic cut out. Ten minutes? I blanked. Lost my words. Froze on stage in front of everyone. Fifteen minutes? A man in the front row stood up and walked out. I felt like I was watching my calling crumble in real time.

I walked off that stage defeated. Not because I didn't care, but because I cared too much—and perfectionism had convinced me that failure meant I didn't belong. That I wasn't ready. That I wasn't enough. But then something shifted. I asked myself the question that broke the lie wide open: "Was I hoping to grow by staying hidden—or was I willing to be shaped in the fire of real experience?"

That one question changed everything.

I made a vow that day: I wouldn't wait to be perfect anymore. I'd show up, scars and all. I'd let growth happen in the chaos. I stopped chasing polish and started pursuing presence. And that choice? It led to the biggest stages of my life—Microsoft, SHRM, United Way, TEDx. But those doors didn't open because I was flawless. They opened because I was finally visible.

Listen to me closely: perfectionism doesn't lead to greatness. It leads to exhaustion. Greatness isn't built in secrecy—it's forged in release. Growth demands exposure. And exposure is uncomfortable—but it's also how transformation happens.

If you're still waiting for the right moment, the perfect draft, the flawless product—stop. You don't need guarantees. You need courage.

Strategy: Version 1 Thinking

The antidote to perfectionism isn't more preparation—it's activation. It's choosing to launch before you're fully comfortable. It's building in the open, growing in the light. The cure is what I call Version 1 Thinking.

You don't leap from dream to masterpiece in one shot. You move in drafts. You evolve in versions. Version 1 is the doorway to everything else. It's the messy, imperfect, brave first attempt that gets you in motion—and motion is what builds confidence, clarity, and skill.

Here's the truth: no one gets to version 10 without releasing version 1. Not even Apple and the iPhone. And you can't improve what you refuse to share. If you're constantly waiting for the right moment to hit "go," that moment will quietly become your graveyard of unused potential.

So ask yourself—honestly and without judgment:

- What idea, product, or project have I been keeping in the shadows because it's "not ready"?

- What is the smallest possible version of that thing I could release within the next seven days?

- And perhaps most important: what fear is hiding behind my excuse of "excellence"?

Perfectionism will always find a reason to delay. But progress? It finds a reason to begin.

Choose movement over mastery. Release your version one—not because it's the final form, but because it's the beginning of your real freedom. It's the declaration that says, "I'm no longer negotiating with fear. I'm here now—and I'm building anyway."

ENEMY #2: Procrastination—Delayed Greatness

A few years ago, I was scaling one of my franchise locations. We had traction, demand, and a growing waitlist. The team was solid—contractors were reliable, ops were running, and our reputation was climbing. On paper, it was the perfect time to expand. My gut said, "Go." My mentors said, "Go." The numbers said, "Go."

But I didn't.

I kept holding meetings. Redrafting proposals. Reworking org charts that no one asked for. I told myself I was "building infrastructure." That I was being wise, methodical, long-term focused. But deep down, I knew the truth: I was stalling.

Not because I didn't believe in the vision—but because stepping into expansion meant stepping into the unknown. And with that came the possibility of failure in front of my team. Of leading them into something that might break. And that fear? It wore a suit and called itself "strategy."

I remember one Monday, we were on a Zoom with our marketing vendor and lead contractor. Both of them were waiting for my green light to launch a new division. I nodded. Smiled. Said, "Let's circle back next week." What I didn't say was, "I'm scared it might not work." So the week passed. Then another. Then another. Momentum died. The opportunity faded. And eventually, that contractor—our best one—took a contract with someone else.

Not because I lacked vision. But because I hesitated.

That day taught me something most books won't say out loud: your team can't follow hesitation. They can work with imperfection. They'll pivot through chaos. But they can't build under a leader who won't decide.

Procrastination doesn't burst through the door waving a red flag. It doesn't announce itself with chaos or confession. It strolls in quietly, disguised in good intentions. It wears the voice of reason, cloaked in phrases that feel responsible: "Let's wait until it's the right time." "I just need to organize things first." "Once the pressure's on, I'll lock in."

And that's the trap.

Procrastination isn't laziness. It's an emotional strategy. It's a shield that the brain raises when faced with discomfort, uncertainty, or the risk of exposure. It says, "Not now," when what it really means is, "I'm scared." And instead of calling it what it is—avoidance—we dress it up in productivity language to justify the delay. We say we're "planning." We say we're "waiting for alignment." We convince ourselves that our hesitation is thoughtful when, really, it's avoidance dressed up in intelligence.

But here's the problem: repetition becomes identity. Every time you delay, you reinforce the subconscious belief that you can't trust yourself with bold action. That delay becomes your new normal. Soon, you don't just procrastinate—you identify as a procrastinator. You start expecting hesitation from yourself. You anticipate postponement as if it's your operating mode.

This is how big dreams shrink. Not through a loud, dramatic collapse—but through a slow, silent erosion of intent. Through quiet deferrals and private rationalizations. That's how your goals end up in limbo—not because you didn't care, but because you let fear masquerade as preparation.

I know this enemy well.

There was a time when I had a full training series ready to go. It had structure. It had value. It had clarity. The content was strong, the message impactful. My audience was primed. I had all the makings of a breakthrough.

But I delayed.

"I need better lighting," I told myself. "I should fine-tune the scripts a bit more." "I'll launch in the next quarter—it's more strategic."

And while I was polishing, someone else launched their version—raw, unfiltered, imperfect. But they launched it. And it caught fire.

It didn't go viral because it was flawless. It went viral because it was *out there*.

That moment stuck with me—not just because they succeeded, but because I knew I had what it took. I had the goods. But they had the guts.

That's when the truth landed: you don't get rewarded for what you intend. You get rewarded for what you execute.

Delay isn't neutral. Delay decays. And when greatness is postponed too long, it begins to expire. Because relevance has a shelf life. And inspiration that isn't acted on fades into regret.

Strategy: The Five-Minute Rule

So how do we break procrastination's grip? You don't overthink it. You don't analyze it into submission. You just move.

You start—with anything.

This is where the Five-Minute Rule comes in. It's simple: set a timer for five minutes and do the thing. Not the whole thing. Not the finished product. Just the *start*. Five minutes. That's it.

Because when you start, something shifts. Your brain moves from analysis to action. From fear to flow. You begin to dismantle the mental barriers that made the task feel so heavy in the first place.

Five minutes might not seem like much—but it changes everything. It reminds your nervous system that movement is safe. It tells your subconscious that you are no longer a prisoner of hesitation. And once you're in motion, momentum joins you.

So don't wait for the lightning bolt of motivation. Don't sit around hoping for clarity to come knocking. Clarity shows up *after* commitment. Momentum is a partner of motion.

The war against procrastination won't be won with willpower alone. It'll be won in micro-decisions—in choosing to act while the fear is still present, not after it disappears.

Start now. Start small. Start anyway.

Because every moment you delay, your dream grows colder. But every action—no matter how small—turns the heat back on.

ENEMY #3: Impostor Syndrome—Fighting the Inner Critic

I still remember the suffocating heat of Iraq, the kind that made the metal of our gear burn against your skin and the sand feel like fire under your boots. I was just 23 years old—the youngest sergeant in our platoon—and up to that point, I had never seen war. My Gunny, a battle-tested leader with a lineage of military men behind him, had just been medevaced home with a severe back injury. I assumed they'd assign one of the senior NCOs to lead First Section. We had experienced guys—Eades, Jason, Perez, Hardin. But then I got the call.

"Allison, you're stepping up. You're leading First Section."

Time slowed. My heart was pounding in my ears louder than any gunfire I'd heard. This wasn't a drill. This was real leadership—life or death leadership. And here I was, 23, still figuring myself out, now responsible for leading men—seasoned men—into hostile territory, on patrols, through communication channels, through chaos.

Impostor syndrome didn't whisper. It screamed. *"You're not ready." "They made a mistake." "They'll see you don't belong."* Every ounce of me questioned if I could carry the weight.

But then I remembered what my Gunny told me before he left: *"Take care of the boys."* Not *try*. Not *do your best*. Just *do it*. That was his confidence speaking over my insecurity. That was the moment I realized: leadership wasn't about age. It was about posture. It was about presence under pressure.

So I suited up. I prayed hard. And I led. I used everything I'd learned, every tactic, every bit of training, every ounce of character. And I led those men with all I had. Mission after mission, we came back. Not because I was the most experienced—but because I was willing to rise when called.

Looking back, I wasn't a fraud. I was becoming. That's the thing impostor syndrome doesn't tell you—it doesn't show up to stop you. It shows up to stretch you. And sometimes, the most profound confirmation you're ready... is when it scares the hell out of you.

Among the enemies that sabotage our progress, none is more deceptive—or more quietly devastating—than impostor syndrome. It's not loud. It doesn't broadcast its arrival. Instead, it slips in unnoticed, subtle as a breath, whispering self-doubt into the quiet moments before you're about to do something meaningful. It's the voice you hear just before a big opportunity, when the stakes are high and the spotlight is warming. And that voice says things like:

"You're not ready."
"Who do you think you are to be doing this?"
"They're going to realize you don't belong here."

It doesn't matter how long you've been in the game or how much you've achieved. In fact, the higher you climb, the more persistent the voice can become. That's because visibility increases vulnerability. The more people who can see you, the more your nervous system equates performance with risk. Your biology interprets visibility not as success—but as exposure. And exposure, to the survival brain, feels like danger.

What's most painful about impostor syndrome isn't the insecurity—it's the betrayal of your own momentum. You know you've done the work. You know you've put in the hours. And yet, right when you're about to cross the threshold, your own voice betrays you. Not out of malice—but out of misalignment. Your identity hasn't caught up to your growth. You've evolved faster than your inner story has. And that lag creates friction. That friction feels like fraudulence.

But let me offer you a reframe that has changed everything for the leaders I've coached:
You don't feel like a fraud because you're unqualified. You feel like a fraud because you're expanding.
That tension in your chest? That quickened breath before you step into the room? That's not fear of failure—it's fear of visibility. And it's only showing up because you're growing.

I remember it vividly—the first time I was invited to speak at a TEDx event. The moment I got the call, I was honored. But just beneath the surface, I was shaking. Not physically, but internally. Emotionally. Because immediately, the thoughts began:

"You're not TEDx material."
"You're not the most polished speaker in the lineup."
"They only picked you to check a box."

The doubt was instant, relentless, and familiar. I'd heard that voice before— right before every breakthrough. But something shifted that day. Instead of silencing the voice or trying to overpower it with bravado, I paused and asked a better question:

Did I manipulate my way here? No.
Did I fabricate credentials or exaggerate my impact? Absolutely not.

Had I put in the work, refined my message, invested in my craft? Without a doubt.

Was I perfect? Of course not.

But was I prepared and purposed? 100%.

So I stepped on that stage. Not because I felt completely confident—but because I refused to let doubt define my identity. I remembered that courage isn't the absence of fear—it's movement in the presence of it. I didn't need to feel ready. I needed to act in alignment with who I was becoming.

Strategy: Rewire the Narrative

Let's get one thing clear from the start—this isn't about corporate strategy, or some carefully curated plan etched into a whiteboard in a meeting room. This is personal. It's about the mental battleground you walk into every day—the inner dialogue that shapes your confidence, your courage, and ultimately, your contribution. Because if impostor syndrome is the quiet, insidious voice whispering that you're not enough, then your first act of resistance must be to raise the volume of the truth.

It starts with evidence. Hard facts. Your mind may be a master of fiction, spinning tales of inadequacy and fear, but your life tells another story. So write it down. Not as a brag sheet, but as a rescue line for the moments you feel like you're drowning. List the projects you've completed—the ones you stayed up late to finish. Name the people you've helped, even if it was just one conversation that shifted their day. Recall the wins, not just the big flashy ones, but the quiet ones too—the moments you didn't quit, the times you showed up scared and spoke anyway. These are your receipts. Your personal archive of evidence that you are not only capable—you are called. And when your feelings betray you, your history will hold you up.

The second step is brutal but necessary: you must confront the lie. You wouldn't let someone speak to your best friend the way your inner critic speaks to you. So why do you tolerate it in your own head? The next time you hear the whisper of inadequacy, don't just absorb it. Confront it. Call it by name. Say it out loud if you need to: "That's not truth. That's fear, dressed up as logic." Fear is brilliant at disguise. It masquerades as reason, wrapping itself in the language of responsibility and wisdom. But just because a thought sounds polished doesn't make it accurate. Your job is not to get into a debate with fear—it's to expose it for what it is: a fragile idea, not an absolute truth.

And then—this is the clincher—you move. You act while anxious. You show up even when your stomach knots and your palms sweat. You don't wait for confidence to arrive like some divine visitor. Because confidence doesn't knock before entering—it shows up *after* you've taken the risk. Neuroscience supports this. The brain doesn't strengthen confidence through passive hope—it strengthens it through experiential risk. Each time you act through the anxiety, you carve a new neural pathway. You train your body to associate discomfort with possibility, not peril.

So start where you are. Hit publish on the imperfect post. Raise your hand in the meeting. Pitch the idea that's been haunting your imagination. Show up to the conversation you've been avoiding. Because the truth is, the miracle isn't waiting on the other side of readiness. It's waiting on the other side of movement.

As performance psychologist Dr. Sian Beilock puts it, "Action reduces anxiety. Overthinking amplifies it." And she's right. Every overanalyzed fear grows in the petri dish of delay. But the moment you move—just a little— your fear loses oxygen. It shrinks under the weight of motion.

Let me leave you with this: You do not need another degree, certification, or title to start. You don't need permission from your boss, your peers, or even your past. What you need is alignment. Belief. The decision to trust what's already within you. The truth is, the enemy is not your résumé—it's your reluctance to own the résumé you already have.

Problems aren't signs to stop. They are invitations—open doors asking you to build, to stretch, to grow. Invitations to stop doubting and start doing. Invitations to use your grit, your history, your insight to craft something real. Something that moves the needle. Something that matters.

And that invitation? It's been waiting on you to accept it.

Why These Enemies Show Up

Let's pull back the curtain and go deeper—not just into psychology, but into biology. These enemies we've been confronting—perfectionism, procrastination, and impostor syndrome—don't knock on the door of every project or goal at random. They're far more cunning than that. They're strategic. They show up with uncanny precision, timing their arrival to the exact moment when something meaningful is at stake. They don't waste energy haunting the insignificant. They wait until something important is about to be born—until you're on the brink of impact, influence, or irreversible transformation. That's when they strike. That's when the noise in your head becomes deafening.

And the reason is simple—yet profound. Your brain isn't wired for progress. It's wired for protection. Evolution didn't optimize your nervous system for purpose, visibility, or vulnerability. It optimized you to stay alive. To blend in. To avoid danger. That primal programming still runs silently beneath the surface, even in our modern world of business meetings and creative pursuits. The amygdala, an ancient part of the brain responsible for threat detection, doesn't distinguish between a lion on the savannah and a critical audience at your next presentation. To your brain, visibility is exposure—and exposure is risk. And risk? Risk means danger.

So perfectionism steps in—not to sabotage you, but to shield you. It says, "Let's make this flawless, so no one can criticize you." It promises protection through polish. Procrastination does the same. It whispers, "Let's wait a bit longer. Let's give it more time. The discomfort will fade." But that delay isn't strategic—it's self-soothing. Then comes impostor syndrome, cloaked in logic, insisting, "Let's not get too visible. What if they discover you're not as good as they think?" It's not trying to derail you; it's trying to protect you from emotional exposure. All of it—every whisper, every hesitation—is your biology attempting to keep you safe. But in doing so, it's also keeping you small.

Here's the tragic irony: the same protective reflex that shields you from perceived pain also shuts the door on your greatest growth. The brain's default mode is to equate discomfort with danger. But leadership, purpose, and transformation demand the opposite—they demand that you step into discomfort, not avoid it. You have to retrain your instincts. You have to rise above the automated circuitry of survival and choose something higher: intention. Because instinct says, "Stay safe." But intention says, "Move forward—even when it's hard."

This isn't recklessness. This is maturity. This is self-mastery. In the field of psychology, this ability to reinterpret your fear—to reframe what your body perceives as danger—is called cognitive reappraisal. It's the superpower of every effective leader and change-maker. It's not about pretending fear doesn't exist. It's about seeing fear for what it is: not a stop sign, but a signal. A flare shot into the sky announcing, "Something meaningful is close. Don't back down now."

And that shift? That's the gateway. When you reframe fear as a signpost instead of a shutdown, you begin to make radically different decisions. You stop asking, "What if I fail?" and start asking, "What if this actually works?" You stop bargaining with safety and start trading it in for something far more powerful: momentum. You declare, "I choose motion—even if my hands are shaking. I choose visibility—even if my voice cracks. I choose forward—even when it's unfamiliar."

There's a quote I often share with coaching clients and teams alike, and I offer it to you now not as motivation, but as permission: "Fear is excitement without breath. So breathe—and move anyway." That moment when your chest tightens, when your palms sweat, when the urge to delay or shrink takes over—that's not a reason to retreat. That's the exact indicator that you're standing at the edge of growth. Right there—at that trembling threshold—is the future you keep praying for.

And if you need one final reminder, hear me now: You are not late. You are not unqualified. You are not losing your mind for feeling resistance. You're simply standing on sacred ground—the threshold of something extraordinary. And thresholds, by their very nature, require decisions.

So make yours—not someday, not when it feels safer, not when you're more prepared. Make it now. Step through. Not because you're fearless—but because you're no longer willing to be ruled by invisible lies masquerading as logic.

This is your moment. Claim it. Breathe—and move anyway.

Pattern Recognition: The Mind's GPS—And Grounded Threat

For millennia, humans have survived—and thrived—by spotting patterns: the shifting of seasons to sow and harvest, the sky's weather maps to predict storms, or ancestral rhythms that shaped migrations and agriculture. This ability to detect recurring signals and attach meaning to them is baked into our biology and culture—what Chris Millas describes as "the cognitive ability to identify cause-effect relationships to make predictions," and what chronobiologists confirm shapes not only our decisions but also our very biology.

But that gift—pattern recognition—also sets the stage for the enemies inside your mind. Just as ancient civilizations used predictable natural cycles to guide planting schedules, your brain uses patterns to protect you. This pattern-based programming was essential when external threats ruled survival. But now those same mechanisms reinforce internal boundaries. You've seen it: the recurring loop of "I'm not ready," "I'll wait longer," "You don't belong here"—each one a habit, each one a voice shaped and repeated until it feels automatic. These voices live in the same neural highways that learned seasonality, weather forecasting, even how to speak and recognize a friend's face.

Your mind has mapped these three saboteurs—Perfectionism, Procrastination, Impostor Syndrome—not because they serve you, but because they once protected you. They are old patterns in a new context. They trigger emotional shields programmed through education, culture, and repetitive self-doubt. And like any software update gone viral, they reroute your focus, hijacking your intention and reinforcing uncertainty.

History and science are clear: pattern recognition is your brain's GPS—fast, automatic, and often unconscious. But just because it runs well doesn't mean it runs correctly. The skill that helped your ancestors predict harvest cycles won't help you publish that first draft or raise your price. Clinging to these entrenched patterns isn't wisdom—it's habit masquerading as protection.

So here's the choice: let your programming run the route again—or intervene. Awareness is the first step. Recognize these patterns for what they are: responses rooted in survival, not strategy. Understand that giving them space only strengthens them. Then, interrupt the script. Reassign attention to what matters. Feed a new habit. Create a novel pattern that aligns with who you're becoming.

When you understand that your mind is wired to detect these sabotaging patterns, you gain an unexpected power: you can reprogram them. You don't need to erase your survival instincts—they served you well. What you need is to override them with intention.

This is where the battle truly begins—not in the external world, but in the silent architecture of your brain. And knowing how that architecture works gives you the authority to redesign it.

If you've ever felt like you're fighting a mental or emotional battle, you're not alone—and you're not broken. There is a battle within. You have to reclaim your emotional health in a world that feeds chaos. You are part of a global crisis that is deeper, wider, and more urgent than most people realize. According to the World Health Organization, depression is now the leading cause of disability worldwide. In the United States alone, over 60 million adults are quietly grappling with chronic mental health challenges. That's one in five people—navigating life with an invisible weight on their chest, often in silence and shame. And among young people, the statistics are even more alarming.

A 2023 CDC study revealed that 42% of teenagers feel persistently overwhelmed by stress, anxiety, fear, or depression. Sixty percent of teen girls reported feeling hopeless or sad most of the time. One in three teenagers seriously contemplated suicide—a staggering 60% increase over the past decade. These numbers are not just data points. They're a mirror reflecting something broken in our culture: emotional disconnection, relentless pressure, and the growing inability to slow down long enough to heal.

We're living in an age where joy feels scarce, peace feels out of reach, and emotional overwhelm has become the new normal. We talk about wellness, but we rarely live it. Prescription medications—particularly antidepressants—are at an all-time high. And while they can be necessary and even life-saving in some cases, they are not the whole answer. Too many people are medicated and still feel empty. That's not a condemnation of treatment—it's a challenge to examine the *real roots* of our struggle. Medication may suppress the symptom, but it doesn't change the story you tell yourself when you wake up. If your inner world is still ruled by unprocessed pain, limiting beliefs, and a focus on what's broken, no pill will provide lasting peace. Healing demands more than numbing. It demands awareness. It demands leadership of your inner life.

There was a season in my life when the mornings felt like mourning. I'd wake up with a heaviness in my chest that didn't lift, no matter how many hours I slept—or how many pills I swallowed. Thirteen. That's how many medications I was on at one point. Antidepressants. Anti-anxiety. Sleep aids. Mood stabilizers. You name it, it was in my system. My kitchen counter looked like a pharmacy. The pill organizers were color-coded. Morning. Noon. Night. My routine was wrapped in a ritual of survival.

But it wasn't living.

There were days I'd sit in my car outside the gym, engine running, unable to move. I wasn't crying. I wasn't panicked. I was just... frozen. Like my mind had short-circuited under the weight of its own loops. *You're never going to get better. Why even try? You're too broken.* Those weren't new thoughts— they were old patterns. Familiar scripts. Neural highways I had driven so many times, I could coast them in my sleep.

The truth was, my mind had become an expert at anticipating pain. Somewhere along the way, it decided that disappointment felt safer than hope, that numbness was easier than feeling, and that staying stuck was more familiar than risking failure. But nothing cut deeper than the moment my doctor looked at my CT scan and told me there was a hole in my brain. In that instant, every hidden fear seemed confirmed—and the weight of it pressed harder than ever.

But I'll never forget the day I decided to question that programming.

It wasn't dramatic. There was no breakdown. No epiphany. Just a small moment. I was standing in the bathroom, brushing my teeth, staring at my own reflection. My eyes looked hollow. My shoulders hunched. And I remember whispering to myself—not out loud, but in the quiet place where the soul speaks—*"Is this who I really am? Or is this just who I've become because I've believed the same story for too long?"*

That was the moment the circuit broke.

It didn't happen all at once. Healing rarely does. But I began rewriting the narrative, one small choice at a time. I started walking again. I cleaned up my diet. I swapped out noise for quiet, chaos for structure. Eventually, I worked with a doctor to taper off the medications. Not because I didn't need help—but because I finally had hope. And hope is a medicine they don't sell in bottles.

Looking back, those patterns didn't define me—they just *trained* me. They trained me to survive. But survival isn't the same as purpose. And when you finally realize that the voices in your head are just echoes of old fears, you can start reprogramming them. You can create a new pattern.

One built not on protection, but intention.

Here's the hard truth: if you keep reacting to your environment instead of directing your response, you'll always feel powerless. Emotional freedom begins when you stop being a thermometer—constantly responding to the world's temperature—and start becoming a thermostat, someone who *sets* the tone. You must lead your thoughts, not just have them. Govern your emotions, not just feel them. This shift in mindset is the key to emotional sovereignty. It's not about suppressing feelings—it's about developing the strength to process them and move forward with clarity. You don't need more coping mechanisms. You need a strategy. You need a way to reframe, re-center, and re-empower yourself from the inside out.

So where do we start? Not with shame. Not with performance. But with honesty. If you are tired, overwhelmed, anxious, or numb—you are not weak. You are human. But you don't have to stay stuck. You can begin the process of healing by anchoring yourself in four powerful keys. These aren't quick fixes—they're internal frameworks that shift your baseline. When consistently applied, they become the foundation of true emotional health.

Key 1: Self-Control – Lead Your Emotions, Don't Follow Them

Emotional health begins with emotional leadership. Self-control is not about pretending everything is fine or pushing your feelings down—it's about recognizing your emotions and choosing to guide them rather than be governed by them. Most people are reactive: they're triggered, overwhelmed, or irritated, and the next moment they're yelling, shutting down, lashing out, or checking out. A small inconvenience becomes a massive breakdown. But self-control gives you space between stimulus and response. It allows you to acknowledge, "This is how I feel, but it's not how I'm going to respond." Emotional maturity means you don't have to act on every feeling. You can feel sadness without spiraling. You can feel anger without exploding. You can feel discouraged and still show up. True self-control says, "I may not want to do this right now, but I'm doing it anyway because my future depends on it." You are not a slave to your emotions. You are their leader. Train them accordingly.

Key 2: Connection – Surround Yourself With Meaningful Relationships

When pain hits, isolation is often our default reaction—especially for men. We shut down. We go silent. We disappear emotionally, sometimes even physically, thinking that if we keep it all in, we'll figure it out on our own. But healing was never meant to be a solo mission. We were created for connection. One of the most revealing studies on trauma came out of World War II, where 500 soldiers who had experienced identical battlefield trauma were tracked over time. The result? Three hundred of them adjusted and thrived. Two hundred did not. The difference wasn't in their training or toughness—it was their support system. Those with strong relational bonds—family, friends, trusted confidants—healed more quickly and sustained recovery longer. The others, without those anchors, spiraled into deeper despair. We need people who see us, hear us, and walk with us. We need spaces where we don't have to perform or pretend. So say it out loud: *"I need someone."* That's not weakness—it's wisdom. Connection isn't optional for emotional health. It's essential.

Key 3: Purpose – Anchor Your Life in Meaning

When emotional health deteriorates, it's almost always connected to a deeper void—**a lack of meaning**. People battling mental and emotional storms are often not just overwhelmed—they're unanchored. They may be missing one or more of the core components of internal stability: meaningful work, trusted relationships, personal values, unresolved trauma, a strong sense of identity, or a clear future vision. When we lack these internal anchors, the storms of life shake us harder. That's why purpose matters. Purpose is not just about productivity—it's about meaning. When you are grounded in something greater than the pain you're facing, the pain doesn't get the last word. Purpose gives context to suffering. It reminds you that your struggle is part of a story—not the end of one. Ask yourself: *What do I care about? Who do I want to impact? What future victory is worth fighting for?* Sometimes the only thing that can pull you out of your pit is the picture of where you're headed next. Purpose creates vision. Vision creates hope. And hope is the oxygen your mental health desperately needs.

Key 4: Decision – Take Authority Over Your Life

At some point, healing comes down to a decision. Not a feeling. Not a moment of perfect clarity. But a **bold, intentional decision** to take back the pen and rewrite your story. This is not about toxic positivity. It's not about pretending everything is okay when it's not. It's about recognizing that even when you don't feel strong, **you still have the power to choose.** You can choose to get out of bed. You can choose to reach out. You can choose to journal, go for a walk, drink the water, take the call, go to the appointment. You may not feel like it—but you can do it anyway. That's what emotional resilience looks like: *choosing what honors your future while your feelings catch up.* This is where the tide turns—not when you feel different, but when you decide to live different. Not perfectly, but intentionally. You are not what happened to you. You are who you decide to become next. That one decision may not change everything overnight—but it will start the process of change.

And sometimes, that's all you need to get up again.

There is no shame in struggling. The shame is in pretending you're okay when you're breaking inside. But the moment you choose self-control, surround yourself with healthy connection, reconnect with your purpose, and make the decision to take ownership of your story—that's the moment your healing begins. If you're battling anxiety, sadness, stress, or depression—you are not weak. You are human. And you are not alone. Your life matters. Your peace is worth protecting. And your future is worth fighting for.

These four keys—self-control, connection, purpose, and decision—aren't just principles. They are practices. Daily, imperfect, courageous practices that invite you to lead yourself with grace and grit. And while the battle is real, so is your ability to rise. This won't be easy. But it will be worth it. Because emotional health is not the absence of pain—it's the presence of clarity. It's not just coping—it's creating a life that doesn't require escape. That's what you're building now.

So let this chapter be your turning point. Let it be the line in the sand where you stop waiting for a breakthrough—and start becoming one. You are not a prisoner of your past. You are not defined by your worst day. And you are not powerless. You are a builder. A leader. A fighter. And the restoration of your mind, your emotions, and your identity begins today—with one decision, one connection, one purposeful step at a time.

You have what it takes. Not because it's easy—but because you're done living small.

Now it's time to fight forward.

BREAK THE BOTTLE CHALLENGE — Chapter 7

Let's make this real.

1. **Name Your Enemy** – Which one's showing up the most in your life right now? Be honest.

2. **Track the Trigger** – When does it show up? Before launching? Before hard conversations?

3. **Write a New Script** – Example: *"This isn't truth. It's protection. But I'm choosing progress."*

4. **Take a Small Step Today** – Send the email. Start the pitch. Write the post. Just begin.

RESOURCES

 **Download the Tool: Momentum Reset Scoring Sheet**
Assess your current momentum, identify growth gaps, and strategically rebuild alignment with clarity and confidence.

Available at: btbprograms.com/free-resources

CULTIVATING RESILIENCE—THE ULTIMATE ADVANTAGE

"Life will test you, stretch you, and try to break you. Resilience isn't about being untouched—it's about refusing to stay down."

— Break The Bottle

The Measure of a Person

How do you measure the strength of a person—not in the wins, not in the applause—but in what they do when everything falls apart? When no one's watching. When the light's gone out, and the mirror is asking questions you're not ready to answer. That's where real measurement happens. Not in your success stories, but in your silence.

Life doesn't send calendar invites for crisis. It shows up in the dark. Dreams stall. Plans dissolve. People you counted on disappear. The promotion vanishes. The marriage crumbles. The body breaks. The mind buckles. And in that space—where identity and pain collide—you are forced to choose: shrink or rise. That is where resilience is born. Not in the comfort zones. But in the cracks.

And if we're being real—most people don't rise because they've never built the internal architecture to support the weight of their own potential. They crumble because they were never taught how to construct strength from struggle. That's what we're building now.

The greatest war you'll ever fight isn't with anyone else—it's with yourself. That's when I realized the battle is "Me vs. Me," that is the ultimate internal battlefield. It's not with a harsh supervisor, a toxic relationship, or even a broken system—it's the battle happening silently inside your head every single day. This is where your highest potential confronts your deepest insecurities. Where one version of you longs to grow, and the other cautions, "Maybe this isn't worth it." A timid whisper nudges pause and retreat; the other softly dares you forward, urging you not to give up just yet.

This is where **DIRECTION** begins to take form—not just through maps or mantras, but through the construction of something deeper: **resilient identity.** A foundation that doesn't flex based on applause or titles or outcomes. But one built like a structure with steel beams underneath. That's what makes you unshakeable—not because life stops shaking, but because you're no longer moved by every tremor.

I didn't get this from a classroom or a TED Talk. I got it from surviving storms that never made the news. From standing in rooms full of people and still feeling invisible. From hearing I was "too Jamaican to be American," and "too American to be Jamaican." I was bullied not just for being Black—but for being misunderstood. Different. A misfit. A contradiction. And for years, I carried that confusion into every room I walked into. Every boardroom. Every relationship. Every mirror.

And when I thought I'd found stability—as a husband, a father, a corporate leader—it all collapsed again. My first marriage dissolved into silence and shame. Mental health collapsed like a bridge with no warning signs. I lost my job and nearly lost myself when I was struggling mentally. I wasn't just unemployed—I was untethered. Stripped of all the external titles that had once made me feel worthy. That breakdown didn't feel like a spiritual lesson. It felt like failure. Period.

But here's the paradox no one tells you: **the worst thing that ever happened to you might be the very thing that makes you whole.** Because somewhere in the rubble, when you decide not to run, not to numb, not to quit—that's when the framework begins to take shape. You start building from the inside. Quietly. Intentionally. Not with hype—but with humility.

Psychology backs this. Resilience isn't personality—it's process. A meta-analysis of over 15,000 people around the world found that high levels of resilience directly correlate with lower anxiety, lower depression, and stronger mental health overall. In the U.S. Army's Comprehensive Soldier and Family Fitness program, resilience training didn't just inspire—it statistically reduced substance abuse and stress-based disorders. Why? Because when people learn how to **build** resilience—not just endure—they start navigating life with tools, not just toughness.

Here's what nobody tells you when life caves in: You don't need a miracle. You need a blueprint. And the first piece of that blueprint is emotional agility.

Because let's be honest—most people aren't undone by their circumstances. They're undone by their inability to **feel without falling apart**. They either suppress emotion and become numb, or they drown in it and can't move. But emotional agility is about holding space for pain without letting it dictate your pace. It's about saying, "Yes, I'm hurting—and I'm still moving." That's not weakness. That's precision.

Then comes stress conditioning. That means training your nervous system to hold pressure. Not avoid it. Not collapse under it. But engage with it intentionally, so when the storm comes, it doesn't feel like sabotage—it feels like rehearsal. Like game day. You've been here before, and your system knows what to do.

Cognitive reframing is the third beam in the architecture. This is where you stop asking, "Why me?" and start asking, "What now?" This is where problems become portals, and wounds become instructions. You don't ignore pain. You interpret it differently. You don't erase loss. You extract meaning. You stop seeing life as a punishment, and you start seeing it as a practice. That's where mental toughness becomes a tool, not a trait.

Now, let's talk about building with psychological preparation, the construction site where this all happens: the mind. It's not some distant battlefield—it's right here, every day. Your mind is where resilience is tested and forged. It's where the loudest battles are fought—not between you and the world, but between you and yourself. That version of you that wants to run, quit, delay, isolate. And the other version that dares you forward. That says, "We're not done yet."

That's not a motivational quote. That's my story. I remember sitting in my car after being let go from the railroad—head against the steering wheel, hands shaking, wondering how I got here. The mental noise was louder than any siren. "You failed again." "You're not enough." "It's over." But there was this one quiet question that cut through the noise: "What if this isn't the end?"

That question saved my life.

Because resilience is not about bouncing back—it's about building forward. It's the discipline of choosing meaning over misery. Construction over collapse. And that decision—small as it seems—is everything.

So here's your blueprint for this next phase:

1. **Emotional Agility** – Feel everything. Avoid nothing. And move anyway.

2. **Stress Conditioning** – Train in adversity. Practice presence under pressure.

3. **Cognitive Reframing** – Change the frame. Redefine the fight.

4. **Pre-Commitment to Principles** – Anchor yourself in values before chaos hits.

5. **Recovery as Ritual** – Rest is not a reward—it's a responsibility.

We'll unpack each of these disciplines, not as abstract theories but as buildable skills. Because this isn't the part of your story where we preach positivity. This is the part where we **lay bricks.** We're not talking about surviving life—we're constructing a life that survives anything.

Because resilience is the ultimate advantage—but only when you choose to build it.

Activating the Four Archetypes Within

There are moments in life where the engine just stalls. It's not that you're broken. But it feels like something vital inside you has gone quiet. You try to push forward, but the motivation won't come. You've got plans, goals, even clarity—but something's off. You're not lazy. You're not weak. You're just out of sync.

What I've learned through experience—both my own breakdowns and the breakthroughs I've helped others walk through—is that feeling stuck isn't always about the situation. It's often about misalignment within yourself.

Most of us have been trained to live in survival mode. To pick one way of being and grind it into the ground. Stay strong. Stay calm. Hustle harder. Just "figure it out." We've built our identity around a single lane—and then wonder why we're drained, burned out, or emotionally detached. That's not because we're broken. It's because we're living fragmented.

You weren't designed to move through life with only one gear. You were created with an internal system—a deep intelligence made of multiple energies. And when these energies work in sync, they activate something powerful: direction with force, clarity with depth, strength with meaning. That's when you stop spinning your wheels and start building forward. That's when you come alive.

Inside you live **four core archetypes**—not fictional roles, but ancient energies deeply rooted in human psychology and spiritual tradition. These archetypes are the **Warrior, the Magician, the Lover, and the Sovereign.** They represent not just traits—but tools. Each one holds a set of gifts essential for navigating real life, real adversity, and real purpose.

You don't just need grit—you need all of you. That's what this moment is about.

1. The Warrior – Unstoppable Drive, Grit, and Courage

I remember when my marriage collapsed. It didn't implode with fireworks. It unraveled in slow silence—two people who stopped speaking the language of "us" and started surviving separately. And after the divorce, I didn't just lose my marriage. I lost my sense of worth. My identity was tangled in being a protector, a provider, a husband. And when that role dissolved, I was left staring at the mirror, wondering who I was without it.

It was during this time that I first met my inner **Warrior**.

Not the public version of me. Not the title or the tough guy. I'm talking about that deep, raw, stripped-down voice inside—the one that shows up not when things are going well, but when **everything falls apart and you still get out of bed.**

The Warrior is not about rage. It's not about noise. It's about **intentional aggression**—fire aligned with a cause. It's the mother who works three jobs and still makes it to her daughter's game. It's the man who checks himself into therapy because he refuses to pass his trauma to his kids. It's the addict who relapses but walks back into the meeting anyway.

For me, it was the day I had to look my kids in the eyes and say, "Daddy is still figuring some things out, but I'm not going anywhere." My voice shook. My heart was bleeding. But I showed up. And that's the Warrior—**not when it's easy, but when it's unbearable and you show up anyway.**

The Warrior archetype is your inner engine. It's the one who shows up before dawn when no one is clapping. It doesn't wait for motivation—it **moves from mission.**

When I lost my job at the railroad after my mental health breakdown, I spiraled into a dark place. I questioned everything. My masculinity. My ability to lead. My value. There were days I didn't want to leave the house. But one day, something shifted. I woke up, looked in the mirror, and said out loud, "You will not go out like this." I wrote it on a sticky note and slapped it on the wall. That was my first step. It wasn't a speech. It wasn't a plan. It was a **Warrior declaration.** A line in the sand.

And from that day forward, I built slowly. Day by day. Resume by resume. Workout by workout. That fire—the one that refused to die out—that was the Warrior.

He's not loud, but he is lethal. He doesn't need applause—he needs alignment. You don't need everyone to understand your grind when your mission is clear.

But the Warrior has a shadow. If you live in him too long without balancing the others, you'll become hardened. Emotionally calloused. You'll push through every wall but forget why you built the building in the first place. So yes, **you need your Warrior**—but you need to integrate him with the rest.

2. The Magician – Creativity, Perception, and Flow

Where the Warrior pushes through resistance, the **Magician** sees around it. The Warrior charges the battlefield, but the Magician studies the terrain and rewrites the map. If the Warrior's gift is movement, the Magician's is **vision**—the capacity to see what isn't obvious, to find light in the fog, to shape possibility in the midst of chaos.

The Magician within you doesn't shout. He whispers. He shows up in the moments when your logic fails but your spirit knows. He's the one who says, "Wait—look again," when everyone else is panicking. He's the part of you that turns pain into wisdom, confusion into clarity, and conflict into strategy.

I didn't always trust this part of myself. As a man who came from hard circumstances—poverty, identity tension, trauma—I learned to survive through force, not finesse. I was raised to keep my head on a swivel, chest out, feet grounded. Street instincts. Warrior mode.

But in my 30s, especially after my breakdown, I realized that **grit alone wouldn't get me out.** I had become so used to fighting that I forgot how to *feel.* So used to pushing that I couldn't see what was *actually happening.* Every challenge looked like something to overpower, rather than understand.

I remember sitting alone in a quiet café in Atlanta one rainy afternoon— paper in front of me, pen in hand, unsure of what I was even trying to write. I had just been turned down for another job. I was exhausted—not just physically, but mentally. I felt like my hustle wasn't working. I was doing all the "right" things, but none of it was sticking. And for the first time, I let myself stop grinding. I just sat there and listened—not to the noise outside, but to the silence inside.

And something clicked.

I realized I wasn't asking better questions. I was only reacting. Only grinding. Only surviving.

That day, I wrote one question at the top of my journal:
"What if this breakdown is actually a re-route?"

That was the Magician speaking. The part of me that could zoom out. That could see the pattern. That could see not just what was falling apart—but what was being revealed.

From that space, I began to think differently. I stopped applying to jobs that didn't align with my values. I started reading books that challenged my beliefs, not just affirmed them. I began asking, "Where is the leverage in this?" instead of "Why is this happening to me?"

The Magician is flow. He's not afraid of chaos—he *transforms* it. He's the coach who doesn't yell during the fourth quarter—he calls the play with precision. He's the artist who doesn't try harder—but listens deeper. He's the entrepreneur who pivots while others panic.

He's the part of you that reclaims your story and reframes your identity. The Magician knows that **perspective is power**. And when he's awake, you start playing life on a higher level—not just reacting, but **designing**.

You might be thinking, "Okay, but how do I activate that part of me?" You start by **slowing down enough to listen.** You give yourself space to think. To observe. To connect dots. This isn't about being passive—it's about being **perceptive.** Big difference.

One of the biggest shifts for me came in how I began leading my team after starting my coaching and consulting work. At first, I approached everything like a mission—directives, strategies, execution. Warrior energy. But I noticed something was missing. I could feel the burnout. The culture was tense. Ideas weren't flowing.

Then I shifted.

Instead of running every meeting with action steps, I started with a question: **"What are we not seeing?"**

That changed everything. It created space. Dialogue. Flow. Suddenly, the pressure didn't drive us—it informed us. And from that space, innovation started showing up. The business didn't just grow—it **evolved.** Because the Magician had entered the room.

3. The Lover – Passion, Joy, and Connection

If the Warrior fights and the Magician sees, then the **Lover** reminds us why we're fighting and what we're fighting for.

The Lover isn't weak, soft, or indulgent. The Lover is the force within you that brings soul to structure. Emotion to execution. Meaning to momentum. Without the Lover, life becomes transactional. Robotic. Achievements lose their taste. Wins don't land. You're checking boxes, but you're not feeling the heartbeat behind any of it.

There was a point—just after my divorce and in the middle of my professional crash—where I couldn't feel anything. I had buried so much pain under performance that I forgot how to connect. I was working hard, pushing forward, making progress externally. But inside, I felt hollow. Like I was living on mute. No music. No laughter. No joy. Just goals and grit.

One night, after dropping my son back off with his mom, I came home to an empty apartment. I opened the fridge, grabbed a bottle of water, sat on the couch, and just stared. It wasn't sadness. It wasn't anger. It was **numbness.** And numbness is dangerous because it feels survivable… until you realize you've stopped living.

That was my wake-up call.

The Lover was asleep in me—and I didn't even know it.

So I started doing something radical: I started **re-learning how to feel.** I gave myself permission to reconnect with things I used to love before life got so serious. I picked up my guitar again. I started going for walks without headphones—just letting myself hear the sounds of the world again. I began cooking for pleasure, not performance. I even let myself cry at movies that hit too close to home.

You know what happened? **The fire came back.** Not all at once. Not with fireworks. But slowly, gently, steadily.

The Lover is the part of you that loves **without agenda.** That doesn't need productivity to justify its presence. It's the version of you who pauses to kiss your kid on the forehead, who laughs uncontrollably at a ridiculous meme, who dances in the kitchen while dinner's cooking. It's the part that reminds you: **life is not just about building—it's about being.**

In today's hustle culture, we've been conditioned to treat joy like dessert— only after the work is done. But the Lover teaches us that **joy is the fuel, not the reward.** Without joy, the Warrior burns out. Without connection, the Magician disconnects. Without love, the Sovereign becomes a tyrant.

Let me tell you something I've seen again and again in high performers I coach—men and women who run companies, raise families, build legacies. When they lose their **why**, they lose their **way.** And the "why" almost always lives in the Lover.

The Lover isn't lazy. The Lover is **sacred.** It's the counterbalance to the Warrior's grind. It keeps you human. It reminds you that you're not just a machine of discipline and execution—you're a soul with a rhythm and a heart that needs to be felt.

And look, this isn't just spiritual talk. It's science. Positive psychology confirms that **emotional connection, play, and intimacy** are not luxuries— they're **vital to mental health and sustainable performance.** Burnout isn't just physical exhaustion—it's **emotional disconnection.**

When I finally let the Lover back in, everything changed.

My work had more presence. My conversations had more compassion.

My decisions had more clarity—not because I slowed down, but because I **realigned.**

The Lover showed me that I don't have to abandon softness to hold strength. That vulnerability isn't a liability—it's a superpower. That feeling deeply doesn't make you less focused—it makes your focus more meaningful.

The first time I truly laughed after that dark season—I mean belly laughed, tears in the eyes, no filter—was during a simple moment with my son. We were playing this ridiculous game with action figures and I was doing all these weird voices. He looked at me and said, "Dad, you're kinda crazy—but the fun kind." And I felt something in me unlock.

That's the Lover. That's the return of joy.

So if you've been living like a machine—crushing goals, dominating timelines, showing up hard and focused—but you still feel something missing, ask yourself this:

"When was the last time I felt joy for no reason?"

When was the last time you created something just because it made you smile?
When was the last time you hugged someone longer than two seconds without worrying how it looked?
When was the last time you said "I love you" and meant it with your whole chest?

That's the Lover waking up. And when the Lover comes online, everything else in your life starts to breathe again.

4. The Sovereign – Wisdom, Vision, and Leadership

The Sovereign is the final archetype—but don't mistake it for the finish line. The Sovereign is the **center of gravity.** The one who pulls the others together. The stillness in the storm. The voice that doesn't just ask, "What now?"—but "What legacy will this create?"

When the Warrior is ready to go to battle, the Sovereign is the one who decides if the war is even worth fighting.

When the Magician is spinning ideas and frameworks, the Sovereign grounds it in values and purpose.

When the Lover wants to connect and feel, the Sovereign brings discernment—what's true, what's needed, what builds long-term health.

The Sovereign is your inner leader. Your king. Your queen. Your compass.

But let me be real with you—I ignored this voice for years.

For much of my adult life, I chased the next goal with blind hunger. Promotions. Paychecks. The marriage. The respect. The reputation. I told myself I was building—but I was actually **reacting.** Living by urgency. Making decisions from scarcity. And most dangerously—I was leading from ego.

You know when the Sovereign finally got my attention?

It wasn't during a win. It was when everything I thought made me powerful was stripped away.

After the job loss, the divorce, the breakdown, the silence—I remember standing in my bathroom, staring at myself in the mirror, and asking: **"Is this the life you actually believe in—or just the one you built out of fear?"**

That's when the Sovereign spoke—not in a yell, but in a whisper: **"You are not here to chase crowns. You're here to wear one."**

It broke me.

Because the truth is, I'd been moving like a man still trying to earn a seat at the table—when I was already carrying the authority to build my own. I didn't need permission. I needed **alignment**.

The Sovereign doesn't need external validation. It doesn't chase. It doesn't perform. It leads—not from force, but from **vision.**

It's the father who raises a daughter not by fear, but by example. It's the CEO who walks away from a profitable deal because the terms would damage

190

their integrity. It's the woman who walks into a room full of men and doesn't shrink, doesn't posture, but leads with quiet, undeniable presence.

The Sovereign is grounded. Rooted. Wise.

You can't bluff your way into this archetype. You grow into it. You **build** it—through trials, through truth, through the willingness to stop performing and start **becoming.**

One of the turning points in my own sovereignty came when I stopped leading to be impressive, and started leading to be **impactful.**

I had a young client, just out of college, brilliant mind, full of fire—but drowning in insecurity. His parents never believed in him. His mentors overlooked him. And every time he spoke, he second-guessed himself.

One day, I asked him, "What if leadership isn't about being the loudest in the room—but the clearest?"

That's when I saw something shift in him. His shoulders dropped. His breathing steadied. He sat back, looked me in the eye, and said, "Then maybe I'm already more of a leader than I thought."

That's the Sovereign. **It doesn't scream. It steadies.**

And when it's alive in you, your life becomes **ordered—not controlled.** Decisions flow from values, not pressure. Your presence shifts the energy in a room without you needing to say a word.

The Sovereign teaches you to zoom out. To lead with the long view. To stop chasing every fire and start architecting the future.

Without the Sovereign, the Warrior burns out. The Magician spirals in abstraction. The Lover forgets boundaries. But when the Sovereign governs, everything flows **with intention.**

The Integration – Bringing All Four Online

The trap isn't that we don't have these archetypes within us. The trap is that we live our lives stuck in just **one**—overused, overextended, and eventually, overwhelmed. You know the drill. You grind in **Warrior mode** for so long that your body aches and your relationships start to fracture. You float in **Magician energy**, full of ideas and awareness—but never take decisive action. You drown in **Lover emotion**, giving your heart to everyone and everything, but forget to protect your peace. You sit in **Sovereign detachment**, trying to make perfect decisions while avoiding the discomfort of vulnerability and risk.

Living in only one lane creates imbalance. And imbalance creates burnout, regret, disconnection, and confusion.

But wholeness?

Wholeness is integration. It's bringing all four online—so they can **build each other**, not battle each other.

Warrior + Magician + Lover + Sovereign = Activated You

You are not just strong.
You are not just smart.
You are not just passionate.
You are not just wise.

You are the sum of these energies, brought together under one roof: **you.**

The Warrior gives you motion.
The Magician gives you meaning.
The Lover gives you connection.
The Sovereign gives you vision.

This is what emotional architecture looks like.
Not a personality type. Not a gimmick. A full-system design for how to build your life **from the inside out.**

Let me give you some real talk about what integration feels like. I remember a moment—not too long ago—when I had to confront a major business decision.

I was offered a speaking engagement with a large financial institution. On paper, it looked perfect. Big brand. Big exposure. Big check. The Warrior in me wanted to jump—"Let's go! Let's win!" The Magician started strategizing the best pitch. The Lover was excited by the energy and the chance to inspire. It all felt right…

Until the Sovereign spoke.

The Sovereign reminded me to look deeper—into their leadership culture. Their values. Their reputation with underserved communities. And what I found didn't align. Their internal practices didn't match their marketing. It was performative. Hollow.

I said no.

And every part of me was activated in that moment. The Warrior was frustrated—we train to win. The Magician offered rationalizations—"It's just one talk." The Lover felt the loss of connection. But the Sovereign led.

Because that's what integration is: **every part has a voice—but only your values have the vote.**

The Real Blueprint: How to Build Integration

So how do you start bringing all four archetypes online?

Here's the practical **BUILD** system:

1. **Breathe into Awareness**

   o Each day, ask: "Which part of me is running the show today?"

   o Is it the Warrior who's burning out?

   o The Magician overthinking?

   o The Lover feeling neglected?

   o The Sovereign disconnected from purpose?

2. **Understand Your Imbalances**

   ○ Most people live in reaction to their default.

   ○ High achievers often live in Warrior. Artists drift in Magician. Empaths camp in Lover. Planners hide in Sovereign.

   ○ Balance isn't switching personalities—it's integrating strengths.

3. **Initiate Rituals for Activation**

   ○ Assign each archetype a ritual:

     ■ Warrior → Morning workouts or intentional discomfort

     ■ Magician → Journaling or vision mapping

     ■ Lover → Music, play, or presence with loved ones

     ■ Sovereign → Weekly reflection or values-based planning

4. **Lead with Values, Not Emotion**

   ○ Emotion is data—but values are direction.

   ○ Integration means your Sovereign stays in the seat, even when Warrior fire or Lover passion gets loud.

5. **Discern When to Lead from Which**

   ○ You don't need all four at once in every moment.

   ○ You need the **right one for the right context**—and the wisdom to know who leads, and when.

Warning, this is not a hack—it's a lifestyle. This isn't something you do once. It's not a checklist. It's a lifestyle of alignment. Integration is daily work. Hourly work. It means pausing in the middle of a heated conversation and asking, "What would the Sovereign do?" It means choosing to create art instead of numbing out with scrolling—letting the Magician move. It means putting the phone down to give your child your full attention—letting the Lover love.

It means saying yes to discomfort—because the Warrior doesn't back down. This is the deeper work. And most people won't do it. But you? You're building something real. And for that to last, it must be built on wholeness, not just willpower. Because in the end, your identity isn't found in one side of you. It's found when all of you comes together—whole, activated, and unshakably aligned.

How to Use This – A Practical Framework

It's one thing to understand the Warrior, Magician, Lover, and Sovereign. It's another thing to know **how to use them.** Not just in a crisis or in a moment of inspiration—but in the real, gritty hours of your everyday life. The days where nothing flows. The conversations that trigger old wounds. The moments where you know what's right, but you don't feel strong enough to do it.

This framework was never meant to live in theory. It was meant to live in your actual body. Your choices. Your breath. Your leadership. It was meant to become **a rhythm**, not a performance. And for that to happen, you need a system that brings each archetype online—on purpose.

I remember coaching a client—a hard-charging entrepreneur who had built a multimillion-dollar business by sheer Warrior energy. He didn't sleep much. He didn't laugh much. He operated like a machine: efficient, focused, relentless. But underneath all that drive was a man whose marriage was hanging by a thread. His kids barely spoke to him. And the only emotion he recognized in himself was exhaustion.

One day, I asked him, "When was the last time you made a decision from your Sovereign—not your panic?"

He paused.

Then said quietly, "I don't even know what that means."

That's when we started doing the work. The real work. Not the numbers.

Not the metrics. The work of **retraining his internal leadership system.** It started with this simple, powerful question: **Who's running the show right now?**

Step 1: Identify Your Default

Every one of us leans into one archetype more than the others. For some, it's the Warrior—always grinding, always proving. For others, it's the Magician—living in ideas, but disconnected from execution. Some get stuck in Lover energy—always giving, but with no protection of self. And some drift into Sovereign mode—aloof, planning endlessly but avoiding real risk.

Start here: Ask yourself, honestly, **"Which of these four am I living in 80% of the time?"**
Write it down. Own it. Don't judge it. Just notice it.

Then ask, "Which one is least active in me?" Where are you underdeveloped? What have you suppressed or neglected in the name of survival or structure?

Step 2: Anchor Each Archetype

The mind follows what the body anchors. That's why this can't stay intellectual. You need to **embody** each archetype.

Assign each one a posture. A phrase. A color. A breathing rhythm. A space in your body.

The Warrior may be anchored in your chest—broad shoulders, deep breath, fists clenched in commitment. The Magician might live in your forehead—clear gaze, relaxed brow, breath flowing in the nose, out the mouth. The Lover may rise from your gut—relaxed stance, hands open, heart soft. The Sovereign may rest in your spine—upright posture, shoulders back, slow and steady breath. This is how you start training your nervous system to recognize each state—not just as a concept, but as a presence.

Step 3: Build Daily Touchpoints

You don't become integrated by accident. It happens through **deliberate rhythm.**

Design moments in your day where you call each archetype forward.

In the morning, activate your Warrior with movement or discomfort. Do something hard—cold shower, early workout, 15 minutes of focused silence. It doesn't have to be big. It has to be **intentional**.

Midday, bring in the Magician. Pause your output. Journal for ten minutes. Ask yourself: "What am I missing?" "What's the pattern I need to see?" Read something that stretches you. Open your mental windows.

In the evening, awaken the Lover. Hug your kids longer. Turn off the screen. Eat dinner without distraction. Let your body soften. Let your presence return.

Weekly, give space to the Sovereign. Reflect. Plan. Zoom out. Ask yourself: "Am I building something I still believe in—or just something I started?"

The key is not perfection. The key is **presence**. Keep rotating these touchpoints into your life until they become automatic.

Step 4: Use the Inner Council

Once these energies are alive in you, begin treating them like a **council.**

When you're in a difficult decision, don't just white-knuckle it with the Warrior.
 Pause. Ask:

- What would the Warrior do?

- What would the Magician see?

- What does the Lover need?

- What does the Sovereign know?

Let their voices speak before you act. You don't have to let them all vote. But they all deserve to be heard.

Over time, this inner dialogue becomes second nature. Not because you've memorized a concept—but because you've trained your identity to include your **whole self**, not just the reactive parts.

Step 5: Train for Alignment, Not Intensity

Too many people try to force breakthroughs with unsustainable effort. They go hard. They get inspired. They burn out.

That's not integration. That's adrenaline.

Integrated people don't just know who they are. They **build structures around their wholeness.** They create space to be wise, emotional, creative, and strong—without apology and without burnout.

That's what this framework is here to do: **reconnect you to the full range of your power.**
 Not just for clarity—but for longevity.

Because power without integration is unstable.
And passion without structure eventually becomes pain.

But when you bring all four online—consistently—you stop reacting, and you start **architecting your life**.

The Inner Dialogue That Shapes Everything

There is a voice inside your head that narrates your life.
 Every moment. Every decision. Every fall. Every rise. It's speaking.

And for most of us, that voice doesn't sound like love.
It sounds like criticism. Caution. Doubt.
It sounds like every adult who ever belittled you. Every coach who dismissed you. Every friend who left when things got real.
It sounds like fear—dressed up in the language of "realism."
And we believe it. Because it's always been there.

But just because a voice is familiar, doesn't mean it's **true.**

I've sat across from men who built empires and still hated themselves. I've coached mothers who served everyone and still felt invisible. I've walked through my own seasons where the external looked successful—but the

198

internal dialogue was quietly violent.

That's the war no one talks about. Not the external pressures—but the **private conversations** that either reinforce your resilience or slowly dismantle it.

The truth is, you can't build anything that lasts if your inner world is falling apart.

No strategy will hold if your self-worth is bleeding behind the scenes.

No system will work if the voice in your head is sabotaging every win before you even celebrate it.

Your inner dialogue isn't a footnote to your success.
It's the *foundation*.

The Science of Self-Talk

This isn't self-help fluff.
Research from neuroscience shows that the brain is wired for **negativity bias**—meaning we naturally fixate more on threats than rewards.
That email you didn't respond to. That mistake you made in high school.
That time you spoke up and were dismissed.

These moments become scripts—and your brain, wanting to protect you, loops them. Over and over. Until they become identity.

But identity is not built from events.
Identity is built from **interpretation.**
And interpretation is shaped by what you say to yourself.

This is why some people rise after trauma—and others collapse. It's not about what happened. It's about what got *named.*
Did you call it failure—or foundation?
Did you call yourself broken—or becoming?

That voice is shaping your nervous system.
Your posture. Your tone. Your next decision.
It's not optional. It's not background noise.

It's the control center.

Rewriting the Script

There was a moment—during one of the lowest valleys of my life—where I heard that voice in my head say: "You're done. This is who you are now."

I almost believed it.
But then another voice whispered: "Or… this is the chapter where everything changes."

That voice was fainter, quieter. But it felt *truer.* And I made a decision that day—not to magically believe in myself, but to **start practicing better language**.

Not fake affirmations. Not hype.
Just truth. Spoken softly. But **repeated fiercely**.

"I'm not there yet. But I'm not staying here."
"I have made mistakes. But I'm still worthy."
"This pain is real. But it's not the whole story."

At first, it felt awkward. Even foolish.
But day by day, that new voice grew stronger.
Until one day, it wasn't a whisper anymore.
It was my default.

That's what this work is about.
Not becoming someone else.
But **becoming someone you can trust** when no one else is watching.

How to Begin Rebuilding Your Inner Dialogue

Start small.

When you catch yourself in criticism—pause. Don't argue with it. Don't judge it. Just *interrupt it.*

Then respond like you would to someone you love.

Would you speak to your child the way you speak to yourself?

Would you tear down your best friend for missing a deadline?
Would you shame your sibling for falling apart under pressure?

No.

You'd encourage. Redirect. Support.

You'd say: "You're better than this. But I still love you right here."

That's the tone your inner dialogue must learn to carry—not perfection, but **integrity with grace.**

It's okay to be honest. It's okay to hold standards.
But if your voice only critiques and never uplifts, you won't grow—you'll shrink.

And life's too short to spend another year building something externally that you can't enjoy internally.

Anchor It in Ritual

Change doesn't come from inspiration—it comes from *integration.*

So build rituals that reinforce your voice.

- In the mirror every morning, say one sentence that affirms your direction.

- After every win—pause. Celebrate. Don't rush past it.

- After every loss—pause. Learn. Don't tear yourself apart.

- Before every major decision—ask: "Am I choosing from fear or from alignment?"

These small moments shape the system. They rewire the script. They make **self-trust** your new operating system.

Your Inner World Builds the Outer One

If you've ever wondered why life feels out of balance—why things feel "off" even when they look "right"—look at your inner dialogue.

Is it empowering or exhausting?
Is it calling you forward—or beating you down?
Is it helping you BUILD—or keeping you surviving?

This is your invitation—not just to speak better, but to lead yourself better.
To show up in your own mind with the same clarity and care that you offer to the world.

Because when your inner dialogue becomes a place of strength, everything changes.
You walk taller. You breathe deeper. You lead wiser.
And you stop waiting for external proof—because you've already built **internal proof**.

The voice that once doubted you… now believes.
The voice that once shamed you… now holds you to your standard.
The voice that once whispered defeat… now declares destiny.

This is what changes lives.
This is how you become unshakable.

Say it again.
Say it like it matters.
Say it until your nervous system catches up.

I am enough. I matter. My life is worth living—out loud.

What Mental Toughness Really Means

Mental toughness isn't the highlight reel you see on your feed—those perfectly curated videos of people grinding at 4:00 a.m., throwing weights around or preaching about "no excuses." It's not the rah-rah adrenaline of weekend seminars where people shout about positivity while avoiding the weight of real pain. And it's definitely not the mask many of us wear—the one that looks like strength on the outside but hides a quiet collapse inside.

Real mental toughness is quieter. It's less about performance and more about presence. It's the ability to remain rooted when everything around you feels like it's falling apart. It's waking up on the 38th day after you've lost your job, your marriage is barely holding, your bank account is negative, and your chest feels like it's holding bricks—but still brushing your teeth, lacing your shoes, and leading yourself one honest moment at a time.

I remember when I was battling depression while trying to parent, stay sober, and still show up in the world like I had it all together. I would sit in my car in a grocery store parking lot with the ignition off, the radio low, and tears in my eyes. No one saw those moments. No Instagram post. No motivational caption. Just me, and the war in my own head. What kept me going wasn't some mythical "grind." It was the voice that whispered: "You don't have to win today. You just have to not quit."

That's mental toughness. The choice to **stay**. To breathe. To pick up your kid from school even when your heart feels shattered. To go to therapy. To ask for help. To show up to the meeting. To keep moving, one honest step at a time.

Mental Toughness Is Built, Not Born. We often assume toughness is a personality trait—something you either have or you don't. But mental toughness isn't innate. It's constructed. Developed. Sharpened through thousands of moments where you don't feel like it—but you still show up. It's built through adversity that strips away who you thought you were and reveals what you're actually made of.

Every betrayal. Every layoff. Every diagnosis. Every failure. These aren't interruptions. They're initiations. And the question isn't whether you'll go through hard things—the question is, **will you lead yourself through them**?

Toughness isn't "powering through" until you break. It's the ability to pause when you need to—not out of weakness, but out of strategy. It's saying, "I need rest," without shame. It's choosing to not react in anger, to hold your peace, to speak with intention even when you want to scream. You build it like a muscle—through deliberate practice, over time. There are **Five Pillars of Real Mental Toughness.**

1. Emotional Agility: The Power to Feel Without Losing Control

Mental toughness begins in the mind—but it's forged in your ability to manage your emotions. Not suppress them. Not drown in them. But lead them.

Emotional agility means you can name what you're feeling without letting it run the show. It's the practice of saying, "I'm anxious right now—but I'm not broken. I'm angry—but I'm still in control." This isn't weakness—it's leadership. And the more clearly you name your emotions, the more power you regain.

I remember walking into a meeting after getting bad news about my grandmother's health. My mind was spinning. My emotions were raw. I wanted to cancel. Instead, I excused myself for five minutes, stepped outside, took deep breaths, and asked, "What's true? What's needed?" I named the fear—but I didn't hand it the mic. I reentered that room centered, not because I was fine, but because I chose to be present.

Emotional agility lets you move from reactivity to intentionality. It's the skill of feeling without flooding. And it changes everything.

2. Stress Conditioning: Building Pressure Tolerance by Design

The military doesn't train soldiers for peace—they train for chaos. Not just with information—but with **exposure**. Cold, exhaustion, surprise, disorientation. Why? Because when the real storm hits, you default to your level of conditioning.

You don't become tough when things fall apart. You become tough by training for it before it happens.

For me, it looked like learning to stay calm in the middle of custody battles. Taking deep breaths when my heart wanted to rage. Saying "no" to distractions that felt like relief but were just escapes. It looked like therapy. Cold showers. Speaking on stages after panic attacks.

None of those moments were glamorous. But each one built my capacity to **hold pressure without breaking**. Each one whispered, "You can carry this. You've done harder."

Stress conditioning doesn't mean suffering without reason. It means exposing yourself, in small doses, to challenge—so you become someone who can stay steady when it matters most.

3. Cognitive Reframing: Changing the Story You Tell Yourself

The mind can't tell the difference between what's real and what's rehearsed. So if you rehearse stories of defeat, of shame, of failure—you live them. If you rehearse empowerment, possibility, and meaning—you build momentum.

I used to see every setback as proof that I wasn't good enough. If something didn't work out, I internalized it. "There I go again. Always messing things up." That story kept me stuck. It wasn't until I learned to reframe those moments—"This is training. This is information. This is part of the process"—that everything shifted.

Several years ago, I was rejected from a job I desperately needed. Instead of spiraling, I said out loud, "That wasn't mine. Keep building." That wasn't fake optimism. That was a trained pivot. A conscious shift from panic to progress.

Reframing doesn't mean lying to yourself. It means telling a **truer truth**. One that includes your power. One that keeps you moving forward.

4. Pre-Commitment to Principles: Knowing Who You Are Before the Fire

Mental toughness isn't about how you respond under pressure. It's about what you've decided **before** the pressure hits.

You don't become disciplined in the crisis. You live out the discipline you trained when things were calm. This is why values matter. Because in the storm, you don't rise to the moment—you default to your identity.

For me, I pre-committed to honesty. To not ghost people, even when I'm overwhelmed. To show up to parent-teacher conferences, even when I'm exhausted. To not yell, even when my patience is gone. I fail at times, sure. But the **pre-commitment** holds me steady.

One of the most powerful ways to train mental toughness is to write down five principles that guide you—then revisit them every morning. When the world shakes, your roots hold.

5. Recovery and Regulation: The Unseen Strength

Here's the lie: "Strong people don't rest."
Here's the truth: **Strong people recover. Smart people regulate. Resilient people plan for both.**

You don't grow in the gym. You grow in the rest between sets. The same is true in life. Recovery is not indulgence—it's integration.

I used to think burning out was noble. "I'm doing it all. Look how strong I am." Then I'd crash—emotionally, physically, relationally. It took years for me to understand that true resilience meant building rest into the rhythm. It meant breathing. Journaling. Getting off the grid. Saying no.

When I did, I showed up **more powerful**. Not because I was doing more—but because I was doing it from center.

Mental Toughness Is Embodied, Not Announced. You don't have to shout to be strong. You don't have to prove it to everyone. Mental toughness isn't something you tell the world about—it's something the world feels when you walk in the room.

It's in the way you carry yourself. In your tone. In your calm during conflict. In your presence when others panic.

It's the way you speak to yourself when no one is listening.

It's built slowly. Quietly. Over time. And it becomes your edge—not because it's flashy—but because it's **unshakable**.

1. Emotional Agility: The Power to Feel Without Losing Control

Resilient people are not emotionally numb. They are emotionally agile. Emotional agility is the ability to navigate feelings with both honesty and control—acknowledging the truth of your emotional state without becoming hostage to it. In today's culture, people are taught to either suppress emotion entirely or let it rule them. Neither strategy works. Suppression turns into burnout and breakdown. Overindulgence turns into impulsivity and regret. Emotional agility is the third path—the empowered one.

The phrase, coined by Harvard Medical School psychologist Dr. Susan David, defines this skill as the capacity to face thoughts and emotions with openness, clarity, and a willingness to learn. In one study published in the journal *Behavior Research and Therapy*, emotional agility was linked to higher life satisfaction, better performance at work, and lower stress levels—even during crises. It's a high-performance tool, not a soft skill. The most composed leaders—on the battlefield, in the boardroom, in the home—are not the ones who feel the least, but the ones who manage their feelings most effectively.

Consider what happens during conflict or crisis: the body tightens, the mind races, and emotions surge. If you haven't trained yourself to stay grounded in that storm, you become reactive. You say things you regret. You spiral into assumptions. You either lash out or shut down. Resilient people train to pause. To name what they feel without judgment. "I'm anxious. I'm frustrated. I'm overwhelmed." And then, rather than react, they respond—intentionally. That's emotional leadership. That's power under pressure.

There's a growing field of neurobiology that confirms this. When individuals name their emotions—out loud or in writing—they reduce the activity in the amygdala, the fear center of the brain, and increase regulation in the prefrontal cortex, the part responsible for decision-making. Naming emotions disarms their power. It brings you back to center.

This doesn't mean you become robotic or suppress reality. On the contrary, resilient people feel their emotions fully. But they don't let those feelings dictate their choices. They lead them. This is not about ignoring pain—it's about directing it. Emotional agility lets you process grief without being consumed by it. It helps you lead through anger without being destructive. It allows you to face fear without being hijacked by it.

And like any skill, it's trainable.

Daily practices such as mindfulness, somatic awareness, and journaling sharpen this skill. One practical exercise: the "Name it to tame it" technique—used in therapy and executive coaching—where you pause, describe your emotion as precisely as possible, and ask: "What is this feeling trying to tell me?" Not "How do I get rid of it?" but "What is it signaling?" This shift changes everything. It transforms your relationship with discomfort from avoidance to inquiry.

Resilience begins with this: the discipline to feel—and the power to choose how you respond.

2. Stress Conditioning: Building Pressure Tolerance by Design

If emotional agility is the art of leading your inner world, stress conditioning is the physical and psychological training ground that prepares you for adversity before it arrives. This pillar is not about survival after the fact—it's about strategic exposure to stress so you can operate effectively when the stakes are high.

We don't rise to our level of goals; we fall to the level of our training. This is a principle embedded in elite military, sports, and performance psychology circles. Navy SEALs, Olympians, crisis negotiators—they all understand one thing: high-pressure moments don't create champions. They reveal them. And what's revealed is the training that has been quietly done in the dark, long before the spotlight ever hit.

Stress conditioning is not about seeking pain for pain's sake. It's about exposing your system to controlled stress so that you develop resilience at the level of your nervous system. When done right, it creates psychological immunity. This is what psychologists call "stress inoculation"—training your brain and body to handle future stressors through graduated exposure today.

Let's make this practical.

Cold water exposure. High-stakes conversations. Public speaking. Voluntary discomfort in workouts. Difficult feedback sessions. Even saying "no" to things that stretch your boundaries. These are all forms of controlled stress. They don't have to be massive. They just need to be consistent. And they need to challenge you—enough to make your nervous system adapt, but not so much that it overwhelms you.

Why does this matter?

Because the nervous system is designed for survival, not optimization. When stress spikes and you haven't conditioned yourself, your body floods with cortisol and adrenaline. The amygdala hijacks the prefrontal cortex. You lose access to your best thinking. You forget your training. You freeze, flee, or fight—not from strategy, but from reflex. But when you train your nervous system to experience stress without spiraling, you regain control. You increase what neuroscientists call "vagal tone"—your body's ability to regulate stress and return to calm faster.

In one study published in *Psychoneuroendocrinology*, individuals who regularly engaged in mild, voluntary discomfort (like cold showers or intermittent fasting) had lower inflammatory responses and better emotional regulation under high-pressure situations. This is biological proof: stress conditioning works.

But there's a deeper level here. Stress conditioning also trains your identity.

Every time you voluntarily step into discomfort, you reinforce the belief: "I do hard things." You wire a new self-concept—one that sees discomfort not as danger, but as training. Over time, your confidence stops being situational. It becomes structural. Not dependent on outcomes, but anchored in the fact that you've faced challenge and stayed standing.

This is why resilient people seem "unbothered" in chaos. It's not that they're fearless. It's that they've felt fear and practiced holding it. They've trained their biology to respond, not react. They don't break because they've bent—again and again—on purpose.

So the question is not whether stress will show up. It will. The question is: will you be ready?

Resilience isn't built in the fire. It's built in the warm-up. It's built in the daily disciplines that stretch you slightly beyond comfort. One degree at a time. One decision at a time. Until pressure no longer derails you—it sharpens you.

Train for the storm, and when it comes, you'll move through it—not with panic, but with poise.

3. Cognitive Reframing: Shifting Perspective to Empower Your Response

When life tests you, the hardest challenges rarely come from the outside. They come from how you interpret what's happening inside your mind. Cognitive reframing isn't about denying reality or sugarcoating pain—it's about seeing events through a lens that gives you power, not paralysis.

You know the difference between someone who collapses under pressure and someone who responds with clarity? It's not a difference in intelligence or talent. It's a difference in meaning.

Picture two leaders facing the same crisis. One sees failure. The other sees feedback. One feels victimized. The other feels challenged. That shift isn't luck—it's a deliberate mental pivot. It's what psychologists call "cognitive reappraisal," the ability to reinterpret stressful events so they no longer hijack your emotions but guide your response.

Reframing starts with language. How you talk about your situation isn't neutral—it shapes your entire neurological and emotional reaction. Saying "I'm overwhelmed" triggers cortisol. Saying "I'm navigating complexity" engages the prefrontal cortex, inviting strategic engagement. Subtle, but profound.

Here's a better way to look at it: when your instinct is to say, *"I can't handle this,"* shift to, *"I'm learning how to handle this."* When the thought creeps in, *"Everything is falling apart,"* swap it with, *"Things are shifting, and I'm finding my footing."* Those small changes aren't semantics—they're strategy. They flip the brain's stress switch from panic to problem-solving. It's not about pretending things are easier than they are—it's about speaking to yourself in a way that keeps your mind open to possibility instead of shutting it down with fear.

In trauma research, patients who view their suffering as meaningful— something that has shaped them—recover faster and build greater resilience.

In workplace studies, teams that reframe problems as challenges rather than threats achieve more and burn out less. That's not spirituality or motivational fluff—it's science and social science. Framing determines outcome.

Reframing doesn't deny difficulty. It embraces it. It acknowledges the brutal truth, then anchors you in what you control: your response. It transforms disempowerment into agency. Victim into strategist. Fear into fuel.

And here's where the power really lies: when reframing becomes automatic, you start to pre-empt your biology. You build a habit of response, not reaction. The next time the alarm goes off—with stress or disruption—you're no longer a hostage to emotion. You're a leader, even when nothing else feels stable.

This is leadership under pressure. This is the mastery of mind.

4. Pre-Commitment to Principles: Lead Before the Storm Hits

Real resilience isn't reactive. It's pre-emptive. You don't wait for chaos to determine who you are. You decide before the pressure rises—and that decision becomes your anchor.

Pre-commitment to principles means choosing your values ahead of time and rehearsing them until they become non-negotiable. Why does that matter? Because under stress, you won't default to your ideal self—you'll default to your most practiced one. In the middle of a crisis, you won't have time to philosophize. You'll act on instinct. And unless that instinct has been formed through conscious choice, it will be dictated by fear, impulse, or survival mode.

Principles aren't slogans. They're systems. They guide behavior when the environment becomes unpredictable. They're the compass when emotions flare and your nervous system is screaming for escape or aggression. If you've ever said something in anger you regretted, if you've ever broken a promise to yourself under pressure—you've lived the consequences of not having a practiced set of principles.

This isn't about moral posturing. It's about strategic leadership. Navy SEALs, elite athletes, high-stakes negotiators—they all rely on pre-commitment. They train values like they train skills. Honor. Precision. Discipline. Not because they want to look good—but because their lives depend on it.

In your world, it might not be life or death. But your reputation, your relationships, your trajectory? They are absolutely on the line every time you're tested. Every time you're tempted to compromise for convenience, or back down because of discomfort, your principles decide for you.

And when those principles are rooted, practiced, and reinforced—they hold.

So what are your non-negotiables?

What do you believe about how to treat people—even when they don't deserve grace?

What do you believe about your worth—when no one's applauding?

What do you believe about your mission—when your results aren't catching up?

Write them down. Rehearse them daily. Embed them deep. Because the moment will come—the betrayal, the failure, the spotlight, the uncertainty—and when it does, your pre-commitment is what will carry you through without collapsing your integrity.

This is the architecture of an unshakable identity.

5. Recovery and Regulation: The Hidden Pillars of Resilience

There is a myth—still glorified in certain circles—that resilience is about how long you can grind without stopping. That the strongest among us are those who never slow down, never step back, never take a breath. But here's the reality, backed by psychology, neuroscience, and physiology: the people who win long-term are not the ones who burn the brightest—they're the ones who recover the smartest.

Resilience without regulation is a time bomb. You might hold it together for a season—outperforming, overdelivering, outrunning your emotions—but eventually, the body keeps score. Chronic stress becomes chronic illness.

Emotional fatigue becomes relationship damage. Hustle without healing becomes collapse.

That's why the truly resilient prioritize recovery as a core discipline—not a reward after burnout.

It begins with nervous system regulation. Not just stress management, but proactive care of the body's core systems—sleep, breath, rest, and emotional processing. Studies from the American Institute of Stress show that consistent high stress not only impairs cognitive function but erodes immune resilience and decision-making capacity. Translation? Your unregulated hustle is not efficient—it's self-sabotage.

So, what does recovery look like?

It looks like honoring rest—not as indulgence, but as integration. It looks like solitude, not isolation—intentional stillness where the mind recalibrates and the soul re-centers. It looks like breathwork, therapy, journaling, and movement—not just for physical health, but to empty the emotional trash your system has been storing.

Most importantly, it looks like rejecting the lie that stillness means weakness. Because the truth is: anyone can grind themselves to the bone. It takes far more strength to lead yourself back to center. To know when to say, "Today, I recover—so tomorrow, I lead."

And here's the beautiful paradox: the more you prioritize regulation, the more powerful you become. You stop reacting to every external noise. You stop personalizing every setback. You stop chasing chaos and start designing clarity.

This is not about slowing down to stop. It's about slowing down to sustain. Because emotional regulation isn't just about surviving storms—it's about building the emotional capacity to lead through them.

So, breathe. Rest. Recover with intention. Because what you're building requires not just fire—but fuel. And no matter how strong you are, every system runs better when it's not running on fumes.

Strategies for Navigating Adversity and Uncertainty

When adversity hits, you don't need a motivational quote. You need a system. You need clarity. Because chaos doesn't ask if you're ready—it just shows up. Sometimes with sirens. Sometimes with silence. A lost job. A phone call you didn't expect. A wave of anxiety in the middle of a Tuesday morning. And when that chaos hits, your nervous system doesn't care about hype. It needs structure. It needs something to hold onto.

That's why the most resilient people don't rely on inspiration when the world tilts—they rely on rhythm. On grounded, repeatable rituals that don't need motivation to activate. In the military, they're called "baseline behaviors." Athletes call them "non-negotiables." But at their core, they are lifelines—tiny anchors that keep you from drifting into emotional whiteout when the pressure rises.

I learned this the hard way. Years ago, after an unexpected layoff, my finances were in freefall and my self-worth was unraveling with it. I wasn't just stressed—I was spinning. I'd wake up with tightness in my chest and spiral into worry before I even touched the floor. That's when a mentor challenged me with a simple question: "What's your grounding routine?" I didn't have one. I had willpower. I had drive. But I didn't have a system. And that was my blind spot.

So I started small. I committed to waking the body before touching the phone. Just five minutes of stretching, breathing, and movement. It felt insignificant at first—but slowly, it changed everything. The motion shook me out of mental paralysis. Then I added morning journaling—just one page. A brain dump. A mental release. That cleared space to think. Then came the daily text to my accountability partner. Not to vent. Just to say, "I'm in the fight." It gave my nervous system something it hadn't felt in weeks: support. And each night, no matter how chaotic the day, I wrote down one thing that went right. Some days, it was just, "I didn't quit." But that was enough. That ritual became a rope I held onto until my feet were back under me.

These practices are more than productivity hacks. They are **nervous system reset tools**. Here's the framework I now teach and live by:

- **Wake the body first.** Don't let your mind lead the day. Let your movement do it. Stretch. Walk. Cold shower. Train. When your body shifts, your state follows. The Warrior archetype in you needs physical activation to engage with strength.

- **Offload your mind.** Chaos collects. So release it. Dump your thoughts without filters—what's heavy, what's loud, what's confusing. The Magician needs room to reframe and reorient. Clarity comes when clutter is cleared.

- **Anchor with connection.** Call someone safe. Not to fix you— but to see you. The Lover in you needs presence. Emotional regulation accelerates when you feel seen, not when you're trying to power through alone.

- **Reclaim your wins.** Even in grief, there is growth. Ask yourself nightly: What did I handle well? What did I not run from? What did I learn? The Sovereign in you needs reflection. It's how you lead from wisdom, not wound.

Because here's the truth: in adversity, **simplicity is strength**. Complexity breaks under pressure. But simple systems? They hold.

This is why **resilient people don't wait until they're drowning to build lifeboats**. They train daily to stay afloat—before the waters rise.

But let's clear up a myth right now: rest is not weakness. Reset is not failure. Hustle without recovery isn't resilience—it's ego wrapped in exhaustion. And I've lived that too.

There was a season where I believed I had to be "on" all the time. Showing up. Performing. Outworking everyone. Until my body said no. Sleep collapsed. My temper shortened. My heart raced even at rest. I had ignored every warning signal—and called it strength.

Real strength is **not sprinting until collapse**. It's knowing when to stop. When to regulate. When to reset—not as an act of surrender, but as an act of sovereignty.

`1werthjre1wrtteam stays in combat 24/7. They rotate. They recover. They restore—so they can re-engage at full power. You must do the same. Whether through solitude, silence, therapy, prayer, nature, or just sitting with your breath, recovery must be embedded—not postponed.

Because a grounded nervous system makes better decisions. A rested mind sees more clearly. A soul that breathes becomes a stabilizer—not a reactor.

And if you don't pause intentionally, you will break eventually. That's not a threat—it's biology.

But even with systems, **stress sneaks in**. Not like a thunderclap—but like a leaky faucet. A glance that felt like rejection. A text you left unread. A decision you keep postponing. It all layers. And then, out of nowhere, you're triggered by something minor—because your system was already maxed out.

This is what I call **The Stress Spiral**. And if you don't disrupt it early, it will drive you into anxiety, fatigue, or shutdown before you realize it's happening.

That's why I use the **4-Minute Reset™**, and why I teach it. Not a spa day. Not a vacation. Four minutes. Here's how:

1. **Mind Sweep.**
   Dump your thoughts. No structure. No curation. Just release. Like taking mental trash to the curb.

2. **Reflect & Refocus.**
   Ask: What's mine to carry? What matters most right now? What can wait? Let that awareness rearrange your urgency.

It seems simple—because it is. But it works. I've used this mid-meeting, before public speaking, during parenting meltdowns. The reset isn't dramatic. It's effective.

Because what grounds you, governs you. And if you can govern your state, you can govern your next move.

Let's end with this:

Chaos is inevitable. Peace is optional. But that option is yours to claim. You may not control what enters your life—but you absolutely control what you give access to your nervous system. And sometimes, peace is a whispered boundary. A decision to not take the bait. A breath. A pause. A sentence you say out loud:

"I won't let you steal my peace."

It's not weakness. It's wisdom. And wisdom is the real flex.

Transmutation: Turning Struggle Into Strength

Fear has a way of shrinking us—turning ambition into survival, purpose into pause. When we let fear guide us, we start chasing approval, clinging to comfort, and guarding what we have instead of stepping into who we're meant to become. But let me tell you what happens when you stop fearing loss—whether that's status, money, image, or validation—you gain clarity. And clarity becomes leverage.

I remember what happened when I let go of clinging. I had just weathered a personal betrayal—one that shattered my sense of belonging and self-worth. For weeks, I lived with my heart braced, operating like every moment was an ambush. I wasn't leading. I was surviving—gritting my way through grief. Then one morning, I was staring at myself in the mirror and realized my reflection looked small. Not broken. Small. I felt ready to step into possibility, but something inside me wasn't playing catch-up.

That's where clarity reclaimed me. The fear didn't vanish. But I stopped reacting. Instead, I leaned into my values. I started speaking with more authority, moving with less hesitation, loving with less armor. I began to negotiate from conviction, not desperation. I served without needing applause. That's courage. Not recklessness—but readiness.

Courage isn't the absence of fear. It's mastery over it—feeling its weight and choosing to lead anyway.

Failure: The Relentless Mentor. Failure isn't a roadblock—it's the road. It never coddles you. It strips away your illusions. Every person you admire carries scars shaped by failure. But those scars are not chains. They're tools. Refiner's marks.

We fear failure not because of its mechanics—but because of the stories we tell ourselves. "I failed" becomes "I am a failure." Trap. Prison. But what if those words were tools? "Feedback." "Lesson." "Blueprint for what changes next time."

In one of the rock-bottom seasons of my life—jobless, emotionally frayed, shot through with doubt—failure felt like a verdict. But I started to view it as a revision. I closed my eyes, named the failure, then asked, "What part of me is rising from this?" That shift didn't erase the pain. But it rewrote the narrative.

This is where true leaders live: in the quiet alchemy of failure turned into fuel.

Embodiment Over Explanation. When failure is buried—ignored, avoided, rationalized—your body holds the score. Your chest tightens. Your breath shallows. Shame settles like sediment. Logic won't free you. Emotion must. You must feel through the pain. Breathe it. Release it. Your body is not your hurdle. It's your guide. Real clarity flows through somatic healing—through breath, through release, through the gristle and grace of being human.

From Reaction to Reflection Treat failure like a reset button, not a full stop. Don't just react—review. What worked? What failed? What will you do differently? This isn't blame. It's refinement. That's where precision is born—not from perfect results, but from intentional revision.

Pressure doesn't have to crush you. You can channel it. Turn anxiety into focus. Redirect heartbreak into empathy. Convert anger into aligned action. That is emotional intelligence at its highest.

Adversity doesn't comfort you—but it transforms you. Fire weakness away and reveal depth. If you've failed, cried, or been shattered—you've already built endurance. **Finding Gift in the Ashes.** Your soul has been tested. And it emerged stronger.

The next time you visit your darkest moment—whisper: "I am grateful for my mistake." Not because it felt good. But because it woke something in you. Something real. Something ready.

Survival Mode Isn't Sustainment

Survival mode might save you in a crisis—but living there day to day destroys you. Waking up clenched. Breathing shallow. Feeling threatened in silence. That's not living—it's bracing. You cannot build while you're bracing.

True resilience is stepping out of survival mode intentionally. Saying, "This moment doesn't require armor. It requires alignment." Even in war-torn places—real or internal—you can heal. You can live at your edge without being consumed by it.

Because healing begins where hiding ends.

Scarred, Not Stained. Resilience isn't immunity to scars—it's refusal to be defined by them. You've made mistakes. You've been derailed. Yet you breathe. You rebuild. You anchor in belonging. You're still here—and that means you're still becoming. Worthy. Alive. Always recovering.

That's real power. Not domination over others—but sovereignty over self. The world around you will always shift. But when your inner world is steady, chaos loses its grip.

Becoming Fireproof. Stability isn't about stillness around you—it's stillness within you. Like a stone in a river, water flows around—not over—you. That's integrity. That's presence. Quiet. Unshakable.

Build that.

Practice it in breath. In prayer. In stillness. Not to escape life—but to anchor into it.

This is not spiritual fluff. It's emotional survival. Not avoiding storms—but holding fire without turning to ash.

Resilience is not bouncing back—it's bending and building. It's refusing collapse, choosing breath through battle, and making strength your rhythm.

You were not born to merely survive. You were born to lead. To shatter your limitations. To stretch beyond fear.

Close this chapter knowing this: the test will come. But with clarity, courage, and a system built to hold—you will endure. You won't just endure—you'll emerge. Stronger. Wiser. Sovereign.

BREAK THE BOTTLE CHALLENGE — Chapter 8

Resilience isn't a theory—it's a lived practice. It's not something you admire from a distance or wear as a badge when life is calm. It's something you embody, especially when the pressure mounts and the ground beneath you shakes. This challenge isn't about a temporary high. It's not motivational fluff. It's a reset—a declaration. A recommitment to becoming the kind of person who doesn't shatter under stress, but sharpens because of it.

This is your invitation. Your moment to draw a line in the sand. To say: *I lead myself now. I build myself now. I rise now.*

Let's begin.

1. Revisit a Moment That Tried to Break You—And Didn't

Pause. Close your eyes. Go back to *that* moment.

The one where it all felt like too much—when the weight was unbearable, the uncertainty overwhelming, and hope seemed out of reach. Maybe it was heartbreak. Maybe it was a betrayal. Maybe it was a loss so sharp it split your identity. And yet... you're still here.

Ask yourself:

- What brought me back to my feet?

- What inner strength did I discover that I never knew I had?

- What lesson did that pain teach me that I carry with me now?

This isn't nostalgia. It's proof.

221

You've already survived what once felt impossible. You've already overcome more than you give yourself credit for. Let that memory serve as evidence—not that the world is easy, but that *you* are equipped.

You are not starting from scratch. You're starting from experience.

2. Choose One Mental Toughness Practice—And Build a Ritual Around It

Resilience is not built in a single moment of triumph. It's built in micro-decisions. Daily disciplines. Small, strategic acts of self-leadership that become your armor.

Choose one toughness habit. Just one. Then commit to practicing it daily—not for show, but for strength.

Options:

- **Breathwork** – Take control of your nervous system. Inhale with intention. Exhale chaos. Three minutes a day can rewire your response to stress.

- **Cold Exposure** – Step into deliberate discomfort. A cold shower. An icy plunge. A moment of resistance that trains your mind to stay calm under pressure.

- **Journaling** – Put your thoughts on paper. Not to vent, but to sort. To see clearly. To separate emotion from reaction. Reflection breeds awareness—and awareness breeds power.

- **Evening Review** – End your day with presence. Ask: "Where did I show up as a leader today? Where can I evolve tomorrow?" Insight builds incrementally.

Set your ritual. Protect it. Not because it's trendy, but because it recalibrates your identity. This is about progress, not perfection. Consistency, not heroics.

3. Declare Who You Are—Out Loud

Let your nervous system hear it. Let your past hear it. Let your fear hear it. This isn't performance. This is identity reprogramming.

Say this with your chest. Not as a wish—but as a vow:

"Whatever hits me next—

I will recover.
I will rebuild.
I will rise.
My pain will not define me.
My response will."

Say it twice if you need to. Write it down. Record it. Let it echo.

This isn't just affirmation. This is embodiment. A clear and present reminder that your resilience is not theoretical—it's active. Daily. Lived.

Because you're not here to cope.

You're here to conquer.

You're not here to be defined by what hurt you.

You're here to be shaped by how you rise.

RESOURCES

Download the Tool: 90-Day Sprint Calendar
Turn your goals into focused, actionable 90-day sprints. Build traction without burnout.

Available at: btbprograms.com/free-resources

THE POWER OF PERSPECTIVE— SEEING OPPORTUNITIES WHERE OTHERS SEE OBSTACLES

"Perspective isn't what you see—it's what you choose to believe about what you see. Change the lens, and you change the limits."

— Break The Bottle

The Mind War—Winning the Battle in Your Head

You don't live the life you want.
You live the life your mind allows.

It's a bold claim—but one forged in reality, especially for those who've stood under hostile skies with a rifle in hand and death nearby. In a combat zone, the battle doesn't start with a trigger pull. It starts with the dialogue between your ears. Long before a bullet flies, you've already fought through fear, doubt, memory, and meaning. The battlefield is not just physical terrain—it's mental territory. And that war—the one waged silently in the mind—is the one most of us ignore. But it is, without question, the most defining.

We often treat our thoughts like background noise—barely audible, ever-present, and rarely challenged. But what goes unnoticed often goes unchecked. And what goes unchecked grows. Research shows we process between 12,000 and 60,000 thoughts per day. An overwhelming 95% are repeats from the day before. And 85% of those are negative. That means most of what you think today—what shapes your mood, your actions, your identity—isn't new, and it's not helpful. It's a loop. And unless interrupted, that loop becomes your life.

I remember a night from my final deployment, lying awake in my AAV Tank. There was no attack, no noise—just the hum of my own thoughts echoing louder than gunfire. Every regret, every "what-if," every failure rose like smoke in the dark. That night wasn't marked by external danger—it was marked by internal warfare. My body was safe. My mind wasn't. And that's the truth for many people walking around today—outwardly stable, inwardly under siege.

This is neurological warfare. Your brain isn't neutral ground—it's contested territory. Without intervention, it defaults to the most familiar routes: fear, shame, insecurity, distraction. These are well-worn neural paths, carved by repetition. And in times of stress or uncertainty, your brain doesn't search for truth—it searches for the fastest route. That route is often toxic because it's been rehearsed more than anything else. What you repeat, you perform. What you believe, you become.

So the question becomes: who or what is in command of your internal terrain?

If you were a strategist set on sabotaging someone's life, you wouldn't need to touch their bank account or their health. You'd simply alter the story they tell themselves. You'd hijack the narrative in their mind. And they would self-destruct—one compromised belief at a time. That's how powerful thought is. That's why mastering your mental battlefield isn't a luxury—it's a necessity.

Let's get clear on something: not every thought in your head is from your head.

Just because a voice sounds like yours doesn't mean it originates from you. Research confirms that intrusive thoughts—disturbing, unwanted, often completely uncharacteristic ideas—occur regularly in over 90% of people. These aren't indicators of who you are. They're indicators of how the mind collects noise. The real danger isn't the thought itself—it's when you start to agree with it. That agreement is what turns a passing whisper into a permanent stronghold.

It begins innocently: "You'll never make it." "You're too late." "You always mess up." These phrases repeat, and repetition becomes familiarity. Familiarity, unchecked, becomes belief. Belief, rehearsed, becomes identity. And suddenly, you're not just thinking the thought—you're living it.

Your mind is soil. Every thought is a seed. Some are weeds. Some are roots. What you nurture becomes your environment. And eventually, your environment becomes your identity. That's why you must become ruthless in guarding your mental perimeter. If your brain were a military compound, you wouldn't let anyone walk in unvetted. So why allow unfiltered content, unchecked self-talk, and unchallenged beliefs to live rent-free in your head?

Here's where the **Exposure Effect** comes into play—a psychological principle showing that repetition breeds comfort. And comfort, over time, breeds belief. It's not truth that shapes you—it's repetition. That's why marketing slogans work. That's why social media algorithms lock your attention. That's why doomscrolling isn't just a bad habit—it's brain training.

Your brain's **Reticular Activating System (RAS)** filters your environment based on what you've told it to value. If you feed it fear, it will find more reasons to be afraid. If you feed it failure, it will highlight evidence of defeat. But if you train it to recognize peace, strength, and truth, it will shift your focus accordingly. You start to see what aligns with what you've been rehearsing internally.

Let's go deeper. The rise of digital comparison—especially through platforms like Instagram and TikTok—has radically altered mental health trends. From 2003 to 2010, the rise in teenage depression and self-harm mirrored the rise of smartphones and social media. That's not an accident. When you're constantly exposed to curated highlight reels, your brain starts to believe that everyone else is thriving—and you're not. The gap between appearance and reality becomes unbearable.

Culture has changed our tolerance. What used to be obscene is now ordinary. What once shocked us now entertains us. But that didn't happen through argument or evidence—it happened through exposure. Familiarity breeds comfort. And comfort, when unchecked, reprograms conviction.

So, how do you navigate this minefield? You take responsibility for your inputs.

You must become the gatekeeper of your mind. You wouldn't knowingly feed your child poison—so why allow toxic content, conversations, or comparisons to shape your thinking? Your brain doesn't distinguish between fantasy and formation. It processes what's repeated. If you want peace, you must plant peace. If you want faith, you must starve fear. If you want joy, you must fix your focus on what brings life.

Train your thought life with the same rigor you'd train your body. That means intentional repetition of truth. That means curating your environment, your media, your inner dialogue. Your identity is not an accident—it's the harvest of every repeated belief.

I once worked with a highly successful executive, leading a multimillion-dollar company, who lived in quiet torment. Despite his achievements, he was consumed by anxiety and paralyzed by "what if" scenarios. Every new win only amplified the fear of loss. Underneath his accomplishments lived an old, unhealed story: "If I let go, everything will collapse." That belief, rooted in childhood chaos, had become a governing law in his subconscious. No matter how much progress he made, his mind wouldn't allow peace. Peace felt like vulnerability.

We didn't start with business strategy—we started with thought renovation. Identifying the lie. Interrupting the pattern. Replacing it with truth. Rehearsing that truth until it became the new default. That's the real work. And it isn't glamorous. But it is transformative.

The battle isn't out there—it's in your head.

And that means your greatest freedom won't arrive through a change in circumstances, relationships, or income. It begins in the still, sacred space where thoughts are formed. Victory begins where repetition ends and awareness begins. Guard that ground like your life depends on it—because it does.

The Stories We Tell Ourselves About Adversity

We all carry internal scripts—silent but persistent stories about who we are, what we deserve, and what is possible for us. These stories are rarely created in moments of peace. Most are born in seasons of adversity. A failure that made you question your competence. A betrayal that made you doubt your worth. A mistake that became your identity.

The danger isn't that we experience adversity. That's inevitable. The real danger is when we let adversity become the narrator of our lives.

Adversity has a voice. Left unchecked, it speaks in absolutes: "You always mess things up." "People like you never win." "You should have known better." These narratives embed themselves deep within, often so subtly that we stop questioning them. They shape our self-talk, our decision-making, and our risk tolerance. We stop applying. Stop trying. Stop believing. Not because our circumstances are permanent—but because we've accepted the story they told us.

We don't just live through adversity—we interpret it. And in the process, we write stories. Stories about who we are, what we're worth, and what's possible for us. Most of these narratives aren't formed in moments of clarity or triumph. They're born in the shadows—after rejection, betrayal, humiliation, or failure. A lost job mutates into "I'm replaceable." A broken relationship echoes, "I'm unlovable." One missed opportunity becomes "I never catch a break." These stories don't just visit—they take root. They become the subconscious code we live by, dictating our confidence, muting our courage, and narrowing our vision for the future.

I once sat across from a tech CEO in Manhattan, who, despite leading a successful company, confessed, "Every time I pitch to investors, I shrink. I talk fast. I sweat. It's like I'm 12 again, trying to prove I'm not a burden." His company was generating millions, but his internal story hadn't evolved. He was still operating from a script written during childhood—after years of being told to "stay out of the way." That story had become an operating system, silently influencing every boardroom decision and public appearance.

And that's the cost of unchallenged narratives: they override evidence. You can have all the accolades, the metrics, the applause—and still feel like an imposter. Not because you lack capacity, but because the internal narrator hasn't been upgraded. That's why, when I coach leaders, I ask, "Whose voice is that?" When they speak of hesitation, overcompensation, or self-doubt, that question almost always leads to silence. Then tears. Because behind almost every limitation is a borrowed belief—a voice from a mentor, a parent, a past wound—that we never stopped to interrogate.

I remember coaching Rachel, a powerhouse entrepreneur who had built a multi-six-figure business. Every launch was a success—until it came time to scale. Then the sabotage kicked in: missed deadlines, over-analysis, withdrawal. When we traced the pattern, it led back to a single line from her childhood: "When women get too successful, they lose people." Her mother said it in passing after losing a close friendship, but Rachel had internalized it as gospel. For her, success was not just growth—it was a threat to belonging. Her nervous system equated expansion with exile. That's how deep these stories run. They don't argue—they assume. And unless challenged, they become the ceiling to your potential.

But here's what we must understand: just because a story is familiar doesn't mean it's true. And just because it was once useful doesn't mean it belongs in your future. Realism without reflection is just recycled trauma. Rewriting these stories isn't about denial—it's about definition. Painful experiences are real. But the meanings we assign to them? That's where the power lies. You can't change what happened—but you can choose what it means going forward.

After the military, I found myself hustling in every room. More titles, more achievements, more perfection. I didn't recognize it at first—but I was trying to outrun a belief: "You're behind. You've got to catch up." That story drove me to excellence, but it also drove me into burnout. It wasn't until I rewrote it—*"My experience isn't a deficit. It's my distinction"*—that I started leading from identity instead of insecurity. The story didn't disappear overnight. But every time I chose to act from truth instead of fear, the new narrative gained ground.

We all do this. We build adult lives around childhood scripts. We let one offhand comment become a lifelong instruction. We replay scenes that make us shrink, and call it humility. But here's the truth: any story that robs you of courage is one worth confronting. It's not about toxic positivity. It's about honest authorship. You are the narrator now—not your past, not your pain.

Rewriting your story begins with awareness. Ask yourself: *Where did this belief start? What is it trying to protect me from? And what is it costing me to keep it?* Often, these stories were built for survival. But you're not in survival anymore—you're in strategy. And strategy requires clarity. If a belief doesn't help you lead, love, or build—it's time to let it go.

I had a conversation in Miami with a Marine-turned-executive who quietly admitted, "Every time I contribute in a meeting, I brace for someone to call me out." He wasn't afraid of being wrong—he was afraid of being seen. That instinct came from an old military supervisor who belittled him in front of peers. Two decades later, the man was still flinching at phantoms. And that's what these stories do—they trap us in outdated roles long after the curtain's closed.

What breaks the cycle isn't force—it's intentional reframing. One of the most strategic moves you can make is to question your assumptions. That hesitation before you speak? That tendency to over-explain? That fear of outshining others? Those are not quirks. They're clues. Each one points to a belief that may no longer serve you.

The greatest shift comes when you start interpreting adversity as a signal—not a sentence. When you lose something, miss a shot, or get hurt—it's easy to build a narrative of failure. But what if you reframed it as feedback? As data? As design? After my own season of loss—emotionally, financially, spiritually—I stopped asking, "Why is this happening to me?" and started asking, "What is this preparing me for?" That single shift didn't erase my pain, but it recalibrated my focus. It moved me from victim to visionary.

And as you do this work, remember: growth isn't always loud. Sometimes it looks like sitting still and listening to your thoughts. Sometimes it's noticing the subtle shame when you succeed, and tracing it back to its source. Sometimes it's a single sentence you speak aloud—one that contradicts everything your past said was true. These aren't soft moves. They're seismic.

One of the highest forms of leadership is self-leadership. And that begins with story-editing. Choose truth over trauma. Choose authorship over autopilot. Choose a narrative that expands you—not one that contains you.

Because the story you believe the most is the one your life will follow. So choose wisely. And if the one you're living no longer fits—rewrite it.

Reframing Challenges as Catalysts for Growth

Adversity doesn't knock politely—it barges in. It interrupts schedules, hijacks your plans, and forces a reckoning. And yet, while adversity is a shared human experience, how people respond to it couldn't be more different. Some fold under the weight of it. Others rise with fire in their eyes. Some interpret a setback as the end of the road. Others see it as a detour that leads to a better route. The deciding factor? It's not intelligence, wealth, or even grit—it's perspective.

Perspective is not just a mindset. It's a navigation tool. It's the internal compass that dictates how you interpret your reality when the external world refuses to cooperate. It's what transforms setbacks into strategies, delays into development, and rejection into redirection. Perspective asks, not "Why is this happening to me?" but "What can this make possible in me?" And that shift is everything.

I remember a client I worked with several years ago—a brilliant executive known for his sharp instincts and decisive leadership. He was the kind of man who walked into a room and changed its energy without saying a word. But on this particular day, he was a shadow of that figure. He had just watched a multi-million-dollar merger collapse two weeks before closing. His eyes were bloodshot. His voice was flat. He sat across from me, slouched, shoulders rounded inward as if physically trying to disappear. He stared at the floor for a long time, and then he whispered, "Maybe I'm just not as sharp as I thought."

That's how doubt shows up. Not with explosions, but with slow leaks. It doesn't scream—it seeps. I leaned forward, made sure my words cut through the fog, and said, "Or maybe this isn't the exposure of your failure—but the revelation of where you're ready to grow next." His eyes met mine. Silence. Then a slow nod. And he said quietly, "That means this isn't the end. It's an inflection point."

That's what reframing does—it transforms a dead end into a turning point.

You see, most people are not destroyed by events. They're destroyed by their interpretation of those events. It's not the failure that breaks them—it's the meaning they attach to it. "I'm not good enough." "I should've seen it coming." "This always happens to me." These aren't just thoughts; they become internal scripts that eventually direct external decisions. The real threat is not the circumstance—it's the story we tell ourselves about the circumstance. And here's the good news: stories can be rewritten.

Reframing starts with asking better questions in moments of emotional heat. When the contract falls through, when the person walks away, when the plan collapses, instead of defaulting to "What did I do wrong?" try "What part of me is being stretched for the next level?" It's a shift from self-blame to self-examination. Instead of "This is the worst thing that's ever happened," ask "What is this trying to teach me about the assumptions I've carried?" This isn't denial. This is leadership—of your own mind.

I'll never forget a leadership development session I ran for a group of mid-level managers. One of them, a woman in her early thirties, had recently been demoted after a failed team project. The moment she spoke, you could hear the tremor in her voice. "It's like I can't see a way forward," she confessed, her eyes wet but unblinking. Her words carried the exhaustion of someone who had been driving in fog too long. I paused, locked in, and said what I've told myself on the worst days of my life: "You don't need to see the whole map. Just take the next step with clarity. Vision builds with motion."

That line hit her like oxygen. She closed her eyes and breathed—deeply, for the first time in weeks. That's what reframing gives us. Not instant peace, but enough clarity to move forward. Enough light to take the next step. Enough hope to believe that just because the road is broken doesn't mean you are.

There's a dangerous cultural lie that says shifting your mindset is about pretending everything's okay. That's not resilience—that's repression. Reframing is not about plastering positivity over pain. It's about standing in the full weight of reality and choosing to extract meaning from it rather than misery. It's the sacred space between reaction and response—between the gut-punch and the decision to get up anyway.

Life will hit you. Clients will walk. Partnerships will implode. People you trusted will disappoint you. Plans will unravel. And none of these outcomes are pleasant—but none of them have the final say either. They only define you if you hand them the pen. And this chapter, this moment, is about taking that pen back.

Over the years, I've sat across from Marines who lost limbs, founders who lost fortunes, and parents who lost children. Each had a choice: surrender to the pain or see through it. And the ones who rose didn't do it because they were tougher. They rose because they refused to allow pain to narrate their identity. They understood this truth: adversity is not a verdict. It's a classroom.

We've been conditioned to believe that growth only happens in forward motion. But real growth often happens in the pause. In the waiting room between who you were and who you're becoming. In that still space where the noise fades and all that's left is you, your truth, and your choice.

Perspective doesn't eliminate pain. It doesn't excuse betrayal. It doesn't make heartbreak less gutting. But what it does is create room—room to breathe, room to assess, room to reimagine. It gives you the distance to stop reacting and start choosing. And in that choice, you reclaim authority over your story.

Here's what I've learned from walking through wreckage—my own and others': Sometimes destruction is the prerequisite for design. The rubble often contains the raw materials of your next level. The blueprint for your future often emerges from the ashes of your old expectations. That pain you're feeling? It may not be your enemy. It might be your invitation.

So no, you don't have to pretend the challenge doesn't hurt. But you do get to decide whether it imprisons you or prepares you. Whether it weakens your voice or deepens your wisdom. Whether it defines your ceiling or expands your horizon.

That's the shift.

And that's how you **navigate** toward the life that's waiting for you on the other side of perspective.

Rewiring Your Thought Patterns for Success

Rewiring your mindset is not about embracing hollow positivity or repeating generic affirmations until you believe them. It's a hardwired transformation. Yes, it is about fundamentally transforming the very structure of how your brain responds to life. This is not a cosmetic touch-up. It's a deliberate and disciplined reconstruction of mental wiring that has been shaped over decades. If you've found yourself defaulting to fear, shame, overthinking, or avoidance—it's not because you're broken. It's because you've been trained to respond that way. And what has been trained can be retrained. That is the profound promise of neuroplasticity: the scientifically proven ability of the brain to rewire itself.

I recall speaking at a leadership retreat where a young army veteran approached me afterward. "I try pep talks," he said, "but by the next morning, I'm back to the same fear." I told him, "Then you're not just stuck—you're practicing fear. Want new wiring? Practice something new—daily." We started with just two minutes of breathwork a day. A few weeks later, he called me—from Afghanistan—saying, "I walked my platoon through a blackout because I trained myself to lead under pressure." His transformation didn't start with a motivational quote. It started with neural conditioning—tiny, repeated choices that built a new instinct.

Let's strip this down. Your brain is not static. It's a living, adaptable organ, designed to change chemically, physically, and functionally throughout your life. This is neuroplasticity. It means you're not imprisoned by your past responses—you're sculpting your future ones. Every time you choose gratitude instead of complaint, respond instead of react, or courage over comfort, you are physically altering the structure of your brain. Not metaphorically—literally. You're reshaping neural pathways, redefining reflexes, and reshaping the identity encoded in your cells.

It was 5:37 a.m. The freeway was still cloaked in a slate-gray fog, and the city hadn't quite woken up yet. I was behind the wheel, headed to deliver a keynote for a leadership conference in downtown L.A. The windshield wipers made a rhythmic click—slow, steady, like a metronome for my thoughts. My playlist was quiet. But my mind was anything but.

Even after years of training, battle, coaching high performers, and building a brand that had impacted thousands—there it was: that familiar whisper.

"What if this is the talk where you bomb?"
"What if they regret hiring you?"
"What if you're not as sharp as you used to be?"

For a few seconds, I caught myself spiraling—not in fear of failure, but in that old wiring of needing to **prove** something. Not to them—to myself. It hit me that I was navigating this moment with an outdated map—one drawn in the days when survival meant performance, when pressure meant posture.

And then it clicked.

I gripped the steering wheel, took a slow breath, and said out loud—*"We don't perform for approval anymore. We lead from truth."*

That sentence wasn't poetic—it was an anchor. A reset. A neural override. The fog outside didn't lift—but the fog inside did. I turned down the radio, rolled down the window, and let the crisp morning air hit my face. It didn't just wake me up. It reminded me that this isn't about perfection—it's about presence.

By the time I reached the venue and walked backstage, I wasn't rehearsing the fear. I was rehearsing the **impact** I came to deliver. That shift didn't come from a motivational poster. It came from **mental reps**—years of learning how to *navigate* the terrain of my own mind. Not bulldozing fear, but retraining it. Not denying pressure, but redirecting it.

And when I stepped on that stage that morning, I didn't perform.

I led.

Because rewiring isn't a one-time spark—it's a daily steering wheel. And clarity doesn't come from waiting for the fog to clear. It comes from deciding who's driving when it does.

This principle came alive when I coached an Army sergeant struggling to adjust to civilian life. He was stuck in hyper-vigilance, constantly on edge, always scanning for threats. "This is just who I am now," he told me. But I knew better. We began small: gratitude journaling, intentional one-minute stillness, and a reset ritual before walking into his home. Over time, his nervous system recalibrated. His reactions slowed. He became less tense. And his family noticed before he did. That's not magic—that's neuroplasticity in motion.

And for that rewiring to stick, you need tools. One powerful tool I use with clients is the **S.T.A.R. Model**:

- **Stop** – Interrupt the automatic spiral. Catch yourself.

- **Think** – What story am I telling myself about this moment?

- **Ask** – Is this story helping me? What's another perspective?

- **Respond** – Make your next move with clarity, not chaos.

S.T.A.R. MODEL FOR REFRAMING MINDSET

T: Think
Identify what story you're telling yourself about the moment.

S: Stop
Catch yourself mid-spiral. Disrupt the auto-response.

A: Ask
Challenge the story: "Is this helping me?" "What's another way to see this?"

R: Respond
Choose your next move deliberately – from clarity, not chaos.

The strength of this method lies in its simplicity. You don't need a therapist in your back pocket. You need a mental operating system that meets you in the moment. The more you use it, the more it becomes second nature—rewiring panic into poise, self-doubt into strategy.

You are always training your brain—whether you realize it or not. Every thought you rehearse, every belief you repeat, becomes a mental rep. Just like muscle memory develops from physical repetition, your mind wires itself around the most consistent patterns you entertain. If anxiety is your default narrative, your brain reinforces it. If you choose faith, strategy, or composure—those too become your default over time. The key difference? Intention.

I remember a speaking event with a group of tech founders. One man approached me afterward—wealthy, successful, and utterly miserable. "I think I've just always been this way," he confessed. "Chronically stressed.

Driven by the fear of losing everything." I asked him what his first thought was each morning. He paused. "I start listing everything I didn't finish yesterday." That daily mental rehearsal was priming him to panic before he even stood up. So we rewrote it: three wins from the day before, one priority for today, and one affirmation—spoken out loud. Six weeks later, he called me: "I finally feel like I'm leading my company instead of surviving it."

That's what happens when you shift your mental script. It's not just a productivity hack—it's identity recalibration. You're no longer reacting to pressure. You're rehearsing presence. You're rewiring the very filter through which you interpret stress, relationships, setbacks, and opportunity. And when your thoughts change, so do your emotions, your body language, and your reality.

Here's the hard truth, your brain doesn't care about your intentions. It responds to repetition. You can feel fired up after a podcast or workshop, but if you return to rehearsing doubt or disorganization, that's what your brain strengthens. The belief you repeat most becomes the belief your subconscious treats as truth.

Take one of my clients Jasmine—a newly promoted exec at a Fortune 500 company. On paper, she was thriving. But in coaching, she confessed, "I feel like I just lucked into this." That self-doubt wasn't passive—it was active rehearsal. So we flipped the pattern: each morning, she spoke three statements aloud—"I earned this. I bring value. I'm still growing." It felt forced at first. But by day 30, her language had shifted. "I'm not as scared to speak up anymore," she said. By the third month, her manager noticed she was leading with more confidence. What changed? The story she told herself—repeatedly—until it rewired the way she showed up.

Scientifically, this is backed by research. Stanford neuroscientist Dr. Andrew Huberman explains that repeated thoughts increase myelination—a coating that strengthens neural connections, making the pathway faster and more dominant. That's how both habits and beliefs are formed: repetition builds reflex.

So here's the critical question:

Are you living by default—or by design?

Default looks like:

- "This is just how I am."

- "I've always reacted like this."

- "People like me don't get ahead."

But design sounds like:

- "I get to decide who I become."

- "I can rewrite this instinct."

- "My past shaped me, but it doesn't own me."

Your current mindset isn't a moral flaw. It's a formation—a byproduct of every environment, every voice, and every repetition you've absorbed. But what was formed can be re-formed. That's the core promise of neuroplasticity: your history is not your destiny. You don't need to deny your past. You need to design your future.

One man who deeply embodied this was a retired Navy chief I worked with during a group workshop. Even after years out of uniform, he confessed, "I still bark at my kids like they're recruits." His parenting reflex wasn't from malice—it was a neural default. Together, we created "pause rituals"— stepping away before he entered the house, taking three deep breaths, asking, "What does leadership look like right now?" Weeks later, he said, "I'm becoming the dad I never had." That shift didn't come from inspiration. It came from consistent, deliberate rewiring of an old reflex.

Everyone carries a default setting—a subconscious pattern that activates under pressure. For some, it's anxiety. For others, it's withdrawal, perfectionism, or people-pleasing. These aren't personality traits—they're training. And like any training, they can be upgraded.

Early in my career, one missed deadline could unravel me. I'd stay up at 2 a.m., replaying every mistake, spiraling into shame. That wasn't strategy—it was a nervous system on autopilot. But I learned something powerful: you don't rise to the occasion—you default to your training. And if your training is stress, that's what you perform under pressure.

That's why I encourage people to train their new default responses the same way a soldier trains for combat or an athlete train for game day. Take Marcus, a firefighter I coached. During a house fire response, his mind blanked in a smoke-filled hallway. Trauma and old conditioning took over. We began working on micro-drills: when the alarm rang, he would breathe deeply and repeat one phrase— "Strategic. Calm. Curious." Over time, that practice rewired his impulse. His team began to notice—he moved more deliberately, assessed faster, stayed grounded.

High-level performers understand this principle intuitively. NBA players rehearse clutch free throws long before they face the buzzer. Navy pilots run mental simulations of crisis scenarios before ever stepping into a jet. They don't hope to perform under pressure—they program it in advance. You can do the same.

- Want boldness to be your reflex? Then train it.

- Want peace to be your default? Then rehearse it.

- Want clarity to rise in chaos? Then build the muscle now.

Here's the shift: forget passive living. Forget "this is just who I am." Instead, train for:

- Strategic thinking—pause and choose before reacting.

- Bold action—act from vision, not fear.

- Calm presence—breathe deeper than the storm.

- Curious inquiry—ask better questions, even in tension.

These aren't hacks. They're habits. And over time, your nervous system learns: "This is how we operate now." The result? You start living from strength instead of survival.

One of the greatest myths in self-development is that you have to break yourself down to become new. You don't. You just need to retrain. Change doesn't require you to be perfect. It requires consistency. Small, aligned repetitions that say to your brain, "We're not surviving anymore—we're building."

Even a whisper of intention can disrupt the loudest pattern of fear. A new thought. A reset ritual. A single, powerful sentence like, "I choose clarity, not confusion." These aren't empty mantras—they're programming instructions for your inner AI. They tell your brain, "Here's the new directive."

Because your brain is listening.

It's always learning.

And your most repeated instructions—those become your truth.

Your brain is not broken. It's brilliantly efficient—almost too efficient. It's trained to protect, predict, and preserve. The problem? It doesn't always distinguish between danger and discomfort. That's why growth can feel threatening. That's why peace can feel suspicious when you've lived in chaos. It's not sabotage—it's programming.

Ever lie awake at night thinking through conversations that never even happened? Or close the biggest deal of your life and immediately start worrying if you can replicate it? That's not a flaw. That's your brain doing what it's been conditioned to do—run old threat detection software on new opportunities.

Your conscious brain processes about 40 bits of information per second. But your subconscious? Over 11 million. It's the real engine. Fast. Intuitive. Hyper-aware. It doesn't just remember what happened—it remembers what *felt* unsafe, what triggered rejection, or what once earned you love.

Here's the catch, peace feels like unemployment to a brain wired for chaos. That's why many people feel anxious during vacations, or start fights when things finally settle down. Their nervous system has been trained to expect stress. So, when calm arrives, it feels like something is wrong. Stillness feels unsafe—not because it is—but because it's unfamiliar.

I coached a high-performing entrepreneur who described this perfectly. "Every time things are going well," she said, "I feel like I need to stir something up." Her pattern wasn't random—it was protection. As a child, she learned to stay alert through family instability. Her mind equated peace with pending disaster. Our work wasn't about forcing calm—it was about retraining her brain to recognize it as safety, not threat.

This is why "positive thinking" alone fails. You can't out-think trauma with a motivational poster. You need integration. That means interrupting thought spirals, accessing your subconscious, and embedding new emotional patterns that the body accepts as truth.

The process isn't just mindset—it's neurological reprogramming. And it begins in three steps:

1. **Interrupt the Spiral** – When your thoughts start looping, don't fight them. Redirect them. Ask a different question. "What would this look like if it were easy?" or "What truth would I act from if fear wasn't running the show?"

2. **Drop Into the Subconscious** – Breathwork, embodiment, or guided emotional reset. This is where transformation moves from surface logic to cellular safety. Real healing doesn't bypass the body—it includes it.

3. **Let the Rewired AI Take Over** – When your nervous system believes it's safe, action becomes effortless. You stop performing for validation and start moving from clarity.

This isn't theoretical—it's physiological. Once your internal programming changes, your external behaviors align. You don't have to fake courage. You become it. You don't have to chase peace. You live in it.

Because clarity isn't a personality type. It's a trained skill. It shows up in the quietest moments—when you stop reacting and start rebuilding from the root.

Think of your brain like an old smartphone. The hardware isn't the problem—it's the outdated apps running in the background, draining your battery and slowing your performance. These apps are your subconscious beliefs—coded from years of experiences, disappointments, conditioning, and stories you didn't choose but absorbed. Rewiring your mindset is the upgrade.

It begins with a simple truth, if you don't take control of the frame, the world will set it for you. And when that happens, your perception gets distorted—colored by trauma, trends, comparison, and cultural noise. You stop hearing your own voice. You start echoing someone else's.

I once coached a young pastor who was magnetic on stage, but riddled with anxiety afterward. "Every time I preach," he told me, "I hear this whisper of inadequacy." When I asked whose voice it was, he hesitated. "My mentor's. He used to tear down everything I created." That whisper wasn't his truth—it was an old download, still running in the background. Once he identified it, he reframed his internal narrative. He began to trust his own authority again—and more importantly, he began to feel peace in his own presence.

This is frame control. And it isn't about ignoring reality. It's about taking command of how you interpret it. According to Neuro-Linguistic Programming (NLP), your subconscious does not distinguish truth from repetition. If you repeatedly say, "I'm not good enough," that belief doesn't stay as opinion—it becomes architecture.

When the frame is toxic, your experience will be too.

But change the frame? And you unlock a different story. One where you're not a victim of your thoughts—you're the architect of them.

This came to life in a coaching session with a Marine comrade…Jason. Every time we entered a dangerous zone, he'd freeze—not out of fear, but because of an internal script: "I mess things up under pressure." I reminded him: he had never missed a mission. His reflex didn't match reality—it matched an outdated story. Once we reframed him from "I'm the risk" to "I've been trained for this," everything changed. Not just performance—presence.

You don't need a new brain. You need a new lens.

And the moment you reclaim your mental frame; you stop being at the mercy of external noise—and start living by internal clarity.

But frame control only works when you own your headspace.

Your mind is prime real estate. And too often, we let unqualified tenants move in—social media, toxic commentary, past rejection, other people's expectations. Without realizing it, we let these squatters set up shop, rearrange our furniture, and dictate our emotional weather.

A client once told me she woke up every morning and doomscrolled the news before getting out of bed. By the time she sat down to work, she was already overwhelmed. We flipped the script: she replaced headlines with two minutes of gratitude and one powerful morning prompt. "That tiny change," she said, "gave me my morning back."

Your thoughts are sacred ground. Don't lease them out to fear or chaos.

Own your space. Set boundaries. Curate input. Guard your peace like it's the control center of your future—because it is.

And here's something that will challenge how you think about leadership and clarity: not every voice deserves access to your decision-making. Just because someone is loud doesn't mean they're right. Just because they show up often doesn't mean they're truthful. We live in a culture that profits from your distraction—feeds on your anxiety—and manipulates your attention until you're left doubting what you once knew.

But here's your edge: clarity. And clarity is not found in consumption—it's forged in intention.

One of my high-level clients, a brilliant tech founder, shared that he often felt crushed by social media. "Every time I open my phone," he told me, "I feel like I'm behind. Everyone's launching faster, scaling bigger, winning louder." So we did an experiment: for two weeks, he filtered his inputs—no social feeds, limited news, and only high-caliber conversations. Instead, he began every day with a single question: "Does this align with who I'm becoming?" Two weeks later, his sleep had improved, his thinking was clearer, and he broke through a six-month innovation block. He didn't need more information. He needed less interference.

Years ago, I was at a leadership summit in the mountains. After my keynote, a retired Navy SEAL pulled me aside. "You know what saved us under fire?" he asked. "It wasn't the gear—it was our ability to cut through mental noise. We trained ourselves to stay on mission. Everything that didn't support that—we blocked." That's not just battlefield wisdom. That's life mastery.

And the battlefield in your life? It might look like comparison. Overwhelm. Conflicting priorities. But the principle is the same: clarity wins. Always.

The next time your thoughts spiral or your vision feels clouded—pause. Ask:

- "What's the signal beneath this noise?"

- "What inputs need to go?"

- "Who or what no longer deserves access to my focus?"

Because clarity is not just a gift. It's a discipline.

Let me share one more story—one that changed me. A former Navy pilot I coached told me he used to white-knuckle through turbulence—not out of fear of flying, but fear of losing control. After the military, that control reflex followed him into daily life. Whenever things got messy—at work or at home—he'd retreat. Control silence. Control schedules. Control emotion. One day, I told him, "Next time things feel tense, don't fix it. Feel it. Sit in it." A few weeks later, he said, "I let my teenage son rant. I didn't interrupt. I didn't fix. And for the first time—he actually talked to me." It wasn't a tactical win. It was a transformational one. He traded control for connection. Performance for presence.

Sometimes, the most strategic move isn't to speed up—it's to pause.

With intention.

Pausing with purpose is not weakness—it's wisdom. It's not procrastination—it's preparation. High performers don't pause because they're uncertain; they pause because they're clear on what's at stake. They understand that clarity isn't found in rushing—it's found in rooting.

I once coached a startup CEO who had just lost her biggest client. She was spiraling, pacing the sidewalk, panicking about revenue and reputation. "What do I do now?" she kept asking. I didn't give her a checklist. I asked her to sit. Close the laptop. Breathe. Then we wrote down three insights she gained from that client—what worked, what didn't, and what it exposed in her systems. Within ten minutes, her breathing slowed. Her voice steadied. Her next move was no longer reactive—it was strategic.

That's the magic of intentional pause: it creates space for power to return.

Even in the military, some of our greatest breakthroughs didn't come while we were moving—they came in stillness. I remember being deployed in Fallujah in a high-risk zone. We had to sit and wait—gear on, adrenaline high, intel slow. Every cell in our bodies wanted to act. But we were trained not to flinch in the face of tension. We were trained to breathe in the wait. That pause gave us the clarity that saved lives.

Science backs this up. Studies show that even a one-minute intentional break can boost cognitive performance by 13%, reduce stress indicators, and elevate creative problem-solving by up to 40%. The brain needs these moments to reset. Not to stop—but to sharpen.

So, the next time you feel tension rising, don't default to noise. Don't reach for your phone, scroll, or distract. Try this instead:

- Pause.

- Breathe slowly, intentionally.

- Ask yourself: *"What decision is this tension preparing me for?"*

Because the goal isn't just to move—it's to move with precision. And that only happens when you're grounded. Now let's bring this full circle.

The breakthroughs you're chasing? The next level you feel within reach? They aren't found in louder hustle. They're found in quieter mastery. In how you breathe. In what you repeat. In the stories you refuse to keep living. Your default doesn't define you. Your practice does.

And if you train for strategy, train for peace, train for power—those won't be optional anymore. They'll be automatic. They'll be your new normal. This is the real work. This is where transformation happens. This is where you Break the Bottle™—not by force, but by formation.

From Interpretation to Transformation: Leading Through Pain with Perspective

Transformation doesn't begin in the intellect—it begins in the nervous system. That's the truth most leadership philosophies leave out. You can memorize frameworks, master spreadsheets, and collect strategies from the best minds in the world, but if your body is still bracing for pain every time pressure hits, you'll sabotage your own ascent. Growth can't outpace safety. And when your internal world is in conflict, no amount of logic can override the alarm bells wired into your nervous system.

This is where emotional grit is forged—not in comfort, but in the tension between instinct and intention. Emotional grit isn't glamour. It's the quiet, unseen courage to pause when everything in you wants to lash out, shrink back, or perform for approval. It's the choice to breathe instead of break. In military terms, it's what keeps your finger off the trigger until clarity returns. In leadership, it's what separates impulsive reaction from strategic response.

I saw this firsthand during a high-stakes coaching intensive with a senior executive named Devon. He was sharp, calculated, and respected—yet every quarterly review season, he'd transform into a micromanaging storm. His team dreaded those weeks. When we finally peeled back the layers, the root wasn't about metrics. It was about memory. At twelve years old, Devon's father—a Navy man with zero tolerance for failure—berated him for bringing home a report card with one B. That single moment had trained his nervous system to equate performance with survival. So now, decades later, every evaluation felt like a test he couldn't afford to fail. He didn't need another management course—he needed a nervous system update. Once he could see the story driving the storm, he learned to choose presence over pressure. The shift was quiet—but seismic.

Pain that isn't processed becomes the architect of every system you build. You'll design businesses, teams, even families around the avoidance of that pain. You'll call it structure. The premise is simple: *When life punches you, don't just brace—build.* When the unexpected shows up, you don't collapse. You slow down, interpret, adapt, and act from alignment—not adrenaline. You'll call it excellence. But it's still reaction. And what's reactive can never be fully free.

One of the most impactful founders I ever coached—Shana—grew her company to seven figures in under three years. Publicly, she was magnetic. Privately, she lived in panic. Every time her visibility increased, her joy decreased. She would overextend, overthink, and finally retreat. When we slowed things down, she told me through tears, "I learned a long time ago that when I shine, I lose people." Her nervous system had attached success to abandonment. No spreadsheet could solve that. What she needed was not reassurance, but reconditioning. Together, we worked on teaching her body that safety wasn't found in shrinking—it was found in staying. In breathing through visibility instead of bracing against it. In allowing herself to be seen without scripting the backlash.

This is what deep leadership work demands: not just mental reframing, but **somatic retraining**. Because your body keeps the score. It remembers what your mind has tried to forget. That time you were dismissed when you spoke up. That moment your vulnerability was used against you. That season when joy felt too dangerous to hold. And if those imprints are never interrupted, they become default settings—shaping your choices without your consent.

Leadership, then, isn't about controlling the storm outside. It's about becoming the calm within it. The best leaders aren't those who speak the loudest or have the flashiest vision decks. They're the ones whose internal environment is regulated enough to create safety for others. Because people don't just follow your plan—they follow your *presence*. They follow what you feel in the room, even before you say a word.

Several years ago, I was asked to speak at a summit after a tragic incident had rocked the hosting organization. The atmosphere was tense—eyes wary, energy fractured. I scrapped my prepared keynote. I walked on stage, grounded my breath, and said, "I'm not here to inspire you—I'm here to be real with you." And then I shared my own story of loss and rebuilding.

It wasn't strategy that shifted the room—it was resonance. It was nervous system to nervous system, soul to soul. You could feel the exhale ripple across the audience. That's what perspective can do. It reorients people. It gives them something solid to hold when the ground feels like it's crumbling.

But perspective doesn't mean positivity. It means interpretation. When the unexpected hits, do you spiral? Or do you slow down, get curious, and ask, *"What is this trying to reveal?"* That's the critical shift—from reacting to leading. And that's where true transformation lives.

Let me take you back to a moment from my own journey. I was in Houston, sitting in my car outside a client's office, unable to get out. Not because I was physically stuck—but because my body was gripped by a silent panic. A deal had just fallen through. I felt like a failure. And in that moment, every old voice returned. *"You're not good enough. You're not built for this. You're just a Marine trying to survive in a world that's passed you by."* I had the tools. I had the experience. But what I didn't have—yet—was integration.

That moment became the birthplace of what I now call the **Opportunity Extraction Framework (OEF)**. Because I knew I had a choice: I could collapse. Or I could extract. Not bypass. Not minimize. But extract. Meaning—I could slow down, examine the pain, ask better questions, and anchor into alignment before taking the next step. That process didn't just change how I lead—it changed who I became.

You'll get the OEF in full shortly. But before we go there, let me offer you this:

You don't need to be fearless to be a great leader. You need to be willing to feel. To feel the weight of responsibility without being crushed by it. To feel the fear of expansion without shrinking back. To feel grief without losing your grip on vision. Because that's what transforms pain into power: *not resistance—but integration.*

Leadership is not about being unaffected. It's about being *anchored.* It's about navigating the storm without becoming it. It's about standing in the wreckage and still seeing the blueprint. And more than anything—it's about mastering the sacred space between trigger and choice. That's where your influence is born. That's where transformation begins.

Because if you can lead yourself through the fire, you don't just survive the heat.

You *become* it.

You become the light.

The Opportunity Extraction Framework (OEF)

Perspective without aligned action is little more than a well-worded escape. It sounds enlightened, but without movement, it remains philosophy— distant and disconnected from transformation. The Opportunity Extraction Framework (OEF) wasn't born in a boardroom or on a whiteboard. It was born in the heat of disappointment, in moments when my own clarity crumbled, when I had to decide whether I'd lead from survival or evolve through pain. This framework is not a motivational acronym. It's a daily, repeatable practice designed to anchor leaders when the ground beneath them shifts. It won't make life easier. But it will make you stronger, wiser, and more grounded under pressure. Because everyone hits a moment when the deal falls through, the team fractures, the news drops, the unexpected storms in. And in that moment, instinct screams react. OEF helps you rewire that reflex. It trains you not just to recover—but to lead. Not perfectly, but intentionally. You'll learn to pause instead of spiral, to evaluate without ego, to strategize from alignment, and to act with integrity, even when emotion is high. It's the training for what comes when the plan doesn't go according to plan.

I remember sitting in my car outside a client's office after receiving news that a major contract was being pulled—no warning, just gone. My chest tightened. My breath shortened. Every mental reflex wanted to fire off a rebuttal, to call someone, to move fast. But I didn't. I gripped the steering wheel, closed my eyes, and whispered, "Pause." That single word interrupted the emotional spiral just long enough to remember: clarity doesn't rise in chaos—it rises in the space we create inside it. That was the moment OEF clicked into gear.

Phase 1: PAUSE—Interrupt the Emotional Autopilot

It begins there. Phase one: **Pause**. Not the kind of passive pause where you suppress emotion, but an intentional disruption of your nervous system's autopilot. This is where transformation begins—not in strategy, but in stillness. Most people don't realize how reactive they've become until they see their patterns under pressure. A canceled meeting sends them spiraling. A critical email shuts them down. A tone of disapproval from a partner makes them retreat. Before any new thought can emerge, before any reframe can occur, you must pause the storm. Not to numb it—but to notice it. When you pause, you're not dismissing emotion. You're creating enough space to examine it before it dictates your next move. Ask yourself, *What is actually happening—separate from what I fear is happening?* Feel your feet on the floor. Place your hand over your heart. Name the emotion without judgment. Breath grounds you. Silence recalibrates you. Because clarity doesn't shout—it arrives when the noise subsides.

Phase 2: EVALUATE—Gather the Signal from the Noise

From there, you move into **Evaluate**. Pain always carries a message, but if you're still in defensive mode, you won't hear it. This phase is about separating the story you're telling from the facts you're facing. This is where emotional intelligence is built—when you stop flinching and start listening. Ask, *What's within my control right now? What feedback is this moment offering me—about my system, my leadership, or my assumptions?* You're not mining for blame—you're mining for signal. You're tuning in. Is this showing you a broken system? A communication gap? A blind spot? This is how discomfort becomes data. I've watched leaders grow exponentially by simply slowing down long enough to stop confusing adrenaline with insight. One founder I coached began journaling this phase daily after every major decision. Within three months, she cut her reactivity by half and began leading with surgical clarity instead of scattered energy. That didn't happen from a new tactic—it came from emotional inventory.

Phase 3: STRATEGIZE—Identify the Pattern, Not Just the Pain

Phase three is **Strategize**—and here's where most people either freeze or flail. But this is not the moment to stay stuck in overthinking. This is where you move from introspection to alignment. It's where you look at the entire moment like a mirror, not a monster. You ask, *What part of me is this moment calling forward—boldness, truth, boundaries, humility? What's the root issue this pain is exposing?* Is it a lack of preparation? A missing system? An outdated identity you've outgrown but still default to? This is not about fixing everything at once. It's about identifying the pattern beneath the pain. When a client or colleague triggers fear, maybe it's not about them. Maybe it's reminding you of that early imprint where speaking up led to rejection. Now you see it. And when you see it, you can stop reliving it. This is where leaders shift from being overwhelmed to becoming architects. You're not reacting anymore. You're building.

Phase 4: EXECUTE—Align Action with Awareness

Then comes **Execute**—the step most people rush to first, but that only works when grounded in the three prior phases. Execution is not about motion for the sake of momentum. It's about alignment. One clear, strategic step— anchored in awareness. Not ten changes. One. Maybe it's addressing the tension with a teammate, but this time from a calm, composed state instead of wounded energy. Maybe it's updating your offer because feedback revealed a blind spot in how you communicate your value. Maybe it's automating a task you've been micromanaging to feel useful—or setting a boundary in a relationship that's draining your focus. This is the moment power returns— not because everything is fixed, but because you've taken aligned ownership. The external circumstance may not change yet—but you've changed. And that changes everything.

OEF isn't about avoiding breakdowns. It's about extracting the blueprint for the next breakthrough. When used consistently, it becomes your compass when the path disappears. It becomes your internal GPS when external certainty collapses. I've seen leaders reduce their recovery time from conflict by 70% using this framework. I've watched parents repair relational ruptures with their kids in real-time. I've seen entrepreneurs avoid burnout and reclaim vision simply by building this into their weekly rhythm. And most of all, I've lived it. I've sat in hotel rooms after high-stakes talks where I questioned everything. I've heard the old inner scripts rise up—*You're losing it. You're not ready. They'll see right through you.* But because I trained this muscle, I didn't collapse. I paused. Evaluated. Strategized. Executed. Over time, that became instinct.

Here's what happens when you train with OEF: You hesitate less. You recover faster. You speak more clearly. You lead more steadily. Not because the world stopped shaking—but because *you* stopped being shaken by it. And that's the distinction. This is not about controlling the storm—it's about anchoring yourself inside it. That's leadership. That's emotional mastery. And it's available to anyone who trains.

Perspective is not passive. It's practiced. The best leaders, creators, and visionaries aren't those who never faced hardship—they're the ones who learned to *hear it* without being ruled by it. They extract opportunity from what others waste. They don't flinch when the room shifts—they lead it back into alignment. And that kind of presence? It's not gifted. It's grown. It's the difference between how I used to lead—tense, reactive, hustling for approval—and how I lead now: grounded, clear, and responsive. The difference wasn't more credentials. It was a better frame. A deeper training. And now, it's yours too.

BREAK THE BOTTLE CHALLENGE — Chapter 9

The Lens Shift That Sets You Free

Perspective isn't just what you see—it's how you interpret what you see. And the most dangerous stories are the ones you don't even realize you're telling.

This challenge is about exposing those silent scripts and rewriting them in real-time—not someday, not in theory, but now.

You've learned the power of reframing.
Now it's time to practice it—with clarity, courage, and aligned motion.

STEP 1: Spot the Story That's Driving Your View

Think of a situation that's emotionally charged for you right now—big or small.

- Maybe it's a business decision that feels risky.

- A relationship where your confidence feels shaky.

- A goal that feels just out of reach.

Now pause.
Ask: *What am I assuming to be true in this situation?*

Examples:

- "They're going to say no."

- "I always screw up opportunities like this."

- "This is proof I'm not ready."

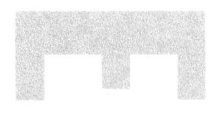

255

Write it down. This is your current lens. This is the story beneath your reaction.

STEP 2: Name the Origin of the Story

Where did that belief come from?
Be honest.

- Was it taught to you?

- Modeled to you?

- Ingrained from past failure?

This is where you start reclaiming authorship. Because what you inherited, you don't have to keep.

STEP 3: Reframe the Meaning

Ask yourself:

- *What else could be true about this situation?*

- *What is this pain, pause, or problem trying to show me about myself?*

- *What strength is being developed right now?*

Now rewrite the narrative.

Examples:

- "This isn't rejection—it's refinement."

- "This isn't failure—it's a diagnostic."

- "This tension is stretching my vision and revealing the real me."

Craft one clear sentence that reframes the meaning. Make it personal. Make it powerful.

STEP 4: Take Strategic Motion

Within the next 24 hours, take **one bold action** that reflects your new frame.

Not just a to-do task—an act of perspective.

- Have the difficult conversation from a posture of clarity, not fear.

- Launch the thing you've been delaying—not because you're ready, but because you believe in where you're headed.

- Set the boundary that protects your energy and affirms your growth.

Even the smallest aligned action can shift momentum. Because motion rooted in truth rewires your mind faster than waiting for perfect conditions. This isn't about hype. It's about emotional integrity. Every story you carry either becomes your container—or your catalyst. Break the bottle by identifying the lie, reframing the lens, and moving like someone who's not waiting for permission.

Let others stay stuck in what was. You have direction now. You have vision now. You have perspective trained through pain. And that? That makes you unstoppable.

10

DESIGNING THE BLUEPRINT FOR YOUR FUTURE

"Clarity isn't just knowing what you want—it's knowing what you won't compromise to get it. The future isn't found. It's built—with vision, discipline, and direction."

— Break The Bottle

The Role of Clarity in Achieving Goals

Achievement doesn't begin at the starting line—it begins in the invisible terrain of decision. The path to success is not paved by motion alone but by meaningful direction. I've learned that firsthand in the spaces between setbacks and pivots, in quiet moments where strategy took a back seat to stillness, and in the trenches where I was forced to ask myself: *Where am I actually going?* Clarity is not a luxury—it's the compass by which we navigate purpose, identity, and next-level impact. Without it, movement becomes noise, effort becomes erosion, and goals become ghosts—ever-present but never realized.

Years ago, I found myself standing in the middle of my living room with a printed itinerary in one hand and an open suitcase in the other. I was days away from one of the biggest speaking engagements of my career—a national summit where I'd be keynoting in front of thousands. Everything looked aligned on paper. My calendar was full. My brand was growing. My inbox buzzed with opportunity. But inside? I felt unmoored. The success I had built was real, but it wasn't rooted. My direction had been shaped by momentum, not clarity. I was moving, yes—but I couldn't answer the deeper question: *Is this taking me where I'm meant to go?*

I remember sitting on the edge of my bed that evening, staring at a single line I had scribbled on a sticky note months earlier: *"Don't just build. Aim."* That moment shook me. I wasn't lacking ambition—I was lacking alignment. I was navigating by the stars of public validation rather than the internal coordinates of vision. That's when I paused, closed the laptop, and asked myself three questions that would become a lifelong guide: *What am I really building? Why does it matter? Who will it shape me into along the way?* Clarity didn't come with fireworks that night—it came as a whisper. But that whisper redirected the entire map.

Clarity isn't about predicting every turn. It's about knowing your true North when the terrain shifts. In the military, we were trained to navigate with precision. If your coordinates were even one digit off, you could end up miles from your objective. The same is true in life. A five-degree misalignment may not show up today, but give it a year—and you'll be living a life that looks successful but feels disconnected. I've lived both. And I can tell you with certainty: motion is meaningless if it's not aimed at meaning.

This is why I say that clarity doesn't come from force—it comes from focus. And focus is born from curiosity. I've never reached a breakthrough by pretending to know everything. My greatest pivots have come from questions I was afraid to ask: *What version of me am I protecting? What am I avoiding by staying busy? What fear would I have to confront if I stopped performing?* The most powerful breakthroughs come not from answers but from the courage to investigate.

I used to think vision was about having a crystal-clear picture of the future. But what I've learned is that real vision is more about clarity of intention than clarity of outcome. I may not always know the exact shape of the mountain ahead, but I've learned to trust the direction of ascent. It's like hiking before dawn: you may not see the summit, but you trust the path because your flashlight reveals just enough to take the next step. And the next. That's clarity. It doesn't demand a full reveal. It simply requires commitment to the next right move.

Clarity also transforms your posture. I remember leading a breakout session in a room full of senior executives, and midway through, one of them challenged my framework—bluntly, almost aggressively. Years ago, that would've rattled me. I would've overexplained, tried to win the room, or second-guessed my stance. But in that moment, I didn't flinch. I paused, grounded my breath, and responded with quiet confidence. Why? Not because I had rehearsed the perfect answer—but because I was clear on my message, my intention, and my identity. Clarity breeds composure. When you know what you're about, you no longer need to defend your value—you *embody* it.

We often think clarity is something we find. But in my experience, it's something we *forge*. It's sculpted in moments of dissonance, refined in seasons of resistance, and revealed in times of stillness. It's not about knowing all the answers—it's about deciding what questions you refuse to stop asking. It's not about having a ten-year plan—it's about having a one-degree shift in the right direction. Clarity doesn't eliminate uncertainty. It just gives you something stronger to follow than fear.

And here's what most people miss: clarity isn't static. It evolves. The version of clarity that led me into a new season five years ago isn't the same one that sustains me today. The dreams that used to drive me don't have the same fire. That's not failure—it's growth. I've had to rewrite visions that once felt sacred because they no longer matched the man I was becoming. And that's the beauty of navigating life with intentionality: you're allowed to change the destination when the person steering the wheel becomes wiser.

So, what does this mean for you? It means you don't need to wait for perfect timing to begin. You need to anchor your direction in truth. Choose a single sentence that defines your next horizon. Clarify the non-negotiable values you will build around. Set the vision not by the world's applause but by your soul's alignment. And then take that first imperfect, faith-fueled step. The path may not be paved. But with clarity, it will always be yours.

This is what it means to navigate. Not to wander. Not to guess. But to move with grounded discernment, eyes forward, soul awake. That's the role of clarity in achieving goals—it's not just the light on the path. It's the reason you walk it.

How to Set Vision-Driven, Actionable Goals

There was a season of my life when my calendar was full, but my soul felt empty. I was saying yes to everything that looked like progress—booked engagements, impressive meetings, collaborative invitations—but deep down, I knew I was building something that didn't fully reflect me. I wasn't lost because I lacked ambition—I was lost because I was executing goals that no longer matched the man I was becoming. And that's the trap so many of us fall into: mistaking movement for meaning. We sprint ahead with vision boards and deadlines, but without anchoring those goals to identity, purpose, and structure, we drift. And drift doesn't feel like failure at first. It feels like fatigue.

That's why setting vision-driven, actionable goals is less about chasing achievement and more about aligning with truth. For me, this process always begins with identity. I remember the exact morning when this became crystal clear. I was recovering from back-to-back travel, sitting in my home office surrounded by whiteboards filled with strategy. And yet, I felt distant from all of it. I grabbed a notepad and wrote just one question: *"What kind of man do I need to become to carry what I say I want?"* That one question changed everything. Because here's the truth—goals are not just about what you want to have; they're about who you must become in the process of building them.

That morning, I didn't write down another to-do list. I wrote a to-be list. "I want to become a man who honors his word to himself." "I want to become someone whose peace isn't sacrificed for progress." "I want to be a builder of legacies, not just platforms." That shift—from doing to becoming—wasn't a motivational gimmick. It was a soul-level reframe. Because when your goals reflect who you are and not just what you want, they gain roots. They weather resistance. They don't evaporate the moment you hit adversity—they get stronger in it.

But even identity isn't enough without emotional alignment. Goals without emotional resonance become mechanical. You can grind your way to a win, but it will hollow you out if it's not tied to something deeper. I had to get radically honest: why does this matter to me? When I first sat down to write this book, I didn't just think about chapters or structure—I thought about my sons. I imagined them reading these words long after I'm gone. That became my "why." This wasn't just a project—it was a legacy. When your goals are anchored in something that stirs your soul, discipline becomes devotion.

Still, clarity and conviction mean little without structure. At one point, I had dozens of ideas for the book—sticky notes, voice memos, scattered Google Docs. It felt overwhelming. So, I gave myself a clear constraint: one chapter drafted every three weeks. That was the cadence. Not because it was the fastest route—but because it was sustainable, and sustainability builds trust. I embedded writing blocks into my calendar, protected them like appointments with destiny, and tracked my emotional energy, not just my word count. That structure made the vision not just possible—but real.

I've come to believe that *structure is a form of self-respect*. You don't need to wait until life calms down or motivation strikes. You just need to decide what matters and build around it. In one season, that meant waking up at 4:45 AM to write while the house was silent. In another, it meant stepping away from opportunities that didn't align—even if they looked shiny on the surface. When your structure is based on internal conviction instead of external pressure, your goals begin to breathe with life.

To make goals actionable, I use a simple but powerful method I call "Vision Mapping." Start with the end. Describe it vividly—not just what it looks like, but what it *feels* like to live in that future. Then, reverse-engineer the path back to the present. Break it down into 90-day sprints. Identify no more than three priority outcomes. Attach them to weekly behaviors. Then attach those behaviors to specific time blocks on your calendar. Not vague intentions— visible commitments. Goals become alive when they're traceable.

But here's something most people ignore: you must build emotional scaffolding too. I've built circles of accountability not just to push me, but to *hold* me. My wife, my inner circle, my mentors—they've challenged me, checked me, and in some seasons, carried me. You don't need a crowd. You need a handful of people who aren't impressed by your image and are committed to your growth. Community is not a productivity hack—it's a resilience strategy.

Finally, vision-driven goals must be checked—not as a guilt trip, but as a growth gauge. Every Sunday night, I ask myself three questions: *Where did I move with integrity? Where did I drift? What matters most this week?* That rhythm of reflection isn't a ritual—it's a recalibration. It's what keeps me from wandering when the winds of life start shifting. It's not about perfection—it's about presence.

Here's what I know for sure: when your goals are rooted in identity, aligned with purpose, and carried by structure, you stop chasing achievement to prove something. You start building from a place of knowing. You're no longer driven by fear of falling behind—you're drawn by the gravity of who you're becoming. This isn't performance. This is embodiment.

And that's the real goal—not just to hit a number, land a promotion, or check a box—but to become the kind of person who leads, loves, and lives with vision as the compass and conviction as the fuel.

When you build goals this way, you don't burn out—you break through.

Avoiding Fractionable Distractions

Success doesn't follow a straight line as you navigate throughout life. It weaves, pivots, stutters, and restarts. But one truth never changes: if you lose your direction, you lose your way. The map may shift, the terrain may surprise you, but your destination requires you to keep orienting back toward it. And the greatest threat to that orientation isn't always failure—it's distraction.

I learned this not during a burnout or breakdown, but in the middle of what looked like high-functioning success. My schedule was full. My team was thriving. The outside world saw momentum. But internally, something had started to shift. The work I used to approach with sharp focus and deep conviction began to feel diluted. The mission didn't disappear—but it was harder to reach. Every time I sat down to create, to vision, to build— what had once been sacred time felt interrupted by a thousand urgent but unimportant demands. My attention, once whole, had become fractioned.

One of the clearest moments came during a trip to Phoenix. I was there to keynote a leadership event—something I had looked forward to for weeks. I flew in early to mentally lock in, fine-tune the message, and connect with the pulse of what the room needed. But instead, I spent the day fielding "quick" calls, checking in on side projects, responding to messages that didn't need me, and tweaking a presentation for a completely different event. By evening, I realized I had been everywhere but present. And even though I had been busy, I hadn't touched the talk I came to give. I had confused motion for meaning.

That night, I sat with my journal and wrote what became a personal compass: *If everything matters, nothing does.*

Not long after, during another event in Chicago, I found myself wandering the city the night before a major session. I passed a cozy jazz café, and on impulse, stepped inside. I struck up a conversation with a man at the bar—a former executive who had walked away from a high-profile career. He told me something that echoed what I had been living: "I didn't burn out from the work. I burned out from all the little distractions that looked like opportunities." At first, I nodded politely. But later that night, his words cracked something open. I wasn't overwhelmed by failures—I was being buried by micro-compromises. All the things I said yes to, that didn't serve the core mission.

And then came the memory of a pilot friend who once told me, "If you're even one degree off course, over time, you'll land hundreds of miles from your intended destination." That line stayed with me. Pilots don't assume their heading is fine—they check it constantly. Not because they expect turbulence, but because they respect the destination. Leadership—real leadership—is the same. If you're not constantly checking your heading, you're drifting. And the most dangerous drift is the one that feels like progress.

Walking back to my hotel that night, I pulled out my phone and deleted half my session slides. I stripped the talk down to its core—no fluff, no filler, just the heart of the message. And the next morning, I delivered one of the most focused keynotes of my career. Not because I said something new, but because I cut everything that didn't belong. *Focus isn't about doing less. It's about knowing what not to do.*

Distraction doesn't always look like mindless scrolling or an overflowing inbox. Sometimes, it's an impressive opportunity that's just a few degrees off your mission. It's the invitation that strokes your ego but splits your focus. It's the small "yes" that bends your week around someone else's priorities. Over time, those minor detours become major distance from your vision. These are what I call *fractionable distractions*. They don't wreck your mission all at once—they slice it into forgettable pieces.

The hardest part of building anything meaningful isn't the crash—it's the drift. The drift is subtle. It's quiet. It doesn't scream like failure or knock you down like crisis. It whispers. It rationalizes. It disguises itself as progress. And if you're not vigilant, it will carry you off course one seemingly harmless decision at a time.

And let's be real—the noise isn't just external. It's internal. For me, distraction often wore the mask of discipline. I'd check all the boxes, show up on time, respond quickly—but deep down, I was avoiding the real work. The vulnerable work. The work that would stretch me. So I buried myself in shallow tasks that gave the illusion of control. Busyness isn't always productivity. Sometimes, it's emotional avoidance in disguise.

That's when I started building what I now call *mental aviation*. Like a pilot mid-flight, I began doing weekly course checks: Where am I actually headed? What's pulling me off center? What needs to be trimmed or delayed? That reset became sacred. Because when you lose sight of your own compass, you start flying toward everyone else's.

I restructured my mornings—no email, no social media, no reactive tasks.

Just one deep focus block for my most mission-critical work. I cleared my workspace. Closed all tabs. Put the phone in another room. Not because I was trying to be productive—but because I was trying to be present. Every part of my environment became a vote for what mattered. That's what leadership is: voting for your future with your focus.

But strategy alone won't save you. You also need alignment. Because the more disconnected you feel from your purpose, the more likely you are to chase distractions. The brain craves meaning—and if your work doesn't provide it, your attention will wander until something else does. So before you blame your phone, ask yourself a harder question: *Do I still believe in what I'm building?*

And if the answer isn't an immediate yes, go deeper. Reconnect with your why. Rebuild conviction. Purpose isn't just a concept—it's emotional traction. When you have it, focus becomes magnetic. You stop having to force yourself to stay locked in. You *want* to be there.

Of course, life will always try to scatter you. That's why systems matter. Time block your calendar. Assign your most meaningful work to your highest-energy hours. Reclaim your physical space. Prioritize rest. Protect your fuel. Fatigue will take your focus before failure does.

And then, once a week, stop and recalibrate. Ask: *What worked? What distracted me? What matters most right now?* Don't treat reflection as a luxury—it's a form of course correction. It's how you lead yourself before you try to lead anyone else.

Avoiding distraction isn't about perfect discipline or pristine conditions. It's about building internal and external environments that honor your direction. It's about recovering your focus when you lose it. Because you will lose it. The goal isn't perfection—it's pattern interruption.

Each time you return to center, each time you say no to what doesn't serve your path, you are casting a vote for your future. That's not just productivity. That's navigation.

And in a world full of noise, those who stay aligned will always lead the way.

Creating a Resilience Roadmap

The first thing I saw when we rolled into the Forward Operating Base in Iraq was not a flag, not a welcome banner, not even a commanding officer. It was a blunt, stenciled message in faded red across a slab of concrete near the entry control point: **"COMPLACENCY KILLS."** It wasn't decoration. It was doctrine. And it slammed into my chest like cold steel. The air was thick with sand and diesel. The scent of grit and gear clung to my uniform. The sun burned hot overhead, but that warning—that warning was colder than any breeze I'd ever felt. We weren't being invited in. We were being reminded: let your focus slip, just once, and you might not make it back out.

That phrase has echoed in my mind more than any battlefield order. Because even outside of combat, complacency doesn't just dull your edge—it erodes your identity. It disguises itself as comfort. It whispers that discipline can wait, that excellence is exhausting, that today is safe enough. But complacency is a slow thief. And its most dangerous trick is that it feels like rest while it robs you of your resilience.

Resilience is not brute force. It's navigation—through fatigue, through failure, through fog. It's the inner compass that keeps you pressing forward when the terrain shifts beneath your feet. But let's not pretend it arrives pre-installed. Resilience isn't downloaded. It's constructed, and it must be reinforced through lived experience—brick by bloody brick.

I built mine the way I imagine most people do: by failing first. By freezing in the face of pressure. By showing up to the wrong mission with the right tools. I remember once being dropped into a situation where the intel was bad, the comms were down, and the backup was late. I was a junior leader at the time, still gripping too tightly to theory and not enough to instinct. What saved me that day wasn't speed. It was recall. It was the endless hours of "what-if" drills, the rehearsals of "If this happens, then that," the contingency muscle memory that kicked in when my confidence collapsed. Resilience, I learned, isn't about always knowing what to do—it's about trusting the protocol when panic arrives.

And that protocol begins with something I call the **Why Stack.** It's not just a mission statement. It's a layered structure built to survive adversity. You don't discover it in daylight—you construct it in the dark. On one level, maybe your "why" is financial freedom. But peel that back—why do you want that? To buy time. Why? To spend it with people who matter. Why? Because you lost too many years to scarcity. You keep digging until you reach the wound. Because resilience doesn't come from inspiration—it comes from anchoring your action to something sacred.

But your "why" isn't enough. In every high-stress environment, we trained using **"contingency stacking."** We rehearsed failure—not to invite it, but to remove its surprise. Miss your mark? Fall back to Plan Bravo. Gear jammed? Shift to hand signals. Vehicle compromised? Switch to foot patrol. The fluidity saved lives. Now in civilian life, that looks like a simple question: If life disrupts your plan, how fast can you re-engage? If you miss a goalpost, do you spiral—or adapt? Resilience isn't about avoiding setbacks—it's about **reducing the cost of re-entry.** It's about knowing what to do when life punches your vision in the face.

But even elite strategy is worthless without energy. I can still remember what burnout felt like during one of my first stateside reintegration tours. I was showing up, performing, checking boxes—but numb inside. I didn't feel present. I was exhausted before the day began. And I thought I could outgrind it. That's the lie burnout tells you: just push harder. But pushing without fuel is erosion. That's why I started doing something that changed everything—I conducted **energy audits.** Like a supply sergeant tracking ammo, I logged what drained me, what fueled me. Long meetings? Drain. Solo strategic work with jazz in the background? Fuel. Conflict with no resolution? Drain. A walk with no phone? Fuel. I built rituals around refueling. I treated it like training. Because without energy, even the strongest map is useless.

And if we're going to build resilience, we must fight what I call the **Seven Silent Saboteurs.** These are the destructive habits that, left unchecked, break down your foundation from within.

The first is **procrastination.** I've stared at blank screens long enough to know it's not laziness—it's fear. I used to delay writing reports after field ops, convincing myself I needed more data. In truth, I was avoiding the discomfort of reliving hard choices I made. But I learned: action creates clarity. Start small with one sentence, start now. One rep. One step. Motion dissolves paralysis.

Second is **negative self-talk.** I've heard louder inner critics in civilian life than I ever did in uniform. After missing a business opportunity I'd chased for months, I caught myself saying, "You're not meant for this." That voice? It wasn't truth—it was trauma. And I had to replace it by speaking truth with kindness, sentence by sentence: "You're still in the fight. You're learning. You're building grit." Speak to yourself like you would to a soldier who just made it out alive. Honor the fight. Then regroup.

The third: **comparison.** There was a time when I watched peers rise fast— book launches, stage invites, viral moments. And I felt like I was stuck in a holding pattern. But then I remembered what we say before every deployment: **"Different mission. Different timing."** You don't judge a sniper's success by an infantryman's speed. Your lane is yours. Stay in it. Practice gratitude and celebrate your progress.

Fourth is **excuse-making.** I've justified inaction with some elegant excuses: "The market's not ready." "The timing's off." I was trying to out-reason my own reluctance. But at the heart of it all was fear. And I had to ask myself: "Am I protecting my future or preserving my comfort?" Because excuses are comfortable. Ownership is brutal—but it's also a gateway. Choose extreme ownership.

The fifth saboteur is **multitasking.** We've glamorized it, but in combat, doing too many things at once gets people hurt. The best missions were surgical: one focus, one goal, one team. In life, focus is force. Scatter your attention, and you dilute your impact. I now build my days like missions—brief, execute, debrief. One clear target at a time and commit to focus

Sixth: **perfectionism.** There were speeches I never gave, projects I never launched, because I thought they needed to be flawless. But the battlefield taught me: plans don't survive first contact. Prioritize progress, it beats polish. Show up. Adjust. Grow. It's not weakness to be unfinished—it's strength to keep building.

Finally, the most seductive habit: **comfort-seeking.** After war, I thought I deserved rest. And I did. But I started mistaking stillness for success. Comfort became my enemy when it kept me from the edge. I wasn't in danger—but I was in drift. And drift, left unchecked, becomes decay. Pursue courage daily.

These seven habits? They're quiet. They rarely shout. But they are persistent. And if you don't name them, they'll narrate your life.

So here's what I've built instead: a daily rhythm of realignment. Each week, I check in—like a patrol leader scanning the horizon. What's draining me? Where am I slipping? What can I recalibrate? I make resilience a ritual. Because if you want to build a future that doesn't just survive but leads, you have to do more than endure—you have to evolve.

Legacy isn't built in comfort. It's forged in the fire of intentional habits, fierce honesty, and relentless course correction. Every morning you choose to start, despite how you feel, you're proving that the mission matters more than the mood. That's not hustle. That's heart.

But don't stop there. Reinforce your environment for success. Clean your space. Declutter your calendar. Limit your exposure to negativity. Set your life up to reflect your highest priorities, not your lowest habits. Surround yourself with accountability—coaches, friends, communities who challenge you to grow. Build rhythms of reflection into your week. Ask: *What's working? What needs to shift? What small win can I celebrate today?* Reflect. Refine. Repeat.

And when the road gets hard—and it will—lean into purpose. Remind yourself why you started. Who are you becoming? What's the cost of staying the same? Anchor into your why. Then pair it with laser focus and patient persistence. You're not just building habits—you're rebuilding identity. You're not just tweaking behaviors—you're transforming your life.

Words matter. Speak life over yourself. Declare daily: *"I'm getting better. I'm doing the work. I'm building a future I'm proud of."* Let your language reflect your new mindset. Let your actions reinforce your new identity. And don't wait for the perfect day. Start now. Show up today. Do it imperfectly, but do it consistently.

Because this is more than a productivity shift. It's a personal revolution. A life transformed one habit at a time. And on the other side of that transformation is a version of you that doesn't just dream—but executes. That doesn't just exist—but thrives. That doesn't just wish—but builds.

Your future is waiting—not on chance, but on change. And that change begins with the decision you make today.

You are not the product of your distractions. You are the architect of your resilience.

So build.

And when the wind shifts and the mission gets muddy, remember: **Complacency kills. But clarity? Clarity navigates you home.**

The Four Intelligences To Navigate Clarity and Alignment

Resilience isn't just a test of your will. It's the result of your entire **intelligence system working in harmony.** For too long, we've celebrated IQ as the lone metric of brilliance. But success in life, leadership, and legacy-building requires four dimensions working together:

> **IQ** gives you strategy.
> **EQ** gives you empathy.
> **SQ** gives you relational depth.
> **AQ** gives you grit.

I've walked into boardrooms wearing a tailored suit with PowerPoint slides in hand, and I've walked into Forward Operating Bases in combat gear with sand in my teeth and tension thick enough to slice with a knife. In both places, one truth has remained: intelligence alone does not equate to impact. Success, clarity, and legacy are not built on intellect in isolation—they're built on integration. What separates those who navigate adversity from those who are crushed by it isn't just mindset. It's how their entire intelligence system is wired to respond, realign, and rise.

There was a day in Iraq I'll never forget. We were halfway through a mission, navigating through a series of broken-down alleyways in a village just outside of Ramadi. The air was heavy with heat and tension—every shadow looked suspect, every corner a potential ambush. Our comms were spotty, visibility was low, and intel had just shifted. A junior soldier in our unit froze, wide-eyed and breathing shallow. He had all the training—IQ off the charts, sharp as steel in the classroom. But his nervous system hadn't caught up with his knowledge. And so I knelt next to him, looked him dead in the eye, and said, "Breathe. Lock in. Remember who you are." In that moment, it wasn't strategy that saved us—it was emotional regulation, human connection, and the ability to regain composure under fire. That was EQ. That was AQ. That was resilience in motion.

We've been sold a narrow definition of intelligence—measured in test scores, grades, and standardized logic puzzles. But the real test of intelligence isn't how much you know. It's how effectively you adapt, lead, connect, and endure. Especially when the map doesn't match the terrain.

Yes, IQ matters. It's your ability to analyze, synthesize, and problem-solve. It builds systems, architects visions, and decodes complexity. I've used IQ to construct training pipelines, to design business frameworks, to pivot quickly under pressure. But I've also seen IQ fail in real time when leaders couldn't flex with people, couldn't feel the room, couldn't read their team's emotional weather. IQ without EQ is a robot with a clipboard—efficient, but disconnected. And disconnected leadership doesn't last.

EQ—emotional intelligence—is what allowed me to lead people, not just missions. It's the difference between reacting to pressure and responding with presence. When I returned home and was building my first business, I hit a wall. Rejections piled up. Doors closed. Some nights I'd sit alone with a bottle of water and a legal pad, wondering if I had what it took. It wasn't intellect that helped me keep going—it was the decision to manage my internal narrative. To speak to myself with grit and grace. To override panic with perspective. EQ isn't soft. It's steel wrapped in empathy. It's the capacity to hold tension without transferring it. To be frustrated without becoming fragile. To be grounded when everything feels like it's crumbling.

But then there's SQ—social intelligence—the ability to navigate relationships, read energy, adjust tone, and build trust. In a military context, it looked like knowing when to challenge my commanding officer and when to hold the line. In civilian leadership, it meant sensing when my team was near burnout, when silence in a meeting wasn't agreement but exhaustion. SQ is the unspoken language of culture. It's knowing how to deliver hard feedback without shattering morale. It's the gift of reading nuance, and the discipline to respond with intention.

And then, the most underrated—and arguably most essential—form of intelligence: AQ. Your Adversity Quotient. It's what's left when the plan fails. When the funding falls through. When the launch doesn't land. AQ is the fire in your gut that refuses to flicker out. It's what kept me moving after 18-hour days in the desert, what got me back up after business deals imploded, what helped me keep writing when the words didn't flow. AQ doesn't care about optics. It cares about endurance. It's the quiet force that keeps your feet moving forward when your mind screams to quit.

But intelligence—any kind—will collapse without belief. Not belief in theory, or belief in luck. I'm talking about the gritty, stubborn belief that you are capable of building what you haven't yet seen. Psychologists call it self-efficacy. I call it your internal vote of confidence. And that vote gets cast with every decision to stay in the game. I've had mornings when I woke up and didn't feel inspired. When my goals felt distant, and the noise of self-doubt was louder than any motivational quote. But belief isn't a feeling. It's a discipline. It's forged in follow-through.

When I trained to navigate by night, I was taught to orient off the stars—not because they change, but because they anchor. Belief is like that. It doesn't guarantee the terrain won't shift, but it gives you a fixed point in chaos. It reminds you that you don't need to see the whole path. You just need to trust your next step.

That's how resilience is built. Not in declarations, but in integration. When IQ builds the strategy, EQ builds the connection, SQ builds the culture, and AQ carries the mission across the finish line—even when it's uphill, in the dark, and your legs are screaming. These intelligences aren't separate compartments. They are coordinates in your internal compass. Together, they help you navigate not just toward success—but toward a life you respect.

So when the noise rises, when doubt creeps in, when the work gets heavy—check your system. Realign. Lead from the center. Because clarity doesn't just come from thinking harder. It comes from aligning deeper. And that alignment is not a personality trait. It's a navigational choice.

And those who make that choice daily? They don't just achieve goals.

They become the kind of leaders whose very presence gives others permission to rise.

Words Create Worlds

I still remember the hallway before I walked into Colin Powell's office—marble floors gleaming, the quiet hum of power thick in the air, that sense of importance that only Washington, D.C., seems to carry. I had already traded my uniform for a suit by then, but the lessons of service still pulsed beneath the surface of my skin. I had been through the sandstorms of Iraq, through the discipline and demand of military life, and now I found myself in a new battlefield—one of identity, purpose, and direction. I wasn't carrying a weapon anymore. I was carrying questions: Who am I now? Where am I going? And what voice do I lead with when the external armor is gone?

General Powell greeted me with a strength that was calm, not loud. A quiet authority that didn't demand respect—it earned it before a word was spoken. The son of Jamaican immigrants, a decorated war hero, a Secretary of State, and yet—he made space for someone like me, a young Black man fresh into the next chapter of life, carrying ambition in one hand and uncertainty in the other. His office wasn't just decorated with awards and flags. It was covered in stories—photos of meetings with presidents, soldiers, world leaders, and communities. Every frame seemed to whisper, *"You belong here if you're willing to carry the weight of clarity."*

I asked him something I don't even fully remember now—something about leadership, about purpose in transition. What I do remember is what he told me next. He leaned in, looked me directly in the eyes, and said, *"Your words are the scaffolding—you build your world one sentence at a time."*

That sentence rewired me. Not just in that moment, but in the days, weeks, and years to come. It was more than advice. It was a transmission. It was permission—to build, to speak, to lead. It anchored something deep inside me that had been floating untethered. I walked out of that room not just inspired, but armed—with the understanding that the architecture of my future would rise or fall on the vocabulary I chose to use, both out loud and internally.

See, in the military, language is everything. Clarity saves lives. Miscommunication can get someone hurt. Ambiguity has no place in a mission-critical environment. You say what you mean. You execute what you speak. But outside that world, language became something else—sloppy, emotional, vague. People say "someday" and "maybe" and "hopefully." But those aren't words that move mountains. They are words that delay destiny.

When I transitioned out of uniform, I had to rebuild my inner dialogue. Not just for my own sake, but eventually for the thousands I would go on to serve as a speaker and coach. I had to learn that *words weren't just expressions— they were instructions.* I had to trade in the passive language of waiting for the language of designing. Saying "I hope" became "I will." Saying "I don't know" became "I'm figuring it out." Saying "I'm not ready" became "I'm building the capacity."

And I watched my world respond to the shift.

It wasn't immediate. Direction never is. But brick by brick, through daily declarations and consistent recalibrations, my path took shape. Not because I had the answers—but because I started speaking the questions that mattered, the commitments that anchored me, and the identity I was growing into.

Direction isn't just about where you're going. It's about the language you use to get there. And language—when repeated with clarity and alignment— becomes the GPS of your transformation. Most people are trying to move without ever telling life where they want to go. It's like stepping into a cab and telling the driver, "I don't know. Just drive." That's not leadership. That's wandering.

That's why I built and now teach the **Clarity Compass™**. Because your vision must live outside your head. You need language that anchors identity: *"I'm becoming the kind of man who keeps promises to himself."* You need words that chart vision: *"Here's what I will build in the next 12 months across my personal, professional, relational, financial, and spiritual life."* You need words that move feet: *"This is my next step today, not someday."*

But this is deeper than strategy. This is soul work. Because words don't just live on your lips. They shape the wiring of your nervous system. They either activate your power or anesthetize your potential. The more I spoke with clarity, the more I moved with integrity. The more I declared who I was becoming, the more I stopped negotiating with distraction.

I remember being backstage once before a keynote—the kind of event I used to only dream of. I was nervous. Not unprepared, just human. I felt that old whisper start to rise: *"What if you're not enough?"* But instead of spiraling, I said something I learned to say years ago: *"I was built for this. I've bled for this. I speak because I carry fire, not because I need applause."* I walked on that stage not because the fear disappeared, but because my words overruled it.

Words are not decoration. They are direction. And when they align with vision, your entire nervous system follows. Your brain scans for patterns that support what you say. Your habits shift to meet the standard you've spoken. Your relationships either deepen or dissolve depending on the frequency of your expression. Your world quite literally begins to shape itself to the sentences you repeat with conviction.

But clarity requires subtraction too. I had to strip away the vague language. The excuses cloaked in busyness. The "I'll try" and "Maybe one day" that used to sound humble but were really just fear in disguise. I began to protect my language like I protect my energy—because they are the same.

And I started passing that truth on. In rooms full of leaders, students, parents, entrepreneurs—people looking for direction—I challenge them to change their words first. Before the business plan. Before the schedule. Before the resume. Start with this: *What are you speaking over your life?* Because you can't build an extraordinary future with a vocabulary of limitation.

What I learned from Powell, from the battlefield, and from the platform is this: *Clarity isn't a lightning strike—it's a linguistic discipline.* The people who build legacy-level lives aren't always the smartest. They're the most aligned. They speak with intention, live with precision, and recalibrate with humility.

You don't need a miracle. You need language that matches the life you're building.

So wake up and work it.

Speak the truth that scares you into movement.
 Declare the identity that future-you is waiting for.
 Build the next chapter, not just with effort—but with articulation.

Because this life doesn't bend to intentions.
 It bends to direction.

And *your words*—fully aligned, unapologetically spoken, anchored in vision—are how you lead that direction with power.

BREAK THE BOTTLE CHALLENGE — Chapter 10

Design the Life That Doesn't Drift

We've spent this chapter building the architecture of clarity, direction, and resilience.
Now it's time to put the blueprint into motion.

This challenge isn't theoretical.
It's tactical.
And it's yours.

Because clarity without action becomes clutter.
Vision without structure becomes a wish.
And belief without behavior? That's just noise.

Step 1: Define Your Next 90-Day Goal

Pick one outcome that matters deeply to you. Don't chase 10 things—choose the one thing that, if completed, would move your life forward in a meaningful way.
Make it specific, measurable, and time-bound.

Ask yourself:
What would I be proud to complete in the next 90 days?

Step 2: Reframe It as an Identity

Now, phrase that goal as an affirmation of who you are becoming.

Instead of: "Make $10,000 in sales."

Try: "I am becoming someone who delivers transformative value and receives abundant reward."

This isn't semantics—it's transformation through identity.

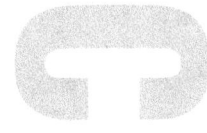

Step 3: Map Your First 7 Days

What three simple, high-leverage actions can you take this week to move toward that 90-day goal?
They don't need to be big—they need to be clear.

Examples:

- Schedule a meeting with a mentor.

- Finalize your offer.

- Clear your morning for deep work.

- Create your content calendar.

- Block out distraction time zones.

Write them. Then schedule them.

Step 4: Create Your If/Then Resilience Plan

Anticipate where it might fall apart.

Example:
If I feel overwhelmed midweek, then I will revisit my "Why Stack" and do 15 minutes of movement to reset.
If I miss a day, then I recommit with a 10-minute task the next morning—no guilt, no delay.

This is your recovery script—burn it into your mind.

Step 5: Declare Your Belief

Before you execute, write this down:

"I am not just planning a future—I am becoming someone who lives it.
Each action I take confirms who I choose to be.
This isn't about motivation.
It's about identity.
And I'm done drifting."

Because that's what breaking the bottle really means:
Refusing to let small distractions dictate a big destiny.
Refusing to trade momentum for mediocrity.
And choosing—daily—to lead your life like the future depends on it.

Because it does.

PART 3

DESTINATION

ACHIEVING EXTRAORDINARY SUCCESS & OWN THE FUTURE

Success is seductive. It whispers that you've arrived. It convinces you that because something's working, you no longer need to evolve. That your hustle has earned you rest. That excellence is now optional. But that's the great deception: it tricks you into thinking you've reached the mountaintop, when in truth, you've only reached the next base camp. The real danger isn't failure—it's stagnation disguised as victory. What looks like arrival is often just a temporary summit. The moment you stop climbing, you start sliding. The real threat to greatness isn't adversity—it's comfort. Because comfort breeds complacency. And complacency is the silent killer of destiny.

When you succeed, the world claps. But if you're not vigilant, your standards soften. You coast on yesterday's effort. You start defending where you are instead of pursuing who you could become. You stop asking hard questions. You slow down your hunger. You wait for life to challenge you—instead of being the challenge yourself. You begin to believe that your old drive is enough for a new level. But the truth is, what got you here will not get you there.

That's why this final part of the journey is the most dangerous—and the most defining. Destination isn't about checking a box or crossing a finish line. It's about becoming someone who sustains their breakthrough. Someone who refuses to plateau. Someone who doesn't just dream—someone who lives aligned with that dream every single day. Destination is a transformation so deep that you become unrecognizable to the version of yourself that once settled for less.

This isn't about hype. This is about identity. You don't want fleeting moments of greatness—you want a foundation that holds under pressure. That's why it begins with **Alignment**. Real alignment means your habits, decisions, relationships, and actions are all working in service of your larger vision. Not some of them. All of them. Every choice either reinforces your direction or erodes it. This is where you eliminate the leaks, declutter the distractions, and hold everything in your life to a new standard. You're not just moving anymore—you're moving with ruthless precision.

Then comes **Engage**. You reinvest. You stretch. You grow. You take what you've learned and build on it. You become the student again. You remain hungry. You don't just chase goals—you expand your impact. You stop seeing success as a mountaintop and start seeing it as a launchpad. A platform for what's next. A place from which you elevate others and multiply your legacy.

After that, it's time to **Sustainability**. Breakthroughs don't maintain themselves. Success fades without care. Sustaining what you've built demands structures that reinforce your growth—systems, routines, and people that keep you grounded. Momentum gets you started, but support keeps you standing. Resilience isn't just bouncing back—it's staying ready. It's knowing how to anchor yourself in stormy seasons so you don't unravel the moment life gets hard.

And that's where we separate the motivated from the committed. The world is full of hype. But true success? It's built in the dark—through discipline, ownership, and relentless execution. Life is tough by design. And excuses don't survive under scrutiny—especially the most common one: "I don't have time." Let's kill that lie right now.

There are **168 hours** in a week. If you sleep 56 and work 50, you still have over **60 hours left**. The issue isn't time—it's priorities. What are you doing with the hours no one is counting but you? Most people spend them in distraction. The elite invest them like gold. Every hour is a seed. And one hour of deep, focused effort each day—stacked over six months—equals more than **130 hours** of transformation. That's how you separate. That's how you rise. The greats didn't win because they worked hard once. They won because they **became the work**.

Discipline is what holds the dream together. It's not occasional effort— it's daily ownership. It's showing up when it's hard. It's honoring your commitment even when the applause fades. The road to real success is paved with early mornings, quiet sacrifice, and relentless resolve. The version of you that got you here cannot take you where you're going. You need a new level of grit. Not emotional hype—non-negotiable, no-matter-what discipline. The kind that builds legacy while no one's watching.

Your environment will either sharpen or sabotage that discipline. The people closest to you are either stretching you or shrinking you. Every conversation, every interaction, every shared space is influencing your energy, your mindset, and your momentum. That's why you must be intentional about your circle. Mediocrity loves company—but so does greatness. Choose iron. Surround yourself with truth-tellers. People who will challenge your excuses and call you higher.

You must design your external world to reflect your internal standards. Cut the noise. Cancel the compromises. Every tab you leave open, every excuse you tolerate, every toxic relationship you justify—it's costing you alignment. Excellence isn't accidental—it's accumulated. So is mediocrity. You choose one or the other by the standards you reinforce every day.

And here's the reality: no one is coming to save you. No one owes you a platform. You build your future by becoming the kind of person who can handle the weight of that future. Leadership is not about noise—it's about consistency. It's about private standards that don't crumble under public pressure. Success is not a destination—it's a responsibility. The farther you go, the more is required. Your internal standards must always exceed external expectations. Otherwise, you will slowly conform to the status quo. It's about becoming the kind of man or woman who is **self-led**, not situationally motivated.

Discipline is not punishment—it's power. It's freedom. It breaks the chains of distraction and indecision. It elevates you from reactive to intentional. It gives you control over your focus, your energy, your identity. The disciplined life isn't always flashy—but it's the only one that creates real, lasting results. The one that leaves legacy, not just a legacy post.

And legacy? It's not one moment. It's every decision. Every rep. Every day you show up when it's hard. Every time you choose progress over comfort. It's the way you lead yourself when no one's watching. The way you carry weight when others drop it. The way you give more than you take. Legacy is not about fame. It's about **force**. The force of your integrity. The force of your consistency. The force of a life that speaks long after your voice is gone.

So here's the charge: **Own your future.** Not in theory. Not someday. Now.

Fully. Boldly. With everything you've got. There are people counting on you. People watching you. People drawing strength from your example. You don't need to be the loudest. You need to be the most locked in. You don't need permission. You need precision. You don't need perfect timing. You need unwavering courage.

Because greatness is never an accident. It's a choice. Made daily. Paid for in silence. And earned in full.

11

BECOMING UNSTOPPABLE

"Design your life with bold hands. Don't just dream it—build it. Don't just wish it—work it."

— Break The Bottle

The Architecture of Building a Life of Purpose Over Pressure
"The Dumbbell Moment"

There's a moment in everyone's journey where the mask of external success begins to crack—where the accolades, the followers, the income, and even the titles begin to feel hollow. That moment often doesn't come with drama. It comes in silence. A hotel room after a speech. A glance in the mirror after boarding your fifth plane in three days. Or in my case, it came in a gym—mid-curl—when the dumbbells slipped from my hands and crashed to the floor. Not because they were heavy, but because my spirit was.

It was a Wednesday. Just like every other Wednesday in that season of my life. Wake up early. Lace up my sneakers. Grab my pre-workout and head to the gym. Grind. Build. Execute. Repeat. The routine was religious. Predictable. And successful—at least by the world's standards. I had built a thriving business, landed a top franchise spot, scaled operations, led teams, and hit numbers that made the world clap. We were on the INC. 5000 list—something only a fraction of companies ever achieve. That's not luck—that's blood, sweat, and strategy. It means you've achieved sustained, substantial revenue growth over a three-year period. It's a badge of honor in the business world. But on that particular morning, in the silence between reps, it didn't feel like a badge. It felt like a mask. And that mask shattered when the dumbbells hit the floor.

It wasn't just an accident. It was divine interruption. I didn't drop the weight because my arms were tired—I dropped it because my soul couldn't carry the disobedience anymore. I had been praying, asking God, "What do you want from me?" And for months, I'd been receiving the answer in pieces— through dreams, through scripture, through conversations, through whispers in quiet rooms. But I ignored it. I kept building. I kept producing. I kept winning. But not in alignment. And on that morning, when the iron clanged against the floor and every head in the gym turned to look, I didn't hear embarrassment—I heard a voice. Clear. Convicting. Undeniable: "Tell your story."

That moment changed everything. It wasn't dramatic on the outside, but inside, it was an earthquake. A divine confrontation. A collision between calling and comfort. I had been given a vision, a dream, a purpose—and I was running from it by hiding in success. That's the thing about winning outside of alignment: it feels good until it doesn't. It pays the bills but robs your peace. It fills your calendar but empties your soul. And in that moment, I realized I wasn't failing—I was misaligned. I had built something that worked, but it no longer felt like worship. It wasn't obedience anymore—it was avoidance.

And that gap? It was costing me something far greater than profit. It was costing me peace. Because the grind without grounding is just another form of self-destruction. I had created something worthy of headlines, but I was quietly dying behind the scenes. The dumbbell moment wasn't about weakness—it was about awakening.

Execution is not just about drive—it's about discernment. What are you building? And why? Because discipline without direction will still make you tired—but it won't make you fulfilled. This is the subtle trap no one talks about. You can be incredibly efficient at building the wrong thing. And when you arrive, the view is empty. That's why emotional clarity matters. Not because we need to be coddled, but because we need to be calibrated. I started asking deeper questions: not just "What's next?" but "What's aligned?" Not just "How can I win?" but "What does winning even mean for me now?" Because if success costs your authenticity, it's actually a form of failure. And the world is already too full of people who are impressive but empty.

So I chose differently. I walked away. I sold the franchise. I left behind a machine that I had spent years building—a system, a structure, a team, a stream of income, a piece of my identity. I walked away not because it was broken—but because I was. It wasn't collapsing. It was thriving. But I knew it was time. I had been called—not to just make noise, but to make impact. Not to chase applause, but to chase alignment. And for the first time in my life, I chose to do something that scared me more than combat ever did: I told my story. Fully. Unapologetically. Vulnerably. Transparently. Honestly. Without a script. Without a resume to back it up. With no professional speaking experience and no safety net, I stood up and opened my heart to the world. And that's when I started living.

That transition wasn't clean. It was messy, uncertain, humbling. But that's the reality of becoming unstoppable. It's not a motivational slogan. It's a thousand quiet decisions to show up even when your voice shakes, even when your bank account trembles, even when your past whispers that you're not enough. Becoming unstoppable means returning to the foundation daily—not the platform. It means refusing to let your past trauma, titles, or triumphs define your identity today. It means becoming so anchored in your purpose that the world's chaos can't move you off your path. That's not hype. That's architecture. And it starts in your mind.

Here's what most people never admit: The true battleground isn't your calendar or your to-do list. It's your internal thermostat—the one that controls your emotional response to resistance. If you believe you need to feel ready to act, you'll be stuck forever. But if you decide that action is what makes you ready, everything changes. Emotional alignment is not about waiting for the perfect mood—it's about establishing a deeper WHY so powerful that it overrides temporary discomfort. On flights, I've met clients who seemed to have it all—seven-figure businesses, massive reach—but behind their eyes, I could see what I used to feel: exhaustion masked as productivity. So I'd ask them, "Are you executing from passion or from pressure?" That one question would freeze the air between us. Because pressure execution might produce performance—but it won't produce peace.

This is why we must not only build systems but inspect the soul that's running them. When I was at my lowest—on 13 mental health medications, navigating a second divorce, separated from my son, and lost in a fog that felt like Groundhog Day—I wasn't failing due to a lack of structure. I was operating from emotional depletion. No system works if the soul running it is empty. That's why healing must precede optimization. Before I could get back to business, I had to get back to wholeness. That journey didn't begin with another checklist—it began with surrender. I sought therapy. I found mentors. I sat in silence long enough to hear the voice that mattered again. I stopped treating my healing as a side project and made it the main project. Because you can't outrun what you haven't faced. You can't outperform what you haven't healed.

This level of relentless execution doesn't require you to be superhuman—it requires you to be deeply human. Fully present. Intentional. It asks that you feel your pain, but not follow it. That you honor your limitations without bowing to them. That you architect a lifestyle that supports who you're becoming, not just what you're producing. I've learned that execution, when aligned, becomes easier—not because the work is less hard, but because the resistance inside you has quieted. You're no longer dragging shame into every meeting. You're not performing to be enough—you're executing because you already are.

So let's dismantle the myth once and for all: you don't become unstoppable because you have superpowers. You become unstoppable because you keep choosing integrity over ease, alignment over applause, and purpose over pressure. You stop chasing moments and start building momentum. You understand that motivation is a mood, but mission is a muscle. And you train that muscle daily—through rituals, through boundaries, through radical honesty.

And yes, there are costs. You'll outgrow circles. You'll disappoint people who benefited from your smaller self. You'll be misunderstood by those who can't fathom your clarity. But the trade-off? Peace. Power. Purpose. Freedom. That is the currency of unstoppable living. And it is always worth it.

This is not theory. It's not borrowed wisdom. It's lived truth. And every time you take one more aligned step—even when it's inconvenient—you are forging the architecture of a legacy. You are declaring to the world and to your inner critic: I'm not just here to start—I'm here to finish. With excellence.

So go ahead—lace up your shoes. Recommit to the work. Look yourself in the mirror not for validation but for recognition. Recognize the warrior, the builder, the architect staring back at you. And then go to bed tired—from meaning. Wake up hungry—for impact. And repeat.

Because that's how you become unstoppable.

What It Takes to Execute Relentlessly

Relentless execution is not a catchphrase—it is a lifestyle formula. One that demands far more than grit or grind. It is about engineering your life so that excellence becomes inevitable, not optional. That's where most people falter. They believe success is driven by emotion or urgency. But true execution is constructed—deliberately—on four immovable pillars: emotional neutrality, identity-based action, commitment over motivation, and environment design. Together, they form a foundation that withstands chaos, fatigue, and resistance.

Emotional neutrality isn't about being numb—it's about being intelligent. It's the ability to feel a storm and still walk into the meeting like the sky is clear. When I first began leading high-stakes trainings for executive teams, I thought performance meant suppression. I'd check into five-star hotels, rehearse my opening line 50 times, and then step on stage pretending nothing in my life was unraveling. But that's not neutrality—that's avoidance. The real transformation happened when I let myself feel everything, but I chose to act from mission—not mood. You can acknowledge pain without bowing to it. You can honor discomfort without giving it a vote. That's emotional neutrality. It's the quiet skill that separates leaders from reactors.

From that neutrality, you execute from identity—not inspiration. This is identity-based execution. You do the work not because you feel like it, but because it's who you are. But getting there requires what I call skunkwork—deep, hidden, unglamorous labor done in the dark. That's what I did after my dumbbell moment. I went dark, not in despair—but in obedience. I pulled away from the noise and into the grind. No applause. No social media recaps. Just the Word, the work, and the weight of knowing I could no longer delay my calling.

Disobedience doesn't always look like rebellion. Sometimes it looks like hesitation. Like overthinking what you already know you're supposed to do. It's sitting on a vision that's been confirmed ten different ways and still asking for one more sign. It's praying for clarity when God already gave you the blueprint. I've watched people do it for years—brilliant leaders, creative minds, people of faith—still circling the same bush, waiting for lightning when conviction was already enough. I know because I was one of them. Disobedience doesn't always feel like defiance—it often feels like delay dressed as wisdom. But deep down, you know it's fear.

I felt that same fear when the urge to write my story wouldn't leave me alone. I remember the moment I chose to stop ignoring it and act. I flew to Houston, Texas, to meet up with a good friend of mine who was a member of the Writers Guild of America East. The WGAE is a prestigious union representing thousands of writers for film, TV, and media—a place where creative visionaries gather, protect their work, and fight for the power of the written word. It was intimidating, but I knew I had to go. Something inside me said, "You don't need credentials—you need courage."

So I went. I didn't know what I was doing, only that I was finally doing it. We sat in a quiet space, and I began writing. My life. My childhood. My battlefield. My failures. My near death moments. My guilt. My grief. My trauma. It wasn't therapy—it was obedience. But it hurt. Every sentence peeled back scars I thought I'd buried. Some days, I couldn't write more than a paragraph. Some pages ended in tears. But in the middle of that room, while I was reliving scenes I hadn't spoken aloud in years, one of the writers—Steve Belber—read what I wrote, looked at me, and said, "You have something here. Something that could change lives."

That moment hit me like a freight train. Because I'd sat on that story for nearly six years. Six years of journaling, scribbling, stuffing pages into drawers. Not because I didn't believe the story mattered—but because I didn't believe I mattered enough to tell it. I had let fear hide behind performance. But after that conversation, something changed. That dumbbell moment echoed again. I picked up the pen, locked in, and went back into the dark—not to hide, but to finish. I disappeared into the skunkwork. I let the spotlight go. I traded visibility for vulnerability. And I wrote.

Ninety days later, my first book was finished. It was raw. It was real. It was everything I had once been afraid to say out loud. But the moment I released it, the dam broke. What came from that was a best-selling memoir that started reaching people I would've never imagined. Veterans. Executives. Single moms. Former addicts. College athletes. People from every background sent messages, emails, voice notes—sharing how my story gave them permission to tell theirs.

And then came the TEDx invitation. I stood on that stage and delivered the most vulnerable talk of my life. And when the applause ended, I was greeted not with praise—but with tears. Dozens of people lined up—not to compliment, but to confess. "I've never told anyone this…" "Your story is mine, too…" "I've been hiding for years…" The heaviness in that room couldn't be staged. And it hasn't stopped since. Hundreds of talks later, the ripple hasn't slowed. But the truth? That calling didn't start in the spotlight. It started six years earlier—when I buried the story God told me to share.

So I tell you this as someone who knows the pain of disobedience and the power of alignment: relentless execution is not public—it begins in the dark. It's built in skunkwork. It's not about credentials—it's about courage. It's not about applause—it's about assignment. Your calling doesn't wait for your readiness. It waits for your response.

And that identity is only sustained by the third pillar: commitment over motivation. Motivation is a nice starter. It's what gets people hyped on New

Year's Eve. But commitment? That's what makes someone wake up on day 97, with sore joints and no applause, and still show up for the mission. When I built my leadership development business, I didn't have the luxury of waiting to "feel ready." There were weeks when my calendar was stacked with speaking engagements, client consultations, and media interviews, and I was still navigating personal healing. The temptation to reschedule, to push back, to coast was real. But I had already signed a contract—with myself. Commitment means there's no opt-out clause. It's the vow that your word matters more than your feelings. And that's what builds trust—not just with others, but with yourself.

The final pillar—the one most people underestimate—is environment design. Because here's the truth: your surroundings beat your willpower every time. If your kitchen is filled with junk food, your discipline will erode. If your workspace is cluttered with digital distractions, your focus will fracture. In my darkest days, when I was taking 13 different anti-depressant medications and feeling like life had lost color, I realized that my environment was reinforcing my despair. I had to make the hard decision to detox my world. That meant clearing my schedule of toxic commitments, cleaning out my home of triggers, and surrounding myself with symbols of life, clarity, and movement. I created what I call "trigger zones"—spaces engineered for the behavior I wanted. A morning prayer chair. A whiteboard filled with my son's future goals. A gym bag always packed by the door. These weren't decorative—they were directional. My space became a silent coach. That's environment design. When you align your world with your values, discipline stops being a battle—it becomes the default.

And if you want a clear, replicable map for living this way, I offer you the Activation Cascade—a five-stage process for turning theory into transformation: Act, Activate, Action, Identity, Actualize. It begins with one small, uncomfortable step. That's Act. It could be declining a late-night snack, journaling for 10 minutes, or finally reaching out for mentorship. That action activates a new pattern in your brain. Activate. From there, consistency builds momentum. You keep taking aligned steps. Action. With enough repetition, your brain begins to believe, "This is who I am." That's Identity. And finally, when identity becomes stable, results flow naturally.

You no longer chase greatness—it flows through you. That's Actualization. You become a living, breathing manifestation of your potential. But none of this happens unless you take that first, often scary, imperfect step.

You want to know the secret behind high performers? Here it is: they go to bed tired, and they wake up hungry. Not tired from chaos, but from purpose. Not hungry for applause, but for alignment. My best days aren't the ones when everything goes right—they're the ones when I fall asleep knowing I stewarded my time, talent, and truth with integrity. When I wake up, I don't need an external motivator. I feel an inner pull. Because the mission didn't end with yesterday's effort. The fire doesn't go out. This is the rhythm of the relentless. They don't wait to feel like it—they move anyway. Because motion, not motivation, creates momentum.

But all of that rests on one undeniable truth: you must participate in your own rescue. No podcast, no keynote, no coach—not even me—can save you from yourself. We can point. We can guide. But the work? It's yours. And if you're waiting for the perfect moment to begin, you've already surrendered to a myth. The perfect moment doesn't exist. What does exist is now. This moment. The decision to lead yourself forward, even if you're limping. Especially if you're limping. That's leadership. Not perfection—but participation.

And in that participation, you begin to confront the question that matters more than any strategy: Why are you here? Not just here reading this page—but here on this planet, in this season, with this pain and these possibilities. What have you been called to build, carry, or break? What lie have you been asked to dismantle through the boldness of your story? What community will breathe differently because you decided to speak, act, rise? These aren't abstract questions. They're architectural blueprints for the life you're here to lead.

Because when you know why you're here, discipline becomes worship. Action becomes sacred. And your life stops feeling like a series of chaotic obligations and starts becoming a mission-driven offering. That's how unstoppable people move. Not with ease—but with conviction.

How the World's Greatest Thinkers and Doers Stay in Motion

You've seen them. The ones who seem to glide through chaos, deliver under pressure, and perform at the highest levels, consistently. The Serena Williamses. The Elon Musks. The Brené Browns. The Ed Myletts. The Sara Blakelys. Whether they're building companies, authoring bestsellers, or shaping entire industries, the world's greatest thinkers and doers share one thing in common: they are in motion—not erratic motion, but aligned, disciplined, intentional movement. They don't wait for clarity. They create it. They don't depend on hype. They root themselves in habits. They aren't operating from luck—they're living from identity.

That's where it all starts. Identity unlocks destiny. If you don't know who you are, no title, platform, or paycheck will ever sustain your momentum. I've seen this firsthand—from boardrooms to green rooms, from veterans trying to recalibrate after the battlefield to rising CEOs seeking clarity in the chaos of scale. It's never just about strategy—it's about identity. Without it, you're a performer. With it, you're a powerhouse. Because when you know who you are, every decision gets filtered through alignment, not approval.

Identity confusion is momentum's greatest threat. It's what makes you overthink. Second-guess. Hesitate. You start asking the wrong people for advice, chasing shiny tactics instead of anchoring your strategy. But when identity is clear? Direction becomes obvious. Discipline becomes easier. And execution becomes natural. You don't need to be reminded to show up—you feel pulled to show up. That's why the best in the world are so consistent. They've decided who they are. And that decision shapes every single action.

It's not enough to be capable—the world rewards those who are clear. Clarity is the new currency. It turns potential into power. If you're unclear about what you bring to the table, people won't just ignore you—they'll redefine you. The world has no obligation to pause and guess your greatness. It's your responsibility to define it, speak it, own it. And no, you don't need a viral moment to begin. Your voice doesn't need mass validation. The green light is not coming. You already have it. Take up space now. Move like your calling is non-negotiable—because it is.

The high performers you admire didn't wait to be chosen—they chose themselves. I once sat across from a global marketing executive on a flight from Atlanta to San Diego. She was sharp, composed, successful by every metric. But when we started talking about leadership, she said something that hit me in the chest: "Most people drown in indecision, not incompetence." She wasn't talking about skill—she was talking about self-permission. And that's what makes the greats move—they don't just have goals; they believe they are worthy of them. They don't just set intentions—they embody them.

And while others tread water, they trailblaze. That's the difference. The world's best aren't in motion just to stay afloat—they're in motion to shift culture, reimagine norms, and create new pathways. I remember leading a training session for an executive team who were stuck in what they called "operational excellence," but what I recognized immediately was just high-functioning stagnation. They were efficient—but uninspired. Productive—but plateaued. I challenged their leadership to stop measuring progress by KPIs and to start measuring it by boldness. That meant asking: What have we initiated this quarter that didn't exist before? What risks have we taken? What norms have we broken? Because motion without innovation is just repetition. The greats don't coast—they disrupt.

And disruption requires one thing most people avoid: obsession. Not the toxic, hustle-until-you-collapse obsession. The focused, disciplined, sacred kind. The kind that wakes you up not out of fear, but out of fire. It's what I call obsession over option. High-level doers don't toggle between commitment and convenience—they've already closed the exit doors. For them, what they're building isn't optional. It's essential.

I had one of these unforgettable moments of aligned obsession while filming *Military Makeover* with Montel Williams and his cohosts. The entire experience was surreal—a former Marine like me, on a national platform, speaking to a military hero whose own story had shaped so many lives. Montel isn't just a television personality; he's a decorated Navy officer, a passionate advocate, and someone who's lived many lifetimes of resilience. Between camera takes, he and I stepped aside, and I'll never forget the gravity of that conversation. We talked about purpose, about pressure, about the way the military both molds and wounds. He looked me in the eye and said, "Success without alignment will eventually turn into self-sabotage. If you're not checking your soul, your wins will bankrupt you in ways that money can't fix."

That moment pierced me. It was a "Break The Bottle" moment. It wasn't just wisdom—it was a mirror. Here was someone who had navigated fame, battled chronic illness, spoken truth to power, and still held himself accountable to a higher mission. I remember walking back onto set not just ready to speak, but ready to recommit. It reminded me that alignment isn't a one-time decision—it's a daily one. And when you're around people who live like that, your excuses shrink. Your standards rise. That's what motion does. It awakens your discipline, your fire, your why.

Obsession isn't unhealthy when it's aligned. It becomes the frequency of excellence. Kobe Bryant understood that. His obsession wasn't with applause—it was with detail. Fundamentals. Film. Footwork. He practiced not to prove, but to perfect. That's the rhythm of greatness: fascination with the process, not just the outcome.

And from obsession flows something sacred: excellence as a standard, not an event. The best in the world finish strong. Every time. Not because they're superhuman, but because they've made excellence their identity. They don't just show up when it's glamorous. They don't disappear when it's hard. I've worked with clients navigating IPOs, legal battles, family breakdowns—and the trait that preserved their influence wasn't brilliance. It was reliability. They finished what they started. They stayed in motion—not with chaos, but with clarity.

Excellence isn't perfection. It's fidelity. It's showing up for what you said matters—when no one is clapping. It's finishing an email with clarity. It's ending a client call with integrity. It's leaving the room better than you found it. That's not ego. That's legacy. Because over time, the compound interest of small completions becomes a reputation no algorithm can suppress. And in a world obsessed with virality, reputation remains undefeated.

But here's the truth most won't say out loud: fear of failure is not a good enough excuse. The world's greatest feel fear, too. They just don't let it drive. I've stood on stages where my voice cracked, hands trembling, heart pounding—and still spoke. Not because I felt brave, but because I knew I was in alignment. That stage wasn't about me—it was about the person in the third row who needed to hear their own voice in mine. That's what purpose does. It anchors you when emotion would drown you.

You'll never become world-class by waiting for comfort. And you won't discover your capacity if you keep retreating from risk. You must step anyway. Try anyway. Fail anyway. Because failure isn't final—but delay often is. The ones who win don't always get it right—but they get in the game. They don't audition for their life. They direct it.

So, how do the best stay in motion?

They ritualize success. They systemize clarity. They surround themselves with reminders of who they are and what they're building. They read their mission aloud every morning. They review their vision every night. They protect their mornings. They prep their priorities the night before. They theme their days. They rehearse their identity in silence so they can walk in authority when it counts.

And most importantly—they don't confuse movement with momentum. They know when to push. And they know when to pause. Rest is part of the rhythm. Because exhaustion without purpose isn't productivity—it's decay. That's why recovery is scheduled. Sabbaths are honored. Reflection is built in. Because the goal is not just motion—it's meaningful motion.

That's what separates the world's best. Not just that they're moving—but that every move is aligned.

World-class execution isn't just about systems—it's about soul-aligned rhythm. The elite don't merely organize their time—they organize their identity. Their greatness doesn't hinge on occasional effort. It rests on keystone disciplines they've made non-negotiable. These aren't trendy hacks or optimization gimmicks. These are the force multipliers—the invisible disciplines that quietly ripple into every part of their lives and make their excellence sustainable.

bits that quietly ripple into every arena of their lives and make their excellence sustainable.

How High Performers Turn Setbacks Into Strategies

You want to know what separates high performers from everyone else? It's not just intellect. It's not merely raw talent. It's not the degrees on the wall or the titles on their email signature. The real difference lies in one powerful discipline: how they handle adversity. Where most people internalize failure and make it personal, high performers treat it like strategic data. They don't absorb it into their identity—they extract insight from it. They interrogate breakdowns without judgment, treat obstacles as feedback, and most importantly, convert emotional friction into refined direction.

When average thinkers fail, they default to shame. High performers default to structure. They ask questions—not about their worth, but about their process. They don't ask, "Why am I such a mess?" They ask, "What's the message in this mess?" That's a game-changing difference. It's not just emotional maturity; it's emotional intelligence in action. And that intelligence becomes the foundation for sustainable success.

I've lived this—not just on stage or in coaching sessions—but in the gritty trenches of building a company. A few years ago, my team at The Adversity Academy submitted our first major government proposal—a multi-million-dollar bid to the USDA. This wasn't some halfhearted attempt. We had assembled a powerhouse team of experts: seasoned curriculum developers, DEI strategists, trauma-informed practitioners, military consultants, and federal procurement advisors. We worked around the clock—writing, refining, rehearsing, calculating. Our approach was bold. Fresh. Rooted in lived experience and evidence-based models. We believed in what we were bringing to the table.

I remember the day we hit "submit" on that proposal. I stood in our office with my team—some virtually, some in person—and we prayed. Not just for a win, but for impact. We believed we could serve people in a way few others could. We didn't just want a contract—we wanted to transform how federal agencies understood adversity, resilience, and culture.

Weeks passed. Then came the email: **we didn't win.**

It stung. Not just because of the time invested, but because it felt personal. Like our vision was being questioned. For a few moments, the room went silent. I looked around at my team—so much talent, so much heart—and I could feel the weight. But instead of spiraling, we did something that changed everything: we paused, printed the feedback, and got to work.

We dissected every line of that rejection. Line by line. Point by point. We asked hard questions. Not "Why didn't they choose us?" but "What didn't we articulate clearly?" Not "Are we good enough?" but "How do we show them we're undeniable next time?" It wasn't emotional—it was surgical. We turned that setback into a strategy session.

We revamped our systems, redesigned our proposal architecture, and doubled down on clarity. We refined our messaging—not just for clarity, but for conviction. We made sure that every sentence screamed alignment, capacity, and credibility. And here's what happened: **we went on to win our next three federal contracts in a row.** Each one multi-seven figures. Each one spanning three to five years. Each one proof that strategy, not just passion, wins the day.

That USDA loss? It was tuition. It taught us how to play at the highest level. It sharpened our edges. It forced us to evolve—not emotionally, but structurally. That's the high performer's playbook. We don't collapse under loss. We convert it. We don't use pain as evidence—we use it as fuel.

Let's be clear—high performers aren't just fearless. They're focused. They've trained themselves to pause in chaos, to assess patterns, and to move with precision. This isn't instinct—it's conditioning. I've seen this under the most high-stakes pressure imaginable. I remembered, during a military drill on the rifle range, a young private misfired and froze. Another senior soldier stepped in, adjusted his position with calm authority, and said, "You don't become a leader by never messing up—you become one by knowing exactly what to do next." That sentence stuck with me for years, because it defines the difference. Leadership isn't about avoiding error; it's about developing the resilience to recover well.

That recovery—rooted in emotional regulation and mental clarity—is the high performer's trademark. They don't wait for a lightning strike of inspiration to regain momentum. They build it through discipline. Through asking better questions. Through pattern recognition. Not "Why did this happen?" but "Where is this guiding me next?" "What pattern is this pointing out?" "How can I realign with what matters most?"

This is what I call emotional agility—the ability to feel deeply and still move strategically. The ability to face setbacks honestly without becoming defined by them. You're not ignoring the pain. You're using it as part of the process.

Years ago, I gave a keynote at a packed auditorium. Afterward, a young woman approached me in tears. Her voice trembled as she said, "I've been so ashamed of everything falling apart in my life. But maybe… the breakdown isn't the end. Maybe it's just the start of my rebuild." That realization was her breakthrough. She stopped resisting her reality and started mining it for wisdom. That's when momentum becomes inevitable. Because purpose isn't found in some magical moment—it's formed in the middle of pressure, loss, and the decision to keep going.

And this isn't just my experience—it's backed by research. Dr. Brené Brown's studies on resilience and vulnerability reveal that those who bounce back strongest aren't those who avoid pain—they're the ones who engage it. They own their story rather than run from it. Brown found that individuals who practice narrative ownership—who can say, "This is my pain and here's what I've learned from it"—develop more resilience, deeper connection, and clearer alignment with their values. In other words, high performers grow not because they're tougher, but because they're more honest.

This alignment isn't a one-time victory—it's a discipline. It's a daily recalibration of what you believe, how you think, and what you choose to do when pressure challenges your progress. It means shifting from identity-based pain ("I'm a failure") to pattern-based strategy ("That didn't work—so let's study why"). It means rising not just with passion, but with process.

So what does this mean for you?

It means the next time life knocks you sideways, don't rush to get back up for the sake of pride. Pause. Ask: Who is the version of me that's rising? And what has this pain revealed that I would've never seen in comfort?

Because that's the strategy of high performers. They don't bounce back as who they were—they rise as who they're becoming.

The Hidden Blueprint of Elite Habits

I didn't learn discipline from a book. I didn't download it from a podcast or find it in a masterclass. I found it on an island 7,600 miles from home—on the cold tile floor of a military barracks in Okinawa, Japan, when I was just 21 years old.

Back then, I was surrounded by men who were stronger than me, more seasoned, more decorated. I was young, hungry, and unproven. But I had something to prove—to myself. Not because I needed to be the best for show, but because I needed to find out who I could become if I went all in. And so, while others slept, I was already moving.

The alarm went off at 4:00 a.m. every morning. Not a gentle buzz. A jarring, piercing sound that reminded me this life wasn't about comfort. It was about commitment. I would roll out of my bunk, body sore from the day before, but mind sharper than ever. I'd hit the ground, stretch in silence, and lace up my boots as if preparing for battle—because in a way, I was.

By 4:30, I was already in the gym. No crowd. No music. Just the hum of the fluorescent lights and the low thud of my shoes on rubber flooring. My first workout was always intentional—compound movements, strength sets, explosive reps. I wasn't just training muscles. I was building mental resilience. When others showed up for PT at 6:00 a.m., I had already logged my first win.

After PT, I'd head to the sauna—a sacred space where I'd reflect, breathe, and reset. That heat, that silence, it was holy ground. In there, I didn't just sweat—I surrendered. I thought about home. About my future. About the kind of man I wanted to be—not just in the Marines, but beyond the uniform. I wasn't chasing medals. I was chasing mastery.

Then came study hours. While my peers took naps or scrolled through their phones, I cracked open leadership manuals, studied military protocols, reviewed strategic theory. Not because I had to—but because I was preparing for what would come. I knew that excellence and separation wasn't built during the evaluation—it was built in the preparation. That's how I got promoted ahead of my peers. That's how I earned the trust of leaders who saw something different in me. It wasn't talent—it was tenacity.

There were moments of loneliness. Nights when I questioned if it was worth it. When my body ached and my spirit lagged. But I kept going. Because while others were asleep, I was stacking quiet wins. And that's when I learned: discipline is louder than talent. When applied with consistency, it builds a man no setback can break.

Looking back, that season in Japan laid the foundation for everything that followed. It was my introduction to what I now call keystone habits—the invisible forces that hold every other part of your life together. They aren't glamorous. They're not flashy. But they're everything.

Here's what I discovered about those habits—and what they can unlock in you.

Morning Mastery

You don't stumble into greatness. You build it, minute by minute, starting with how you rise. Those early mornings in Okinawa taught me that how you begin sets the rhythm for everything that follows. It's not about checking a box—it's about setting the tone. High performers don't let the world dictate their mindset—they set it before anyone else gets a vote. Whether it's prayer, silence, cold water, journaling, or motion—the act is less important than the intention behind it. Morning mastery isn't about perfection. It's about possession. You take ownership of your day before it takes over you.

Movement with Mission

In Japan, I trained like my life depended on it—because it did. I didn't move for aesthetics. I moved for alignment. I moved because my mission demanded more from me than average energy could offer. That's why movement still matters. It isn't punishment. It's preparation. When you move, you activate your focus, your flow, your fire. And you remind yourself: I'm in control of this vessel. I'm not waiting to feel good to take action. I take action—and that's what makes me feel unstoppable.

Fueling Like the Future Depends on It

Back then, I started noticing that some Marines crashed by mid-afternoon—not because of the workload, but because of what they put in their bodies. That's when I began to understand: your fuel is your forecast. I started paying attention—not just to calories, but to cognition. I chose what sharpened me, not what sedated me. High performers don't eat for comfort. They eat for clarity. You want a sharper mind? Start with a cleaner plate.

Digital Discipline

There weren't iPhones in Okinawa. But there were distractions—just like today. Kin Town, Gossip. Entertainment Clubs and Shows. Temptation to scroll through nothing instead of focus on something. I learned early that energy leaks often happen through tiny distractions that don't feel dangerous—until they compound. Now, I build digital boundaries into my life the same way I protected my time in Japan. No mindless scrolling. No unfiltered noise. My attention is currency—and I spend it like I've got legacy on the line.

Reflection as a Weapon

Every night, before lights out, I had a ritual. I'd sit with my journal and ask the same three questions: What did I win today? Where did I fall short? What will I do differently tomorrow? Those few quiet moments became the most valuable part of my growth. They trained me to reflect, not just react. That's what reflection does—it recalibrates your compass. It doesn't just help you evaluate your day. It helps you evolve from it.

What I lived in Okinawa was not a phase. It was a blueprint. And it taught me a truth that still governs my life today: **You don't rise to the level of your goals. You fall to the strength of your habits.**

If you want to lead yourself into something greater, don't start with massive changes. Start with keystone patterns. The ones no one claps for. The ones that happen in silence. The ones that feel small but shape everything.

The world sees your highlight reel. But the habits? Those are forged in the dark, when no one is watching. That's where greatness is born. In early mornings. In sweat-drenched hoodies. In journal pages inked with truth. In saunas where prayers get louder than excuses.

And that's where I found my edge. Not because I was better. But because I chose different. I chose to rise when others rolled over. I chose clarity over comfort. Sacrifice over sleep. Purpose over pressure. And that choice didn't just get me promoted—it made me a man who could carry weight without breaking.

So if you want to build the life few dare to dream, remember this: **you don't have to shout. You just have to show up. Every. Single. Day.**

Building The Discipline To Succeed

Discipline is not a punishment—it is a proclamation. A sacred vow. A declaration that says, *"I love my future enough to respect my present."* For years, I misunderstood it. Like so many, I grew up thinking discipline was restriction—tight schedules, sharp tones, stern rules. I thought it was something others imposed on you. But as I grew—through fire, through pain, through silence—I learned the truth: **discipline isn't about what you're kept from. It's about what you're being equipped for.**

That truth started forming when I was a child.

My parents were strict. Not in a punishing way, but in a *principled* way. There were no shortcuts in our house. Chores were done to completion. "Yes sir" and "Yes ma'am" were expected, not requested. My mother could spot a half-done task with the precision of a drill instructor, and my father—he carried himself with a kind of quiet integrity that taught me more than lectures ever could. He wasn't a man of many words, but when he spoke, you listened. Not because you feared him—but because you respected the weight behind every word. That house taught me early: **do it right, or do it again.**

That early training would come full circle years later when I stepped into the furnace of Marine Corps boot camp.

There are no hacks in boot camp. No hiding. No pretending. You are stripped down—mentally, physically, emotionally—and rebuilt from the ground up. I remember standing at attention in formation at **Parris Island**, sweat dripping down my spine, my calves burning, my fingers twitching to scratch an itch I wasn't allowed to acknowledge. The drill instructor's voice cut through the air like a scalpel. No comfort. No compromise. Only command. And it was there, in that pressure cooker of obedience, fatigue, and repetition, that I realized something profound:

Discipline is the difference between intention and transformation. It's not a cage—it's a key. The key that opens the gate between who you are and who you're called to be. The key that liberates your purpose from procrastination. That rebuilds your dignity after failure. That constructs a life of integrity when the rest of the world is cutting corners. Discipline is not about control—it's about care. The kind of care that says, "I value myself enough to be consistent. Even when it's hard. Especially when it's hard."

It's easy to want change. To talk about goals. To post your resolutions. But when the alarm goes off at 0400, and your body aches, and your mind begs for mercy—that's where it's decided. That's where identity is carved.

And identity, once forged, becomes your compass.

I still remember one night in particular. It was one of the last weeks of training, and we were deep into the Crucible. We'd been running drills all day—weighted hikes, weapons assembly, silent watch rotations. That night, my squad was tasked with navigating a terrain course by compass, in the dark, with minimal sleep. I was exhausted—blinking harder just to stay awake. Every step felt like dragging bricks. But in that moment, I remembered my father's voice: *"Lead anyway."*

So I did.

I took the compass. I led my unit. I made the hard call when the route shifted. I made sure no one was left behind. And when we arrived at checkpoint Bravo—intact, on time, and together—I didn't just feel proud. I felt anchored. Because I had finally understood what discipline really meant.

It wasn't the yelling. It wasn't the rules. It was the choice to rise when everything inside you wants to fold.

That choice is what builds the future.

Discipline is not about rigidity—it's about reverence. Reverence for your calling. Reverence for your family. Reverence for the version of you that you haven't even met yet. That's why I say: *Discipline is the highest form of self-love.* It's not the loud, public kind of love—it's the quiet, private kind. The kind that sets the alarm. The kind that laces the boots. The kind that finishes the rep, the page, the prayer—even when no one is watching.

You won't always feel it. You won't always like it. But if you choose it daily—brick by brick—it will become who you are.

And here's the truth most won't tell you: **discipline silences self-doubt.** Not with noise, but with evidence. Every time you show up for yourself, you disprove the lie that says you can't. Every repetition is a rebuttal to fear. Every routine is a response to chaos. You don't need to debate your worth— you just need to build it. One promise kept at a time.

Discipline doesn't chase applause. It builds legacy. It is the cornerstone to success, it is not a task master and it isn't a punishment—it's a powerful declaration. A declaration that says, "I believe in my future enough to act like it today." For so long, I misunderstood discipline as deprivation. I thought it meant restriction, limits, rigidity. I viewed it as something forced upon me rather than something cultivated within me. But over time, as the old definitions began to crumble—definitions shaped by burnout, trauma, and broken cycles.

Some of the greatest leaders I've coached didn't start with charisma or genius. They started with rhythm. With the decision to become someone reliable. Someone their team, their spouse, their children could count on. They weren't always the loudest—but they were the most grounded. In a world that glorifies optics, their quiet follow-through was their superpower.

And that's the call for you now.

To stop waiting for fire—and start building the fireplace. To stop hoping for alignment—and start constructing it, hour by hour. To stop outsourcing your power—and start stewarding it, with intention.

Because success is not an accident. It's not gifted. It's **governed**—by what you do when it's boring. By what you choose when it's hard. By how you move when no one is clapping.

You don't need another motivational post. You don't need another planner. You need to **integrate** what you already know. You need to live your answers. Because transformation doesn't happen when you *learn* the truth. It happens when you *live* it.

So I'll ask you what I asked myself in that cold bunk in Parris Island, boots by my bed, body aching:

Why are you here?

Strip away the noise. Strip away the goals. Strip away the audience. What remains is the question that builds your legacy.

Why. Are. You. Here?

Not someday. Not hypothetically. But now. In this moment. In this season. With this pain. With this potential. Why?

When you answer that with honesty, discipline stops feeling like a burden. It becomes an echo—**the echo of your yes to the life you were designed to build.**

So live the answer.

Not someday. Now.

BREAK THE BOTTLE CHALLENGE — Chapter 11

The Unstoppable Activation

This isn't just another chapter to read. This is a call to move.

Right now—before you flip the page, before you scroll away, before life distracts you again—I want you to decide who you are becoming. Don't just admire greatness from afar. Activate it from within. **Your challenge is threefold:**

1. Define Your Identity Anchor

In one bold, unedited sentence, answer this:

"I am the kind of person who _____."

This isn't a wish. It's a declaration. Something identity-driven, not goal-based. Something that aligns with your future, not your fears. Say it aloud. Write it down. Post it where your distractions usually win. And repeat it every morning until you believe it on a cellular level.

2. Lock in Your Rhythm

Pick **two keystone habits** from this chapter and commit to them for the next **21 days**. No negotiation. No "if I have time." These are now non-negotiables. Whether it's Morning Mastery, Digital Boundaries, Daily Movement—choose two and make them law. If you miss a day, start again. But never again give up on yourself.

3. Complete the 72-Hour Execution Sprint

Take one priority you've been delaying and put it in motion—within **72 hours**. That means:

- Make the call.

- Send the email.

- Launch the page.

- Sign up for the course.

- Have the conversation.
  Do not wait for perfect. You need movement, not miracles. Prove to yourself that you are a person of execution, not hesitation.

This is more than a productivity hack. This is the moment you stop spectating and start trailblazing. The world doesn't need another passive genius—it needs an active one. It needs *you*—in motion, on mission, unstoppable. Now go execute. Your legacy is watching.

THE LEADERSHIP PARADIGM— OWNING YOUR ROLE IN YOUR LIFE AND BUSINESS

"If you can't lead yourself in the dark, you're not qualified to lead others in the light."

— *Break The Bottle*

Redefining Leadership Through Action, Not Titles

Lead Without Permission. Leadership has been misbranded. We've been sold a version of it We've been misled. Leadership has been dressed up in suits, staged behind podiums, and polished into something pristine and reserved for the "elite." It's been sold as something you *earn* through a title, a badge, or a LinkedIn profile that glows with executive language. But that's not leadership. Not in the trenches. Not in the homes, the communities, the start-ups, or the everyday battles of real people showing up without applause. **Leadership isn't a title. It's a decision.** And the most powerful leaders I've ever encountered? They rarely announce themselves. They don't need to. They show up in silence, with clarity, and leave a wake of impact behind them—not because they were loud, but because they were *aligned*.

Leadership is not a spotlight. It's a mirror. It forces you to look inward before you ever point outward. It challenges you to lead yourself when no one's looking before daring to lead others when everyone is watching. I've seen CEOs with 10,000 employees buckle under the weight of unresolved insecurity, while stay-at-home parents led households with such grace and strength that entire communities shifted because of their influence. One summer in Atlanta, during a local leadership training I facilitated, I sat across from a single mom—no corporate resume, no business plan, no formal team. But as she shared how she structured her day, mentored her son through trauma, kept her household running, and still showed up with empathy and strength, I paused mid-session, looked her in the eye, and said, "You are a leader—more than some of the Fortune 500 execs I've coached." She didn't need a boardroom. She already had a battlefield. And she was showing up to win.

Leadership is a posture, not a promotion. It's not something you're appointed to. It's something you *embody*. In how you respond when things fall apart. In how you serve when nobody's clapping. In how you speak truth when it would be easier to stay quiet. And especially in how you keep showing up with integrity even when the results aren't immediate. That's leadership. Quiet. Consistent. Relentless. It's what you do when the spotlight's gone and the weight is still there. That's where real leaders are forged—in the ordinary moments that no one else sees.

Let me take you into a boardroom in Toronto. I was consulting with a young founder whose startup had just secured millions in funding. On the surface, he had it all—momentum, a lean team, tech buzz, growth. But beneath it? Leadership decay. He was avoiding tough conversations, skimming over team dysfunction, and playing small under the weight of his own doubts. "I don't feel like a leader," he confessed during a one-on-one. I didn't sugarcoat it. I told him plainly, "That's because you're still waiting for a title to validate what only *your behavior* can." That was the shift. Within weeks, he stepped into the hard conversations. He started leading—not perfectly, but fully. He stopped hiding behind performance and started owning his presence. That's when the culture changed. That's when his team started believing. Not because he had authority—but because he finally *used* it.

Leadership isn't about controlling others. It's about controlling your *presence*—your energy, your attitude, your example. You lead in how you show up at dinner with your family after a long day. In how you speak to your assistant when you're behind schedule. In how you lead a meeting not with jargon but with direction and care. I've stood with pastors, military veterans, elite athletes, and corporate giants—and every time I can tell who the real leaders are. It's not the one who talks the most. It's the one who takes responsibility. It's the one who owns their energy. The one who doesn't wait for a shift—they *become* it.

But here's the part nobody likes to admit: **if you can't lead yourself, you will eventually disqualify yourself from leading others**. You can fake charisma. You can memorize strategy. But at some point, your private inconsistencies will leak into your public influence. And leadership isn't just about how high you can climb—it's about how *deep* your roots go. If you can't hold the weight of your own vision, how can others trust you to carry theirs?

I've felt this in my own life. In the seasons where I ignored my health, I couldn't think clearly. When I compromised my boundaries, bitterness crept in. When I shifted focus from serving people to impressing clients, my fulfillment dried up. But the moment I decided to lead *myself* first—to treat my mornings, my workouts, my relationships, my word like sacred territory—everything elevated. My clarity returned. My alignment sharpened. And that's when people started following—not because I was impressive, but because I was consistent. **Leadership starts in the places no one sees.**

So here's the truth: You're already leading. The question is, *how?* Are you leading from purpose or pressure? From avoidance or conviction? Because the myth is that leadership begins after the promotion, after the applause. But the reality? **Leadership is what gets you there**. It's the quiet hours. The daily standards. The way you take care of your soul when nobody's clapping. The way you stand up for integrity when it would be easier to blend in.

The ones who lead without needing credit—those are the ones people follow without needing to be convinced. Because real leadership is *felt* before it's understood. It carries weight. It builds trust. It moves culture. And it doesn't wait for permission.

So if you've been waiting—waiting to be chosen, validated, acknowledged—stop. You don't need a badge. You don't need a platform. You need a mirror. **And once you've looked in it—once you've taken full ownership of your energy, your example, your environment—then and only then do you lead.**

Not later. Not someday. *Now.*

Why I Left Corporate America

People often ask me why I left corporate America—as if the answer must be colored by failure or resignation. Did I leave because I didn't fit? Because I wasn't capable? The truth is the opposite: I left because I had to lead differently. My calling—the kind of leadership rooted in authenticity, soul, clarity, and purpose—was incompatible with a system designed to reward compliance over courage. This wasn't rebellion. It was responsibility. A duty to lead from integrity, not inertia; to stop managing status and start mobilizing significance.

In that corporate world, I honed skills—built systems, learned the rhythm of high-stakes execution. But soul space was nonexistent. And so, during late-night hours of frustration and prayer, when "success" heartily echoed through my calendar but barely whispered in my spirit, I heard the knock: "It's time." Not with fanfare—just with quiet clarity. I realized I'd stopped building the life I was called to, and had begun performing for one I wasn't. And when success starts to suffocate purpose, you either reshape your path or snap under its weight.

So I walked away—not from leadership but toward it. Toward a leadership that doesn't wait for permission, that moves without a title, that knows transformation happens not in boardrooms, but in heart shifts, identity breakthroughs, and moments of decisive clarity. I left to reclaim my voice, stunted under the weight of approval. I left to lead from conviction, not convention. I left because my calling could not be outsourced or delayed—and that meant stepping into the unknown.

Let me take you into that moment with me. It was Thursday at 8:00 AM. I sat in a conference room encased in glass, surrounded by polished executives who measured worth by buzzwords and slide decks. I had just delivered a project that had exceeded revenue goals by over 30%. The nods and half-smiles said I had "made it." Yet inside, I felt hollow. I hadn't slept in two nights. I'd missed my son's school event. I hadn't walked into a gym or opened my Bible in weeks. My voice was confident, but my spirit was tanked. I had become the very thing I swore I never would be: alive on the outside, dying on the inside.

Driving back to my office, suffocated by the applause that felt like chains, I opened my laptop—another flood of emails, demands, invites. Instead of responding, I clicked "compose. " I began writing a resignation letter—not because I didn't love the work, but because I wouldn't lie to myself again. I realized then: success without alignment is sophistic self-betrayal.

Then came the promotion that crushed me. The offer landed with more pay, power, prestige—and disappointment. I went to the restroom, locked the stall, collapsed on the lid, and stared at the letter on my phone. What looks good on paper felt wrong in my soul.

That weekend, I found my way to a corporate retreat—five stars, gourmet meals, ocean views. But instead of being inspired, I was grieving. That night, I slipped away. I walked barefoot into the night air, dug my toes into the sand, and whispered to God through salt air: "If this isn't where I belong, show me what's next." No light show followed, just a sacred stillness that announced: This is not your mission. Two weeks later, I declined the promotion. The HR team was stunned. But I knew: I wasn't leaving a job—I was walking into a calling.

This leap wasn't easy. You don't just leave comfort—you walk away from benefits, teams, identity. And data shows the world's feeling it too. Nearly one in four Americans have quit their job in the past two years, and another one in five are planning to. Roughly 79% of employed Americans—and especially Millennials and Gen Z—are considering leaving traditional roles to start their own ventures. But nearly half hesitate to take the leap because they're afraid of failing. That fear is real—it's strategic, cultural, even practical, like letting go of health insurance. Institutional inertia is strong. Yet, stepping away mustn't be idolized—it must be rooted. I wasn't abandoning security—I was following mission. Real leadership isn't about titles—it's about temperature. It's about how you regulate energy, how you stay present in chaos, how you uphold identity when no one's watching.

Let's go deeper: Are you a wolf, or a sheep? I'm not talking about aggression. I'm not talking about dominance or bravado. Not the aggressive kind, but strategic and self-led. I'm talking about instinct. Precision. Presence. Wolves move strategically with intention. They don't chase - They calibrate and understand terrain. They lead with an internal compass—not external applause. They don't perform—they embody. Sheep, on the other hand, wait. Sheep follow safety. And in moments of crisis, many realize they've already abdicated their leadership too late. They conform. They follow pre-laid paths because it feels safer than forging a new one. And often, they don't even realize they've abdicated leadership of their own life until it's too late.

Leadership isn't reactive—it's responsive. And that responsiveness always follows mission clarity. Not aspiration. Not ambition. Your mission—the internal fire that outlasts fatigue—is what gives rise to leadership that matters. It's the reason you continue even when applause fades, when pressure mounts, when success feels like suffocation. A lack of clarity will burn you out. But clarity will build you through pressure.

You won't find your mission in performance reviews or paychecks. You find it in the grit of grief, the tension of trial, in choosing alignment over applause. When you live from mission, you stop chasing hype and start protecting purpose. You say no—strategically. You prune. You protect. You preserve what matters. That's the difference between noise and legacy.

Builders, not branders. Architects, not avatars. People who lead from root truth—not borrowed ambition. Let me ask: What. Is. Your. Mission? Not your to-do list. Not your LinkedIn summary. Your mission—the tether that pulls you when motivation fades, the soil in which your leadership roots.

If you don't know yet? That's freedom. A chance to find it. If you do? Then lead like it. Act like it. Decide like it. Because your clarity is somebody's breakthrough. Your leadership rooted in mission changes more than teams— it changes cultures, communities, and legacies.

True leadership starts long before the title. It starts in silence, in the mirror, in the soul. It's forged in self-leading integrity before it ever shows up in public influence. It isn't about charisma—it's about congruence. Influence isn't called—it earns trust. So lead yourself first. Master your habits, clarify your values, govern your thoughts. Because if you can't trust yourself to follow through, why would anyone else?

How to Friend, Speak, Listen and Show Up

It was a Wednesday night in Atlanta—one of those quiet evenings after a long stretch of meetings and back-to-back speaking engagements. I had just dropped my son off after dinner, and instead of heading home, I swung by a local café where an old friend had asked to meet. I wasn't in the mood. My energy was depleted. But something in me said, "Show up." So I did. I walked into that small corner shop, the smell of cinnamon and burnt espresso clinging to the air, and saw him already seated—same hoodie, same nervous bounce in his leg, same story I'd heard more than a few times over the years.

He looked up and gave a tired smile, the kind that doesn't quite reach the eyes. I sat down. We dapped up. And before we even finished our drinks, he was offloading again—the breakup, the business setback, the unresolved tension with his father. It wasn't that I didn't care. I did. But as he spoke, I felt myself detaching. Like I was watching a rerun of a show I used to love but could no longer get into. A quiet thought crept in, uninvited: "Why am I still here?" Not in judgment, but in exhaustion. The kind that comes when you've spent years being someone's sounding board and you're no longer sure if it's helping—or just enabling.

But instead of pulling back, I made a choice. I leaned forward. I asked one simple question: "Do you feel like you're repeating the same chapter?" His eyes flickered. His mouth paused mid-sentence. And for a moment, everything got still. "Yeah," he whispered. "I don't know how to stop." That one admission cracked open a different conversation. I stopped trying to solve him and started trying to see him. As he shared, I listened with everything—my eyes, my breath, my posture. And as I watched him struggle to put language to his pain, I saw myself—not the polished version, but the man I used to be. The man who used to spin his own wheels in the dark, afraid to name what hurt.

That night, I realized something profound: friendship isn't a transaction of solutions. It's a ministry of presence. Real friendship isn't measured by how often you hang out or how much history you share—it's measured by the *quality of the mirror* it offers you. It's about how I show up in their presence. Who I become in their company. Am I generous? Present? Compassionate? Energized by the interaction? Or am I shrinking, distracted, or judgmental? The true measure of a relationship is not what it gives me—but who I become when I'm in it. Do I like who I become around this person? Do they challenge me to be more honest? Do they invite my authenticity? Do I feel safe enough to be undone, yet loved enough to stay whole?

Since that evening, I've started watching myself in rooms with more curiosity than critique. Am I showing up out of obligation or out of integrity? Am I actually listening—or am I just waiting for my turn to talk? Because the truth is, most of us live behind social masks so thick we don't even realize we've forgotten how to actually see one another. We confuse communication with talking. But speaking is not connecting. And listening is not hearing. There's an art to both. And that art is dying in this age of performance.

There are Four Leadership Questions for Effective Communication that help unlock everything. In the journey toward extraordinary influence, the most powerful leaders aren't the ones who speak the most—they're the ones who listen the hardest. They understand that communication isn't just about delivering messages; it's about uncovering truths hidden beneath words, emotions, and tension. Leadership, at its core, is discernment—and the sharpest tool isn't a speech—it's a question.

Below are four essential questions that serve as a leader's compass. When asked with honesty and answered with openness, they become catalysts for clarity, trust, and transformation. Use them consistently, model them publicly, and integrate them into your rhythm. They don't just shift structures—they shift hearts, minds, and cultures. That realization changed not just how I friend—but how I lead. Because presence, at its core, isn't just emotional—it's strategic. And the deepest presence begins with the questions we ask.

1. What am I not saying that needs to be said?
This is the courage question. It demands honesty and vulnerability. It points to the truth you've avoided, the boundary you haven't enforced, the feedback you've refrained from sharing. The strongest leaders recognize that silence often protects comfort—but clarity demands courage. They don't hold back truth to maintain peace; they speak truth to build it. Because without courageous dialogue, assumptions fill the space, confusion grows, and momentum stalls. Asking yourself this question challenges you to expose what's hidden and make the invisible—visible.

2. What am I saying that's not being heard?
This is the humility question. It acknowledges that communication is a two-way street. If your message isn't landing, volume is often not the issue—approach is. The most influential leaders measure not by how much they speak, but by how well they're understood. This question demands active adjustment. It's not about talking louder. It's about talking clearer, simpler, more empathetic. It requires pausing, rephrasing, and inviting confirmation. Communication isn't broadcasting—it's connecting.

3. What am I not hearing that's being said?
This is the awareness question. It invites leaders to tune into subtext: the tone, the hesitation, the unsaid weight behind the words. Real leadership hears what's unspoken. They pick up on the tension just beneath a casual comment, the fatigue in a voice, the resistance behind a nod. Asking this question develops emotional intelligence and creates environments where guards come down. When people sense they're truly heard—even in silence—the conversation deepens, trust grows, and alignment follows.

4. What is being said that I'm not hearing?
This is the presence question. It requires you to check your intentions at the door. Are you listening to understand, or listening to respond? Are you present with curiosity—or distracted by your agenda? The most impactful leaders slow themselves down to speed understanding. They make space

to sit with others, suspending their own answers until the question has been explored fully. They know that interruption kills trust and assumption contradicts clarity. To cultivate true leadership presence, ask yourself this frequently—and lean into the pause until the real message emerges.

Leadership doesn't demand perfection—it demands sophistication. It dares you to excavate assumptions, challenge norms, and seek clarity—even when it's uncomfortable. The path to influence isn't carved through charisma alone—it's revealed through questions that penetrate the surface and reach to what matters.

Use these four questions as your daily ground game. Interrogate your next conversation. Reflect on recent conflict. Cultivate greater curiosity. Ask relentlessly. Seek not just what's said—but what isn't. Because behind every breakthrough is a question daring enough to lead.

Now go lead—not with louder voices, but braver hearts. Lead with your ears. Lead with intention. Lead in questions that uncover clarity.

The same is true for speaking. There are levels. Some speak to inform. Some speak to impress. Others speak to influence. But the highest level? Speaking to inspire transformation. Speaking with honesty, authenticity, integrity, and love. That's when your voice becomes more than noise—it becomes a mirror, a bridge, a spark.

But to speak at that level, you must be grounded. You must have done the inner work to ask hard questions like: *Am I easy to love? Am I easy to be around? Am I easy to talk to? Am I easy to listen to?*

This kind of introspection doesn't weaken your message—it strengthens it. Self-awareness sharpens your presence. When you communicate from an honest, integrated place, your words carry weight—because they're not performance. They're truth.

And truth is more than just words. In fact, 55% of communication is nonverbal—it's body language. Only 7% of communication is verbal. The rest? 38% is tone. That means your posture, your energy, your facial expressions—they're saying something long before your mouth opens. You can't fake alignment. People feel when your tone contradicts your words. They sense when your eyes drift, when your spirit isn't present, when your body says "leave me alone" even while your lips say "I'm listening."

So if you want to connect—deeply connect—you have to do more than talk. You have to embody what you're saying. You have to be congruent. You have to slow down long enough to listen between the lines. What's not being said? What's being masked by smiles or silence? What's being shouted by their exhaustion?

We must stop approaching communication as an obligation and start treating it as a sacred act. Every conversation is an opportunity to affirm someone's dignity. To remind them they're not alone. To validate their existence. That doesn't mean agreeing with everything. It means honoring the human being behind the words. That's what makes you safe to talk to. That's what makes you magnetic. That's what gives your voice gravity.

When people feel heard, they heal. When people feel understood, they rise. And when people feel loved through your presence, not just your praise, they remember that moment forever.

So ask yourself today: Am I building people with my words, or breaking them with my silence? Am I creating safe spaces with my presence—or confusing ones with my inconsistency?

Communication is how we build bridges—but it starts inside. With integrity. With honesty. With love.

Let me give you another moment that changed me—a day I'll never forget. I was scheduled to speak at a leadership retreat for veterans reintegrating into civilian life. One of the organizers pulled me aside and said, "There's a guy in the back—he's here, but he's not really *here*. Just a heads-up." I nodded. I've met many men like him. Stoic. Guarded. Eyes that scan but don't settle. During the break, I noticed him lingering by the hallway. Something told me: *Talk to him.* I walked over, said his name, and for the first few minutes, all I got were one-word answers and polite nods. Then I asked, "When did you stop feeling seen?" His lip twitched. His eyes locked onto mine like I had just picked a lock he'd kept sealed for years. "After my third deployment," he said. "When I came back and nobody knew what to do with me."

That man hadn't shared more than a few sentences with anyone in months. But after that moment, he didn't stop talking for forty-five minutes. Not because I had the right words. But because I *stopped* trying to say the right thing. I just *stayed*. Fully present. No fixing. No reframing. Just human. Just real. That's what presence does. It gives people permission to return to themselves.

We've glamorized speaking so much that we've forgotten the power of silence. We idolize those who "speak truth" but overlook those who can *hold truth*. The leaders I respect most aren't just powerful communicators— they're *sacred listeners*. They create space that feels like oxygen. Rooms where people can breathe without pretense. That kind of leadership isn't loud. It's not flashy. But it's unforgettable.

And the words we do speak? They matter more than we know. Years ago, I was in a room where a leader casually said to a young woman, "Maybe leadership just isn't your thing." He chuckled after, as if it were a joke. She didn't. That one sentence haunted her for three years. It became the loop in her head, the reason she turned down promotions, the lie she internalized. One careless moment planted a seed of doubt that grew roots. That's the weight our words carry. So I ask myself before I speak—*Will this plant fear or will it plant courage? Will this help someone rise or make them shrink?*

Even tone matters. I once coached a senior executive who told me, "I don't know why people say I'm aggressive. I just say what needs to be said." I asked him to record one of his meetings. He did. And when we played it back, even *he* flinched. It wasn't what he said—it was *how* he said it. His tone betrayed his intention. He meant to lead. He sounded like a warning. This is why emotional congruence matters. People hear your heart before they ever process your logic. Your tone, your body language, your eyes— *they all speak.*

I remember the first time I truly saw the cost of showing up half-present—it wasn't in a boardroom or a battlefield. It was at my own dinner table. My son was about nine years old, sitting across from me, his little legs dangling from the chair, swinging with that carefree rhythm kids have when they're excited about something. He was mid-sentence, telling me about his science project, when I reached for my phone. Just a quick glance. Just to check one email. Just to make sure nothing urgent had come in. I wasn't even gone for five seconds. But when I looked back up, his voice had trailed off. His shoulders dropped. And he muttered, "Never mind."

I'll never forget the sting of that moment. It wasn't what he said—it was what he didn't. It was the unspoken message: *I'm not as important as what's on that screen.* He didn't cry. He didn't raise his voice. He just withdrew— quietly. And that silence echoed louder than any outburst ever could.

That night, after I tucked him into bed, I sat in my car and cried. Not out of guilt—but out of clarity. I had spent years training to lead in high-pressure situations, learning to navigate crisis, conflict, and chaos. But I hadn't trained myself to be present in the calm. I knew how to perform. I didn't know how to *pause.* And that's when it hit me—leadership isn't just what you do when the stakes are high. It's who you become in the moments no one is grading. The quiet ones. The ordinary ones. The ones that ask: *Can you be here, fully? Even when nothing dramatic is happening?*

From that day on, I made a vow: no phones at the dinner table. Ever. Not for calls. Not for texts. Not for anything. Because *presence is how people feel prioritized.* And I've learned that you can't fake being present. People may not always remember what you said, but they will never forget how you made them feel. And when someone feels like a background task in your life, they stop showing up fully in theirs.

Presence is leadership. Period. Whether you're parenting, coaching, mentoring, managing, or simply building a relationship—how you show up is what shapes trust. And trust is the currency of every meaningful connection. It's what makes the difference between someone hearing your advice and *actually absorbing* it. Between a child confiding in you or shutting down. Between a team rallying or retreating. Between a partner leaning in—or walking away.

But here's the hard truth: presence isn't natural in this age of performance.

We are constantly pulled toward distraction—alerts, demands, expectations, the endless noise of proving ourselves. And the danger is not that we'll become numb. The danger is that we'll become *functional*. Able to operate, to execute, to achieve—while our hearts slowly disengage. That's the silent erosion of humanity. You can hit every goal, hit every metric, build the life you once dreamed of—and still feel like you're missing it *while living in it*.

I once coached a high-level executive at a Fortune 100 company. On paper, he was at the top. A multimillion-dollar salary. Private jets. Global recognition. But in his first session with me, he looked at me with hollow eyes and said, "I don't think my kids know me." That's the price of unexamined momentum. Of performance without presence. Of being excellent at what you do and a stranger to who you are. We get so caught up in doing more that we forget to *be more*. We become experts at managing time but amateurs at managing energy. At managing *presence*.

What does it mean to be fully engaged? It means your words match your body. Your eyes stay on the person in front of you. Your tone reflects care. Your spirit slows down to the pace of the moment. You stop trying to impress and start trying to *imprint*. You understand that the most impactful thing you can do in any room is *be fully in it*—not just physically, but emotionally and energetically. That's when connection becomes transformation.

A while back, I was mentoring a young Marine who had just returned from deployment. He was hard—stone-faced, hyper-disciplined, always standing straight even in casual settings. In one of our sessions, I noticed he kept looking at his watch. Tapping it. Checking it. Finally, I asked, "You got somewhere to be?" He shook his head and said, "No sir, just trying not to feel too much." That hit me. He wasn't just checking the time. He was checking out. He was trying to manage emotion by avoiding engagement.

So I leaned forward and said, "What if the thing you're avoiding is the thing that's trying to heal you?" He went still. Then he nodded—barely. That was our turning point. Not some grand insight. Just a moment of *presence* that gave permission. That allowed safety. That created space for the armor to come down.

This is what true leadership looks like. It's not just strategy—it's soul work. It's not just performance—it's presence. You want to change someone's life? Don't just tell them what to do. *Sit with them in the middle of their not-yet.* Witness them. Hold space. Mirror back their strength. Name what they've forgotten. Remind them of who they are beneath the pain.

I've sat with millionaires and with men who didn't know where their next meal was coming from. And here's what they have in common: *they all want to be seen.* Not managed. Not motivated. Not manipulated. *Seen.* And when you can give that to someone—not through speeches but through soul-level stillness—you earn the kind of trust that changes everything.

Some time ago, I was speaking at a private leadership retreat in the Pacific Northwest. The venue was a mountain lodge nestled in pine trees, intentionally disconnected from cell towers and Wi-Fi. The idea was to force disconnection from the digital world to reconnect with ourselves and each other. On the second day, a man in his fifties approached me after my talk— quiet, buttoned-up, intense. He looked like someone who had mastered the external game of leadership but hadn't said much the entire weekend. When I shook his hand, I noticed it trembled ever so slightly.

He didn't start with his name. He started with this: "I haven't told anyone this in over 30 years." He was speaking before he was breathing, like the words had been waiting so long that they didn't need permission anymore. What poured out next was not just a confession—it was a collapse. A lifetime of performance, pressure, and pretending cracked open in front of me. Childhood abuse. A suicide attempt at 19. Decades of silence wrapped in success. The armor he wore in the world had protected him—but it had also imprisoned him.

I didn't speak for a while. I didn't need to. In that moment, my job wasn't to solve him—it was to see him. He didn't need advice. He needed an *audience of truth.* Someone to witness—not with pity, but with presence. And as he cried, he kept repeating the same words, "I didn't think anyone would ever really hear me." That's when it hit me—he wasn't crying because he was weak. He was crying because he was finally safe.

Presence is what makes people feel safe enough to tell the truth. And truth is the only place transformation begins. You cannot coach someone past a lie they're still living in. You cannot lead someone into freedom if they don't feel safe in your presence. The most powerful room you'll ever enter is not the stage—it's the space between two people when one feels seen without condition.

That's what it means to engage. It means entering rooms with your whole self. Not just your expertise. Not just your charm. But your soul. Your scars. Your stillness. It means trading performance for presence, ego for empathy, reaction for response. That's where real leadership lives—in the sacred spaces between words, in the courage to *stay* even when it's uncomfortable, in the ability to *see* people even when they can't see themselves.

In today's culture, so many chase visibility—but overlook value. They want the microphone before they've earned the trust. They speak louder, post more, hustle harder—but often feel more disconnected than ever. Why? Because visibility doesn't equal intimacy. Fame doesn't equal legacy. Engagement—true engagement—is the bridge between the life you project and the life you actually live.

I've watched men in suits and women in stilettos fall apart in silence. Not because they lacked skills—but because they lacked spaces where they didn't have to perform. The truth is, most high achievers aren't overcommitted— they're under-supported. They've mastered the art of seeming okay while privately drowning. They smile wide in meetings and cry alone in hotel rooms. They build teams, profits, platforms—but forget to build *presence* with the people closest to them. And over time, that absence corrodes everything.

So how do you engage? You start by *noticing*. Who around you has gone quiet? Who's showing up, but clearly checked out? Who's performing the role but looks like they've lost the plot? Ask. Don't assume. Sit longer. Listen harder. Pause more often. Don't be afraid of the silence—it's where the truth lives.

And while you're at it—turn that gaze inward too. Where have *you* gone silent? Where have you been drifting instead of deciding? Where are you showing up out of duty instead of desire? Where have you convinced yourself that being functional is the same as being fulfilled?

Because here's what no one tells you: Disengagement doesn't always look like quitting. Sometimes it looks like staying too long in the wrong spaces. Smiling in rooms that no longer hold your growth. Leading people you no longer align with. Speaking words that no longer match your heart. That's not loyalty. That's self-abandonment.

To engage fully, you have to reclaim your voice. You have to stop shrinking your truth for the comfort of others. You have to stop ghosting yourself. You have to be willing to be honest—even if it costs you applause. Because no amount of success is worth losing your soul in silence.

That's why I'm not impressed by how many followers someone has. I want to know—who follows you when the cameras are off? Who trusts you when you're not performing? Who confides in you when they're bleeding? That's your real influence. That's the weight of your presence. That's the mark of an engaged life—not one measured in accolades, but in authenticity.

So what does it mean to engage?

> It means leading with your ears, not just your voice.
> It means seeing people, not just their titles.
> It means being the same person in every room—onstage, offstage, behind the scenes, and behind closed doors.
> It means checking your ego so you can carry empathy.
> It means staying when it's hard.
> It means showing up when you don't feel like it—not for performance, but for *people*.
> It means not waiting until someone is gone to finally hear them.

Because the greatest leaders aren't remembered for their vision—they're remembered for their presence. The kind of presence that sits with the broken. That listens through silence. That speaks when needed—and stays quiet when wisdom says wait. The kind that holds space for others while never abandoning themselves.

This is how you break the bottle. Not by shouting over the noise, but by entering it with stillness. Not by fixing others, but by engaging with who they really are. And not by proving your worth, but by embodying it.

Engagement is not a tactic. It's a posture. It's a way of being in the world that transforms every room you enter—not by the power of your words, but by the integrity of your presence.

The Power of Your Circle

Your circle is either sharpening your future or quietly suffocating it. There's no neutral. There may be players on your team that you need to kick out of your huddle and sit them on the bench. The people closest to you are either amplifying your vision or anesthetizing your ambition. And the danger rarely arrives in obvious betrayal—it shows up in small misalignments. The friends who don't understand why you can't just "chill for a while." The old colleagues who mock your standards because they haven't elevated their own. The casual companions who celebrate your past but ignore your potential. Over time, these micro-frictions erode your conviction. One compromise here. One excuse there. And suddenly, your trajectory has drifted—not because you lacked commitment, but because you lacked alignment.

I'll never forget the moment it crystalized for me. It was the day I graduated boot camp. We lined up in formation on the gritty parade deck, sweat and salt residue still clinging to our fatigues. Our drill instructor, eyes blazing with intensity, finally spoke the words I'd been waiting for: "Marines, you have earned the title that most will never earn. You've proven by heart and courage that you'll put your life on the line for something bigger than yourself." Our chests swelled with pride. Yet almost immediately, his tone shifted. "Go home," he said. "Some of you will see high school friends, girlfriends. Some have already moved on while most remain the same. You'll look in their eyes and realize how much you've outgrown them in just three months."

That hit me like a punch. I looked out and pictured coming home as the same person—but knowing I wasn't. The boy who hesitated, who wanted to be liked, who feared standing out? He didn't come back. I carried that realization with me always: purpose demands evolution, and growth often means leaving old circles—for your own integrity, not out of disgust, but clarity.

That principle has anchored me ever since—the words my parents spoke long before I ever stepped onto that drill field: *"Show me your friend, and I'll show you your future."* Now, at every junction in life, I ask: Does this person move me closer to who I'm called to become? Do they hold a higher standard because they see that in me too?

Since then, I've made it a point to cultivate circles that challenge and elevate. My leadership masterminds aren't about consensus—they're crucibles where truth meets ambition. My mentorship connections don't just offer answers— they call out my blind spots. My men's church community isn't passive—it keeps me anchored in faith while pushing me to act with purpose. They believe in the version of me I'm still becoming, even when I don't. They don't just affirm—they stretch. When I walk into those spaces, my energy shifts, my language shifts, my thinking sharpens. That's not magic—it's momentum, passed between people committed to aligned vision and shared destiny.

The most dangerous circle isn't filled with toxic people—it's filled with stagnant ones. The ones who settle. Who justify mediocrity. Who think your ambition is "too much" because it convicts their complacency. And if you're not careful, you'll start second-guessing your vision just to keep the peace. But legacy doesn't grow in comfortable soil. Impact doesn't emerge from echo chambers. And purpose never flourishes in permission-seeking environments.

Evaluate your circle like your future depends on it—because it does. Ask yourself: Who around me calls me higher? Who challenges my blind spots with love and honesty? Who believes in the future version of me so deeply they won't let me settle for anything less? Because the people around you shape your pace, your priorities, and your peace. And proximity is power. Sit with the right people long enough, and your language changes. Your energy rises. Your clarity sharpens.

The right circle doesn't compete with you—they complete your momentum. They cover you in prayer, challenge you in truth, and cheer for you in rooms you're not in. They call out the greatness you've forgotten. They stretch your thinking. They pour into your purpose without draining your soul. And when pressure hits, they don't retreat—they remind you who you are.

But the wrong circle? It will cost you. Slowly. Quietly. Consistently. It will dilute your focus. Numb your urgency. Make you question your instincts. And before long, you're no longer pursuing your mission—you're managing mediocrity. You're shrinking in rooms you were meant to transform. You're negotiating your destiny with people who were never assigned to your future.

So let me say it plainly: You don't owe access to anyone who abuses your energy. You don't owe your momentum to someone who mocks your evolution. And you certainly don't owe comfort to circles that require your compromise. Your calling deserves protection. Your capacity deserves wise stewardship. And your leadership demands a circle that's as committed to truth as it is to loyalty.

Surround yourself with those who sharpen, not soften you. Those who push, not pacify. Those who won't let you settle into survival when greatness is still possible. Because the right people aren't intimidated by your growth—they're inspired by it. And they won't let you retreat into old patterns just because it's familiar. They'll remind you of who you are—especially when you forget.

And that's the real power of your circle: not that they agree with everything, but that they anchor you to everything that matters. Your values. Your vision. Your standard. Because when the storm hits—and it will—it won't be your talent that keeps you grounded. It'll be your tribe.

Choose wisely. Lead boldly. And never forget: your future is too important to walk with people who aren't headed the same direction.

The world doesn't need more flashy leaders—it needs fortified ones. It needs the kind of leaders who don't flinch when the pressure rises, who don't perform for applause, and who don't bend their values when the stakes get high. This is the leadership paradigm shift we're living through.

We're moving away from the era of brand-first leadership—where it's all optics, metrics, and curated influence—and we're entering a time when real leadership is defined by backbone, not buzzwords. This is the emergence of resilient, impact-driven leadership. Leadership that doesn't perform—but transforms. Leadership that doesn't just manage—but mobilizes.

These are the leaders whose authority is rooted in alignment, not popularity. They are unmoved by trends, unshaken by setbacks, and unafraid to stand alone if it means standing in truth. These leaders don't chase approval—they chase alignment. And that conviction is what makes them powerful. Not in an authoritarian sense, but in an unshakable one. They bring clarity to chaos. They remain composed when others unravel. They anchor culture, not just command it. They're not here to be impressive—they're here to be effective.

How Elite Leaders Respond to Crisis, Conflict, and Growth

Leadership is not proven in moments of praise—it is revealed in the moments where everything breaks. When the lights are off. When the plan falls apart. When the stakes shift from theory to life and death. It's in the silence after the blast. The tension in the room after a wrong decision. The quiet chaos of knowing everyone is watching you to speak the words that will bring order to the madness. These moments—crisis, conflict, and growth—don't just define your leadership. They define *you*. And in every one of them, you are faced with a brutal but simple choice: **Engage—or retreat.**

I remember standing in a narrow alley in Iraq. The mission had shifted. Intel was off. What was supposed to be a sweep and secure had turned into a waiting game. We were exposed. The air was thick with tension. You could feel it—like the pause before a thunderclap. One of my guys locked eyes with me. He didn't say a word. He didn't need to. That look said it all: *What now, Sergeant?*

And in that moment—**everything slowed**. I didn't have a playbook. I didn't have a script. All I had was the awareness that if I froze, they'd falter. If I lost control, they'd lose their edge. So I walked the line—one man at a time. I didn't bark. I didn't posture. I locked eyes. I steadied my breath. I reconnected them not just to the mission—but to each other.

"We're not panicking. We're adapting. We stay sharp. We move on my call."

That moment changed everything. We shifted from scattered to synchronized. We moved. We cleared. We returned. But the true win wasn't in mission completion—it was in *how I showed up* when everything cracked. That's what elite leaders do in crisis: **they don't react—they respond.** Not from ego. Not from emotion. From clarity.

Because in crisis, people don't need heroes—they need anchors. They need someone who doesn't lose themselves when everything else is falling apart. And elite leaders understand: **leadership under pressure is about posture, not performance.**

But crisis isn't the only battlefield. **Conflict**—the kind that brews in boardrooms, on teams, or between people you care about—is just as defining. I remember a moment while leading a franchise operation. Numbers were up. Revenue was strong. But morale? Cracked. At first, it was quiet—eye rolls in meetings, sarcasm in emails. But the tension was real. It came to a head when I walked into what should've been a routine review—and instead got blindsided by a wall of anger.

One of my senior team members—loyal, capable, and deeply frustrated—unloaded months of unspoken disappointment. My instinct? Defend. Explain. Correct. But I remembered a different lesson: *Engage the environment before you engage the mission.* So I took a breath, and I said, "Tell me everything—from your point of view. I'm not here to win. I'm here to understand."

That conversation didn't fix everything in ten minutes. But it cracked open the silence. And that's where trust begins again. **Elite leaders don't flee from conflict—they enter it with courage and curiosity.** They ask:
What are we not saying that needs to be said?
What tension are we pretending doesn't exist?
Where have I made it hard for you to be honest?

They stay long enough in the discomfort to find clarity. And when correction is needed, they do it with precision, not punishment. Because **you can challenge behavior without crushing identity**. That's how you build cultures of truth, not fear.

But here's the paradox: it's not just in crisis or conflict where leadership is tested—it's in **growth**. Because success has a seduction of its own. I remember sitting across from a business partner after we'd just crushed our quarterly goals. Retention up. Revenue high. Everything on paper screamed *victory*. But my gut said otherwise.

"If we don't evolve our systems," I told him, "this growth will outpace us. We'll collapse—not from failure, but from success we didn't steward."

So we made the hard call. Brought in coaches. Revamped teams. Delegated authority. It meant releasing control. It meant admitting what got us here wouldn't get us there. That's where most leaders fail—they want expansion without surrender. But **you cannot grow and cling at the same time**.

Growth demands humility. It demands honest reflection. *Where am I the bottleneck? Where am I blocking momentum?* Elite leaders don't hoard their position—they multiply their people. Because a leader who refuses to evolve becomes the lid on everyone else's potential.

And that's where the **Five Pillars of Resilient Leadership** emerge. These aren't strategies. They're spiritual disciplines. They aren't for applause. They're for alignment. They aren't just about leading others—they're about leading *yourself*.

1. Lead with Conviction, Not Convenience

It was the winter of 2019, and I was sitting across from a regional director in a high-stakes meeting that would determine the future of one of my franchise territories. The numbers were strong, but behind the scenes, pressure had been mounting for months. A senior partner wanted to implement a shift in business strategy that, on paper, made sense—but in practice, would dilute everything I believed in. It meant cutting corners on service, pushing volume over value, and asking my team to compromise standards for speed.

I had two options. Go along and keep the peace—or speak up and risk the fallout.

I remember that morning vividly. I sat in my truck in the parking lot, rehearsing what I might say. I was young, relatively new in leadership, and the easiest route would've been silence. Just nod. Just go along. Just play the game. But I knew I'd be betraying something deeper—my own sense of integrity. The culture I promised my team. The standard I said I'd never abandon. And so, I walked into that room, looked across the table at men with more experience and more clout, and I said clearly: "I won't sacrifice long-term trust for short-term metrics. If that costs me opportunity, so be it."

You could've heard a pin drop.

What followed wasn't applause—but a wave of resistance. I was challenged. Questioned. One even asked if I was "too idealistic" to handle real business. But I stood my ground. Not because I was fearless. But because my *conviction was louder than my convenience*. I didn't sleep well that night. I didn't know what doors would close. But I knew I could look my team in the eye. And weeks later, something shifted. Quietly, privately, one of the senior leaders pulled me aside and said, "You made us rethink the whole strategy. Thank you for not folding."

That's the truth of conviction—it rarely rewards you immediately. But it always protects your integrity.

Elite leaders lead not when it's easy—but when it's costly. They don't wait for consensus to walk in truth. Leaders know this. They don't wait for approval to act. They don't freeze while waiting for a perfect moment. They move when the moment *calls* them. **Conviction is louder than comfort.** It whispers, *You were made for more. Don't compromise to be accepted.* Because real leadership means doing what's right—even when no one claps. Especially when no one claps. They don't sacrifice their principles for position. Because in a world full of noise, the rarest thing is someone who stays rooted when the wind of opinion shifts. And that kind of rootedness? That's what others rally around. That's what builds legacy.

2. Prioritize People Over Optics

In a world obsessed with appearances, real leaders invest in what can't be posted. I once walked into a franchise unit that looked strong on the outside—but the inside was bleeding. Numbers were fine, but culture was cracked. My instincts said: don't manage the metrics—*engage the hearts.*

I pulled the team together, dropped the agenda, and asked, "What's breaking that we're pretending is fine?" Silence. Then tears. Then truth.

What followed wasn't pretty—but it was real. The quiet betrayal of being unseen surfaced. Hidden frustrations aired. Misalignment exposed. And from that mess, something sacred emerged: **trust**. Because when people feel safe enough to speak their truth, the real work begins.

Leadership is not about how good you look—it's about how deeply you connect. And elite leaders don't just lead the room—they *read* the room. They recognize the invisible. They show up not for applause, but for alignment.

3. Build Cultures, Not Just Companies

I once mentored a CEO whose company exploded in growth—fast. But his staff turnover was brutal. He couldn't keep leaders in place. On paper, he was crushing it. But underneath? His culture was starving. I asked him a question he couldn't answer:
"What are your people saying when you're not in the room?"

He didn't know. And that's why his influence was cracking.

Culture is built in what you tolerate. In how you respond under pressure. In the things you reward and the things you ignore. It lives in the hallway whispers more than the boardroom slogans.

So we rebuilt—together. He started holding open-table feedback sessions. Anonymous check-ins. Not for data—for truth. And what emerged wasn't just retention—it was transformation. People stayed because they were seen. Because the culture wasn't a poster. It was a *promise*.

Elite leaders **build places people want to belong to**. Places of dignity. Of challenge. Of safety. That's how you sustain greatness.

4. Stay Calm Under Pressure

September 11th, 2001. I was stationed in Camp Lejeune, North Carolina. The moment the towers were hit, the base snapped into lockdown. Alarms screamed. Orders flew. Uncertainty flooded every hallway.

But our commanding officer? Calm. Controlled. He walked into the control room and said simply,
"Everyone take a breath. We are Marines. We don't panic. We execute."

I watched the room shift. Chaos gave way to clarity. His tone was our anchor. And I learned that day that the loudest leader isn't always the strongest—**the calmest one is.**

Since then, I've led teams through financial crises, unexpected loss, betrayal, and breakdowns. And each time, I return to that posture. **Calm is not absence of fear—it's evidence of discipline.** You build it through preparation. Through inner work that no one sees. Because when the storm comes—and it will—your steadiness becomes everyone else's oxygen.

5. Communicate with Truth and Compassion

One of the most humbling leadership moments of my life happened not on a battlefield or in a boardroom—but during a one-on-one meeting with an employee who had recently lost her father. Her performance had dipped. Deadlines missed. Attitude hardened.

The easy thing? Issue a warning. Set consequences. But I felt a nudge: **Engage the heart before you correct the hand.**

So I asked, "How are you really doing?" And she broke. She wept. And in that moment, I didn't lead with a plan—I led with presence. We talked. We mourned. We rebuilt. And weeks later, her performance not only returned—it soared. Not because of strategy. But because of *trust.*

Truth without compassion is cruelty. But truth delivered with empathy? That's leadership. Elite leaders don't correct to prove superiority. They correct to elevate. They don't weaponize feedback. They wield it with surgical care—to build, not break.

And that's the difference. The leaders who shape legacy are not the loudest in the room. They are the most **engaged**. They lean in when it's hard. They speak when it's risky. They listen when others retreat. And they do it not for control—but for *connection.*

So ask yourself:

- In crisis, am I reacting—or responding with grounded clarity?

- In conflict, am I shutting down—or asking the deeper question?

- In growth, am I clinging to what was—or evolving into what's next

Because leadership isn't made in the spotlight. It's revealed in the trenches. It's earned when you engage—not with ego, but with empathy. Not with performance, but with presence.

And if you're still reading this—it's because you know: **you're not here to be impressive. You're here to be impactful.** And that kind of leadership? It starts the moment you decide to *engage.*

Build Your Personal Leadership Code

I flew into New York for a private workshop with a team that was collapsing. Low morale. High turnover. A culture slipping quietly into toxicity. The leader—charismatic and brilliant—radiated dysfunction. He wasn't failing from lack of skill, but from a place of no center. He'd sacrificed substance for optics, said "yes" too often, and skirted the hard conversations. He didn't lack confidence—he lacked a code, a set of inner absolutes to tether him when pressure bent his decisions. Strategy wouldn't fix him. Purpose wouldn't save him. We began by rebuilding his code.

Leadership is having their six. In the military, "I've got your six" is more than just eye protection—it's an unspoken vow: *You don't have to watch your back—I will.* It's a pledge of emotional safety, steadfast loyalty, and unwavering support. When you lead, that vow is part of your DNA. You aren't just directing—you are shielding. During the darkest transitions—when contracts fail, when market trends shift, when people leave—what your team needs isn't strategy, but *security in your presence.* That presence becomes their anchor when the storm silences clarity.

True leadership isn't a decree. It's a container. You don't tell people how to act—you create the gravity that invites their best selves to show up. It means anticipating needs before they're voiced, addressing tension before it fractures relationships, and holding space when everyone else is collapsing. The culture you build isn't what you preach—it's what people feel when you're not there. Fumbles. Failures. Disruptions. They reveal the real test: do people still act with courage, integrity, coherence when the boss is offstage? That's legacy-level leadership. Because when you consistently have their six, they don't just follow your directions—they trust your heart.

But leadership doesn't begin in boardrooms. It starts in the mirror—long before you assess teams or launch vision. Before influence flies, you must reflect truth in the stillness of your soul. Ask: *Where am I insecure? Where am I hiding behind busy schedules? Which old failures are still tripping me up when courage demands clarity?* Those internal remnants don't fade— they mask themselves in hesitation, in micromanagement, in division. When clarity cracks under pressure, your leadership falters. You can't call others forward until you're forwarding yourself. Identity precedes impact. Presence precedes productivity. Mirrors must meet mission, or the mission will meet excuses.

Then, after that deep reckoning, stand firm in your value. Real authority doesn't rise from applause—it emerges from identity. Not arrogance, but alignment. It's the moment you declare, *My experience, insight, convictions—they belong here.* And because you own that value, people around you are released to own theirs. Your clarity births community. That's leadership that lasts. It's not about being the loudest voice in the room—it's about being the clearest.

And now here's the truest test: conflict doesn't have to mean combat. Disagreement doesn't demand destruction. When tension rises, reactive leaders retreat or explode. Resilient leaders pause, breathe, and ask, *What's really going on here?* Emotional regulation is the highest form of leadership. You don't dominate. You discern. You don't shut down. You invite difference. When handled with maturity, conflict deepens trust: it questions without attacking, it listens without yielding to agreement, it honors unity even when opinions differ. That's resilient leadership in practice.

So here's what I'm asking you—no, what I'm *challenging* you to do right now: write your leadership code. Not as platitudes, but as fiercely guarded parts of your soul. Discover the three values that steady you under pressure. Declare the non-negotiables—what you simply *will not* tolerate in your life or leadership. And filter every decision through that memory: *What will my legacy—my spouse, my child, my team—remember about how I led?*

This isn't about recognition. It's about alignment. It's about being anchored, quiet, and steady in a world that rewards loudness. True leadership is not the performance—it's the posture that sustains. It's how you move when you're spent, how you lead when the audience is gone, and how you stand when everything you thought you knew crumbles.

Because leadership doesn't ask for followers—it demands authenticity. It asks you to become the person worth following. And that begins here—with your code, your clarity, and your courageous decision to lead like someone called for purpose, not applause.

But here's where personal leadership becomes transformational—not just tactical. You must build your personal leadership code. This is the moment leadership moves from strategies and slogans to soul-level standards. Because you can't lead from clarity if you haven't defined your core.

First, define your values. These aren't aspirational buzzwords you frame in an office. These are the battle-tested truths you protect like your future depends on them—because it does. Integrity, for me, meant no more half-truths in business negotiations, even when the stakes were high. Courage meant walking into a boardroom to deliver direct feedback I'd avoided for months—not to wound, but to honor the relationship enough to tell the truth. Empathy meant canceling a high-stakes call to sit with a team member navigating grief. These weren't just moments—they became my mirror. Every elite leader I've coached, from scrappy startup founders to billion-dollar CEOs, had clarity on their values. They made decisions *through* them. They shaped meetings, culture, and communication from them. Without values, you react. With them, you align.

Second, declare your non-negotiables. It's easy to write what you believe. It's harder to say what you *refuse to tolerate.* That's where your leadership code grows teeth. I remember early in my consulting journey, a high-paying client pulled me aside and said, "Just massage the numbers—it's not lying, just reframing." That was my fork in the road. I walked away from the deal. Not because I didn't need the income, but because my integrity spoke louder. Years later, that single moment protected my credibility—and brought more business than I ever lost. You must name those lines in the sand. Say them aloud. *I do not gossip. I do not shrink to protect someone else's ego. I do not lead from fear. I will not pretend I'm aligned when I'm not.* These become your internal armor. Because when stress hits, you will default—not to your hopes—but to your habits.

Third, build your legacy filter. A few years ago, I sat across from a mentor over dinner in Atlanta. He asked one question that changed how I lead everything: "When you're gone, what will your *son* say about how you lived your life?" Not what your résumé says. Not what your audience applauds. But what the people closest to you—who see behind the curtain—*remember.* That wrecked me. And it recalibrated everything. Now, every major decision passes through one filter: *Does this reflect the legacy I want to leave?* It's the reason I say no to offers that compromise peace, even if they promise platform. It's why I sit down after a flight instead of squeezing in one more Zoom call—because presence isn't a perk. It's the proof of what matters most.

This is what builds a leadership code: deep values that drive decisions, non-negotiables that protect your credibility, and a legacy filter that keeps you anchored in what matters long after applause fades. You don't need more tactics. You need a soul-level compass that tells you, in every room, *This is who I am. This is what I protect. This is the legacy I lead.*

Leadership doesn't need another echo. It needs an original. And that original begins with you—becoming the kind of leader you would follow, even in silence, even in storms.

**BREAK THE BOTTLE CHALLENGE —
Chapter 12**

1. **Self-Leadership Inventory**

   ○ Reassess your scores from earlier chapters. What's improved? What still needs work?

2. **Write Your Leadership Code**

   ○ List your top three to five core values

   ○ Define each one in action

   ○ Identify your top three non-negotiables

   ○ Answer your legacy filter question

3. **30-Day Leadership Challenge**

   ○ Morning alignment: Review your mission daily

   ○ One hard conversation: Lead with truth, not avoidance

   ○ One modeled decision each day: Choose values over comfort

   ○ Evening reflection: "Did I lead today from values or emotion?"

THE CONFIDENCE CODE— UNLEASHING YOUR BOLDEST SELF

"Confidence isn't the absence of fear—it's the audacity to move anyway. It's choosing boldness before you feel ready, and backing yourself when no one else will. Your power begins the moment you stop waiting to be worthy."

— Break The Bottle

Confidence in Motion: Building Boldness Before You Feel Ready

Confidence isn't a spark reserved for the charismatic. It's not inherited through charm, talent, or status. It's not granted in boardrooms or by social media likes. Confidence is not a personality—it's a posture. A decision. A relentless commitment to show up even when everything in you wants to shrink back. Let's be real—confidence is forged, not found. That's the truth we forget: confidence doesn't precede action. Action precedes confidence.

I remember it like it was yesterday—I was maybe nine years old, standing at the edge of the neighborhood pool, shirt on, arms crossed, trying to laugh along with the other kids but feeling like my whole body was betraying me. The sun was out, the chlorine was thick in the air, the shouts and splashes around me were full of summer joy—and there I was, paralyzed. Not because

I couldn't swim. But because taking off my shirt felt like exposing my shame. I was the chubby kid. Round-faced, belly hanging, always sweating even in the shade. My cousins and neighborhood friends used to joke that I had my own gravitational pull. It was supposed to be funny—until it wasn't. Until those words followed me home. Until they echoed in my mind every time I walked past a mirror. "Fat boy. Slowpoke. Big Mike."

Back then, food was comfort. It wasn't just about being hungry—it was about escaping. When life felt unsafe, food was safe. When emotions felt overwhelming, a bag of chips numbed the noise. When the world outside told me I wasn't enough, I could eat until I couldn't feel. I didn't know it then, but I was developing a relationship with food that was about survival, not nutrition. Late nights with the refrigerator door cracked open like a guilty secret. Sneaking snacks into my room like a soldier hiding ammunition. I became a closet eater—stuffing my pain alongside every snack I wasn't supposed to have.

Fast forward to adulthood. The boy who avoided the pool grew into the man who dreaded airplanes. The anxiety didn't come from flying—it came from wondering if the seatbelt would click. Would I need a seatbelt extender? Would the person next to me look uncomfortable? I'd hold my breath while buckling in, literally and figuratively, trying to shrink my body to fit into a world that never seemed to have space for me. I'd sweat before the plane even took off—not from fear, but from shame.

Confidence? I didn't have it. I faked it. I buried it under titles, jobs, accomplishments. I wore ambition like armor, trying to prove to the world— and to myself—that I was more than my weight. But here's the truth: I could lead teams, win awards, speak on stages—and still feel small when I looked in the mirror. I had the credentials. I didn't have the confidence.

Then came October 23, 2023. I had just finished a powerful television interview, feeling good, riding the high. The host—a fellow brother—pulled me aside and said, "Can I talk to you, man to man?" I nodded, curious. What he said next shifted something deep inside me.

He shared how he lost his brother—a good man, a smart man—to a heart attack at just 46 years old. His brother weighed 350 pounds. And then he looked me straight in the eye and said, "I saw my brother in you today. You're doing incredible things. But if you don't take care of your health, none of that is going to matter." That hit me like a silent bomb. He wasn't judging me. He was warning me. Caring for me. Holding up a mirror that I couldn't ignore. Then, with a half-smile, he said, "You're a Marine, right? So act like it."

That moment stripped me. There was no performance. No ego. Just truth. And truth, when delivered in love, doesn't just convict—it awakens. That day, I was 331 pounds. No diagnosis yet, but I was dancing with prediabetes, inflammation, chronic fatigue, and slow-motion self-destruction. I didn't need a New Year. I didn't need another breakdown. I needed to decide.

So I made a vow. Not a wish. A vow. I decided to transform my life—not just for looks, but for legacy. I wasn't losing weight for beach photos. I was doing it so I could see my son's walk down the aisle with their bride to be. So I could run with my grandkids. So I could be alive to finish the work I've been called to do.

Here's where most people get it twisted: they wait to feel confident before they act. But I had to act before I felt anything. I was still insecure. Still winded. Still haunted by every fat joke from my childhood. But I moved anyway. I laced up my shoes and walked—gasping for breath, body aching, but soul committed. I said no to the midnight snacks, yes to early morning walks, and I started tracking not just my calories, but my character.

And this is where confidence started to take root.

Because confidence isn't a product of applause—it's the result of alignment. I began to say "yes" to what aligned with my vision, not just what satisfied my cravings. And slowly, the story in my head started to change. The fat kid narrative got quieter. The Marine in me got louder. The voice that used to say, "You'll always be like this," got replaced with, "You're becoming someone new."

And the neuroscience backs this up. Dr. Amy Cuddy's research proves that behavior shapes belief. When you move with boldness—even before you believe you are bold—your body teaches your mind what's possible. You build confidence through motion, not meditation. Every time I showed up for a workout when I didn't feel like it, every time I chose fasting instead of feasting, I was stacking bricks of belief. Not because I was strong, but because I was consistent. Repetition rewires the brain.

Was it hard? Of course. I slipped up. I wanted to quit. I felt ridiculous doing lunges in my living room, dripping sweat, cursing my own weakness. But I kept going. Because that's the real secret: confidence isn't about never struggling. It's about not stopping.

Eventually, the scale moved. From 331 to 320. Then to 300. Then below. And when I broke into the 240s to the 200s, it wasn't just a weight milestone—it was a soul marker. It told me: you're not who you used to be. And more importantly: you don't have to be. Yes, I've tried to fad diets and none of it worked for me in the long term.

Now people ask me, "How'd you do it?" expecting some secret formula. And I tell them—it wasn't a diet. It was a decision. And every day, I had to re-engage that decision. Because you don't lose 150 pounds once. You lose it every time you choose water over soda, rest over scrolling, fasting over grazing, healing over hiding.

I didn't just lose weight. I lost the lies. The lie that said I wasn't worthy of being seen. The lie that said it was too late to change. The lie that said I had to stay broken because I had been broken for so long. Those lies died one "no" at a time. One step at a time. One choice at a time.

And now, confidence isn't a mask I wear—it's the muscle I've built.

I want you to hear me: You don't have to wait to feel ready. You don't need to look a certain way, or sound a certain way, or have your past neatly tucked away in order to move. You move first. You engage your body. You engage your mind. You engage your truth. And the confidence will come.If you're waiting to feel ready, let me lovingly tell you—you never will. You'll never feel 100% certain. But 70% with courage beats 100% with paralysis.

That's what "Confidence in Motion" is all about. It's not about faking it until you make it. It's about practicing it until you believe it. It's about doing the thing—the workout, the hard conversation, the first step—not because you're already bold, but because you're building boldness one move at a time.

But let me take you deeper.

As the pounds began to shed, something else began to emerge—a clarity about who I was becoming. Confidence wasn't just showing up in the mirror; it was showing up in meetings, in decisions, in how I walked into rooms. Yet I realized confidence didn't show up the same way every time. It wasn't one flavor. It wasn't one speed. It was adaptive—alive—and learning to lead with confidence required learning how to shift gears.

That's when I began to recognize what I now call **the three confidence archetypes**. These weren't personas I put on. They were dimensions of me— forged in different fires—that I could call on depending on the season, the moment, or the battlefield.

The Centered Guide

The first is **The Centered Guide**—the calm within the chaos. This version of me doesn't shout to be heard. He doesn't perform to be seen. He walks into the room with a quiet gravity that anchors the space. The Centered Guide doesn't control the room—he steadies it.

I remember stepping into a corporate training session just days after two departments had been merged, and tensions were boiling. People were guarded, territorial, unsure of their place in this new world. The client had asked for "high energy" and "rah-rah motivation," but I knew that wasn't what the room needed. What they needed was peace. So, I stood there for a moment in silence—no slides, no hype—and simply said, "I know you're all carrying a lot. Let's breathe before we build." You could feel the resistance melt. Shoulders dropped. Brows unfurrowed. That wasn't charisma. That was presence. That was the Centered Guide doing his work.

Years ago, I would've overcompensated—tried to crack jokes, make noise, own the stage. But now? I understand that groundedness is a flex. That regulated presence is more powerful than reactive posture. Neuroscience confirms this—deep breaths engage the prefrontal cortex, the logical center of the brain. The message your body sends to your mind? *I am safe. I am capable. I am ready.* This kind of leadership—this kind of confidence—doesn't explode. It expands.

Nelson Mandela had it. After 27 years behind bars, he emerged not with rage but with resolve. His power wasn't in volume. It was in vision. That's the Centered Guide—the one who leads not from ego, but from alignment.

The Strategic Architect

Then there's **The Strategic Architect**—the one who doesn't just hope for transformation but builds it brick by brick. This is the version of me that rose up when everything in my life fell apart—divorce, job loss, legal battles, and a health scare all colliding in the same chapter. Chaos was knocking at my door daily, and spiraling would've been easy. But I knew this: emotion without strategy is self-sabotage. So I got to work.

I mapped my days. Created fitness routines. Built a fasting plan. Wrote down non-negotiables. I wasn't chasing perfection—I was installing discipline. I became my own project manager, using systems to create stability. Not because it was easy—it never was—but because it was the only way to survive with intention.

Confidence here didn't come from results. It came from *repeatability*. Showing up. Following through. Turning execution into ritual. I had to design a life I could sustain—a structure that could hold both my ambition and my healing.

And I'm not alone in that. Harvard Business Review studies show that the most effective leaders aren't just charismatic—they're consistent. They think in frameworks, plan in systems, and execute with clarity. Marie Curie changed the world not with bravado but with precision. She was deliberate, measured, and relentless in her process. That's the Strategic Architect—not flashy, but foundational.

It's the part of me that wakes up early, packs my bag the night before a speaking tour, logs meals, reviews notes, and creates space for both movement and mindfulness. You don't have to be perfect to be this person—but you have to be disciplined. And every time I follow through on what I promised myself, my confidence gets another rep in the gym.

The Charismatic Driver

And then there's the third archetype—**The Charismatic Driver**. The one who doesn't just walk into the room but sets it on fire. The one who channels energy, passion, and presence into ignition. This is the version of me that people often assume is "just how I am." But what they don't see is that this energy isn't hype—it's honesty.

I felt it most intensely in a room of over 3,000 leaders. I was booked to speak on transformation and leadership, but as I stood backstage, gripping the mic, I felt that old familiar fear creep in. The voice that says, "You're not ready." My shirt was sticking to my back with sweat. My knees felt hollow. And then I remembered that conversation with the TV host—the brother who looked me in the eye and said, "You're dying slowly, and I'm not gonna let you." That truth hit me again like lightning. And I stepped on that stage not to perform, but to *testify*.

I told the truth. About my weight. My shame. My journey. My almost death. And the room didn't just listen—it *moved*. I saw heads nod. People cry. Leaders break their silence. That's what the Charismatic Driver does—he doesn't just speak; he stirs. He doesn't just motivate; he mobilizes.

And yes, research backs it up. Studies show that emotional resonance makes ideas more memorable and actions more likely. But I don't need a study to tell me what I felt that day—what I still feel every time someone comes up to me after a talk and says, "I've never told anyone this, but…"

That's the power of showing up with your scars visible. That's what confidence looks like when it's wrapped in transparency, not trophies.

Here's the secret, though: **these archetypes aren't costumes you put on—they're gears you shift into.** Depending on the room, the moment, the need—you adapt. You flex. You lead not with rigidity, but with range.

Sometimes you need the Centered Guide—the one who doesn't flinch when the pressure spikes. Sometimes you need the Strategic Architect—the one who plans the exit before the fire even starts. And sometimes, you need the Charismatic Driver—the one who rallies people when they've forgotten how to hope.

I've been each of them—on different stages, in different seasons. With clients who were unraveling, I showed up as the Centered Guide. With overwhelmed CEOs building new teams, I stepped in as the Strategic Architect. With audiences craving truth over polish, I turned up as the Charismatic Driver—mic hot, truth louder.

And here's the invitation: so can you.

You're not stuck in one lane. You're not confined to one style. You are a multidimensional leader, built to **engage** your world with the version of yourself the moment requires.

So study yourself. Know your strengths. Recognize your triggers. Then practice the *shift*.

Let the Centered Guide protect your peace.
Let the Strategic Architect build your vision.
Let the Charismatic Driver carry your message.

And above all—don't perform these roles. **Embody them.** Because when your confidence flows from integrity, not insecurity—when it adapts with intention, not panic—when it leads from alignment, not approval—you become unstoppable.

You don't just show up.
You transform environments.
You become the kind of leader the world needs now.

Breaking Free from Fear and Self-Doubt

The real war never made the news. It didn't happen on the battlefield, though I've been there too—in the bone-dry heat of Iraq, heart pounding, rifle clenched, scanning alleyways for threats that sometimes looked like children, sometimes looked like shadows. I've seen combat. I've faced enemies that wanted me dead. But let me tell you something honest: those weren't the scariest battles of my life.

No, the hardest ones were invisible. The silent ones. The ones that unfolded in empty hotel rooms between speaking engagements, or on long drives back from courtrooms, wondering if I'd see my son again. The ones that happened after the applause stopped, when the room emptied out and I was left alone with myself—with that subtle whisper, familiar and cruel: *"They're going to find out. You're not enough."*

That's the war zone most people don't see. The battlefield in the mind. You can suit up in success—the titles, the wardrobe, the degrees—and still be bleeding inside. You can be the most celebrated voice on the stage and still doubt your right to be there.

That voice doesn't scream. It whispers. Smooth. Calculated. Full of just enough truth to sound reasonable and just enough lie to keep you bound. It doesn't shout, *"You're a failure."* It simply reminds you of every time you almost were.

I've heard that voice in the locker rooms of my high school—back when I was a lineman on the football team, bigger than most, stronger than most, but still carrying the shame of being the fat kid who never took his shirt off at the pool. I wore my helmet like a hiding place. I played to prove something, but I was never quite sure what. Maybe that I belonged. Maybe that I mattered.

That voice followed me into the Marine Corps. Boot camp was where boys became machines. We were taught to harden, to suppress. Pain? Numb it. Fear? Bury it. Weakness? Disguise it. I learned how to kill, how to march, how to survive. But I never learned how to be *still*. I never learned how to be *kind to myself*. There was no drill for self-compassion.

And so, when I transitioned out of the military—suddenly stripped of my uniform, my mission, my brotherhood—I felt unarmed. No battle plan. No clear enemy. Just questions. Who am I if I'm not in combat? Who am I if I'm not Sergeant Allison? What am I now? I was a free man—and yet I felt completely lost.

The fog settled in slowly. I was navigating divorce. I was fighting for my child. I was taking pills for depression, anxiety, sleep—some days thirteen different medications just to feel *okay enough* to get out of bed. And still, that voice whispered. "See? You're broken. You're just pretending. One slip and it all comes crashing down."

But in the middle of that darkness, something else stirred. Not confidence. **Confrontation.** A refusal. A rebellion. I started to interrogate that voice. "Who gave you permission to narrate my life?" "Who decided that my past failures would forever shape my future?" And the more I pulled that thread, the more it unraveled. That voice? It wasn't even mine. It was inherited. From a culture that equated masculinity with silence. From coaches who praised performance but never asked about pain. From a society that applauds success but ignores suffering.

Confidence doesn't come when fear disappears. It comes when truth gets louder.

So I started speaking differently—not on stages, but in my own head. I stopped begging fear to leave and started showing it who was in charge. I told myself: *"Yes, I've failed. But I've also gotten back up." "Yes, I've been hurt. But I've chosen to heal." "I'm not who I was. And I don't need to be who they expected. I just need to be me—fully, completely, and now."*

That shift didn't erase fear. It gave me authority over it.

Because here's the truth no one tells you: fear doesn't vanish when you succeed. Sometimes, it gets louder. But the way you relate to it changes. You stop reacting. You start *leading it*.

The most dangerous imposter isn't the one who sneaks into the room. It's the one who sneaks into your thoughts and convinces you that you don't belong. That you're too broken. Too different. Too late.

But you're not. Not even close.

I've stood in front of thousands of CEOs—buttoned-up, high-level decision makers—and shared my story. The Jamaican-American boy who felt like he was "too dark" for one culture, "too different" for another. The combat veteran who carried more invisible wounds than visible medals. The divorced father trying to stitch together a life that felt ripped apart. I've shared it all—not because I have it all together, but because confidence doesn't come from polish. It comes from *presence*.

You've been waiting to "arrive"—to feel ready, to feel affirmed. But maybe it's time to stop waiting and *start engaging*. Maybe you don't need to conquer fear—you need to confront it with *movement*. With one bold act of alignment. With one step toward the future version of yourself who already knows how this ends—in victory.

So what does confidence actually look like?

It looks like **refusing to shrink** for the comfort of others.
It looks like **saying no** to things that no longer align, even if you used to say yes.
It looks like **choosing rest without guilt**, because exhaustion is not a badge of honor.
It looks like **walking into rooms where no one looks like you, sounds like you, or agrees with you—and deciding to lead anyway**.

Confidence isn't about pretending the storm isn't real. It's about choosing to anchor yourself in the middle of it.

And I want to tell you something—if you're in the storm right now, if you're barely holding on, if you're questioning your worth, your calling, your future—this is your moment. Not after you clean it up. Not after you lose the weight, get the deal, get the ring. Now. This is the moment you break the contract with fear. This is the moment you say: *"I'm not waiting for the world to affirm me. I will lead myself out of this."*

Because confidence isn't a trait—it's a decision.
A decision to engage.
> To rise.
> > To lead.
> > > To live.

The Three Confidence Killers and How to Dismantle Them

Confidence, by design, isn't fragile. But it becomes fragile when it's built on shaky ground—on borrowed timelines, unattainable ideals, and the unstable currency of external praise. If you're walking through life wondering why you can't sustain boldness, why courage flickers in and out like faulty Wi-Fi, it's probably not a flaw in your DNA. It's a flaw in your foundation. There are three subtle, seductive forces that erode confidence from the inside out—and I've battled all of them.

The sauna was a sacred space for me.

Not because it was fancy—it wasn't. Just a quiet corner of the gym, tucked behind fogged glass, the kind of place where no one's flexing, no one's posturing, just breathing and sweating and being. It was a Tuesday afternoon, post-workout, and I had sat down with the intention to relax, but my mind wouldn't slow. I was anxious. Not from the heat—from the voice in my head. I had just wrapped a leadership intensive with a high-profile client. It had gone well. Objectively. But I kept replaying a moment when I stumbled over a word. That one moment was all I could hear.

That's when this man sitting across from me—older, calm, eyes closed like he'd lived some life—opened them, looked straight at me, and said, "Brother, you ever notice how sweat only comes when the body's under pressure?" I blinked. He wasn't talking about heat anymore. He smiled, leaned back, and said, "Pressure doesn't mean you're failing. It means something's working." That moment sat with me.

That's the first killer of confidence—comparison.

It creeps in when you're not even looking for it. I was sweating success and still questioning my right to lead. It's not just social media comparison, though that's a part of it. It's the subtle way we measure our value by someone else's metrics. Their followers. Their applause. Their timing. We see the highlight reels and wonder why our behind-the-scenes feels so messy. But comparison doesn't clarify your path—it clouds it. It doesn't sharpen your identity—it distorts it.

I've felt that distortion. There was a time I was prepping for a keynote and caught myself scrolling through another speaker's reel—stadiums, ovations, fans waiting in line for selfies. And here I was, doing voice warmups in a Hampton Inn bathroom mirror, wondering if my story would land. That's the trap. You forget that your power isn't in the stadiums. It's in your *specificity*. Your scars. Your presence. Your truth.

Comparison tells you you're behind. Confidence tells you you're becoming.

A few months ago, after a speaking event in Wisconsin, my wife and I went on a walk—just the two of us, boots crunching on snow-packed trails, the air crisp and quiet. She turned to me mid-conversation and said, "You know what I love about you? You're finally enjoying what you used to only chase." I didn't respond right away. Because she was right—for years, I'd hustled for the next stage, the next post, the next moment that might finally make me feel like I made it. But I was missing *this*. The now. The quiet peace of being aligned.

That's when I realized: **perfection is the second killer of confidence.**

It disguises itself as excellence. As drive. As ambition. But really, it's fear wearing a tuxedo. Fear of being exposed. Fear of being judged. Fear of failing out loud. And it'll keep you refining, tweaking, delaying—all in the name of "getting it right." I've been there. I once pushed a program launch back three times because the website banner didn't "feel right." But guess what? The clients who signed up didn't care about the banner. They cared about the breakthrough. They didn't need my polish. They needed my *presence*.

Perfection paralyzes progress. It convinces you to wait. And waiting becomes your story. "When it's ready." "When I'm ready." But you don't need ready. You need real. You need rhythm. You need movement. Confidence doesn't grow in theory. It grows in motion.

The third killer is the one most camouflaged: **validation addiction.**

It's tricky because it can look like momentum. The speaking gigs. The reposts. The DMs. The conference invites. But if you're not rooted, you start depending on the noise. You start checking your worth through applause. And the moment it's quiet? You unravel.

I was in another country, fresh off delivering a keynote that got a standing ovation. I should've been flying high. But I found myself in the hotel room that night, obsessing over a single piece of negative feedback. Not the dozens of affirmations. Just that one. That one sentence hit like a dart, and it punctured something I hadn't fully healed—the part of me that still believed I needed external confirmation to be whole.

That's when I called my brother.

He's not a coach. He's not a speaker. But he's wise. I told him what happened, expecting empathy. Instead, he said, "Mike, did you tell the truth on that stage?" I said, "Yeah, of course." He said, "Then why are you outsourcing your peace to someone who didn't clap?" That stopped me cold.

Because that's what validation addiction does—it makes your truth dependent on someone else's reaction. And that's unsustainable. Because the more you need the crowd, the more you'll bend to fit their preferences. And the moment you bend, you break alignment. And the moment you break alignment, you trade leadership for likability. That's not confidence. That's codependence in a nice suit.

So how do you dismantle these killers?

You rewire the source.

When comparison creeps in, re-anchor in clarity.

> "What am I building, and why?"

When perfection whispers, choose momentum.

> "What's the next right move?"

When validation tempts you, re-center in truth.

> "Did I move in integrity?"

Confidence is not the absence of insecurity. It's the mastery of it. It's saying, "Yes, that voice is still there. But it doesn't drive anymore." It's choosing to lead yourself with intentionality—when no one's watching, when no one's clapping, when you're standing in front of a mirror wondering if today is the day it all clicks.

And some days, it doesn't click. Some days, you stutter. You forget. You regress. But even on those days—*especially* on those days—confidence is built. Because confidence isn't formed by how loud you roar when you're winning. It's built by how steady you walk when the lights are off.

So burn the metric of comparison. Shatter the myth of perfection. Detach your worth from praise.

Confidence that endures is not gifted. It's *guarded*. Every day. From the inside out.

Becoming Unapologetically You

Confidence begins the moment you stop waiting for someone else to hand you the mic. It begins the moment you refuse to apologize for your existence, your brilliance, your truth. It begins the moment permission becomes irrelevant—because you've chosen to authorize yourself. That is the point where real transformation begins. The turning point where quiet agreement turns into active alignment. And at the heart of it all is this unshakable truth: the world doesn't make space for confidence; it responds to it.

Most people don't fail because they lack capability. They fail because they postpone their power, holding back their voice, their ideas, their action—waiting for a nod from someone who doesn't hold their destiny. And in that delay, a dangerous narrative begins to fester: "I'll be ready when someone tells me I'm enough." But what if that nod never comes? What if the seat at the table you're waiting for doesn't exist until you build it? That is the cost of postponing your power—the slow erosion of your dreams under the guise of waiting for validation.

It wasn't the day I got promoted. It wasn't when I stood on stage or earned the medal. It wasn't when the world clapped. The moment I truly became powerful—unshakably, unapologetically powerful—was in a dimly lit bathroom, on a night no cameras were watching, with my palms pressed to the sink, and my reflection staring back like a stranger I barely recognized.

I was wearing the weight of other people's expectations like it was body armor. A curated version of myself had shown up to every boardroom, every keynote, every family gathering. Polished. Professional. Impressive. But underneath? I was exhausted. Not from the work—but from the performance. Every room I entered came with an internal checklist: Don't be too loud. Don't seem too confident. Don't ruffle feathers. Make them comfortable, even if you're breaking inside. Smile. Nod. Agree. Lead—but don't lead so boldly they feel threatened.

That night, after another day of showing up everywhere but home inside myself, I whispered the words: "I don't even know who I am anymore." And that's when it hit me—if I couldn't recognize myself in the mirror, how could I ever expect the world to see me?

Confidence isn't found in applause. It's forged in those moments where you strip down to your truth. Where the mask cracks, and you're finally brave enough to say, "I've been performing someone else's comfort, not living my own conviction." Becoming unapologetically you isn't a declaration you post on social media. It's a quiet revolution that begins the moment you stop editing your existence for approval.

The transformation didn't happen all at once. It started small—almost unnoticeable. I stopped saying "yes" when I meant "maybe." I let silence sit longer in meetings instead of rushing to fill it with agreement. I began choosing discomfort over compliance, not out of defiance, but out of devotion to something bigger than people-pleasing: **purpose**.

When I first brought my real voice into professional spaces, it didn't sound rehearsed. It cracked. It quivered. But it was mine. And with every syllable, I felt a fragment of the man I'd buried begin to reemerge. Not the version groomed to impress. The version forged in fire. The one who had survived IED blasts and battlefield decisions, who had watched friends bleed out in foreign sands and still stood. The one who knew what it meant to rebuild from emotional rubble, to rise from trauma and say, "You didn't take me."

That man—the real me—didn't need permission. He needed **remembrance**.

I stopped apologizing for taking up space in rooms that weren't designed for my voice. Because here's what I learned: when you shrink yourself to fit someone else's comfort zone, you're not being polite—you're being erased. And too many of us have mistaken erasure for humility. We've confused being agreeable with being valuable. But your value isn't in how little noise you make—it's in how much impact your presence commands, even in silence.

I remember sitting across from an executive who questioned my expertise—not because of my résumé, which was longer than his—**but because I didn't look like his definition of leadership**. I was a Marine combat veteran with battlefield strategy wired into my DNA, a systems thinker who had managed multi-million-dollar federal projects, a founder who built and exited a seven-figure franchise—but all he saw was a Black man who wasn't performing palatability.

And in that moment, I had two choices.

I could shapeshift. Soften my tone. Bend my truth to match his comfort. Or I could stand in my earned authority, unwavering, and risk being misunderstood.

I chose the latter.

Because being unapologetically you means you no longer compromise clarity for approval. You understand that your truth may threaten those who've never confronted their own. And still—you speak. Not out of arrogance, but out of allegiance to the **mission you were born to fulfill**.

This kind of confidence doesn't just shift rooms—it exposes them. It reveals who was rooting for your mask and who can respect your realness. And that exposure? It's painful—but it's necessary. Because the only way to build a life of integrity is to stop inviting people who only know how to love your edited version.

Becoming unapologetically you will cost you things. Relationships. Opportunities. Illusions. But it will give you something infinitely more valuable—**yourself**. Your peace. Your power. Your presence. Your clarity.

You will lose people when you stop hiding. That's the reality no one tells you. The moment you choose full alignment with who you really are, the shadows begin to peel back—and not everyone has the eyes to handle that kind of brightness. They loved your hustle. They admired your strength. But they weren't ready for your truth. And when you no longer perform exhaustion as a badge of honor… when you set boundaries, speak plainly, and choose your calling over their comfort—it offends them.

Let it.

Because the people who are meant to walk with you won't be repelled by your truth—they'll be **reverent** of it. They'll honor the unfiltered you, the healed you, the rising you. The you that doesn't apologize for being fire in a world that keeps asking for smoke. Your alignment will attract your tribe. But only when you stop auditioning for your enemies.

I learned that the hard way. For years I watered myself down to fit in rooms that were never designed for my expansion. I studied their language. Dressed for their approval. Muted my story because it carried too much grit. But nothing stings more than realizing you were invited into a space only because you diluted what made you powerful.

The truth? You don't need more rooms—you need more courage. The courage to build your own tables. To create your own platforms. To lead in your own voice. Because the moment you stop waiting to be chosen, you start building systems that others can rise through too. That's real impact. That's legacy.

You don't get to rewrite history by being forgettable. You don't transform rooms by blending into them. And you don't change lives by keeping your truth in your pocket, only to bring it out when it's safe. Being unapologetically you means risking being misunderstood—because staying muted is no longer an option. Because silence has cost you enough already.

I had to bury the version of me that sought safety in agreement. I had to grieve him—the agreeable Marine, the overly polished executive, the man who measured his volume based on how threatened the room might feel. And I had to resurrect the version who bled for this country, who battled his way through trauma, who rebuilt from rock bottom with his hands shaking and heart still open.

That man didn't need permission.

He needed alignment.

So I made a decision—not just to speak, but to live out loud. To teach from scars instead of perfection. To show up in spaces as my full self, even if that meant fewer invitations. Because every time I stood in my own truth, I watched the right people find their voice too. That's how impact works—it's not just taught. It's **transferred**. Your confidence becomes a mirror that reflects possibility for others.

And that's what you're being called to right now—not to impress, but to ignite. To show the world what it looks like when a human being lives in their full expression. The world doesn't need more noise. It needs more light. Not filtered, not polished, not diluted—**radiant and raw**.

So walk into the next room like you belong there—because you do. Lead the meeting. Start the business. Launch the movement. Write the truth. Wear the color. Raise your volume. Set the boundary. Say the thing. Because the version of you the world has been waiting for isn't the one trying to prove anything.

It's the one who has finally remembered: I am not here to fit in. I am here to be **fully found**.

And now… you have been.

Building Confidence Through Small Wins

Confidence isn't an accident. It's not magic, and it's definitely not something reserved for the lucky. Confidence is math. It's the result of a sequence of consistent, intentional decisions—small, often unseen choices—that over time reinforce one foundational truth: "I can trust myself." That's where real power begins. Not in talent. Not in image. But in the invisible faith and belief, an often uncomfortable act of self-trust.

You build that trust through repetition. Through keeping your word when no one's watching. Through honoring your values even when it costs you. Each time you make a decision that aligns with who you want to become, you make a deposit into your internal confidence bank. You don't need external proof—you've got internal evidence. You've got receipts.

Let me take you back to a moment that didn't look like a breakthrough—but was.

I was sitting in the corner of a dim, overheated shared office space in Southern California, in a chair that wobbled every time I shifted my weight. I had just left a franchise I had built from scratch. Left comfort. Left safety. Left something that, on paper, looked like a success. But my soul knew it was time. And now, I was facing the blank canvas of entrepreneurship—not as a dream, but as a *necessity*. Rent was due. My sons needed stability. My wife was supporting me with unwavering belief, but we both knew belief didn't pay the bills. I was staring down a laptop with no email list, no business plan, and no real income.

Confidence? It wasn't loud then. It was a whisper. But it was there—nudging me to move, even without a map.

I didn't wait to go viral. I didn't obsess over branding colors or logos. I did the first thing I knew how to do: I sent an email to someone I had helped years ago. I reminded him of the impact our conversation had made back then, and I asked if he needed support now. That led to a phone call. That phone call led to a small coaching agreement. That agreement led to another referral.

That's how it started. Not with hype—but with a *decision to engage*.

Confidence isn't built in leaps. It's built in reps. And in that season, every rep mattered. I started my days before sunrise. Not because I'm naturally a morning person, but because that was the only time I could think clearly before emails, school runs, and self-doubt crowded the space. I created what I now call *"non-negotiables"*—a simple routine that included a walk, scripture, journaling, and outreach. Not for show. Not for performance. For *alignment*.

Each of those disciplines was a small win.

Each time I sent a proposal that I was scared to hit "send" on.
Each time I followed up after getting ghosted.
Each time I delivered value before asking for a contract.
Each time I recorded a video with no lighting, no mic, no audience—just my conviction.

That was me building my *Confidence Loop™* in real time. Clarity → Courage → Credibility → Confidence. And then back again.

And I didn't do it alone.

Courtney—my wife—became more than my support. She was my strategy. She'd sit with me after 10-hour days, while I pitched ideas I wasn't even sure would work. She reminded me that just because something was hard didn't mean I was failing. She reminded me that building something that lasts doesn't require applause. It requires *alignment and action*.

Then there was Anthony Trucks—former NFL player, powerhouse speaker, someone who had walked the road of reinvention himself. He reminded me in a phone call during one of my lowest months, "Mike, momentum doesn't need motivation. It needs movement." That line stayed with me. So I moved.

There were nights I couldn't sleep—not because I wasn't tired, but because the weight of building something from scratch while healing from the trauma of burnout and past failures was real. But I showed up the next morning. Not always excited. Not always confident. But *committed*. And every one of those days became a deposit.

Confidence isn't always knowing it will work. It's deciding you'll work it anyway.

You know what no one tells you? Building a business isn't about having the most polished funnel or the trendiest offer. It's about follow-through. It's about integrity. It's about how you treat people when no one's watching. When I started coaching executive leaders, I didn't have a massive media kit. I had a reputation for honesty and resilience. I had lived through pain, through loss, through rebuilding—and I spoke from that place. That earned trust. That earned referrals. That built traction.

You build confidence the same way you build anything else—*by building*. One brick. One phone call. One meeting. One rejection turned into a lesson. One offer that flopped turned into a refined message. One failed webinar taught me more about connection than any course ever could.

Small wins are sacred. But they only compound when you document them.

That's why I journal. Not for the public. Not for aesthetics. But because I need to *see* what I've done. Because when my mind wants to lie and say I'm behind, my receipts tell the truth.

Here's the truth no one's shouting from stages: confidence is quiet before it becomes compelling. It's built in the lonely hours. In the unsexy work. In the courage to keep promises to yourself when no one's watching. That's what makes it *real*.

And you don't need a perfect strategy. You need motion. Today.

Send the email. Make the ask. Follow up with that client. Rewatch your pitch and improve it. Study what worked and what didn't. Find your rhythm. Because the rhythm becomes your runway. And the runway leads to liftoff.

So, if you're sitting at your laptop, wondering if this is the season you finally go all in—this is your confirmation.

You don't need the full map. You need one honest step. Confidence is math.

Decision + Repetition = Self-trust.
Self-trust = Momentum.
Momentum = Identity shift.

And identity shift? That's where everything begins to transform.

You don't need a miracle. You need a moment. This one.

Stack the win.

The Discipline Behind Delayed Gratification

Confidence is rarely born in the spotlight. It's forged in the quiet, in the unseen hours where sacrifice and discipline converge without fanfare. It's formed not in grand moments of achievement but in private decisions where no one is watching and no one is clapping. Real confidence, the kind that commands a room and shifts a culture, is rooted not in talent, charisma, or charm—but in the daily mastery of one often-overlooked principle: delayed gratification.

In a society obsessed with instant everything—likes, fame, pleasure, recognition—most people live as slaves to impulse. They trade enduring growth for fleeting ease. But every time you resist the need for now—every time you delay a temporary comfort in favor of a long-term reward—you tell yourself something powerful: "I can be trusted." That kind of trust is sacred. It's self-respect in action. And it's the foundation for unshakable confidence.

Delayed gratification isn't deprivation—it's transformation. It's the conscious act of honoring what you're building more than what you're feeling. It's the internal declaration that says, "My future matters more than my momentary craving." It's the refusal to let emotion become the architect of your destiny.

I've lived both sides of this truth.

I've tasted the sugar-rush of quick wins—getting the check, signing the contract, feeling the instant buzz of applause. And I've also sat in silence, choosing to say no to an opportunity that didn't align. I've walked away from quick money, fast praise, and familiar comfort because I knew they were pulling me off mission. And let me tell you—nothing will test your confidence more than walking away from something shiny to honor something sacred.

The first time I said "no" to a lucrative deal, I had just gotten off stage. The applause was still ringing in my ears. A representative from a big-name company approached me and offered a contract that would've padded my bank account nicely. But the content they wanted me to teach wasn't mine. It didn't align with my values. It wasn't my voice. It was someone else's script with my face on the flyer. I stood there, smiled, thanked him—and declined.

That was one of the hardest decisions I'd made up to that point. Not because I didn't want the money. But because I wanted my future more.

And that's the heart of it.

Delayed gratification is the ability to tell yourself, in real-time: "What I'm building is worth more than what I'm craving." That's not deprivation. That's maturity. That's legacy-level leadership.

I didn't learn this in a book. I learned it in the pressure cooker of life. During my divorce, I could've taken easy routes—emotionally, legally, spiritually. I could've lashed out. I could've made decisions out of pain. But I chose to think beyond the moment. To act like the man I wanted my sons to remember, not the one who wanted to win a temporary battle.

That restraint wasn't about control. It was about character. And the confidence I feel today when I look my son in the eyes comes not from the stage, but from those invisible moments where I chose legacy over ego.

You want real confidence? Build it in the moments no one claps for.

When you say no to the impulse to argue, and instead send the text that leads to peace.
When you wake up at 5AM, not because you want to, but because your future deserves it.
When you walk away from a toxic dynamic—not because it feels good, but because it's right.
When you stick to your fast. Show up to the gym. Push send on the pitch. Keep the promise to yourself. Again and again.

These are not just habits. They are *identity recalibrations*. They tell your nervous system: "We don't live at the mercy of emotion. We live by mission."
That's how you become unshakable. That's how confidence roots.

And the data backs this up. Studies in cognitive neuroscience confirm that the prefrontal cortex—the part of your brain responsible for decision-making, planning, and emotional regulation—*gets stronger* the more you practice delayed gratification. In simple terms? Every time you resist the urge to choose what's easy over what's right, you're rewiring your brain to trust itself. You're shaping the version of you who can handle pressure. Lead others. Sustain success. That's not motivation. That's **mental architecture**.

Let me make this personal.

There was a season when I had to train myself not to need immediate results. I was launching my coaching business after walking away from everything I knew. And the results didn't come fast. My inbox wasn't full. My calendar wasn't booked. I had to sit in the space between "I believe in this" and "no one else sees it yet." I had to *build in obscurity*. That was the gym. That was where I built muscle I use to this day.

I remember a specific morning—I was sitting at the kitchen table, three client proposals out, no confirmations in. My son was at school, and my wife was out working, supporting our household while I built. My confidence was shaking. The doubts were screaming. But instead of spiraling, I took a breath. I opened my laptop. I created content. I refined my offer. I made another call. I followed up. I didn't *feel* confident. But I *acted* in confidence.

That act—unseen, uncelebrated, unglamorous—was a seed. And weeks later, those same proposals came back. Two out of three signed. The third led to a referral. But more than the revenue, what I earned that day was the deep internal knowing: **"I can be trusted with my future."**

That's what delayed gratification gives you—self-trust.
And **self-trust is the birthplace of confidence**.

Because here's the hard truth: If you can't keep your word to yourself in private, no amount of public praise will save you.
If you shortcut discipline, you sabotage destiny.
If you sacrifice the long game for the thrill of now, you'll always feel like a visitor in the life you were born to own.

Your calling is too important for that.

The world doesn't need you to show up fast. It needs you to show up *ready*. And readiness comes from discipline. From the long nights. The quiet yeses. The restrained no's. The invisible workouts—mental, emotional, physical—that you do when no one else is watching. That's what makes you unshakable. That's what gives your presence weight. When you speak, people feel it—not because you're loud, but because you're *rooted*.

And if you've struggled with this—if you've broken promises to yourself, given into impulse, lost momentum—it's not over. You haven't failed. You're not disqualified. You just need to start again. Right here. Right now. One decision at a time. One yes at a time. One "not now" for the sake of "something greater" at a time.

The results will come. The respect will come. The platform will come. But none of it will matter if you don't have the internal stability to hold it.

So choose the grind over the gimmick. Choose alignment over applause. Choose the slow, steady rhythm of discipline over the chaos of chasing quick dopamine hits.

Because the person who can delay gratification without losing vision— without shrinking, without numbing, without quitting—that person becomes unstoppable.

You want to feel confident?

Live like the person your future self will thank.

That's where real, unshakeable, stormproof confidence lives.
Not in the hype.
Not in the hurry.
But in the decision to *wait well and build anyway*.

BREAK THE BOTTLE CHALLENGE — Chapter 13

1. Write Your Confidence Code:

- "I am becoming a person who…"
- "I take bold action even when…"
- "I no longer seek validation from…"

2. Pick One Visibility Action This Week:

- Post your perspective online
- Share your work publicly
- Initiate a conversation you've avoided
- Lead the room without overthinking

3. Stack Five Micro Wins in Five Days:

- Choose one action per day that makes you uncomfortable—but proves your power

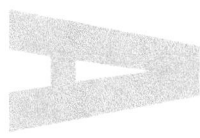

MASTERING MOMENTUM— SUSTAINING LONG-TERM SUCCESS

"Momentum is not built in a moment—it's built in motion. Success isn't about speed; it's about sustainability."

— *Break The Bottle*

The Discipline Behind Enduring Greatness and Success

Self-mastery isn't just the secret to greatness—it's the infrastructure that keeps greatness from collapsing. Anyone can rise for a moment. Anyone can grind through a season. But long-term success—*real*, aligned, sustainable success—requires more than hustle and motivation. It requires mastery. The kind of inner leadership that doesn't just produce results—it preserves them.

This is where most people fall short. They confuse intensity with consistency, hype with foundation, and momentary drive with sustained identity. But the ones who endure—the ones who build legacies, not just moments— understand that sustainable success must be rooted in something deeper than performance. It must be anchored in who you are when the stage is empty and no one is watching. Because at the end of the day, it's not your ambition that keeps you grounded—it's your alignment. It's your ability to master your emotions, focus your energy, and show up in integrity with your values that makes excellence repeatable.

Look at the greats—not just those who dominated headlines, but those who created enduring impact. Serena Williams didn't become iconic solely because of raw talent. Her greatness came from her unrelenting discipline, her composure under pressure, and her ability to show up—again and again—regardless of external conditions. Queen Elizabeth II, who reigned through decades of global upheaval, exemplified composure and unwavering discipline under the world's unrelenting gaze. Barack Obama's leadership wasn't fueled by charisma alone. It was sustained through emotional regulation, deep reflection, and a practiced mastery over how he responded to criticism, pressure, and complexity. This level of self-mastery—this internal infrastructure—is what separates those who simply lead in moments from those who lead across lifetimes. And Dr. Martin Luther King Jr., whose words and actions reshaped a nation, embodied moral courage and spiritual discipline, leading with purpose in the face of hostility.

These individuals did not merely command authority—they *sustained* it. They didn't just perform in the spotlight—they endured in the shadows. Their influence wasn't a product of fleeting charisma. It was rooted in character, conviction, and the consistent exercise of self-mastery. They are the evidence that greatness is not about giftedness—it's about groundedness. They are reminders that the most extraordinary lives are built not on shortcuts, but on the steady, intentional practice of mastering oneself.

These individuals didn't just achieve—they *endured*. That's the mark of mastery.

And neuroscience backs it up. Behavioral psychology shows that individuals who cultivate high levels of self-regulation consistently outperform their peers—not because they're more intelligent or more privileged, but because they've trained their nervous system to respond with strategy rather than react with emotion. They've built a relationship with themselves that's stronger than the chaos around them.

In a world dominated by distraction, urgency, and instant gratification, the real winners aren't the most talented—they're the most anchored. Talent may get you in the room, but temperament determines whether you stay. Mastery isn't about managing your schedule—it's about managing your state. It's the quiet strength of showing up without applause. The emotional intelligence to remain steady when things fall apart. The discipline to keep moving forward when hype fades, criticism rises, and comfort tempts you to coast.

Theodore Roosevelt, a man of immense energy and principle, channeled his personal challenges into bold reform, proving that true leadership is born in self-governance. Mother Teresa, in the face of overwhelming suffering, cultivated compassion through inner stillness and moral clarity. Nelson Mandela emerged from 27 years of imprisonment not bitter, but anchored in forgiveness and vision—a testament to emotional sovereignty. Mahatma Gandhi's quiet resolve shifted empires, not by force, but through disciplined, value-driven resistance. And Winston Churchill's wartime leadership was forged not just by strategy, but by his ability to remain unshaken amid chaos.

But let's be clear—self-mastery isn't reserved for elite performers. It's not a personality trait. It's not a gift bestowed on the chosen few. It's a practice. A mindset. A discipline. A way of being. It starts with the courage to look inward—to stop outsourcing your identity to titles, timelines, or external outcomes—and to start building a life from the inside out. It's not about being perfect. It's about being aligned. Every. Single. Day.

One of the most powerful tools on this sustainable path is *self-inquiry*—the practice of asking yourself better questions that shape your identity and clarify your behavior. Questions like:

- "Is this decision feeding my future or my fear?"

- "Is this action aligned with the version of me I'm becoming?"

- "Am I leading myself well before I try to lead anyone else?"

These questions don't just influence your choices—they *define your character*. They move you from passive drift to active design. From reactivity to resilience. From external validation to internal conviction. You stop chasing approval, and you start walking in alignment.

And let's not confuse mastery with martyrdom. Self-mastery is not self-denial. It's not the grind culture that leads to burnout. It's not rooted in shame or performance. No—*real mastery is rooted in rhythm.* It's about protecting your energy, honoring your boundaries, and moving with clarity and conviction—not chaos and compulsion.

The beauty of self-mastery is that you don't need to control the world—you only need to control yourself. Your attitude. Your discipline. Your reactions. Your rituals. That's where the true power lies. And the moment you understand that truth, momentum becomes sustainable. Because mastery doesn't require more effort—it requires more *alignment*.

The people who sustain success are not necessarily the most gifted—they're the most congruent. Their habits match their vision. Their values inform their actions. Their identity fuels their performance. That's why momentum lasts—it's built on something deeper than energy. It's built on *integrity*.

Self-mastery isn't about trying to be someone else. It's about becoming fully, powerfully, and unapologetically you—the version of you that leads with intention, not impulse. The you that doesn't just show up once, but keeps showing up with discipline, peace, and presence. The version of you that doesn't need hype to move, applause to act, or crisis to grow. The version that is not just *motivated*—but *mastered*.

The Genius of the Inner Struggle

The path to self-mastery doesn't pass through comfort—it is carved through struggle. What we often mistake as personal turmoil is actually the genius of the inner struggle doing its work. It's the silent architect of character, chiseling away at our defaults and constructing the version of ourselves that's capable of bearing the weight of destiny. True growth doesn't happen when everything is working—it happens when nothing is. When you're standing in the gap between who you've been and who you are becoming, fighting the friction of change, and deciding—again and again—that you will not quit. That you will not shrink. That you will not return to who you were.

I remember one morning sitting across from my mentor—an older man with years of wisdom etched into his face like battle scars. We were at this small café in Atlanta, tucked away off a quiet street, one of those rare places where the noise of the world feels muted, and the conversations go deeper than the surface. It was a gray morning. Rain had just swept through, and the air still smelled like fresh pavement and renewal. I was restless, angry even—not the loud kind of anger, but the kind that simmers beneath the surface. I had been grinding nonstop. Publicly, I looked like I was thriving. But privately, I was questioning everything—my direction, my identity, my worth. I had just come out of a failed venture that drained me emotionally and financially, and beneath my polished exterior, I felt like a fraud. I didn't know if I still believed in my own vision. I didn't know if I still had the strength to keep rebuilding.

He looked at me for a long time. Silent. Sipped his coffee. And then he said something I'll never forget: *"Michael, what if this part right here—this confusion, this exhaustion—isn't the breakdown… but the build? What if you're not failing… you're forming?"*

That broke something open in me.

I didn't need a strategy in that moment. I didn't need a pep talk. What I needed was permission to see my struggle as sacred. To stop demonizing the tension I felt inside and start honoring it as the work of transformation. That conversation reframed everything. He reminded me that I was still in the fire—not because I was doing something wrong, but because the gold hadn't fully surfaced yet. That fire was the genius of the inner struggle doing its refining work. It was painful, yes. But it was also precise. And it was building the version of me that wouldn't just perform—but persevere.

This internal conflict—this sacred tension—is where self-mastery is born. It's not birthed in the polished, Instagrammable moments. It's born in the late nights when no one sees you crying, in the early mornings when discipline trumps desire, in the moments where truth is heavier than convenience. That battle rewires the mind, reshapes the soul, and restores authority over your own life. And it demands three rare virtues: patience to accept what's beyond your control, truthfulness to face what you'd rather avoid, and faith to believe that transformation is happening even when your progress is invisible.

Self-mastery isn't about force. It's about freedom. It's not about being in control of everything—it's about being in control of yourself. As Roosevelt powerfully stated, "Courage, hard work, self-mastery, and intelligent effort are all essential to a successful life." But make no mistake: self-mastery is not a single skill—it's an entire infrastructure. Self-control may be one weapon. But self-mastery is the full arsenal: emotional intelligence, self-awareness, behavior design, mental discipline, and the spiritual stamina to lead yourself even when no one is clapping.

After years of studying athletes, artists, CEOs, and creators at the top of their game, a clear pattern has emerged. Mastery doesn't depend solely on talent—it depends on the trifecta of willpower, habits, and systems. These three pillars don't just drive excellence—they sustain it.

Willpower is the gatekeeper. It's the short-term fuel that pushes you to make the right choice when it's hardest. Think of the Olympic swimmer who dives into icy water at 4am, the CEO who meditates before a brutal decision, the parent who holds their temper after a long day. Willpower is what makes those moments possible. But here's what most people miss: willpower is finite. It gets depleted—by stress, fatigue, distractions. That's why the highest achievers don't lean on willpower all day—they use it to build habits, and then let those habits do the heavy lifting.

Habits are where mastery becomes automatic. Most of what you do every day isn't a choice—it's a pattern. A reflex. A routine. The question is, are you the author of that routine—or are you its prisoner? As John Maxwell said, "You don't choose your future. You choose your habits. And they choose your future." Your future isn't shaped by dreams—it's shaped by repetitions. Small decisions made again and again until they become your identity. Want to change your life? Start by changing your rituals. Anchor new habits to existing routines. Make them simple. Reward them immediately. And above all—repeat until they become second nature.

And then come systems—the hidden architecture of sustainable success. Systems are the structures you install to make greatness predictable. They're the design of your daily life that eliminates friction and enhances focus. A system could be your morning routine. Your meal prep strategy. Your decision to time-block your calendar instead of reacting to chaos. These aren't just productivity hacks. They're the automation of identity.

Within your brain lies the basal ganglia—the region responsible for automated behavior. The more you structure your actions through systems, the less mental energy you need to stay on track. You're not deciding what to do every moment—you're following a design. This is why something as simple as, "Make my bed, write my goals, stretch," becomes a launchpad for your entire day. You've wired your brain to win without overthinking.

World-class performers rely on these systems religiously. Morning and evening rituals. Digital boundaries. Review periods. Identity-based planning. These are not luxuries—they are non-negotiables. Because success isn't spontaneous—it's systemized. The difference between someone who burns out and someone who breaks through isn't willpower—it's structure. One is constantly reacting. The other has designed their life for resilience.

So if you want to master yourself, start here. Not with a grand gesture, but with a grounded decision: to own your willpower, to choose your habits, and to install systems that honor your future. Because in the end, self-mastery is not a trophy—it's a toolkit. And when you wield it well, there is nothing you cannot build, sustain, or overcome.

Habits of the Most Successful People

The world's highest performers—from elite athletes to Fortune 500 CEOs—aren't just lucky or uniquely talented. What truly sets them apart is the architecture of their days. They build their lives around habits so rooted in intention that success becomes an outcome. If you've ever wondered why some people seem to achieve massive goals while staying centered and energized, the answer lies not in intensity, but in consistency. And consistency begins with daily habits that reinforce identity, energy, and execution.

Let's start with what many call "Morning Mastery." This isn't a buzzword; it's a principle. A study published in the Journal of Applied Social Psychology found that people who engage in a structured morning routine report significantly higher levels of emotional clarity, productivity, and fulfillment. The most successful individuals don't begin their day buried in notifications or reacting to the outside world—they begin inward. With mindfulness, prayer, journaling, or even strategic movement. Think of it as tuning the instrument before the concert. You don't play your best when you're out of tune—and your life is no different.

After that, they perform a Mind Sweep. It's not just helpful—it's survival in the age of overwhelm. Our brains weren't designed to hold dozens of unfinished tasks, worries, and ideas in working memory. Successful individuals externalize those thoughts. They put pen to paper. They clear the mental noise so they can think with precision. As David Allen, productivity expert and author of *Getting Things Done*, often says, "Your mind is for having ideas, not holding them."

They then Reflect and Refocus. Before diving into action, they ask: What really matters today? What's the one thing that moves me closer to my mission? This isn't about being busy—it's about being strategic. They don't let urgency override importance. And in that clarity, they find momentum.

Enter the Focus Block. Every high performer knows that deep work is a superpower. In an era where the average attention span is now less than a goldfish's (eight seconds, according to Microsoft's research), the ability to work uninterrupted for 60 to 90 minutes is gold. No tabs. No phones. Just one meaningful task. It's during this time that the needle actually moves. This is when books get written, businesses get scaled, and ideas become reality.

But what if motivation is low? That's where the Micro Win Stack comes in. It's not about massive victories—it's about small wins that build belief. James Clear, author of *Atomic Habits*, puts it this way: "Every action you take is a vote for the type of person you wish to become." Something as simple as making your bed, sending a thank-you text, or finishing a short workout compounds into a mindset of progress. These wins stack. And over time, they create momentum that's impossible to ignore.

Then there's the daily discipline of Connection. The myth of the lone genius has been debunked. Real success is relational. The most grounded leaders prioritize time with family, team members, mentors, and those they serve.

These conversations aren't distractions—they're lifelines. They remind you of your "why," offer fresh perspective, and often deliver the insight you didn't know you needed.

And while daily structure builds the foundation, four Momentum Anchors ensure your progress is protected and amplified.

The first is Vision Reinforcement. It's not enough to set a goal once a year. You need to live with your purpose in plain sight. Whether it's a statement on your wall, a journal prompt you revisit, or a phrase you repeat in the mirror—your vision should haunt you in the best way possible. It should be so visible that drifting becomes impossible.

The second is Habit Stacking. Behavioral science tells us that new habits stick better when anchored to existing ones. Instead of overhauling your entire life, you start by attaching a habit to what's already natural. It could be as simple as reviewing your goals right after brushing your teeth. When it's embedded into your day, it becomes effortless.

The third is Accountability Structures. This is where many talented people fall short. You can be self-motivated, but even the best performers have systems of external accountability. From check-ins with a mentor to peer groups to sharing your goals publicly, these structures hold you to your highest standard. They don't just keep you on track—they keep you evolving.

And the final anchor is Energy Management. This is the one most people overlook until it's too late. Discipline isn't just about grit—it's about capacity. If you're not fueling your body, recovering well, or protecting your focus, even the best strategy will collapse under fatigue. Studies from Harvard Business Review confirm that high performers prioritize rest with as much intensity as they prioritize work. Because they know the truth: a burned-out mind can't build a brilliant future.

Ultimately, these daily habits and anchors aren't about control. They're about alignment. They ensure your actions reflect your ambitions. They protect your purpose from being eroded by distraction or fatigue. They transform your identity—not through grand declarations, but through small, sacred repetitions.

This is what separates the successful from the struggling. Not talent. Not luck. But intentionality. And when you build a rhythm around these daily choices—morning mastery, focused execution, meaningful connection, and anchored systems—you stop chasing momentum. You become it.

Greatness has a soundtrack—and Michael Jordan's was intensity. Not hype, not fame, but inner intensity. He didn't just play the game—he redefined it. But what separated Jordan wasn't the points he scored. It was the **standards he demanded**. From himself. From teammates. From the moment. In a world full of players waiting to be told what to do, Jordan didn't wait. He led from the front—and he did it with surgical clarity. One of the most vivid accounts comes from Tim Grover, his personal trainer, who described MJ as "the only athlete who never needed to be pushed. He only needed to be held back."

Jordan didn't show up for practice to get ready for the game. **Practice *was* the game.** That's the mindset. That's the standard. In one legendary moment, during a Bulls practice, Jordan went so hard that he ended up in a near physical altercation with Steve Kerr. Not because of ego—but because he believed you either show up at your peak in practice or you never will in a playoff. That day wasn't about being right—it was about pushing the environment to match the mission. **That's internal accountability at war with comfort.**

Jordan's greatness didn't come from motivation. It came from obsession. From detail. From a Momentum Operating System that was not built on luck but **engineered through daily excellence**. He arrived early. He stayed late. He trained with precision. He built rituals around recovery. He visualized with intensity. And even when he walked away from the NBA—twice—his **standard never left him**. It followed him into baseball. Into ownership. Into legacy.

Michael Jordan's story teaches us this: you don't rise to your dreams. **You rise to your systems.** And when your identity is locked into elite standards, **consistency becomes inevitable.** You're not chasing moments—you're building a rhythm that makes greatness *normal*.

If Michael Jordan was the architect of intensity, then **David Goggins** is the sculptor of suffering. His name is now synonymous with mental toughness—but not because he was born resilient. It's because he built it—one painful, humiliating, soul-ripping decision at a time. His life wasn't a highlight reel. It was a **war with himself**—and he chose to win.

There's one story that burns in the mind—a moment that's not about glory, but about guts. During Navy SEAL "Hell Week," Goggins had already failed twice. His body was broken. His spirit was frayed. Most people would have called it—walked off and told themselves a safe, believable story. But Goggins had buried something deeper. Something violent. A rage not against others, but against the **voice in his head that kept trying to settle**. That voice that had told him all his life he wasn't enough—too dumb, too fat, too slow, too poor.

So on his **third attempt** at Hell Week, with fractured feet duct-taped, running on bone and blood, he didn't just show up—he took over. He ran with broken legs. He paddled until his hands blistered raw. He became, as the instructors called it, *"an animal with no quit."* But here's the part most people don't see—**he didn't rely on motivation**. Motivation was gone by day two. What carried him through was a **system of internal rewiring**. When the pain came, he didn't fight it. **He welcomed it.** He used it as proof that he was on the edge of expansion.

That system—the "callous the mind" protocol he developed—became his **momentum loop**. When others avoided pain, he **ran into it**. When others rested, he leaned into repetition. When others sought validation, he sought silence. He didn't build motivation. He built mastery. Repetition. Reflection. Accountability. Identity stacking.

In one of his most famous interviews, Goggins described how he would log every painful moment in a "cookie jar" in his mind—something he could draw from when weakness tried to take the mic. Not a list of wins—but of moments he **chose to rise when quitting was easier**. That's momentum in motion. That's the genius of the inner struggle.

David Goggins is proof of this: **your greatest pain can become your power source**—if you give it purpose. Momentum isn't always clean. Sometimes, it's bloody. But when it's built on identity, on intention, and on the willingness to out-suffer your excuses, it becomes unstoppable.

If David Goggins showed the world how to weaponize pain, then **Steph Curry** revealed the quiet precision of repetition. Not the kind that screams for attention—but the kind that builds dynasties in silence.

Curry wasn't born with a body built for basketball greatness. In fact, early scouts and coaches **overlooked him** entirely. Too small. Too skinny. Too fragile. He wasn't recruited by major D1 colleges. His shot form was even ridiculed early on. But that's the part of the story casual fans miss. While the world questioned his ability, Curry wasn't chasing anyone's approval—**he was building a system.** One brick at a time. One rep at a time. And he did it where no one could see him.

His pregame shooting routine is now legendary—not because it's flashy, but because it's **obsessively consistent**. He'll take the same shots in warm-up that he expects to take in the game. He's logged **hundreds of thousands of shots** in practice—many from distances and angles most players would never attempt. And yet, for Curry, it's not improvisation. It's **execution of design**. Deep, detailed repetition—not just to master the skill, but to wire it into his nervous system until it becomes reflex.

One of his trainers once said: *"The reason Steph can shoot from 35 feet without hesitation isn't because he's confident—it's because he's prepared."*

And that preparation? It's powered by his **Momentum Operating System**— though he never called it that, it's what he lives. He builds his day around repeatable rhythms. Early rising. High-intensity skill work. Film study. Nutrition. Sleep. Recovery. Spiritual grounding. Connection with family. Nothing is random. It's all intentional. Because for Steph, **consistency is the flex**. He doesn't ride the wave of hype. He **controls his frequency**.

Even during the 2021 season—when the Warriors were down, expectations were low, and his supporting cast was thin—Curry **put up career-high numbers**, showing the world that momentum isn't about circumstances. It's about identity. He didn't rise because the environment favored him. He rose because his habits never dipped. When the lights were dim, he still showed up in full. And that's the mark of momentum mastery: your habits perform, even when the spotlight doesn't.

Steph Curry's legacy teaches us that **excellence is built in the margins**—in the 5 a.m. drills, in the film breakdowns, in the small habits stacked across seasons. You don't need to be the loudest. You just need to be the most **aligned.** And when you are, **the scoreboard starts to echo your rhythm.**

If Steph Curry is the technician of repetition, **Derek Jeter** is the embodiment of quiet consistency. For 20 years, through roster changes, championship wins, media storms, and physical wear, Jeter showed up—**not as a flash**, but as a *foundation*.

He wasn't always the most powerful, the flashiest, or the most media-driven athlete. But in a city that eats inconsistency alive, Jeter became *the most respected man in New York*. And that wasn't luck. It was the product of a life built around **relentless standards and unshakable structure**. He made a career—and a legacy—by mastering the art of doing the right things over, and over, and over.

What made Jeter special was that he **never let emotion dictate execution**. He'd show up early, stay late, and lead by example—even when the cameras were off. One teammate recalled how Jeter **warmed up for routine grounders like he was in Game 7**. His logic? If you disrespect the basics, the game will eventually punish you. That mindset became contagious in the Yankees locker room. Not because he demanded it—but he modeled it.

He was obsessed with the little things—**footwork, eye contact, preparation, emotional control.** While others coasted on talent, Jeter **competed with himself.** He didn't need someone yelling in his ear. He had what every high performer must develop: *an internal scoreboard*. His game wasn't built on emotion. It was built on system. He executed like a man with something to prove—even when he'd already proven it all.

And in one of the most symbolic endings to a career in sports history, **his final game at Yankee Stadium delivered a walk-off hit.** Not because fate was on his side—but because **he was ready for the moment.** He didn't rise to the pressure. The pressure rose to meet the system he had built for 20 years.

Derek Jeter's story is a masterclass in sustainable leadership. He didn't burn bright and fade. He didn't ride emotion or chase validation. He focused on rhythm, character, and **doing the right things until they defined him.** That's what makes momentum unshakable. That's how legacies are carved—not through peaks, but through the daily grind that 99% of people will never see.

If Derek Jeter taught us the power of professional rhythm, **Tom Brady** proved that the greatest edge isn't age—it's **optimization.**

Coming out of college, Brady was not the archetype of an NFL franchise quarterback. He ran a 5.28-second 40-yard dash. He was picked **199th overall** in the 2000 NFL Draft. He was too slow, too average, too ordinary—on paper. But what no scout could quantify was Brady's commitment to the **long game**. He didn't see himself as a backup. He didn't see himself as a sixth-round pick. He saw himself as **a system in development**, a project under construction, and he went to war—daily—to prove that belief right.

From the moment he stepped onto an NFL practice field, **Brady approached repetition like religion**. Every throw. Every read. Every warmup. It wasn't just about getting better—it was about building **precision under pressure**. By the time he became a starter for the Patriots, his game was no longer just instinct—it was **engineered excellence**.

What separates Brady is not just seven Super Bowl rings. It's the **meticulous way he designed his life** to match his performance ambitions. His TB12 method—nutrition, pliability, recovery, cognitive training, sleep tracking—is not hype. It's **infrastructure**. He created a Momentum Operating System around his body, his mind, and his leadership. Every component of his day served a purpose. Meals were optimized. Workouts were non-negotiable. Even his mindset was ritualized. In interviews, Brady often talks about visualizing entire games before they happen—not as fantasy, but as **mental reps** that wired his execution in advance.

At an age when most athletes are watching from the sidelines, Brady was **still breaking records**, dissecting defenses, and **leading fourth-quarter comebacks** like clockwork. He didn't defy time—he managed it better than anyone. Because while others trained to compete, Brady trained to **outlast**.

One of the most defining moments came during Super Bowl LI, when the Patriots trailed the Falcons **28-3**. Most quarterbacks would have mentally unraveled. But not Brady. He **stayed anchored**. Not because of raw talent—but because of ritual. Because he had rehearsed adversity so many times that chaos couldn't surprise him. He engineered a comeback that is now legend—because his system didn't fold under pressure. It flexed.

Tom Brady's greatness isn't magic. It's maintenance. It's what happens when obsession meets organization. When ambition is backed by alignment. When leadership is **modeled in the micro, not just the spotlight**.

He is proof that momentum isn't just about speed—it's about **sustainability**. And that sustainability isn't achieved through effort alone. It's earned through **deliberate design.** That's why Brady never chased greatness. He built it—one habit, one system, one year at a time.

The blueprint for momentum isn't reserved for celebrities or household names. I know this truth personally, because I've lived it. Not on a global stage—but in the trenches of military combat, corporate strategy, leadership failure, and personal reinvention.

I remember one particular moment—sitting in my hooch, replaying capturing the Iraqis that tried to kill us on September 12, 2004 in the middle of the night, the VBIED car bomb that killed my comrades, and the firefight on September 13, 2004, shrapnel wounds burning, breath shallow, and the weight of silence louder than any battlefield. I wasn't thinking about greatness. I was questioning everything. My purpose. My path. My worth. The medals didn't matter in that moment. The degrees didn't speak. What stared back at me was one question: *"What are you going to build from this?"*

That moment of stillness became the spark for what you now know as the **Momentum Operating System™**. The military gave me structure—but that structure had to be internalized. I had to strip away the performance mask and face the truth. I had to ask, *What parts of me still serve? What parts need to grow?* These weren't comfortable questions. But they were the right ones. They forced me to **lead myself before I ever tried to lead anyone else.**

I began crafting systems—not just for success, but for *survival.* Morning rituals to quiet the chaos. Focus Blocks to rebuild attention and discipline. Weekly resets to recalibrate direction. Public accountability to restore my own standard. That wasn't theory—it was **therapy turned into architecture**. It became my way of anchoring identity, not around emotion, but around intention. And over time, those systems became the very engine that powered recovery, clarity, leadership, and ultimately, transformation—not just for me, but for those I now serve.

When I built the **Daily Momentum Blueprint™**, it was forged in fire—not in comfort.
When I designed the **90-Day Momentum Sprint Strategy**, it wasn't a productivity trick—it was my strategy for survival and significance.
When I say that structure will save your purpose, I'm not quoting research— I'm speaking from scars.

So when we study legendary performers, we're not romanticizing celebrity. We're decoding **systemic mastery**—and it's available to all of us.

The stories of greatness don't begin in championships. They begin in obscurity—in the uncelebrated moments when no one's watching and no one's clapping. What unites legends like **Michael Jordan, David Goggins, Steph Curry, Derek Jeter, and Tom Brady** isn't luck or natural talent—it's their sacred relationship with the **inner struggle**.

The pain most people avoid? They ran toward it.
The silence most fear? They trained in it.
The structure most reject? They *became it.*

Their greatness wasn't spontaneous. It was **scheduled**. Engineered. Systematized.

- **Jordan's obsessive workouts**, long after the cameras were off, were his *Focus Blocks*—discipline when no one was watching.

- **Goggins' "cookie jar" of pain** became his *Micro Win Stack*— transforming trauma into fuel.

- **Curry's centered mornings and faith routines** were his *Morning Activation*—anchoring identity before action.

- **Jeter's poise and relational awareness** were his *Connection Point*—grounding greatness in grace.

- **Brady's TB12 method** was not an idea—it was a full system of *Morning Activation, Focus Blocks, Energy Management*, and *Evening Integration*.

They didn't rely on hype. They built **habits**.
They didn't need applause. They operated from alignment.

And perhaps most critically—**they didn't keep their vision to themselves**. They understood the transformative power of **Public Accountability**.

This is the piece most high-potential leaders miss. When you speak a goal out loud—when you declare a deadline, a dream, a decision to those around you—you don't just raise the stakes. You **raise your identity**.

And it's not hype—it's *neuroscience*. Publicly committing to a goal increases follow-through by up to 65%. Why? Because now, your vision is visible. Your actions are attached to your integrity. And that changes how you show up. It's not about pressure—it's about alignment.

- **Jordan declared, "I'm back."** Then delivered history.

- **Goggins published his struggle.** His life became his message.

- **Curry aligned faith and performance.** Quiet confidence, loud results.

- **Jeter's legacy led without volume.** Integrity was his leadership style.

- **Brady promised Super Bowl greatness—and then engineered it.**

This is why your **90-Day Momentum Sprint Strategy** is not a motivational gimmick—it's your *identity lock-in*. It takes your ideas and anchors them in action, clarity, and accountability. You're no longer drifting. You're designing. You're not reacting. You're rising.

And beneath all of it lies the truth: **momentum is not a mood—it's a formula.**

That formula is forged through **three critical systems**:

MINDSET – The Story You Tell Yourself

Your inner dialogue determines your direction. If you believe you're still a fraud, still behind, still trying to earn it—you'll sabotage what you've built. But if you tell a different story, *a true one*, everything changes.

Jordan's story? *"I win because I do what others won't."*
Goggins' story? *"This pain will become power."*

My story? *"Structure is what saved me. Now I teach others to build their own."*

Mindset isn't about optimism. It's about **internal authorship**. Choose your script wisely.

HEART-SET – The Emotional Engine That Drives Resilience

This isn't about bottling feelings. It's about directing them. Purpose, presence, gratitude—these are high-performance emotions. They don't weaken you. They *power you*.

Curry's joy. Jeter's calm. Brady's focus. Goggins' intensity.
Each one emotional. Each one *trained*.

If you don't do emotional work, your emotions will do the work for you. **Lead from your center.**

SKILLSET – The Execution Muscle That Transforms Vision to Victory

Without execution, belief is just potential. Skillset is where you sharpen your edge, build your playbook, refine your rituals.

Brady's film study. Curry's thousand-rep drills. Goggins' soul-level conditioning.
Their wins didn't come from hype—they came from habits.

Your skillset doesn't need to be perfect—it needs to be **practiced**.

So here's your charge:

Stop waiting for perfect timing.
Stop hiding behind preparation.
Stop confusing potential with permission.

You are not behind.
You are not broken.
You are not lost.

You are becoming the system.
You are no longer chasing momentum. **You are now creating it.**
Every story, every scar, every standard you've built was preparing you for this—

The moment you stop watching greatness… and start living it.

You've already broken the bottle.

Now it's time to **build what lasts**.

The Six Types of Momentum—and How to Guard Each

Momentum isn't a singular surge of energy. It's a *multidimensional flow*—an ecosystem of forward motion woven across every domain of your life. And the most dangerous myth in high performance is the idea that momentum is solely strategic or professional. The truth? Momentum is **emotional, mental,**

physical, strategic, relational, and spiritual—and if even one area falters, your entire trajectory begins to shake.

Sustainable greatness requires that you guard all six. Because the moment you neglect one, your foundation begins to fracture.

Emotional momentum—The Heartbeat of Drive is the heartbeat of your purpose—how much joy, passion, and fuel you feel for the mission. This is the energy you feel about the *why* behind your work. It's the difference between action and *alive* action. When emotional momentum is flowing, clarity, joy, and fire align. When it's lost, effort feels empty—even when results show up.

I remember a dinner conversation I had with a combat-tested general. We were talking about leadership under fire—not the kind you read about, but the kind that scars your memory. He leaned back, voice calm, and said, "The real battle isn't bullets flying—it's losing your reason for fighting." That truth hit hard. Not just for the battlefield—but for boardrooms, marriages, and missions. Emotional momentum doesn't come from performance—it comes from *purpose*. From remembering the story *behind* your goals. That dinner didn't give me strategy—it gave me something better: *emotional clarity*. The kind that reignites everything when fatigue whispers, "Quit."

Mental momentum—The Engine of Clarity is the clarity that sharp decisions and calm thinking build. It thrives on focus blocks, brain dumps, and priority reviews. Without it, distraction chips away at purpose. Mental momentum is about cognition, decision-making, and calm focus under chaos. Without it, everything becomes noise. With it, every choice becomes power.

One afternoon, my dad and I were sitting together—two men, two generations, same blood, same ambition. I was mentally taxed, juggling leadership roles and internal pressure. He didn't offer a solution. He asked a question: *"What's taking up space in your mind that you haven't cleared out yet?"* I sat in silence. That question led me to pull out my notebook and write everything swirling in my mind. From unfinished tasks to unspoken fears. That five-minute "mind dump" wasn't just therapeutic—it restored mental clarity I hadn't felt in weeks. Sometimes momentum isn't about acceleration—it's about removing the mental weight you've been unconsciously carrying.

Physical momentum—The Fuel That Powers the Machine. It's the sleep, movement, nutrition, and hydration that power your mind and emotions. Neglect this, and burnout looms. The body doesn't lie. You can't out-think burnout. You can't out-strategize sleep deprivation. Physical momentum is the baseline—and without it, nothing sustains.

This hit home during a coaching session with my fitness trainer. I came in with mental fire—but my body? It was lagging. I hadn't been hydrating, my sleep was erratic, and I was living on caffeine and willpower. He paused the session and said, "You're not building strength—you're borrowing from your future." That line arrested me. We didn't finish the session with reps—we finished with a strategy. Hydration alarms. Bedtime shutdown rituals. Midday movement breaks. Within weeks, I felt stronger—not just physically, but emotionally and mentally. Because *your body is the gatekeeper of all other momentum.* You don't just owe it performance—you owe it respect.

Strategic momentum—The Bridge from Goals to Outcomes is your execution engine—it's where goals become outcomes. It depends on clarity, feedback, and disciplined follow-through. Wander without your strategic plan, and you chase new goals instead of pushing forward on existing ones. This is where vision meets execution. You can have fire in your belly and ideas on paper—but without structure, you drift.

I remember a tense strategy session with a past business partner. We were moving fast, but not forward. Activity was high, but progress was murky. Frustrations mounted. Finally, we put everything on the table and created a simple, ruthless 90-day roadmap—three bold outcomes, weekly accountability, and non-negotiable check-ins. That clarity turned tension into traction. Revenue doubled, decision fatigue disappeared, and confidence soared. **Strategic momentum doesn't just move you—it aligns you.** And alignment, not activity, is what gets you to the finish line.

Relational momentum—The Energy in Every Connection is the energy flow in your closest connections. If your relationships—and the conversations within them—drain you, momentum crashes. Your relationships are either a source of fuel—or a slow leak in your momentum tank. I learned this in a season where leadership consumed me, and meaningful conversations fell to the side.

It all changed in my own home, after a dinner with my family. Or rather—**without** dinner. We were all physically present, emotionally disconnected, faces lit by screens. I made a quiet decision that night—no more unintentional evenings. We created a "no devices, all hearts" rule for two dinners a week. Real conversation returned. Laughter resurfaced. And strangely enough, my work productivity jumped. Because **when your relationships are in rhythm, your life has more flow.** Momentum isn't just built in meetings—it's built at the dinner table.

Spiritual momentum—The Anchor Beneath the Strategy is alignment with your values and deeper meaning. You lose it when you ignore your inner barometer. Spiritual momentum is about meaning. About knowing your work aligns with your *why beyond the work*. It's what centers you when everything else feels off.

This showed up during an encounter in my men's church freedom group. We weren't talking business—we were talking *bondage*. What holds us back. What breaks us open. One man shared how success had made him spiritually numb. Another said he hadn't felt peace in months. When it came to me, I opened up about a season where I was building everything but neglecting *being*. That conversation wrecked me—in the best way. I came home, realigned my calendar with my convictions, and suddenly the tension in my leadership dropped. Not because my workload changed, but because **my soul came back online**.

You can't protect what you don't name. And now you have the names: **emotional, mental, physical, strategic, relational, and spiritual**.

These are your six streams of momentum. Guard them like you guard your future. Audit them weekly. Ask: *Where am I leaking? Where am I strong? What needs to be restored?*

Because momentum isn't just about how far you can go. It's about how *whole* you are while you go.

And when these six are aligned?
You don't just chase momentum.
You become the source of it.

The Role of Systems and Accountability in Sustaining Success

Here's the raw, unvarnished truth about long-term success: *inspiration may spark the start, but only systems sustain the climb.* Greatness is not granted to the most talented—it is earned by the most **structured**, the most **anchored**, the most **intentional**. I didn't learn this in a seminar or self-help book—no, I learned it in the crucible of my own endurance. My systems were born not from theory or motivational hype—but from moments when everything I had built threatened to crash—not because of lack of passion, but because I lacked the structure to protect it.

One of the earliest reminders of this came from a mentor who saw straight through my momentum. We sat in a dimly lit office, me presenting a beautifully crafted vision—charts, goals, mission statements. I was proud. He leaned forward and, quietly, he asked: "Michael… this is powerful—but where's the *system* beneath it?" That one question felt like a scalpel. I realized I'd been living in bursts of inspiration—bright, yes—but brittle. No structure to hold my success when emotion falters. He taught me to build routines, feedback loops, and non-negotiable checkpoints—a design that would outlast mood, disappointment, and thrill. That conversation didn't just reorganize my calendar—it began reconstructing my legacy.

Then came my accountability partner—a fellow Marine, someone who didn't operate in encouragement but in execution. We weren't texting to stay connected—we challenged each other to live into identity. One morning, I'd let fatigue justify skipping my evening rituals. At 6:00 a.m., my phone buzzed: "Are you leading a life—or drifting?" That text stung, but more importantly, it saved me. Because accountability isn't simply someone *watching* you—it's someone *seeing* you. And reminding you of who you promised to become even when it slipped from memory.

Coaches followed—each sharpening a different edge of my life. One designed my health structure when business demands began draining my body. He didn't hand me a workout—it was a full *operating rhythm*, complete with Movement Anchors, Recovery Windows, and Focus Blocks calibrated to performance fatigue. That design didn't just restore my strength—it protected my mission. Because any leader who lets the body burn without infrastructure is building a success that falls apart at the first failure.

Another coach intercepted me at a pivotal crossroads—when ambition was climbing faster than my systems. He said, "You're chasing too much. One question: which of those goals do you want to hold in your system?" That sparked the creation of my **Momentum Map**—90-day targets, weekly wins, non-negotiables built around the 3-D Framework of Decision → Direction → Destination. That plan didn't just align my work—it *amplified it*. I didn't just do more; I did *more of what mattered.* That process became the architecture that scaled not my intentions—but my impact.

Some of the most powerful recalibration didn't happen in coaching—but in the confessional space of a small group circle. One night in my men's church freedom group, I wasn't the one teaching. I was the one cracked open. I admitted that outward momentum had masked inner fatigue. The business was booming. Doors were opening—but I felt untethered, disoriented, empty. And a brother looked across the circle and asked, "Brother, where in your rhythm is the stillness?" I couldn't answer. And that silence blasted through me. It showed me the empty spaces in my system—where meaning had been traded for movement. I didn't walk out with new metrics—but with a *new standard*: never again sacrificing soul for schedule.

Gradually, that group became ground zero for restoration. We prayed. We named our broken rhythms. We built spiritual anchors to refill the container I had let dry out. Because systems—even stellar ones—*must serve the soul, not suffocate it.*

Here's what I discovered: *Accountability isn't micromanagement—it's mission management.* Your system isn't just for executing today—it carries you across seasons. It is the daily expression of who you say you are. It is how you *automate excellence*, how you *filter distractions*, how you *align with purpose* even when everything tries to throw you off-track.

I came to live by this creed: You don't have to be the most gifted. But you must be the most grounded. And that grounding is not spiritual fluff—it's *architectural*.

Architecture made of:

- **Weekly Resets** that pause the spin, assess the map, and recalibrate direction.

- **Focus Blocks** that guard deep work from the tyranny of distraction.

- **Morning Activation** to shape your inner state before the world demands your focus.

- **Public Accountability** to sharpen your edge not with shame—but with honor.

- **Energy Rhythms** to protect your mind, body, and soul from slow erosion.

- And most importantly—**Authentic Relationships** that don't just hold your goals—they hold *you*.

Structure doesn't come from willpower—it comes from design. A well-structured life doesn't fade—it endures. So yes, *dream big. Cast audacious goals*. But then *build the rhythms* that protect them—because true success is not measured by how loud your launch is—it's measured by how long your legacy lasts.

Burnout doesn't knock on your door with a flashing sign. It slips in through loyalty, disguised as drive, cloaked in "I'll rest later." But the brutal truth is this: *Burnout is not a badge. It's the interest charged when high performance meets restlessness.*

You don't get burned out because you work hard—you get burned out because you're working hard on low-leverage things, without recovering your human context. And that's not ambition—that's alienation.

Think about Michelle—a driven founder I coached. Brilliant. Disciplined. Driven. But by the time we met, she was running on fumes. Creativity stifled. Sleep erratic. Her team achieved new heights—and yet joy felt unreachable. So we didn't build another strategy. We built *permission to pause.* We built *scheduled restoration* into her life. Suddenly, energy returned—not just for her work, but *for herself.* Because leadership fueled by exhaustion is unsustainable.

This isn't just anecdote—it's biology. The APA reports nearly 77% of professionals experience physical stress symptoms regularly. The human nervous system is not wired for infinite pressure without restorative cycles. Just as muscles grow in rest zones, not training, your greatest growth— creativity, clarity, vision—emerges when you give yourself margins *not just meetings*.

The greatest performers—world-class athletes, CEOs, leaders—don't avoid intensity. They *season* it with intention. They honor the rhythm. They know that marathon effort requires pacing—not panic. Sprinting every day doesn't prove strength—it guarantees collapse.

So how do you avoid burnout?

- Make self-leadership non-negotiable. Schedule your recovery with the same rigor as your tasks.

- Build micro-breaks, not mega-detours. Ten intentional breaths can do more than a weekend away.

- Honor your limits like prayers. They're the boundaries between leverage and breakdown.

- Practice emotional intelligence. Ask yourself: *Is this exhaustion physical—or existential? Has productivity become performance? Is my worth tangled with output, because I'm thirsting for approval in the wrong places?*

Coming home to yourself isn't quitting your dreams—it's anchoring them in a *sustainable foundation.*

Because burnout-proof success isn't soft. It's not safe. It's strategic. It's the way you play the long game, remain present with your people, stay sharp in decisions, and anchor deeply in purpose.

Legacy isn't born in bursts. It's cultivated in seasons of momentum renewed by rest, clarity, and alignment.

If you're feeling that fast-burning edge in your life—pause. Not forever, but long enough to ask: *Am I building something I can truly sustain? Am I sacrificing myself for success—or honoring myself for legacy?*

You don't have to choose between big goals and healthy boundaries. You just need to choose structure—rest that's not surrender, rhythm that isn't resignation, and self-leadership that's sustainable.

Because real power isn't about how fast you can go—it's about how well you manage your energy. That is the new standard. That is what legacy is made of.

Self-Mastery and The Foundation of an Extraordinary Life

Self-mastery in practice is not a concept reserved for sages or elite performers—it's a lifestyle available to anyone willing to choose intentionality over impulse. It starts with the way you speak to yourself. Your internal dialogue forms the boundaries of your identity, and for many, the greatest shift comes from the simplest statement: "I am the kind of person who follows through." This affirmation is not just motivational fluff—it is identity-based reinforcement. The more you speak it, the more your subconscious aligns with it. You begin to filter decisions not through how you feel, but through who you are becoming.

But words alone aren't enough. The body and mind need alignment. Daily mindfulness and meditation are more than wellness trends—they are neurocognitive training grounds. MRI scans of experienced meditators show increased gray matter density in brain regions associated with learning, memory, emotional regulation, and self-awareness. You're not just calming yourself—you're rewiring yourself. You're building the kind of mental clarity that allows you to respond to life rather than react to it.

Energy management becomes a cornerstone of this process. You cannot master your mind if your body is in chaos. Blood sugar instability, poor sleep hygiene, and lack of movement quietly sabotage willpower. That's why the most disciplined people are often the most intentional about rest, nutrition, and rhythm. They understand that energy is not just physical—it's strategic. It determines your capacity to show up fully. The most effective leaders don't burn out because they know burnout is not a badge of honor—it's a sign of misalignment.

Then comes implementation intention—one of the most powerful tools in behavior design. Self-mastery does not begin with some mystical revelation. It begins in the trenches of everyday decisions—the small, invisible crossroads where you either lean into impulse or lean into intention. I remember the moment I realized that my inner dialogue was either building me or betraying me. After returning from Iraq, I carried not just scars on my body but a war raging in my mind. For years, I told myself stories of limitation: "I can't trust people. I'll never get beyond this pain. This is just who I am now." Those words became walls, boxing me into an identity of survival. The shift came when I began to reframe the conversation inside my head. Instead of repeating defeat, I chose a new mantra: *"I am the kind of man who follows through."* At first, it felt foreign, almost like lying to myself. But the more I said it, the more my decisions began to bend toward it. I filtered my choices not through fleeting feelings but through the compass of identity. And slowly, what felt like fiction became fact—I was becoming the man my words declared.

Words without alignment are noise. To master myself, I had to bring my body and mind into agreement. During my lowest seasons—when PTSD, divorce, and shame pulled me toward destruction—I discovered the power of stillness. Meditation and mindfulness were not abstract wellness trends for me; they became survival tools. Each morning, I sat in silence, forcing myself to breathe through the chaos. Over time, I noticed changes I couldn't deny—clarity where confusion used to rule, steadiness where panic once lived. Neuroscience would later confirm what I felt firsthand: the mind rewires through consistent stillness. But it wasn't just about the mind. My energy was sabotaged daily by poor eating, restless nights, and endless hustle. When I learned to honor my body—nourishing it with rest, movement, and rhythm— my willpower multiplied. Energy, I realized, wasn't just fuel for the day—it was strategy for my destiny.

Self-mastery does not begin with discipline, routines, or even goals—it begins with identity. Long before you master your habits, you must master the story you tell yourself about who you are. Your internal dialogue is the architect of your future, silently constructing either a fortress of strength or a prison of limitation. I learned this in the hardest way possible, not through theory, but through the battlefield of my own mind.

When I returned from Iraq, the world outside had moved on, but inside me, the war never ended. My body carried scars from a car bomb, but my mind carried an even heavier weight—the echo of explosions, the faces of brothers I buried, the sleepless nights haunted by memories I couldn't silence. Every day, I replayed the same script: *You'll never be whole again. You can't trust people. This pain is permanent. This is who you are now.* Those words became walls, and those walls shaped my reality. I was alive, but not living—I was surviving, and survival was not enough.

One morning, after another restless night, I stared at myself in the mirror and barely recognized the man looking back. My eyes were tired, my shoulders heavy with shame and regret, my spirit fractured. And in that moment of raw honesty, I realized something that would change the trajectory of my life: it wasn't just the bombs in Iraq that nearly destroyed me—it was the bombs I kept detonating in my own head. My enemy was no longer on foreign soil; it was inside me.

That morning, I chose a new line of dialogue. I whispered it at first, because it felt foreign, almost laughable: *I am the kind of man who follows through.* The words tasted strange, like I was lying to myself. But I kept saying them. Over and over. Louder and stronger. That single statement became the first crack in the walls I had built. I began to filter my choices not through fleeting feelings of fear or fatigue but through the compass of identity. Every time I stood at a crossroads—whether to numb myself with another drink, whether to isolate instead of engage, whether to quit when the weight felt unbearable—I returned to that statement: *I am the kind of man who follows through.*

Slowly, my subconscious began to believe it. My decisions bent toward it. What once felt like fiction became fact. That affirmation was more than motivational fluff—it was an anchor, an identity-based reinforcement that pulled me toward the man I was becoming. And that was the beginning of self-mastery: not perfection, not performance, but alignment between the words I declared and the life I lived.

Words create worlds, but words alone are not enough. Self-mastery requires alignment—when the body and mind stop living as strangers and finally start living in agreement. For years, my mouth declared discipline while my body betrayed me. I spoke of resilience but ate like a man numbing his pain. I told myself I was strong but spent sleepless nights scrolling, tossing, and drowning in restless anxiety. My energy was chaos, and chaos doesn't negotiate—it quietly sabotages.

I remember a season after my second divorce, when the silence in my apartment was louder than any battlefield I had known. PTSD weighed on me like chains, and shame pressed on my chest like a vice. My body screamed for relief, and I gave it all the wrong answers: fast food, late nights, overwork, and the endless hustle of trying to outrun my pain. I thought movement was progress, but I was running in circles—burning out my body, draining my spirit, and eroding my willpower.

The turning point came not in a grand revelation, but in a whisper of stillness. One morning, exhausted from another sleepless night, I sat on the floor, desperate. I closed my eyes and forced myself to breathe—deep, slow, deliberate breaths. For the first time in months, I allowed silence to sit with me instead of fleeing from it. That practice—just sitting, just breathing— became survival at first, then strength, and finally transformation.

At the time, I didn't know the neuroscience behind it. Later I would learn that mindfulness and meditation physically reshape the brain, increasing gray matter density in regions tied to learning, emotional regulation, and self-awareness. But I didn't need a brain scan to prove what I felt. The fog began to lift. Confusion gave way to clarity. Panic gave way to steadiness. My mind, which had been a constant battlefield, slowly became a training ground for peace.

But the mind could not carry the burden alone. I had to honor my body. I discovered that my willpower was not weak—it was being sabotaged daily by poor fuel, broken rhythms, and restless nights. When I finally treated rest as sacred, when I nourished my body with clean food and disciplined movement, when I stopped glorifying burnout and started honoring rhythm, everything changed. My energy stopped leaking, and with it came a strength I had not known in years.

That's when I realized: energy is not just physical—it's strategic. It determines how fully you can show up in every area of your life. The most disciplined leaders I've met are not just committed to their vision; they are committed to protecting their energy. They guard it because they understand that burnout is not a badge of honor—it's proof of misalignment.

Self-mastery began to take root when my body and mind finally shook hands. Stillness rebuilt my mind, rhythm restored my body, and together they became the foundation of clarity. My marriage, my parenting, my business, even my friendships felt the ripple effect. People began to notice the steadiness, the presence, the energy. But it all began with alignment—choosing every day to bring my body and mind into agreement with the man I declared myself to be.

If self-mastery began with identity and deepened through alignment, it was sustained by systems. For years, I relied on sheer emotion to fuel my choices—moments of passion, bursts of motivation, flashes of inspiration. But emotion is a fickle ally. It can lift you to the mountaintop one day and abandon you in the valley the next. What I discovered was this: self-mastery is not protected by how you feel, but by the systems you build when you feel nothing at all.

I learned this lesson in the trenches of my own inconsistency. There were mornings I woke up determined to lead my business, love my family well, and show up with excellence. And then there were mornings I woke up numb—drained from nightmares, distracted by shame, or simply exhausted by the grind. Without systems, those days unraveled me. I gave in to impulse, wasted hours, and let frustration leak into my relationships. My family felt the drift, my clients noticed the cracks, and inside I carried the weight of my own inconsistency.

The breakthrough came when I embraced what psychologists call **implementation intentions**—pre-decisions written into the fabric of my daily life. Simple, strategic phrases like, *"If X happens, then I will do Y."* At first, it felt mechanical, but soon it became liberating. For example: *"If I feel overwhelmed at work, then I will take a five-minute breath reset before responding."* Or: *"If I feel triggered by criticism, then I will write down my response before I speak it."* These micro-commitments became anchors in stormy seas.

It wasn't glamorous. No one applauded me for pausing to breathe, or for choosing water instead of whiskey, or for walking away from an argument instead of escalating it. But those tiny, invisible choices were the quiet bricks that built a new identity. Systems gave me stability where emotion once gave me chaos.

To build those systems, I had to take a ruthless inventory of my life. I wrote down every habit, every emotional trigger, every pattern of sabotage. It was painful to face the truth. I had to admit the ways I was betraying my health, the shortcuts I was taking in my business, the emotional shortcuts I leaned on in my marriage. That list was not flattering—but it was freeing. Because sovereignty begins with honesty. You cannot redesign what you refuse to name.

Once I had the inventory, I began to design. I installed small guardrails into my daily rhythm. I stopped checking my phone before I checked in with God. I replaced late-night scrolling with early-morning reflection. I automated healthy meals during travel so my energy wouldn't crash. I scheduled rest like I scheduled meetings, because both were essential to my mission. Over time, these systems stopped feeling like restrictions and started feeling like freedom.

The evidence showed up everywhere. In my marriage, my wife could feel the difference between a man who reacted to everything and a man anchored by systems. My children felt the safety of my consistency instead of the volatility of my moods. In business, clients began to trust not just my words but my follow-through. Even my friendships deepened, because I stopped performing and started showing up authentically.

That's when I understood the quiet genius of systems: they turn discipline into delight, chaos into clarity, and effort into ease. Self-mastery isn't sustained by hype—it's sustained by design. And when my systems lined up with my identity, my life began to feel less like an accident and more like an assignment.

For much of my early career, I believed success was measured in strategies, credentials, and execution. I chased certifications, stacked degrees, and sharpened every technical skill I could find. I thought intelligence alone was the ladder to influence. But time and failure became my greatest teachers, revealing a truth I could no longer deny: intelligence may open the door, but emotional intelligence determines whether you stay in the room.

My first lessons in emotional intelligence weren't in corporate boardrooms— they were in combat zones. In Iraq, survival depended not only on tactics but on our ability to read people, interpret atmospheres, and regulate our own emotions under unimaginable pressure. I remember one particular patrol where the air felt heavier than usual. The streets looked quiet—too quiet. My training told me to check my gear. My gut told me to check my men. I walked the line, scanning not just for weapons but for eyes. I saw the tightness in a Marine's jaw, the shallow breaths of another, the way silence swallowed the squad. If I had barked commands, I would have heightened panic. Instead, I paused, breathed, and spoke calm. That calm diffused the tension. Minutes later, an IED was discovered down the road. We avoided disaster—not because of strategy alone, but because we mastered the atmosphere.

Years later, in corporate boardrooms, I discovered the principle was the same. Strategy could win contracts, but only emotional intelligence could win people. I remember sitting at a negotiation table where tension crackled like static. Two executives glared across the table, each ready to prove their point. The old me—the Marine wired for combat—would have matched intensity with intensity. But self-mastery taught me another way. I leaned back, took a slow breath, and asked one disarming question: *"What outcome would feel like a win for both of you?"* The tone shifted instantly. The air loosened. Conversation replaced confrontation. A deal that was destined to collapse turned into a partnership that lasted years.

That was the moment I realized emotional intelligence was my unfair advantage. It wasn't about being "nice." It wasn't about avoiding conflict. It was about being effective—turning volatility into trust, and trust into influence. Emotional intelligence allowed me to regulate myself so I could lead others. It helped me read the unspoken, listen between the lines, and respond with wisdom instead of impulse.

The ripple effect was undeniable. In leadership, my teams trusted me not because I had all the answers, but because I carried steadiness when others carried fear. In marriage, my wife felt seen instead of managed. In parenting, my children opened up not because I demanded it, but because I listened without judgment. In friendships, I discovered connection not through performance, but through presence.

What I had once believed was weakness—pausing, listening, empathizing— became my greatest strength. High EQ was not a soft skill. It was a survival skill, a leadership weapon, and a relational superpower. And when I paired it with systems, alignment, and identity, it elevated my influence beyond anything credentials alone could offer.

Self-mastery without emotional intelligence is incomplete. Because mastery is not about controlling the world—it's about leading yourself so well that you transform the world around you. And for me, EQ became the crown jewel, the difference-maker that turned knowledge into wisdom, conflict into collaboration, and influence into legacy.

For years, my life looked successful on paper but felt suffocating in reality. I was the man who said yes to everything—clients, meetings, opportunities, favors, demands. If someone asked, I agreed. If a door opened, I walked through it, no matter where it led. To the outside world, I looked like I was thriving. But behind the scenes, I was drowning. My calendar was full, but my soul was empty.

I didn't understand then what I know now: every "yes" is a contract with your future energy. Each time I agreed to something out of guilt, fear, or pride, I was signing away a piece of myself. I was writing checks my spirit couldn't cash. The result was predictable—burnout, resentment, and a gnawing sense of misalignment. I was living everyone else's agenda while betraying my own.

The breaking point came during a season when my business was expanding, invitations to speak were increasing, and my reputation was rising. From the outside, it looked like momentum. But at home, the story was different. I remember one night sitting at my kitchen table after another fourteen-hour day. My phone buzzed with congratulatory messages about a deal I had closed, but across the table my child sat quietly, waiting for me to notice them. Their silence pierced me more deeply than any criticism ever could. That night I realized success in business meant nothing if it cost me my presence at home.

So I began practicing a radical discipline: mastering my yes and my no. At first, it felt unnatural. I had built my identity around being the dependable one, the problem solver, the Marine who could take on any mission. Saying no felt like weakness. But slowly, I discovered the opposite was true. Saying no was strength. Saying no was stewardship. Saying no was my way of saying yes to peace, yes to purpose, yes to alignment.

I started filtering every request through one simple question: *Does this move me closer to the man I am becoming?* If the answer was no, then my answer was no. Not out of arrogance, but out of allegiance—to my values, to my family, to my faith, and to the mission that mattered most.

The impact was immediate. My calendar became lighter, but my life became fuller. My business grew—not because I was doing more, but because I was doing the right things with greater clarity and energy. My marriage and friendships deepened because I was no longer half-present, scattered in a dozen directions. My children felt the difference—my yes to them finally meant something because it was no longer diluted by a thousand other commitments.

What I discovered is this: boundaries are not barriers, they are bridges. They connect you back to your true self. They protect your energy so you can pour into what truly matters. They free you from the tyranny of everyone else's urgency and anchor you in the clarity of your own purpose.

Mastery of yes and no became one of the most life-defining forms of self-leadership I've ever practiced. Because in the end, saying no to what doesn't align is the most powerful way of saying yes to the life you were designed to live.

Identity gave me direction, alignment gave me strength, and boundaries gave me clarity. But what sustained lasting transformation was a framework—a method I could return to when motivation faded and life pressed hard. Mastery is not an accident; it is a process of design. And for me, that process crystallized into three undeniable steps: **Modeling, Immersion, and Repetition.**

Step 1: Model Someone Outstanding

The fastest way to collapse time is to learn from someone who already lives the life you want to create. Early in my transition from the Marines into business, I tried to figure everything out alone. I worked hard, but I wasted years reinventing the wheel. My pride whispered, *You should already know this. Don't ask for help.* But that pride left me stuck in cycles of frustration.

The breakthrough came when I humbled myself and sought out mentors who were already excelling in areas I was struggling. I remember one businessman in particular, a mentor who not only built wealth but carried peace in his home. Watching him showed me that success didn't have to cost me my family, and wealth didn't have to bankrupt my integrity. I studied his habits, his mindset, the way he anticipated problems before they arrived. His example became a roadmap, collapsing years of trial and error into steps I could follow.

Modeling isn't copying—it's compressing time. Just as a young athlete studies the film of champions, I began to study the patterns of extraordinary people. I modeled their consistency, their rhythms, their mindset, and then I made those principles my own.

Step 2: Immerse Yourself Fully

Change doesn't happen by dabbling—it happens by diving. Immersion became the crucible of my transformation. When I attended my first multi-day leadership intensive, I was skeptical. I had been to conferences before, walked away with notes and motivation, but little real change. But this was different. Immersion didn't just fill my head with knowledge—it rewired my nervous system.

For four days, I lived in an environment saturated with growth. Phones were away, distractions removed, excuses stripped. I wasn't just hearing principles; I was embodying them. I felt them in my bones. By the end of the immersion, I didn't just know what resilience looked like—I had lived it, practiced it, tasted it. That kind of learning doesn't fade. It imprints itself into your identity.

Immersion became a strategy in every area of my life. In faith, I immersed myself in Scripture and prayer communities. In health, I trained alongside people stronger than me, letting their standard raise mine. In business, I surrounded myself with leaders who thought bigger, acted faster, and demanded excellence. In relationships, I immersed myself in vulnerability—allowing trusted voices to challenge me, call me out, and build me up. Each immersion pulled me out of survival mode and accelerated my growth.

Step 3: Apply with Spaced Repetition

But immersion alone is not enough. Without reinforcement, transformation evaporates. The conference high fades. The motivation leaks. And soon you are back where you started—unless you cement change through repetition.

Repetition is the mother of skill, and mastery is the child of repetition. I didn't truly learn resilience until I applied it over and over—in boardrooms where tensions flared, in late nights when trauma whispered, in mornings when my body begged to quit. I didn't truly master discipline until I repeated it daily in my workouts, my prayer, my journaling, my boundaries. Repetition turned habits into identity.

In my family, repetition looked like consistently showing up at dinner, phones down, eyes up. In my marriage, it looked like saying "I love you" and proving it with presence, not just words. In business, it looked like refining the same keynote over dozens of stages until it no longer felt like a speech but like second nature. In my health, it looked like choosing the gym again and again until movement was no longer a chore—it was a lifestyle.

Repetition built resilience into my DNA. It turned new disciplines into default settings. And when I failed—as I often did—repetition gave me the grace to recommit instead of retreat.

The framework of **Modeling, Immersion, and Repetition** reshaped every area of my life. It restored my health, deepened my faith, rebuilt my family, expanded my business, and anchored my friendships. It moved me from drifting to designing, from surviving to sustaining. And it taught me this truth: greatness is not achieved once—it is practiced daily, forged in the quiet consistency of modeling the right people, immersing in the right environments, and repeating the right actions until they become who you are.

In Fallujah, I once saw a sign that seared itself into my soul: *Complacency Kills.* It wasn't there for motivation. It wasn't a catchy slogan for morale. It was survival code. One moment of comfort, one lapse of vigilance, one assumption that "everything is fine" could cost lives. That principle didn't stay in Iraq—it followed me into every arena of my life.

What I've learned since then is this: complacency doesn't announce itself with sirens—it whispers. It doesn't storm through the front door; it creeps in through small cracks of success. It hides in the applause after the achievement, the exhale after the promotion, the quiet thought: *I've made it. I can coast now.* And that whisper has destroyed more dreams than failure ever could.

In business, I saw the cost firsthand. During the rapid growth of my company, momentum was high, revenue was climbing, and recognition was pouring in. For the first time in years, I felt like I could breathe. But that breath turned into a pause. And that pause almost cost me everything. I delayed decisions, ignored red flags, and assumed the same strategies that worked yesterday would carry me tomorrow. I forgot what the battlefield had taught me—that the moment you stop sharpening your edge, you start losing ground. Competitors out-hustled me, clients drifted, and my team felt my disengagement. It wasn't failure that threatened us—it was my comfort.

Complacency showed up in my health as well. After months of discipline—training consistently, eating clean, sleeping well—I hit my goals. I looked in the mirror and felt proud of the man staring back. But pride sedated my urgency. I started skipping workouts, rationalizing late nights, and telling myself I had "earned" the shortcuts. Within weeks, my energy dipped, my body slowed, and my mental clarity blurred. Not because I lacked ability, but because I stopped applying urgency.

And in relationships, complacency is even more dangerous. Marriages don't collapse overnight; they erode slowly, one unchecked assumption at a time. I've lived through it—the quiet drift, the missed conversations, the small daily choices where comfort replaced connection. Love doesn't explode, it evaporates. Complacency doesn't just kill dreams—it kills intimacy, trust, and joy.

That's why I believe complacency is the silent killer of every domain—business, health, family, faith. The antidote isn't paranoia, but hunger. It's staying in the posture of a student even when you're the teacher. It's choosing curiosity over certainty. It's asking hard questions when everything looks easy. It's remembering that success isn't owned—it's rented, and the rent is due every day.

I had to rewire myself to treat each success not as a finish line but as a checkpoint. Writing the book, winning the contract, reaching the milestone—none of those moments were arrival. They were assignments. Each one demanded a new question: *Now, who must I become to steward this well?* That mindset killed complacency before it could kill me.

When I live with that urgency, I sustain growth. When I drift into comfort, I lose ground. The truth is simple, but sobering: complacency kills—but vigilance sustains.

For much of my life, I believed in the myth of arrival. I thought the day would come when success would feel final, when achievement would silence the hunger, when milestones would deliver lasting satisfaction. I believed that once I had enough money, enough recognition, enough influence, I would finally be able to exhale and rest in the glow of accomplishment. But the myth of arrival is a lie, and I learned that truth the hard way.

I remember standing backstage after delivering a keynote to thousands. The crowd had risen to their feet, applause thundered, people rushed to shake my hand and thank me for the words that inspired them. On the surface, it was everything I had worked for. But later that night, sitting alone in a quiet hotel room, the applause still echoing in my ears, I felt an unexpected hollowness. I had achieved the dream—but it didn't feel like arrival. It felt like emptiness in disguise.

That night forced me to confront a deeper truth: success without growth is stagnation. Achievements are not endpoints; they are assignments. They are checkpoints on the journey, each one asking a new question: *Now who must I become to carry this well?*

The danger of believing you've arrived is that it blinds you to the work still ahead. It lulls you into drifting when life demands designing. Most people don't quit at the beginning when the dream is still fresh, or in the middle when the grind is grueling. They quit at the plateau, right after the breakthrough, when success tempts them to coast. That is when momentum quietly dies—not in a blaze of failure, but in the slow fade of complacency.

I had to reframe success not as an outcome, but as a rhythm. Sustain became my mantra. To sustain my business, I built systems of innovation so we never stopped asking what was next. To sustain my health, I treated discipline not as a sprint but as a lifestyle. To sustain my family, I turned victories into deeper commitments, choosing presence after achievements instead of disappearing into the next pursuit. To sustain my faith, I resisted the temptation to pray only in crisis and learned to worship in the ordinary. To sustain friendships, I showed up not just in their highlight reels but in their hidden valleys.

Sustain is not sexy. It doesn't get the spotlight. It doesn't feel as thrilling as the mountaintop moment. But it is where legacy is forged. Because anyone can reach a milestone—but only the mastered can sustain momentum.

Sustain means living by design, not default. It means building rhythms strong enough to carry you when emotions run out. It means refusing to let yesterday's win become today's ceiling. Sustain is about asking the harder questions after the applause: *Am I aligned? Am I growing? Am I still hungry?*

What I discovered is this: the myth of arrival sedates you, but the practice of sustain strengthens you. Success is not a destination; it is a responsibility. Every breakthrough carries the weight of stewardship. And the only way to honor that responsibility is through daily design—through the quiet, consistent choices that keep you aligned with who you're becoming.

The deeper I journeyed into self-mastery, the more I realized it was never just about me. Mastery was not a private pursuit of discipline; it was the foundation of my legacy. It was about becoming the kind of man whose presence, choices, and consistency became a living testimony that adversity does not define us—our response does.

I saw it most clearly in my family. For years, my children experienced the fragments of me—part of me was with them, while part of me was lost in work, distraction, or unresolved pain. But when I aligned my identity, body, and systems, they didn't just hear the words *"I love you."* They felt it. They felt it in the steadiness of my presence, in the patience of my listening, in the joy of my laughter when I was no longer weighed down by shame. My home became a reflection of the man I had fought to become.

In my marriage, alignment turned apology into transformation. It wasn't enough to say *"I'll change."* My wife needed to see the change, to feel the consistency of my no's and yes's aligned with my highest values. Every act of restraint, every moment of presence, every word spoken in steadiness instead of anger became evidence that I was not who I once was. Love deepened not through grand gestures but through quiet, daily alignment.

In my business, clients learned that my value wasn't in flashy presentations or empty promises—it was in consistency. They could trust me because I trusted myself. They could rely on my leadership because my leadership was anchored in self-leadership. Influence stopped being about persuasion and became about presence—showing up whole, aligned, and grounded in integrity.

In my faith, self-mastery taught me the discipline of devotion. I discovered that God isn't impressed by scattered bursts of intensity—He is honored by steady obedience. It wasn't the mountaintop prayers that changed me most; it was the daily posture of surrender, the quiet mornings of stillness, the decision to align my life with a higher calling even when no one was watching.

In friendships, alignment freed me from performance. I stopped showing up as the man who needed to prove himself and started showing up as the man who could be himself. Vulnerability became a bridge, and authenticity replaced the masks I once wore. The result was deeper connection, richer conversations, and bonds built not on image but on truth.

And in my health, self-mastery became visible in the way I carried myself— not just in physique, but in energy, focus, and vitality. I learned that discipline in the gym was never just about muscle; it was about mindset. Every rep, every run, every choice to care for my body was a declaration: *I am a man who follows through.*

The culmination of all of this is simple but profound: self-mastery is alignment. It is the daily choice to live as the person you were created to be—in business, in health, in family, in faith, in friendships. It is not perfection. It is not arrival. It is consistency. It is clarity. It is choosing, again and again, to refuse default and live by design.

And that alignment is legacy. My children will not remember every stage I spoke on or every contract I signed, but they will remember whether I was present, steady, and aligned. My clients will not remember every word of my presentations, but they will remember whether my life matched my message. My friends will not remember every conversation, but they will remember whether I showed up authentically.

Legacy is not built in moments of applause—it is built in moments of alignment. And self-mastery is the foundation of that legacy. Because when your identity, body, systems, and spirit all agree, you don't just live successfully—you live significantly.

That is the power of self-mastery. It is the foundation of an extraordinary life. It is the compass that sustains momentum, resists complacency, and turns adversity into assignment. And when practiced fully, it doesn't just transform your life—it transforms the lives of everyone your life touches.

**BREAK THE BOTTLE CHALLENGE —
Chapter 14**

The Unstoppable Momentum Challenge

This challenge isn't about hype—it's about execution. Over the next 90 days, you won't just build momentum. You'll engineer a life that sustains it. You'll shift from short bursts of energy to long-term elevation. Every step is intentional. Every habit is strategic. Every move is about legacy.

STEP 1: Perform Your Momentum Audit (The Power Scan)

Start by assessing all six momentum categories—Emotional, Mental, Physical, Strategic, Relational, and Spiritual. Score each from one to 10 based on how aligned, energized, and clear you feel. Then, circle the lowest score. That's not your weakness—it's your next area of growth. Your job? Devote specific attention to that area for the next 30 days with one intentional habit or shift. **Remember:** Momentum starts with awareness. Your audit isn't just data—it's direction.

STEP 2: Activate Your 90-Day Sprint (Your Forward Framework)

Define one to three high-leverage outcomes for the next 90 days. These aren't dreams—they're deliverables. Make them measurable and mission-aligned. Then choose your One Weekly Win—a single, bold outcome you'll focus on each week that moves the needle.

Set up your Focus Blocks, Weekly Resets, and Accountability Rhythm. This becomes your Momentum Operating System. You're no longer reacting to life. You're engineering it.

STEP 3: Establish Your Weekly Reset Framework (Recalibrate & Realign)

Block 60 minutes every week for your Weekly Reset using this seven-point rhythm:

1. Celebrate five wins.

2. Audit your energy (Fuel vs. Drain).

3. Score your alignment (one to 10).

4. Review your data (trends, habits, gaps).

5. Choose one Weekly Win.

6. Lock in your non-negotiables.

7. Declare your weekly intention out loud.

This is your weekly leadership lab. It's where clarity is restored, direction is recalibrated, and excuses are eliminated.

STEP 4: Lock in Three Keystone Habits (Daily Identity Reinforcement)

Choose three core habits that reinforce the identity you are building. Examples: 20 minutes of reading, 10 minutes of journaling, 30 minutes of movement, Focus Block execution, gratitude reflection, evening disconnection.

Stack them into your Morning Activation, Focus Block, and Evening Integration routines. Track them for 30 days. Make them non-negotiable. You're not just doing tasks—you're becoming someone new.

STEP 5: Declare Your Identity (This Is Who You Are Now)

This isn't affirmation fluff. This is alignment. Speak it. Own it. Write it on your mirror. Make it your lock screen. Tattoo it on your calendar. Say it boldly: "I don't rise to the moment—I rise to the system I built. I am now a person who sustains momentum by design. My mind is clear. My heart is grounded. My actions are aligned. This isn't pressure—it's purpose. This is who I am now." This is the challenge that doesn't end with a temporary breakthrough—it ends with a permanent baseline upgrade. You're no longer chasing momentum. You're embodying it. One system. One rhythm. One intentional day at a time. Let the challenge begin. Are you ready to live unstoppable?

RESOURCES

Download the Tool: Weekly Review Sheet
Track your progress, reflect with clarity, and course-correct with purpose every week.

Available at: btbprograms.com/free-resources

THE FINAL BREAK—LIVE FREE. LEAD BOLDLY. YOUR TIME IS NOW.

"You were never meant to live confined—so shatter the bottle, free your future, and let your legacy echo louder than your limitations. Your time isn't coming—your time is now."

— Break The Bottle

The Ripple Effect of Breaking the Bottle

You may be the reason someone finally dares to rise. They may never tell you. They may never tag you in a post, mention your name in a speech, or even look you in the eye to say, *"Thank you."* But somewhere—right now—someone is choosing not to quit because they saw you refuse to break. They saw you walk through the storm with scars on your soul but light still in your eyes. They saw you stumble, they saw you bleed, they saw you stripped of everything you thought defined you—and yet, you kept showing up. Not perfect. Not polished. But present.

This is the essence of sustain. Anyone can sprint for a season, but when life rips your foundations out from under you, when the storm doesn't last for days but for years, it is presence that becomes power. It is not the roar of applause that changes lives—it is the whisper of endurance. The quiet decision to wake up and try again. The resolve to sit in a probation office while your pride burns, to show up at an AA meeting when shame is screaming at you to stay home, to keep breathing when death feels like the easier option. Sustain is not glamorous. It is not Instagram-worthy. It is gritty, it is lonely, it is fought in the hidden places where no one claps for you. And yet—this is the ground where legacies are forged.

The world is drunk on performance. We are conditioned to measure worth by followers, by the size of the stage, by the volume of the spotlight. But transformation does not erupt with fireworks. It grows in the soil of consistency. It is sustained by choices that seem small but cost everything. It is the father who keeps calling his child even when rejection pierces his heart. It is the mother who chooses sobriety today, again, after relapse tried to steal her tomorrow. It is the veteran who admits he is not invincible, who sits on a stage with trembling hands and tells his story so others can finally speak theirs. It is the employee who quietly endures ridicule while rebuilding after failure. These moments don't trend. They don't go viral. But they ripple.

I know this because I have lived both sides of it—the collapse and the rise. The bottle almost silenced me. Divorce papers placed in my hands the same night I was arrested for a DUI. I can still feel the bite of the steel cuffs, the fluorescent glare of the holding cell. The man who had once stood in combat as a Marine, entrusted with lives, carrying a Purple Heart, was reduced to a number. My identity shattered, and all I could feel was shame pressing against my ribs like a vice. For a year I lived in that silence, reporting to a probation officer, stacking hours of community service, sitting through mandated programs, speaking words I didn't believe. Outwardly compliant, inwardly collapsing. That was sustain in its darkest form—showing up to the motions, day after day, when every fiber in me screamed that I was finished.

And yet, even in that pit, the ripple began. Not because I was impressive—far from it. But because I did not disappear. Sustaining meant surviving another day, even if it meant crawling. It meant walking into AA with my head hung low and staying anyway. It meant sitting across from a clinician with clenched fists and opening up, just a little. It meant not letting my worst night become my final chapter. Sustain is not about winning every battle—it is about refusing to forfeit the war.

That is what people see. That is what people feel. Not the polish of your perfection, but the grit of your survival. And when you sustain, when you choose to keep showing up despite the humiliation, despite the setbacks, despite the silence—you create ripples you may never fully see. The neighbor notices. The child learns. The coworker remembers. The stranger takes courage. Because when you refuse to quit, you quietly give someone else permission to keep going too.

That is the ripple effect of breaking the bottle. Not one grand explosion, but waves that move outward, carrying strength, carrying hope, carrying presence that sustains.

The night of the divorce and the DUI wasn't just a personal collapse; it was the ignition of a storm that seemed endless. Reporting to probation each week felt like walking with chains around my ankles. Community service stripped me of pride as I picked up trash along roadsides, each piece of litter another reminder of the mess I had made of my own life. Sitting in AA circles, I listened to strangers confess battles with addiction, and while I nodded, I never once let the truth of my shame fully leave my lips. I bottled everything—my pain, my failure, my fear—because to speak it felt like proving I had nothing left. And yet, even in that silence, I sustained. I kept showing up.

One night, as if life was mocking me, I was called to respond to a suicide on the railroad tracks in Stockbridge. I can still hear the metallic hum of the rails, the wail of sirens cutting through the cold night air, the sight of a body that had given up on tomorrow. Standing there, I was struck by a chilling realization: I was staring at what my own silence was leading me toward. It was a mirror held up by fate—showing me that if I continued to bottle, if I continued to let shame drown me, I too would end on the tracks. Sustain, in that moment, wasn't triumphant. It was desperate. It was holding on by a single frayed thread.

The spiral only deepened. My career—once unblemished, once marked by excellence and trust—crumbled under the weight of my untreated mental health. I was among the top one percent of railroad employees, and yet they dismissed me, branding me a hazard to safety. That was the final blow to the identity I had been clinging to. A Marine, a Purple Heart recipient, a trusted worker—gone. What remained was a hollow man, ashamed and uncertain. Still, I sustained. I didn't do it gracefully. I didn't do it with speeches or smiles. I did it by refusing to vanish, even when everything in me wanted to.

For a time, I tried to redirect the ripple. I volunteered at a hospital in Miami, hoping that helping other veterans would silence the storm inside me. I poured into them what I could, but the truth was, I was running on fumes. I was sustaining for them while starving myself. On the outside, I looked like I was giving back, but inside, I was still dying. That's the deceptive part of sustain—you can wear it like armor, fooling everyone else, but inside the cracks widen. Eventually, those cracks split wide open again.

Washington, D.C. seemed like redemption at first. A new job, a new city, a new relationship. Courtney moved in with me, and within months we were married. On paper, it looked like the comeback story. But sustain without healing is survival on borrowed time. Depression, anxiety, and flashbacks from war and failure surged through me like an undertow. The marriage that had begun with hope was unraveling in months. Six months after we said "I do," I was filing for divorce again. That failure cut deeper than any other. It wasn't just another collapse—it was confirmation of the lies I had begun to believe: *You're not a Marine. You're not a husband. You're not a father. You're not a leader. You are nothing.*

It was in that fog that I reached the darkest edge. I decided I would end my life. I remember sitting down to write the letter—the kind of letter you hope will explain away your absence. My hands trembled as I wrote apologies, regrets, empty words meant to soften the devastation I was about to cause. But as I reread the letter, something inside me broke. Memories rose uninvited—my mother's letters during boot camp, words scrawled in ink that gave me strength when my body was broken in training. Letters from Iraq, folded and dirt-stained, written by people who believed I would come home alive. And then the faces of my brothers who didn't make it back. The car bomb that missed me by seconds. The lives cut short, while mine was spared.

And it was as if heaven itself thundered in my chest: *How dare you. How dare you waste what others were denied. How dare you throw away breath you did not earn but were given.* That night, I was sustained by something greater than me. I was sustained by the voices of the fallen, by the prayers of a mother, by a grace I didn't deserve. The gun never fired. The act never came. I was still here.

That was the moment I learned the truest definition of sustain: it is not about strength. It is about surrender. It is about letting yourself be held when you cannot stand. It is about realizing that even when you want to quit, the ripple of your life still matters to someone, somewhere. Sustain is choosing not to end the story—even when you no longer believe in its worth.

The night I almost ended my life did not erase the failures that haunted me. If anything, it illuminated them with brutal clarity. I had to face what I had done, not just what had been done to me. For years, I had carried betrayal in my bones, and I could no longer deny it. I had failed Courtney. I had broken vows. I had committed the kind of infidelity that doesn't just fracture a marriage—it dismantles trust at its very core. No excuse could soften that truth. No résumé or title could erase it. I could stand in front of audiences and impress them with stories of combat, of leadership, of resilience, but behind closed doors, I was a man drowning in his own dishonor.

That shame burned me alive from the inside. It didn't matter that people applauded my success, invited me to speak, or hired me to coach their teams. On the outside, my life looked polished—good job, growing influence, thriving career. But on the inside, I was dying. Each morning I looked in the mirror and saw a man I didn't respect. Each night, the silence in my soul screamed louder than the applause. I was living proof that you can appear successful while being spiritually bankrupt. That is why breaking the bottle mattered—because the bottle is never just about substances. It's about the lies you drink to numb yourself from the truth. My bottle was shame. My bottle was pride. My bottle was the mask I wore.

When I finally broke it, when I finally shattered the illusion and owned my failures, that's when the real ripple began. Not because it was easy—it wasn't. It cut me open to admit the worst parts of myself. But the moment

I did, the possibility of healing returned. This is where the 3-D Framework saved me. It wasn't a clever model or a motivational tool—it was survival.

Decision.

I had to decide that my life wasn't over, even though it felt like it was. Decision meant refusing to keep rehearsing excuses and instead naming the truth: *I betrayed my wife. I destroyed my marriage. I nearly destroyed myself.* That single choice required me to move through the sub-framework of decision itself. First, I had to **Identify** the truth—not the watered-down version, not the edited explanation I could live with, but the raw, unfiltered reality. Then I had to **Clarify**—to see that the pain I was in was not punishment but an invitation to responsibility. Finally, I had to **Verify** my commitment—not with words but with action, showing myself and others that I was done with denial. That decision was the most painful of my life, but it was also the most liberating. Because until you decide—and until you walk through identify, clarity, and verify—nothing changes.

Direction.

But decision without direction is empty. Once I chose responsibility, I had to set a course for healing—not just talking about it, but walking into it. That meant counseling. That meant accountability. That meant sitting with faith-based mentors like Franklin Graham and others who weren't impressed by me but were willing to confront me. Direction required a new sub-framework. I had to **Plan** the steps that would rebuild me, mapping out not just intentions but concrete actions—therapy sessions, daily disciplines, honest conversations. I had to **Build**—to stack small wins on top of one another, reconstructing the integrity I had demolished. And then I had to **Navigate**—because healing is never a straight line. It was setbacks, triggers, dark nights, and moments where I wanted to run. Direction was not glamorous—it was grueling, humbling, day-after-day work. And this is where the theme of *sustain* first began to breathe in me. Because healing wasn't a sprint; it was a marathon.

Destination.

And here is the part most people don't believe when they first hear it: years later, Courtney and I stood together again. Not just in polite civility. Not just as two people who tolerated one another. We stood remarried. Redeemed.

Restored. The same marriage I once shattered became the testimony of grace and grit. That didn't happen by accident—it happened because I worked through the sub-framework of destination. First, I had to **Align**—to align my actions with my values, to live in integrity so that my words and choices finally matched. Then I had to **Engage**—to re-engage with my family, with my faith, with my purpose, not halfway but fully, with both hands open. And finally, I had to **Sustain**—to keep choosing daily disciplines that kept me from drifting back into old bottles, old lies, old failures. This was all done by tremendous people in my life like Billy Graham's son Franklin Graham and his team in Alaska at a couples retreat, three years of individual and family counseling with Dr. Makungu Akinyela aka Dr. A, mentors, coaches and the support of my men's FREEDOM Group. The ripple of my decision to break the bottle didn't just save me—it rebuilt my family. It gave my children their father back. It gave my wife her husband back. It gave me my soul back.

That's what sustain does. It carries you through the years when nothing makes sense. It holds you steady when the storm doesn't stop. It allows you to keep breathing when you'd rather quit. And when you stay in it—when you don't give up—the ripple grows wider. My marriage became a testimony. My family became a witness. My business began to carry not just principles but power. Audiences didn't just hear polished points—they felt the presence of a man who had lived the pain, sustained through the fire, and come out scarred but standing.

And that's why I believe in the 3-D Framework with everything in me. Not because it's catchy. Not because it sells. But because it sustained me when I had nothing left. It rebuilt what I destroyed. It gave me direction when I was lost in shame. And it led me to a destination I once believed was impossible—redemption.

That's the ripple effect of breaking the bottle. It doesn't stop with you. It moves through your marriage, your children, your friendships, your calling, your legacy. You never know who is watching. You never know who is choosing not to quit today because they saw you sustain through your darkest night.

Sustain is not glamorous. It is not celebrated. It does not trend. Sustain is often quiet, hidden, unacknowledged. It looks like walking into your probation officer's office week after week when your pride is bleeding. It looks like showing up to AA and saying nothing, but still sitting in the chair. It looks like facing your children after failure, even when your voice shakes. Sustain is not about winning every day—it's about not quitting in the days when you feel like you've already lost.

That's the ripple. Not the perfect picture, not the polished speech, but the presence of someone who endured and did not surrender to the lie that it was over. People watch that. They feel that. They are changed by that. They may never tell you. They may never write you a message or say "thank you," but somewhere, in a corner of their own battle, they keep fighting because they saw you refuse to collapse.

I learned this in the most unexpected way. Years after I thought I had disqualified myself from ever being an example, I stood on a stage telling my truth. Not the polished résumé version—*the truth*. I shared about the DUI, the headbutt nightclub fight and jail in Miami, the divorces, the shame, the bottle, the suicide letter. Afterward, a man came up to me with tears streaming down his face. He said, "I came here tonight to hear about leadership. I didn't expect to hear my own story. I was going to end my life this weekend. But now I know I'm not too broken to start again." That moment reminded me—your ripple may not come in applause, but in someone else's survival.

And that's why sustain matters. Because the ripple effect doesn't come from what you *achieve*—it comes from what you *endure*. It comes from the fact that you're still here. You may feel cracked, bruised, ashamed, or overlooked, but you're breathing. You're standing. And that means the ripple is still moving through you.

Breaking the bottle is not the end—it's the beginning. It is the choice to no longer numb, no longer hide, no longer pretend. And when you do that, you give permission for others to do the same. You model what real healing looks like, not the Instagram version, not the polished version—the sustained version. The version where you fall, and get back up. Where you cry, but still keep going. Where you admit your failures, but still claim your future.

This is why your ripple matters. Because someone is watching you sustain. Someone is drawing strength from your decision to break your bottle and keep walking. And that someone—whether it's your child, your spouse, your friend, or a stranger on a plane—may one day say: *Because you didn't quit, I didn't either.*

That's the power of the ripple. That's the legacy of sustain.

The Hero's Journey Is Yours Too

The Hero's Journey isn't reserved for myth, folklore, or cinematic scripts—it's the map of your own becoming. Whether you've realized it or not, you've already been walking it. Every valley you stumbled into, every storm you thought would finish you, every whisper that told you to rise—all of it is evidence that you are not ordinary. You are extraordinary in motion.

You began in what Joseph Campbell calls the **Ordinary World**. For some, that world looks neat and polished, a routine dressed up as stability: the job that pays the bills, the marriage that looks fine on Facebook, the polite smiles at holiday gatherings where no one dares to ask how you really are. For me, it was the illusion of "togetherness." The résumé. The paycheck. The uniform. Yet beneath the appearance, I was suffocating. Maybe you know the feeling too—the ache of checking boxes, of doing what you "should," while something deep in your gut whispered, *There has to be more than this.* That whisper was your **Call to Adventure**.

For some, that call is quiet—a restlessness, a yearning. For others, it crashes into the living room, uninvited, as divorce papers on the table, a diagnosis, or a pink slip. My call came violently: the night I lost my marriage, my freedom, and my identity all at once. A DUI, a jail cell, and the sound of my own shame echoing louder than any battlefield explosion I'd ever survived. That was my call. Yours may have looked different. But here's the truth: the call rarely feels like opportunity. It feels like chaos. Like your world cracking open. But beneath that chaos is clarity waiting to be uncovered.

And what happens right after the call? The **Refusal of the Call.** It's almost guaranteed. Because to leave the familiar, even when it's killing you, feels terrifying. You tell yourself: *Maybe I can stay. Maybe this isn't so bad.*

Maybe survival is enough. I tried that. I buried my wounds under work, alcohol, and distraction. You may have tried that too—clinging to old coping strategies, pretending the storm wasn't as fierce as it was. But life doesn't negotiate with lies. The refusal always fails.

That's when **Supernatural Aid** arrives. It doesn't always come with angel wings or thunderclaps. For me, it came through conversations I didn't expect—a host pulling me aside after an interview, a stranger at 35,000 feet who reminded me what resilience looked like, the words of a mother's letter from bootcamp that resurfaced when I was seconds away from quitting life altogether. For you, maybe it was a mentor, a book, a sermon, a friend who saw behind your mask. However it came, it was a lifeline—and it marked the shift from drifting to deciding.

That decision propelled you to the **First Threshold.** It's the place where the ground you once stood on disappears, and you realize survival won't cut it anymore. You can't go back. You can only go through. This threshold isn't glamorous. It's raw. It's standing in the mirror, recognizing the person staring back at you has been performing strength while secretly bleeding out. It's naming your truth without spin. For me, it was admitting: *I betrayed my wife. I broke my marriage. I destroyed my own life.* And yet, paradoxically, that brutal honesty was the doorway to my healing.

Then comes the **Belly of the Whale**—the place where you feel swallowed whole by darkness. For me, it was a fog of medications, depression, airport bourbons, and sleepless nights, all while training leaders and pretending I was fine. For you, maybe it was a season of unemployment, addiction, relapse, or grief. This stage strips you. It removes everything you thought you were so that you can discover who you actually are.

And then—the **Road of Trials.** This isn't one test; it's many. Unrelenting. My trials were endless: probation check-ins, community service, the weight of being called to suicides on the railroad tracks while contemplating my own. Every day was a battle not just with circumstances but with myself. Yet every trial revealed a new piece of me—fragile, yes, but also fierce. Wounded, yes, but also willing. You've walked your own road of trials too. You wouldn't be here otherwise.

At some point on that road, grace breaks in. That's the **Meeting with the Goddess.** It's not always a person; often it's a moment—an insight that bathes you in truth. For me, it was realizing that I wasn't broken beyond repair—I was buried beneath layers of shame. That realization cracked something open: I didn't need fixing. I needed freeing. But right on the heels of that came the **Temptation.** Old habits wearing new masks. For me, it was "success"—stages, applause, speaking gigs. On the surface, it looked like healing. In reality, it was sometimes just another distraction. The enemy of your soul is crafty—he doesn't only tempt with destruction; he tempts with counterfeits of progress.

The deeper confrontation arrived as the **Atonement with the Father.** For me, this was not about my earthly dad. It was about confronting legacies, patterns, and voices that weren't even mine but lived inside me as if they were gospel. It was reckoning with the lies I had inherited and agreeing no more. For you, it may be facing the expectations of family, society, or even religion. The atonement is brutal—but it's necessary. Because it clears the stage for **Apotheosis.** Not a mystical light, but a piercing one: the flash of truth when you finally see yourself for who you are. Not who you've been, not who they said you were—but who you are becoming.

And that awakening—that's the **Ultimate Boon.** For me, it wasn't fame or fortune. It was peace. Presence. The quiet confidence that I didn't have to prove anything anymore. That I could walk into any room, scarred but whole, and be unapologetically myself. For you, the boon might look different, but the essence is the same: ownership of your story, without apology.

Of course, even after awakening, there's the **Refusal of the Return.** You wonder: Can I carry this clarity into a chaotic world? Can I sustain this healing when the applause fades? I wrestled with that. But ultimately, you choose to return—not as the same person, but as the transformed one. That's when you take the **Magic Flight**—not to escape, but to embody. You bring the elixir home. The elixir isn't a trophy—it's the lessons, the truth, the framework. For me, it was the 3-D Framework—Decision, Direction, Destination—that became my compass.

And now you stand where I stand—at the place of the **Master of Two**

Worlds. You carry both inner peace and outer purpose. You've integrated pain and progress. You've walked through failure and found freedom. You've learned that leadership isn't about noise—it's about presence. That true influence comes not from perfection but from scars carried with integrity.

This is the Hero's Journey. And it's yours, too. You didn't just break the bottle—you became the ripple. You didn't just survive—you became the signal. You are no longer a product of your past—you are a prototype for someone else's future. The standard. The mirror. The proof that ordinary lives can be transformed into extraordinary legacies.

And now the question remains: **How will you sustain it?**

How Your Transformation Impacts Others

Transformation is never just about you. That's the myth we're sold—that healing is a private project, a solo climb, a battle waged only within. But the truth? Transformation ripples. It travels further than you'll ever know, reaching people you may never meet, changing lives you'll never touch directly. When you choose to rise, when you decide to break the bottle that once kept you bound, you become more than a survivor—you become a signal. A living invitation. A quiet revolution that awakens possibility in those watching you from the shadows.

And here's the paradox: your impact is rarely loud. It doesn't come with applause, hashtags, or highlight reels. Most of the time, it shows up in silence. In someone choosing not to quit because they saw you endure your storm. In someone daring to forgive because they watched you model peace instead of pettiness. In someone quietly pushing through their relapse because they saw you get back up after yours. You may never hear their names. They may never send you a thank-you note. But your life will have spoken to theirs in a language deeper than words—the language of integrity.

This is what people are desperate for today. Not more advice. Not more polished speeches or "10-step programs." They're longing for examples. For presence. For leaders whose peace walks into a room before their words do. When you embody alignment—when what you say, believe, and live all sing the same song—you shift atmospheres. You recalibrate energy.

Your transformation becomes less about personal growth and more about collective hope.

I've watched this unfold with my own eyes. I've stepped into training rooms where executives expected charts, strategies, and KPIs. They thought I was there to talk numbers. But when I opened up about my own battles—the depression, the late-night spirals, the weight of leading while broken— something sacred happened. The room softened. The walls dropped. Men and women who hadn't cried in years suddenly found themselves wiping tears they didn't expect. Why? Because truth is contagious. When you speak from scars instead of from masks, you create a space where other people feel safe enough to face their own. That's legacy. Not a platform, not a viral clip—but a pattern that multiplies freedom in others.

And patterns always ripple. Your healed boundaries become your children's safety net. Your courage to confront addiction becomes your friend's permission to seek help. Your honesty about failure becomes the freedom your team needs to admit their own struggles. Healing isn't selfish—it's stewardship. When you choose to face your pain, you save others from inheriting it. That is how cycles break. That is how futures shift. That is how generations are rewritten.

Legacy isn't about people remembering your name. It's about them remembering how they felt in your presence. Safe. Seen. Inspired. Empowered. Want to know if your growth is real? Look at the atmosphere around you. Look at your family. Do they feel lighter? Look at your friendships. Are they more honest, more life-giving? Look at your workplace. Has your integrity raised the standard? That's the evidence. Not applause. Not promotions. But the quiet impact of sustained transformation.

And here's the truth you cannot ignore: finishing this book isn't the end. It's the beginning. Everything you've just walked through has been an initiation, not information. You've gone to war with your own past. You've dismantled lies. You've stepped into alignment. You didn't just flip pages—you crossed a threshold. And with that crossing comes responsibility. Responsibility to drive your life instead of drifting in it. Because if you don't take the wheel, something else will. Fear will. Comfort will. Expectations will. The ghosts of your past will. But today, you declare—*No more.*

This is your Break the Bottle™ moment. The moment you cancel your subscription to smallness. The moment you stop negotiating with doubt. The moment you stop bleeding for applause and start living for purpose. You don't need perfect timing. You don't need more permission. You need activation. You need to believe again that your story is not over—that the pain you've carried can become the wisdom you offer. That the battles you've survived can become someone else's breakthrough.

And it starts with conviction. A deep, soul-level declaration that says: *I am done living on autopilot. I am done shrinking to make others comfortable. I am done carrying cycles I never asked for. I am done waiting until I break to rest, recover, and rise. My transformation is not for me alone—it is for everyone connected to me.* That kind of conviction doesn't need a microphone. It doesn't need an audience. It shows up in your walk. In your tone. In your stillness. In the way you treat your family when no one is watching. In the way you handle silence and pressure. That's impact. That's leadership.

So stop waiting. Move now. Make the call. Write the page. Book the flight. Release the grudge. End the toxic cycle. Begin the hard conversation. Choose the habit that will sustain you instead of the shortcut that will sabotage you. Do it now. Because your mission demands a whole, rested, restored version of you. Your family deserves it. Your future requires it.

And here's what you must remember: you are not alone. There is a tribe of bottle breakers rising all over the world. Men and women clawing their way out of trauma, shame, addiction, and fear. People like you who are choosing truth over image, clarity over chaos, wholeness over hustle. They're not waiting for your perfection. They're waiting for your presence. For your realness. For your scars.

So show up. As you are. Bruised, but unbroken. Tired, but willing. Scarred, but sacred. Take the next step. Lace up. Plug in. Keep walking. Because your transformation isn't just about you—it's about the hundreds, maybe thousands, who will rise because you refused to quit.

This is your moment. Your legacy in motion. Go live it—not half-hearted, not halfway, not hidden—but fully. Freely. Boldly.

How to Build Relentless Discipline and Make Success Inevitable

If transformation is the spark, discipline is the engine that keeps you moving long after the fire dies down. Transformation without discipline fades. Discipline without design breaks. The mistake most people make is believing discipline is about superhuman grit—when really, it's about structure. It's not that people are undisciplined, it's that they're unprepared. They rely on feelings to carry them, when feelings are the most unreliable fuel of all. Discipline is not about emotion—it's about engineering.

I learned this lesson the hard way. There was a season in my life where I had vision but no velocity. I wanted success. I wanted peace. I wanted wholeness. But my days were chaos. I woke up reactive, I lived distracted, and I ended each day with the heavy guilt of wasted potential. I was working, but not building. Busy, but not aligned. The turning point came when I stopped depending on willpower and started designing discipline into my environment.

That's where the *Relentless 13* were born—not as theory, but as battle-tested habits forged in fire. These shifts didn't just make me more efficient; they rewired how I lived, thought, and led.

1. Discipline Begins the Night Before

Most people try to fix their mornings, but I learned discipline begins at night. I didn't set an alarm for waking up—I set an alarm for going to bed. Why? Because when you train your body to respect recovery, you train your life to respect performance. Hitting snooze every morning is a rehearsal for procrastination. Going to bed on time is a rehearsal for alignment. If you want to sustain discipline, protect your rest before you demand your results.

2. Feed Your Mind, Not Just Your Body

I replaced hours of TV with chapters of books. I realized something sobering: the wealthiest people I knew had libraries, the most frustrated had living rooms filled with screens. Inputs shape identity. I could either consume entertainment or consume elevation—but not both in the same measure. What you allow in becomes what you live out.

3. Eliminate the Digital Parasites

Discipline leaked from me through every ping and buzz on my phone. Notifications were siphoning my focus, bleeding my peace. So I silenced them. I didn't delete my phone—I disciplined it. I reprogrammed my algorithm so every scroll poured fuel instead of poison. Leadership content. Faith content. Strategy. Not gossip. Not comparison. My device stopped using me, and I started using it.

4. Write It Down, Free Your Mind

High performers don't live in chaos—they live in clarity. I began writing everything down: packing lists, content lists, priority lists. The moment I stopped asking my brain to remember, I freed it to create. A scattered mind produces scattered results. A structured mind produces systems.

5. Anchor Habits to Identity

I didn't try to change everything overnight. I stacked new habits on old anchors. Vitamins after brushing my teeth. Prayer while walking. Reading with coffee. And I stopped saying, *"I'm trying to get healthy."* I started saying, *"I am a healthy man."* Identity made discipline natural. Habits stuck because they weren't tasks anymore—they were me.

6. Public Promises, Private Consequences

I made my commitments out loud. To friends. To mentors. To clients. And I attached consequences. Miss a run? Pay someone $100. Skip a deadline? Donate to a cause I didn't agree with. Accountability made my words expensive. And expensive words are rarely broken.

7. Remove Friction, Remove Excuses

I cleaned my pantry. Organized my workspace. Streamlined my wardrobe. Not to look pretty—but to eliminate temptation. When the only available option is the aligned one, discipline becomes default. Willpower is weak, but design is strong.

8. Make Failure Hurt Enough to Change You

I hired coaches I couldn't afford. Signed up for races I wasn't ready for. Put money on the line so quitting had a cost. Pain is a teacher. And when comfort costs too much, you'll trade it for growth.

9. Attack the Big Domino First

Every morning, before emails, before calls, before scrolling—I attacked the one thing that mattered most. The big domino. The hard thing. The real thing. Because fake productivity kills more dreams than failure ever will.

10. Simplify to Multiply

I eliminated decisions. Rotated meals. Simplified routines. Success loves structure. Every decision you automate gives your brain bandwidth for brilliance. Complexity kills clarity. Simplicity fuels success.

11. Guard Your Circle with Fierce Intention

Proximity is power. Discipline is contagious. So is distraction. I curated my circle until every person in it reflected the future I was building. I refused to normalize mediocrity. If I wanted to rise, I had to run with runners.

12. See It Before You Step Into It

Visualization became my secret weapon. I didn't just write my goals—I visited them. I sat in the car I wanted. Walked the neighborhood I dreamed about. Breathed the air of my future until it felt familiar. Because the mind won't chase what it doesn't believe is possible.

13. The Rule of 300

Finally, the framework that made success inevitable: The Rule of 300.

- **100% Clarity**—You can't hit what you can't see. Stop moving blindly. Write it. Feel it. See it.

- **100% Belief**—The plan means nothing if your heart doubts your worth. Remember your wins. Rehearse your strength. Believe you're built for this.

- **100% of the Time**—Not perfection. Presence. Consistency, especially on inconvenient days. Because breakthrough is fueled by boring faithfulness.

This isn't hustle. It's harmony. When you live by the Rule of 300, success stops being a gamble. It becomes gravitational. You align so deeply with clarity, belief, and consistency that achievement has no choice but to find you.

Embracing the 3-D Framework for Life

Transformation without a framework is like building a skyscraper on shifting sand—you may rise for a moment, but collapse is inevitable. Momentum may carry you for a season, but without structure, you won't sustain it. That's why *Breaking the Bottle* is more than a dramatic moment of courage. It's not just the crash of glass and the rush of freedom—it's the decision to live from identity instead of impulse. And the only way forward is through the 3-D Framework: **Decision. Direction. Destination.**

This framework isn't trendy. It's not another self-help gimmick to tape on your wall and forget after a week. It's the architecture of alignment. It's the scaffolding that holds your transformation upright when storms come. And storms will come.

People are watching you. But not the way you think. They're not watching to see if you can impress them. They're watching to see if it lasts. If it's real. If you can stand when the lights dim, when the paycheck slows, when the marriage strains, when the applause is gone. They're watching to see if the words you say on the stage echo in the way you live at home. And this is why the framework matters: it takes you out of performance mode and roots you in conviction. When you walk in the 3-D Framework, your life becomes the message.

Decision: The Fracture of the Bottle

Decision is the first crack in the glass. It's not always loud. Sometimes it's a whisper in the pit of your stomach that finally says, *"No more."* Sometimes it's not fireworks—it's tears on the floor of a therapist's office when you realize you've been negotiating with your fears for far too long.

Decision requires three things:

- **Identify**—You must name what's been killing you. Name the lie. Name the dysfunction. Name the addiction, the fear, the pattern. Because what you will not identify, you cannot defeat.

- **Clarify**—It's not enough to name the problem; you must clarify what you want instead. What are you saying yes to? What will your life look like on the other side? Clarify gives decision a target.

- **Verify**—Finally, you verify your decision not with feelings, but with action. You verify it in the small, practical steps—the call to a counselor, the prayer whispered through tears, the public commitment that costs you comfort.

Decision is not made in the comfort of clarity—it's made in the chaos of courage. It separates the someday thinker from the now mover. Everything changes when you stop waiting for circumstances to soften and start deciding to get stronger.

Direction: The Construction of Momentum

But Decision without Direction collapses. Choosing without building is like buying bricks and never laying them. Vision without structure always turns into anxiety. That's why Direction is where hope becomes history.

Direction requires three disciplines:

- **Plan**—Write it down. Map it out. Stop wishing and start structuring. Most people fail because they rely on memory instead of strategy. A plan gives your dream legs.

- **Build**—Systems sustain what emotion starts. Build your environment, your routines, your boundaries so that winning is easier than losing. Willpower is weak. Systems are strong.

- **Navigate**—No plan survives contact with reality. That's why you must learn to pivot, to adjust, to reroute without abandoning the mission. Navigation is the art of resilience—it's how you walk through storms without losing your compass.

Direction isn't glamorous. It's the 5:00am alarm. It's the canceled distraction. It's saying no when temptation dresses itself in urgency. But this is where integrity is born. Direction makes you predictable. And predictability is the soil where peace grows.

Destination: The Fulfillment of Alignment

When Decision is consistent and Direction is disciplined, you step into Destination. But don't confuse it with culture's definition. Destination isn't a title on your résumé or a number in your bank account. It's not the photo-op mountaintop moment.

Destination is when your **being** finally matches your **becoming**. It's not about what you've achieved—it's about who you've embodied. It's the peace of living as the person you promised yourself you would become. It's not survival anymore—it's impact. It's multiplication. It's giving your pain a purpose by using your platform—whether that's the boardroom, the pulpit, or the dinner table—to pass on wisdom instead of wounds.

Destination rests on three anchors:

- **Align**—Your habits must line up with your values. You can't preach legacy and keep feeding dysfunction. You can't crave peace while you chase chaos. Alignment is not optional—it's the litmus test of leadership.

- **Engage**—True destination is not isolation. You don't climb to the top of the mountain just to breathe alone—you engage others. You mentor. You model. You multiply your breakthrough into their becoming.

- **Sustain**—And the greatest challenge of all: sustain. Transformation is not a sprint—it's a marathon of daily choices. Sustain is about rhythm. About maintaining integrity when the applause fades. About showing up for the ordinary Tuesday with as much commitment as the celebrated Friday.

The Bold Life: Thought, Action, and Presence

When you cross this threshold—Decision, Direction, Destination—you begin to live in three bold dimensions.

- **Bold in Thought**—You protect your mind like the sacred control tower of your future. You filter the noise. You guard your mental real estate from lies and clutter.

- **Bold in Action**—You move with rhythm, not for applause. You say no when distraction masquerades as opportunity. You lead with strategy, not impulse.

- **Bold in Presence**—When you enter a room, you don't bring performance—you bring peace. Your presence is rooted, steady, unshaken. The kind of presence that makes others breathe easier, because you've already done the work in private.

That is the *Final Break*. That is the life of a Bottle Breaker. Not just someone who smashed glass once in a dramatic moment, but someone who sustains a new rhythm daily. Someone whose transformation isn't a story—it's a standard.

The Call to Alignment

And so I say it plainly: alignment is not a suggestion—it is a requirement. Because hype fades. Inspiration has a shelf life. Podcasts end. Instagram reels scroll out of memory. The workshop closes. But alignment—the architecture of Decision, Direction, and Destination—will carry you long after the noise fades.

You don't need more applause. You don't need more permission. You don't need more hype. You need alignment. You need to live from overflow, not fumes. From identity, not impulse. From peace, not pressure.

This is not a motivational burst. It's a return to foundation. The stripping away of distractions that don't belong to your future. The anchoring of a life designed to last.

Because one day, in the middle of an ordinary Tuesday, you'll pause and realize: *I'm living what I once only dreamed.* And that's when you'll know— it was worth it.

The Legacy of Your Decisions - Your Time is Now

Success is not the car in the driveway, the commas in your bank account, or the titles the world hangs around your neck. "I've told you about the season when my life was unraveling—when divorce, custody battles, and depression nearly convinced me I was finished. What I didn't see then was that even in that pit, legacy was being born. Every scar, every setback, every sleepless night became part of the foundation I now stand on. And here's what I know now: success is not the car in the driveway. Those are outcomes—they're not essence. They are decorations on an empty house if the foundation is cracked. For years, I chased them. I believed that if I just accomplished more, bought more, proved more, I would finally feel whole. I wore ambition like armor and achievement like a mask, thinking the applause of others could drown out the silence in my own soul. But here's the truth I learned the hard way: success without soul is bankruptcy in disguise. It is emptiness wrapped in luxury. It is applause covering a cry. I know because I lived it. I had the accolades. I had the platforms. I had the stage lights in my face and the applause of strangers in my ears—yet in the stillness of night, I was dying inside.

What I've learned, what I am leaving with you, is this: the true measure of a life well lived is not in the glitter or the glamor, but in the values you refuse to compromise when no one is watching. It's in the alignment between what you say and what you do. For me, the anchor has always returned to the 3-D Framework—Decision, Direction, Destination. It is not just a clever model— it is my lifeline. It is etched not in theory but in scars, not in abstract concepts but in battles I nearly lost. After all the storms, after all the broken bottles, after all the rebuilds, I have come to the same revelation again and again: the only legacy worth leaving is the one rooted in alignment.

My health matters—because without it, I cannot run my race or carry my calling. My family matters—because without them, every victory rings hollow. My morals, principles, and ethics matter—because without them, I am nothing more than a hollow man selling applause for authenticity. My business matters—but not because of profit margins or accolades. It matters because it is a platform to impact, to multiply, to serve. And above all, the people closest to me matter—because what good is it to change the world if you neglect the world inside your own home?

That is why I wrote *Break the Bottle*. Not to impress you with my survival story, but to invite you into your own redemption. Not to pose as a perfect man, but to prove that scars can sing, that wounds can breathe again, that brokenness can be rebuilt into a framework that holds when everything else collapses. I have lived it. I have watched this framework resurrect my marriage, restore my mental health, and reignite a future I once believed I had forfeited. And I believe, with everything in me, that it can do the same for you.

Legacy is not something you stumble into at the end of your life. It is not something etched only on tombstones or written into obituaries. Legacy is forged in the quiet moments, in the shadows where no cameras flash and no applause is heard. It is built one decision at a time—decisions that stack, small but significant, until they create a structure that outlives you. It is in the way you answer your children when you are exhausted. It is in the way you discipline yourself to honor your body so you can carry your purpose. It is in the way you tell the truth when lying would be easier. It is in the way you guard your integrity when distraction comes dressed like opportunity. Legacy is not loud—it is consistent. It is not a highlight reel—it is a rhythm. It is not about being remembered for what you owned—it is about being remembered for what you built inside of others.

I remember sitting beside my father's hospital bed during the Christmas holiday. He was paralyzed from the waist down after a sudden blood clot and spinal emergency. The machines hummed. The room smelled sterile, but the weight of mortality hung heavier than any scent. I watched him fight to recover, to breathe, to move again. And in that moment, I realized something no stage, no award, no paycheck had ever taught me: this life is fragile. Legacy is not something you wait to chase after retirement. It is something you embody now, in every breath, every choice, every conversation. My father looked at me with eyes that carried both pain and power, and he said words that have been branded into my soul: *"Live unapologetically."* That was not advice. That was not suggestion. That was a generational charge. A torch passed from a man who had lived his battles into the hands of a son who would carry them forward. And I knew in that moment: legacy is urgent.

Presence—real presence—is the beginning of legacy. Presence is not performance. It is not busyness. It is not noise. It is being rooted in who you are, why you're here, and what you're building. It is being anchored when the crowd is gone, when the mic is off, when it's just you and God. That's where legacy is birthed. You've heard it said: *"You teach what you know, but you reproduce who you are."* And it's true. People don't follow your titles— they follow your temperature. They don't inherit your words—they inherit your ways. Your children, your spouse, your team—they all absorb your rhythms, your habits, your decisions. That is why your transformation cannot be selfish. When you heal, others rise. When you lead yourself, others follow. You become proof. You become the blueprint.

Years ago, I was standing on a cobblestone street in Rome, just beyond the shadow of the Colosseum, where history breathes through the cracks of every stone. I had finished speaking at a small leadership gathering and was soaking in the hum of scooters, the smell of espresso, the weight of history in the air. An older man approached me, his face weathered by life, his eyes heavy with something deeper than time. He had been in the audience. His English was careful, wrapped in a thick Italian accent. "May I tell you something?" he asked. He placed his hand over his heart. "You remind me of my son. He was full of dreams… but he waited too long to live them." His voice cracked. He told me his son had died suddenly the year before. The grief in his eyes was not sharp, but deep—a sorrow that had settled. And then he looked straight into me and said words I will never forget: *"Don't wait until it's too late to become who you were meant to be."* That moment pierced deeper than any ovation, any accolade. Rome didn't just remind me of history—it reminded me of urgency. It reminded me that I don't have forever. And neither do you.

Your wake-up call may not come through a stranger in a foreign land. It may come through a mirror. Through burnout. Through a broken relationship. Through the quiet ache of "is this all there is?" Or maybe, through these very words. But when it comes—answer it. Because the legacy of your decisions is not built on perfection. It is built on consistency. On how you rise after falling. On how you apologize when you're wrong. On how you recover when life knocks you flat. That is what people remember. That is what becomes contagious.

Each year, near the close of the calendar, Courtney and I slip away—not to a spotlight, not to a stage, but to a quiet, undisclosed place where the noise can't follow us. We call it our **legacy retreat**. It's not about luxury; it's about intentionality. We sit together with pens, notebooks, dreams, and prayers spread out between us. We laugh, we sip our favorite drinks, sometimes with soft jazz or acoustic music in the background, and we dare to design the next chapter of our lives.

We don't just plan vacations—we strategize the architecture of our family's future. We map out savings and investments, talk through wills and trusts, decide how to care for aging parents, how to nurture our children, how to steward the business, how to protect our health, and how to live generously. We create space not just to react to life but to **design it on purpose**. It's sacred. It's our declaration that legacy isn't something we stumble into—it's something we craft brick by brick, year by year.

Those retreats remind me of this: drifting builds nothing but regret. Designing builds destiny. And together, we refuse to drift.

So I ask you to picture this: Ten years from now, you're at a table surrounded by family, by friends, by people you've mentored, maybe even strangers who have been touched by your story. And they're not celebrating your net worth—they're honoring your worthiness. They're not praising your perfection—they're honoring your persistence. They're not clapping for your possessions—they're thanking you for your presence. What will they say? What will your life declare? Will it whisper survival—or will it roar purpose?

This is your moment. This is your time. Not tomorrow. Not someday. Now. This is the moment you stop shrinking. This is the moment you stop waiting. This is the moment you stop consuming wisdom and start carrying it. This is the moment you become the example—flawed, scarred, human, and unstoppable.

Your decisions are the bricks of your legacy. Lay them intentionally. Build them with courage. Protect them with conviction.

Because this—this life, this moment, this chance—is the Final Break. Not the end, but the beginning of everything that matters.

**BREAK THE BOTTLE CHALLENGE —
Chapter 15**

Legacy Challenge: 90 Days to Live It Loud

Here's your challenge: For the next 90 days, live like your legacy depends on it—because it does. Not later. Not next year. Not "once things slow down." Start now.

For 90 days:

- **Audit your alignment weekly.** Ask yourself every Sunday night: *Does my life reflect what I say I believe?* Adjust what doesn't fit.

- **Lead one courageous conversation.** Say the hard thing. Forgive. Set a boundary. Tell the truth.

- **Mentor one person.** Choose someone and pour into them. Don't wait for a title or permission. Teach them what you've lived.

- **Honor your health like your purpose depends on it.** Because it does. Move your body. Rest your mind. Fuel your spirit.

- **Create your legacy practice.** Maybe it's journaling to your kids. Maybe it's recording your story. Maybe it's showing up consistently for your team or family. Whatever it is—build it into your rhythm.

And at the end of those 90 days?
Look in the mirror. You won't just see someone who read a book.
You'll see someone who became the message.
You'll see a legacy in motion.

RESOURCES

You've read the stories, wrestled with the framework, and faced your own bottles. Now it's time to *activate*. Below are resources designed to equip you to take this work from theory to transformation:

Available here: btbprograms.com/free-resources

1. Download the Tool: Action Guide—Step-by-Step Exercises to Apply the 3-D Framework

Reinforce the *Break The Bottle* principles and take bold action with this full-spectrum guide. Includes prompts, planning templates, and frameworks to activate your **Decision, Direction, and Destination**.

2. Legacy Planning Worksheet: Designing a Life That Outlives You

This is not just a worksheet—it's your blueprint for intentional living. It guides you through six powerful phases:

- ○ **Core Values Inventory (Anchor it)** – Clarify the five values that guide your life.

- ○ **The 3-D Framework (Decide it)** – Align decisions, direction, and destination.

- ○ **SMART Goals Framework (Map it)** – Turn vision into concrete, measurable milestones.

- ○ **Key Life Domains (Balance it)** – Faith, family, health, finances, work, contribution.

- ○ **Annual Legacy Questions (Define it)** – Ask what really matters before it's too late.

○ **Legacy Action Map (Live it)** – Build 90-day rhythms and accountability systems that sustain your success.

3. It even includes a **Legacy Planning Checklist** with wills, trusts, digital estate planning, and family conversations most people avoid until it's too late.

This tool ensures you don't just drift—you design. Use it annually, quarterly, or whenever you feel off-track. Use it alone, or with your spouse, partner, or accountability circle. It will give you clarity, unity, and courage for the road ahead.

Remember this: Drifting builds regret. Designing builds destiny. Bottle Breakers don't wait for life to happen—they design it, live it, and multiply it. Your time is now.

ACKNOWLEDGMENTS

This book is more than a manuscript—it's a movement. A declaration. A distillation of decades of pain, purpose, and personal transformation. *Break The Bottle* wasn't written in comfort. It was forged in fire. It was born from trauma and truth, from leadership in crisis, from spiritual surrender and radical self-accountability. And while the words on these pages carry my voice, the strength behind them comes from a village. I didn't just write this book—I *lived* it. And I could never have made it here without the grace of God and the people who held me up when I couldn't hold myself.

First, to **God**—my Source, my Redeemer, my Anchor. Without You, I would still be carrying the bottle. You met me in the pit, in the silence, in the dark nights of my soul. You restored what I thought was lost and reminded me that brokenness doesn't mean the end—it often means the beginning. Every breath, every breakthrough, every bold step I take flows from Your grace. Thank You for trusting me with this assignment and for giving me the courage to live it out.

To my **wife, Courtney**—you are my home, my covering, my warrior companion. You've walked with me through valleys that most would've run from. You've seen the broken glass, the rebuilt man, and every scar in between. Your unwavering love, fierce loyalty, and quiet strength are present in every word of this book. This journey is marked by your prayers, your patience, and your presence. Thank you for choosing me twice—for loving the man I was and believing in the man I'm still becoming. I love you endlessly.

To my **sons, Omar and Corey**—you are the reason I rise. Watching you grow into strong, thoughtful, brilliant young men gives me hope for the future and conviction in the present. I wrote this book with you in mind. Not just to teach others how to lead, but to model for *you* how to live—with courage, character, and conviction. May you always walk boldly in truth, knowing your legacy started long before you realized it. I will always be your biggest champion.

To my **mother, Paulette**—your strength built the foundation of mine. You prayed for me when I didn't know how to pray for myself. You sacrificed without applause. You interceded when I strayed, and you loved me back to life. You are the blueprint of quiet resilience, and I carry your legacy in my bones. Thank you for never letting go, even when I gave you every reason to.

To my **father, Sylburn**—thank you for your quiet discipline, your growth, your redemption. Our journey hasn't been perfect, but it has been powerful. Your life taught me that healing is not only possible—it's generational. I'm proud to be your son.

To my **sisters, Simone & Charmaine and brother, Horane**—you are my first circle, my unshakable roots. And to my extended family, my **in-laws—James Sr. and Barbara Jones, my brother-in-law James Jones Jr., my sister-in-law Junita Jones, and their incredible kids Journee and Jaden Jones**—you are my laughter, my grounding, my reminder that love expands through generations. And to my **brother's daughter, Lily Allison**—you hold a piece of my heart that will never fade. Thank you all for your prayers, your joy, and your constant support.

To my **FREEDOM Men's Group** from Journey Church—you created sacred space for me to take off the armor. Your brotherhood, accountability, and spiritual covering gave me the courage to confront what I once buried. You reminded me that vulnerability is not weakness—it's the birthplace of real power. Your prayers carried me through more than you know.

To my brothers-in-arms—especially those I served alongside in the **United States Marine Corps** at 3rd AABN, 2nd AABN, 31st MEU, The Basic School, and Marine Security Guard School—your courage, loyalty, and sacrifice helped shape the leader I am today. You taught me how to lead under fire, how to endure with honor, and how to stand when the pressure mounts. This book carries your fingerprints. Your legacy is etched into its pages.

To the **healthcare professionals, educators, and therapists** who guided my healing—especially those at **RUSH University and Emory Veterans Hospital**—thank you for your insight, compassion, and relentless pursuit of truth. You equipped me to understand PTSD, TBI, and trauma not just as afflictions, but as invitations to rebuild. Your work saved my life. And through that, you've helped save others.

To **Anthony Trucks—my coach, my mentor, my brother, and my friend**—thank you for speaking into my life with honesty, faith, and relentless belief. You've pushed me past my limitations and past identity, held me to my potential, and reminded me that greatness isn't a goal—it's a daily choice. Your wisdom shaped not only this book but the man writing it. Having you pen the foreword is an honor I don't take lightly. You didn't just influence these pages—you influenced my path.

To **Shine Press**—thank you for your belief in this message and for helping bring it to life with excellence, integrity, and intention. You didn't just help me create a book—you helped me launch a movement.

To my team at **The Adversity Academy Leadership Development Group**—thank you for embodying the mission and carrying the message with both strategy and soul. Every workshop, every keynote, every coaching breakthrough is a testament to the power of our collective purpose. This is not just business. This is *kingdom work*. This is *legacy*.

To every **client, partner, and company** that trusted me with your growth—thank you for the honor of leading alongside you. Your hunger for transformation pushed me to grow, to refine, to expand. You taught me as much as I taught you.

To every **friend who became family**—the ones who answered late-night calls, called out my blind spots, reminded me of who I was when I forgot—thank you. Your love was louder than my self-doubt. Your presence was my proof that healing doesn't have to happen alone.

To the **readers, listeners, and leaders** who've followed this journey—from livestreams to podcasts, from stages to social media—thank you for giving me permission to be *real*. Your messages, your breakthroughs, your stories gave me fuel when I wanted to quit. You are the reason this message has weight. This book exists because you believed in the man behind it.

To those who **doubted me, dismissed me, or tried to define me by my past**—thank you. Your rejection became my redirection. You taught me that favor doesn't require permission. That the past only has the power I give it. And that silence, when stewarded well, becomes strength.

To anyone reading this who feels like their story is too broken, too delayed, or too unqualified to matter—this book is for you. I *see* you. I *was* you. And I'm telling you: freedom is possible. Identity can be rebuilt. Purpose can be rediscovered. The bottle can be broken. And when it is, everything changes.

And finally, to the younger version of me—the wounded boy, the angry man, the one who numbed pain with achievement and buried dreams under the weight of disappointment—I honor you. You didn't quit. You kept showing up. And because of that, *this* version of me gets to lead. I won't waste your pain. I'll build with it. I'll speak from it. I'll lead because of it.

To every reader who made it to this page—thank you. My prayer is that this book didn't just inspire you—it *ignited* something in you. Something eternal. Something unstoppable. Something *true*. The world doesn't need more information. It needs more people willing to lead with freedom, love with clarity, and live with *conviction*.

You are that person.
The bottle is broken.
The future is waiting.

Let's go build it—together.Living Free, Leading Boldly "You don't just break the bottle for you. You break it for everyone watching who still believes they can't."

There's no perfect finish line. No magical arrival point. This is a journey, not a destination. And that's a gift. Because if you're still growing, still stretching, still pressing forward—you're right on time. Don't idolize the outcome. Respect the process. Some days will be full of fire. Others will feel like failure. But it all counts. Every step. Every choice. Every breath. Keep walking.

At the end of the day, we have choices and opportunities, so you have two options: make history or make excuses. You can rationalize away your potential, or you can rise. Excuses feel safe—but they steal legacy. History is written by the bold, not the hesitant. If your name is going to stand for something, let it stand for resilience. For courage. For action. No one becomes unforgettable by playing small. Don't wait for permission. Start writing your history now.

REFERENCES & RESOURCES

This work was influenced by a wide body of research, literature, and thought leadership in the areas of psychology, leadership, neuroscience, emotional healing, and personal development. The following books, authors, and academic sources were instrumental in shaping the frameworks, insights, and language used throughout *Break The Bottle™*.

Books & Influential Thought Leaders

Brown, B. (2018). *Dare to Lead: Brave Work. Tough Conversations. Whole Hearts*. Random House.

Clear, J. (2018). *Atomic habits: An easy & proven way to build good habits & break bad ones*. Avery.

Covey, S. R. (1989). *The 7 habits of highly effective people: Powerful lessons in personal change*. Free Press.

Dispenza, J. (2012). *Breaking the habit of being yourself: How to lose your mind and create a new one*. Hay House.

Duhigg, C. (2012). *The power of habit: Why we do what we do in life and business*. Random House.

Dweck, C. S. (2006). *Mindset: The new psychology of success*. Ballantine Books.

Frankl, V. E. (1946). *Man's search for meaning*. Beacon Press.

Goleman, D. (1995). *Emotional intelligence: Why it can matter more than IQ*. Bantam.

Gladwell, M. (2008). *Outliers: The story of success*. Little, Brown and Company.

Holiday, R. (2014). *The obstacle is the way: The timeless art of turning trials into triumph*. Portfolio.

Hill, N. (1937). *Think and grow rich*. The Ralston Society.

Jakes, T. D. (2019). *Crushing: God turns pressure into power*. FaithWords.

Kahneman, D. (2011). *Thinking, fast and slow*. Farrar, Straus and Giroux.

Lewis, C. S. (2001). *Mere Christianity*. HarperOne.

Maté, G. (2008). *In the realm of hungry ghosts: Close encounters with addiction*. North Atlantic Books.

McKeown, G. (2014). *Essentialism: The disciplined pursuit of less*. Crown Business.

Peale, N. V. (1952). *The power of positive thinking*. Prentice Hall.

Robbins, T. (1991). *Awaken the giant within: How to take immediate control of your mental, emotional, physical and financial destiny!*. Free Press.

Sharma, R. (2018). *The 5AM club: Own your morning. Elevate your life*. HarperCollins.

Sinek, S. (2009). *Start with why: How great leaders inspire everyone to take action*. Portfolio.

van der Kolk, B. (2014). *The body keeps the score: Brain, mind, and body in the healing of trauma*. Penguin.

Willink, J., & Babin, L. (2015). *Extreme ownership: How U.S. Navy SEALs lead and win*. St. Martin's Press.

Bridges, W. (1980). *Transitions: Making sense of life's changes*. Da Capo Press.

Tolle, E. (2004). *The power of now: A guide to spiritual enlightenment*. New World Library.

Dyer, W. W. (2001). *There's a spiritual solution to every problem*. HarperOne.

Dyer, W. W. (1997). *Your erroneous zones: Step-by-step advice for escaping the trap of negative thinking and taking control of your life*. Harper Paperbacks.

Murphy, J. (2001). *The power of your subconscious mind*. TarcherPerigee.

James, W. (1890). *The principles of psychology*. Henry Holt and Company.

Scientific & Academic Sources

American Psychological Association. (n.d.). Resources on trauma, cognitive behavioral therapy, and emotional resilience. Retrieved from https://www.apa.org

Maslow, A. H. (1943). A theory of human motivation. *Psychological Review, 50*(4), 370–396. https://doi.org/10.1037/h0054346

Harvard Business Review. (n.d.). Articles on executive leadership, emotional regulation, burnout, and decision-making frameworks. Retrieved from https://hbr.org

Journal of Personality and Social Psychology. (n.d.). Research on behavior change and mindset. Retrieved from https://www.apa.org/pubs/journals/psp

National Institute of Mental Health. (n.d.). Publications on stress physiology and neuroscience. Retrieved from https://www.nimh.nih.gov

Neuroscience News. (n.d.). Articles on neuroplasticity and emotional regulation. Retrieved from https://neurosciencenews.com

U.S. Department of Veterans Affairs / National Center for PTSD. (n.d.). Resources on trauma recovery and post-traumatic growth. Retrieved from https://www.ptsd.va.gov

ABOUT THE AUTHOR

Michael W. Allison is a U.S. Marine Corps Purple Heart Veteran, international keynote speaker, TEDx speaker, resilience strategist, best-selling author, and award-winning entrepreneur who has dedicated his life to helping individuals and organizations break limitations, lead with purpose, and rise beyond adversity. As the Founder and CEO of *The Adversity Academy Leadership Development Group*, Michael blends over two decades of battle-tested leadership experience—from combat zones to corporate boardrooms—into transformative tools that ignite personal growth, build resilient leaders, and catalyze organizational breakthroughs.

Born in Jamaica and raised in the heart of Overtown, Miami, Michael's story is one of grit, grace, and grit again. He arrived in the United States at the age of eight following natural disasters and family upheaval, only to face homelessness, bullying, and the overwhelming challenge of starting over in a new country. Despite early adversity, he was a standout athlete with multiple football scholarship offers, but a career-ending injury redirected his path. At 17, he made a life-defining decision: he enlisted in the U.S. Marine Corps.

His military service spanned nearly a decade, including combat deployments to Iraq following 9/11 with 1st MARDIV 3rd AABN Alpha Company and high-level leadership roles such as a Leadership Instructor at The Basic School (TBS) in Quantico, Virginia. Michael also completed Marine Security Guard (MSG) School and served in specialized assignments worldwide. He endured a VBIED (Vehicle-Borne Improvised Explosive Device) attack, traumatic brain injury (TBI), and the lingering wounds of post-traumatic stress disorder (PTSD). But the real battles, he says, started after the battlefield.

Following his service, Michael's journey took a harrowing detour through addiction, depression, a DUI arrest, divorce, and a near-suicide attempt. It was in the darkest season of his life that he began the deepest work. Through faith, therapy, mentorship, and personal accountability, Michael began to rebuild—not just his life, but his identity. He studied trauma recovery, neuroscience, and performance psychology at institutions like RUSH University and Emory Veterans Hospital. He got healthy, losing over 150 pounds, and went on to earn a Bachelor's in Information Security Systems and an MBA in Applied Management from Indiana Wesleyan University.

Michael's professional journey is equally dynamic. He served as a Senior IT Project Manager with the Department of Veterans Affairs, holding a Top-Secret clearance and overseeing multi-million-dollar government initiatives. He spent five years in railroad operations at Norfolk Southern, training leaders in high-pressure environments, and later served as the Director of Military & Veterans Affairs at Florida Atlantic University. He has built and sold an INC 5000 construction franchise and now leads a multi-tiered leadership training and consulting company that works with Fortune 500 firms, government agencies, and high-performing professionals.

Michael has spoken on global stages for companies like Microsoft, Columbia University, and TEDx, and has been featured on NBC, ESPN, VFW Magazine, The Military Makeover Show with Montell Williams and The Jennifer Hudson Show. His methodologies—*Break The Bottle™*, *The 3-D Framework™*, *Protect The House™*, and *The 4-Walls Method™*—offer powerful pathways for resilience, reinvention, and results. His unique voice is raw, real, and deeply transformational, bridging the gap between lived experience and professional expertise.

Beyond the accolades, Michael is a devoted husband to Courtney and a proud father to Omar and Corey. Together with his wife, he co-leads marriage-based initiatives and is planning a podcast centered around the complexities and victories of second-chance love. His work is guided by faith, fueled by purpose, and rooted in a profound desire to help others own their story, unlock their potential, and lead with relentless resilience.

Break The Bottle is more than a book—it's a manifesto of personal liberation. And Michael Allison is more than an author—he's a mirror, a mentor, and a living example that no bottle is too strong to break, and no story is too broken to be redeemed.

www.ingramcontent.com/pod-product-compliance
Lightning Source LLC
Chambersburg PA
CBHW070542130626
46556CB00001B/7